TWILIGHT OF THE PISTONS

AIR FERRY - A MANSTON AIRLINE

MALCOLM FINNIS

Published in Great Britain by
M.J.Finnis,
Pipkin,
30, Rise Park Gardens,
Langney,
EASTBOURNE,
East Sussex,
BN23 7EY

© 1997 Malcolm Finnis

ISBN 0 9517295 1 9

All rights reserved.
No part of this publication may by reproduced, stored in a retrieval system or transmitted in any form or by any means, electronic, mechanical, photocopying, recording or otherwise without the prior written permission of the author.

British Library Cataloguing-in-Publication Data.
A catalogue record for this book is available from the British Library.

Set from computer disk by
ARIOMA,
Gloucester House, High Street,
BORTH, Ceredigion, SY24 5HZ
Tel/Fax (01970) 871 296

Printed by
Cambrian Printers,
Llanbadarn Road,
ABERYSTWYTH,
Ceredigion, SY23 3TN

All photographs via the author.

CONTENTS

		DEDICATION	IV
		APPRECIATION	V
CHAPTER	1	TO SET THE SCENE	1
CHAPTER	2	STARTING UP	9
CHAPTER	3	1963 THE FRANTIC SUMMER	19
CHAPTER	4	1964 SECOND WIND AND A TAKEOVER	39
CHAPTER	5	1965 NEW MANAGEMENT	63
CHAPTER	6	1966 OIL LIFT AND A NEW LIVERY	89
CHAPTER	7	1967 A DOUBLE BLOW	119
CHAPTER	8	1968 PROPJETS AND FINALE	151
CHAPTER	9	OSCAR GOLF AND YANKEE KILO	189
CHAPTER	10	POSTSCRIPT	201
		LIST OF APPENDICES	223
		GLOSSARY	224
		APPENDICES	225
		BIBLIOGRAPHY	261

DEDICATION

This book is respectfully dedicated to all those who
were on the final flights of Oscar Golf and Yankee Kilo

APPRECIATION

I should like to record my great appreciation for the assistance on the background material for this story to all those works listed in the bibliography, but particularly to:
Strike Force by Robert Jackson - published by Robson Books Ltd.,
Golden Age by Charles Woodley - published by Airlife,
Fly Me I'm Freddie by Roger Eglin and Berry Ritchie - published by Futura, 1981,
Flight and Flight International - published by Reed Business Publishing.

Thanks for permission to include extracts are due to:
The Narrow Margin - reproduced with permission of Curtis Brown Ltd. on behalf of Derek Wood & Derek Dempster. Copyright Derek Wood & Derek Dempster, 1940,
R.A.F. Biggin Hill by Graham Wallace - published by Putnam, 1957,
The Sky Suspended by Drew Middleton - published by Martin Secker & Warburg, 1960,
Nine Lives by Al Deere, permission from Mrs. Joan Deere,
The Story of 609 Squadron by Frank Ziegler - permission from Jane's Information Group,
The Mighty Eighth by Roger Freeman - permission from the author,
The Big Show by Pierre Clostermann - translated by Oliver Berthoud, published by Chatto & Windus,
The Nuremberg Raid by Martin Middlebrook - published by Penguin 1986,
V Force by Andrew Brookes - permission from Jane's Information Group, and
Phil Townsend for articles previously printed in the newsletter of the Kent Aviation Historical Research Society, and for his involvement.

Especial thanks are due to Brenda for her help at the reunion; to Peg and Bob Marshall for their tremendous support, for the second time; to Audry Kennard for her interest and assistance; to Jane Kennard, to Steve Pigg for his unstinting enthusiasm for the project; to Alan and Evonne Jones for their hospitality and for permission to use Alan's fine painting; and to Robbie Thomson, particularly for the Engineers' Handover Books, Eileen Pullinger, Andy Nicol, Ronnie Cox, Jeep Jackson, Ann Rippon, Rose Edgar, Anna Turner (Oates), Hazel Brooks (Baynham), Robert Stitt, Mike Harradine, Rosemary Wood (Tubman), Paul Noller, Ann Bay (Cowley), Jodi Hope, Maura Hunnable, Keith Sissons, Roy Doherty, Ron Blake, Frank Strainge, Maureen Pople, Alan Breedon, Rick Rickards, Don Nay, Lorna Monje (Brownridge), Brian Koering, Brian McAvoy, Hazel Kyd-Grant (King), Mike Waddingham and John Kenton-Page.

Thanks also to: Douglas Whybrow, Richard Grist, Michael Bopst, Patricia Dobson, John Cornwell, J. Burns, John Davey, Tony Merton-Jones, Monsieur V. Ferry, Chas. Finn-Kelcey, Howard Meredith, Peter O'Sullivan, Rene Zurcher, Eddie Fuller, and 'The Isle of Thanet Gazette.' Lastly, but certainly not least, I am most grateful to Moira and Patrick Smith for their patience, encouragement and making corrections to the power 'n'.

I am very conscious of the many people I would like to have made contact with but have not managed to do so. I am sorry the project was not started earlier, hopefully the readers will be glad it was started at all. If I have omitted anyone, in the appreciation or the book, please accept my apologies.

..........the greatest care has been taken in the compilation of this history but any mistakes are the responsibility of the writer alone.

Also by Malcolm Finnis:
The Six Eighty First Comes Back (Novel)

Pictures on the cover are from the following sources:

Front
Hugh Kennard   G-AIVD   at Manston
Stephen Wolf   G-APNP   at Gatwick 15th, August 1968
Painting by Alan Jones G-ASFY   in flight

Back
Air Britain   G-APYK   at Manston
J.J.Halley   HB-AAN   (G-AIVF) at Heathrow, September 1959
Malcolm Finnis   G-ASFY   at Manston, summer 1963
Eddie Fuller Collection G-ARWI
René Zürcher   G-APNO   at Basle May 1966
Eddie Fuller Collection G-AHOW
Hazel Brooks (Baynham) G-AVHE   at Manston
Robert M. Stitt   C-GIBS   (G-APNO) at Abbotsford, Canada, 1995

The author wishes to point out that due to the passage of time, original prints of some photographs vital to the telling of the story are no longer available, and they have had to be reproduced from newspaper cuttings, from photocopies, or from less than perfect prints, with the inevitable loss of quality.

CHAPTER 1
TO SET THE SCENE

Every play must have a setting, for Air Ferry the stage was an airfield described by one Station Commander as being steeped in aviation history; the story was the British aviation scene and travel industry of the 1960s. The story spans just over six years, a long time in the life of many airfields, especially those built solely for use in the second world war. For Manston this represents but one chapter in a long and momentous life.

Manston's past has received extensive coverage, notably by the Station History, and it is not the intention to retell it in detail here. However, no story set in such a famous place would be complete without a reference to earlier times on the airfield, and also of the aviation scene leading up to the start of Air Ferry. Those readers impatient to start the story proper are referred to Chapter 2.

During the winter of 1915/16 aircraft from nearby Westgate sometimes used the area which became Manston airfield as an emergency landing ground. Some months later the limitations of both Westgate and Detling airfields led to the establishment of a Royal Naval Air Station at Manston.

The first world war was being fought across the Channel and Manston was used by fighter, bomber and training aircraft. In 1917 German Gothas raided England, the Royal Air Force was formed the following year and Manston went through a period of considerable expansion. Construction continued after the Armistice and provided accomodation for over 3,600 people, a big station by any standards. Another feature was the provision of underground hangars, in reality buildings in vast scooped out hollows, they were probably unique to Manston and all part of the legend.

Manston, aerial view, pre WWII   (Manston History Club)

TWILIGHT OF THE PISTONS

The training role was extended in early 1920 by the establishment of the R.A.F. School of Technical Training, an important step in ensuring the firm basis of technical excellence which would be so badly needed later on.

The inter war years saw Manston as one of the 'great five' R.A.F. stations of the time with involvement in flying training, as a base for bomber squadrons and for summer camps by Auxiliary Air Force and University Air Squadrons. The station participated in Air Defence of Great Britain exercises and held Empire Air Days.

In 1935 it was discovered a German spy had been studying Manston and his trial in 1936 made the newspaper headlines. Also in 1936 the expansion programme which prepared the R.A.F. for the second world war led to the establishment of the School of Air Navigation. The schools moved away when WWII started and in November 1939 the station transferred to R.A.F. Fighter Command.

Manston's contribution between 1939 and 1945 was quite staggering. Defensive and offensive operations were often inextricably mixed as those six long years saw a gradual shift of emphasis from the early 'backs to the wall' days through to eventual victory. Aircraft flying from Manston endeavoured to clear mines from the sea, covered the evacuation of Dunkirk, and gave protection to shipping in the Channel. As a forward airfield during the Battle of Britain the station was exposed to frequent attacks by the Luftwaffe and was extensively damaged.

Early 1941 saw the pattern evolving which remained, with variations, until the end of the war. The station was used as a forward striking airfield for Manston's own aircraft and as a refuelling and briefing point for aircraft based inland. Virtually the full range of R.A.F. operational code words applied to Manston's operations, carried out by single aircraft and in flight, squadron and wing strength. There were sorties for reconnaissance, low level strikes against enemy targets, fighter sweeps and bomber escorts.

One of the primary roles was the participation in 'Channel Stop', an attempt by the Royal Navy and R.A.F. to deny axis shipping entry to the Dover Straits. The anti-shipping strikes developed into a long and arduous campaign, one well known feature being the passage by the German heavy ships in February 1942, at a time when, although the German forces were deeply involved in Russia, there was still fear that an invasion of Southern England could take place.

There were Air Sea Rescue flights, night operations, support for the landing at Dieppe and counters against the tip and run raids by the Luftwaffe on the southern counties. Just before the Dams raid the station was used for bombing trials at Reculver.

From early 1940 Manston was used by R.A.F. bombers as a diversion and emergency landing airfield and this requirement escalated during the following years as Bomber Command's strength built up, while from August 1942 onwards aircraft of the U.S.A.A.F. found a similar need when in distress. A special emergency runway was built for this purpose in 1944 which was backed up by additional facilities for aircraft repair and specialist medical support, both staffed by British and American personnel. Later on the F.I.D.O. landing aid was added to further enhance Manston's capabilities.

After D-Day Manston's fighters assisted in mastering the V1 menace, transports flew from the airfield in support of the Arnhem landings and the bomber escorts continued. In early 1945 wounded personnel evacuated from the Continent were airlifted into the station, and by the end of the war Manston's aircraft on long range penetration flights were using continental airfields as their forward bases.

Many thousands of aircrew used the airfield, from the unknown to the famous and decorated. Some short excerpts, chosen with great difficulty from the many evocative descriptions of the station, give a brief anthology of Manston at war.

THE NARROW MARGIN   by Derek Wood and Derek Dempster, June 1940

> *Generaloberst Milch went to see Goring on June 18th at command headquarters at Sovet in Belgium. Milch proposed that all available paratroops and air landing forces which remained operational after the battles of Belgium and Holland should be despatched immediately to southern England. There they were to take and hold key fighter airfields such as Manston and Hawkinge and be reinforced by normal troops taken over by air in second or third waves.*

TO SET THE SCENE

R.A.F. BIGGIN HILL   by Graham Wallace   12 August 1940

At 2.30pm 32 Squadron was scrambled to patrol Dover-Hawkinge at 8,000 feet; no enemy aircraft sighted. While the Hurricanes were on the ground refuelling and the pilots snatched a breather, Spitfires from Manston kept watch.

The SKY SUSPENDED   by Drew Middleton   1940

In my mind's eye the pilots still sprawl in the sun at Manston, the German bombers still move aloofly up the Thames, I stand in a Kentish lane and see a tormented Stuka trying to shake off a Hurricane.

NINE LIVES   by Al Deere   12 August 1940

"What the hell's up now," I thought to myself. The answer was soon forthcoming; just below and to my right lay Manston aerodrome, half hidden in mushrooms of smoke which drifted across its now bomb cratered surface. The first of the many attacks that were to be made on Manston had been launched.

All that day the German formations continued their onslaught. First Manston, then Hawkinge, then Lympne and further along the coast the radar stations. Manston was serviceable again in a matter of hours and 65 Squadron, which was airborne shortly after our return to Hornchurch, was diverted there to fill the gap caused by our withdrawal. They had barely refuelled before the second wave was plotted in mid-channel, heading for Manston. The squadron managed to get airborne but only just in time to miss a stick of bombs that exploded behind them as they became airborne. Miraculously, none of the Spitfires was hit, but there were several casualties among the station personnel.

54 Squadron landed at Manston again later that afternoon, after a second engagement, to be met by a very shaken body of airmen and a no less frightened gathering of 600 Squadron pilots. The airfield was a shambles of gutted hangars and smouldering dispersal buildings all of which were immersed in a thin film of white chalk dust which drifted across the airfield and settled on men, buildings and parked aircraft in the manner, and with the appearance, of a light snow storm. The rows of yellow flags, marking the safety lane for landing, and the chalk-coated men and materials were to become symbolic of Manston in the days that followed, and remain as a lasting impression with all those who worked and operated from there in August 1940.

THE STORY OF 609 SQUADRON   by Frank Ziegler   20 January 1943

Then at 12.45, distracted from report-writing by deafening anti-aircraft fire, I saw the sky festooned with convoluting smoke trails, plus one or two parachutes, and was nearly run down by 'Bee' driving furiously towards Typhoon PR G. Next moment I was horrified to see another Typhoon, coming in to land, being fired on by one of a Spitfire squadron that had been told thirty enemy planes were attacking Manston - the Typhoon pilot being Jean de Selys, landing now from a defensive patrol.

...in June 1943

Manston was now easily the busiest airfield in the country right round the clock, for besides at one time having six squadrons of its own, it was also the nearest landfall for shot-up Flying Fortresses and Liberators by day and Lancasters and Halifaxes by night.

THE MIGHTY EIGHTH   by Roger A. Freeman   381 Bomb Group U.S.A.A.F.   1943

The Fortresses finally got to Villacoublay on Bastille Day, July 14th, and wrought considerable havoc. Le Bourget and Amiens/Glisy airfields were also attacked with creditable results. A

TWILIGHT OF THE PISTONS

Fortress 'T.S.' (ostensibly Tough Stuff but generally having a more purposeful if unprintable meaning) of the 381st Group was on its fifth mission as part of the force sent to Amiens/Glisy. The Ridgewell group was attacked head-on and one FW190, either hit by defensive fire or through pilot error, struck the 'T.S.' with a wing. The impact knocked the propeller from the Fort's No. 3 engine, amputated the Focke-Wulf's wing as it slashed almost halfway through that of 'T.S.' and caused the enemy machine to cartwheel over the Fortress disintegrating as it went and tearing away part of the bomber's fuselage skin and fin. 'T.S.' wallowed around the sky, but somehow held together and, under the watchful eye of eight Duxford Thunderbolts, lurched into Manston for a wheels up landing. From its battered fuselage the crew emerged without a scratch. One of the Focke-Wulf's gun barrels was found embedded in the wall of the radio room.

THE BIG SHOW   by Pierre Clostermann   341 'Alsace' Squadron 27 August 1943

We landed on the first airfield on the coast - Manston. Chaos reigned supreme there. The Luftwaffe's reaction, in such an unfrequented sector, had disagreeably surprised everyone. Aircraft were simply piling up. A Fortress had crashed in the middle of the runway. The Thunderbolts, disregarding all the rules, were landing cross and down wind. The perimeter of the field was cluttered up with Spitfires, Typhoons and aircraft of every sort waiting for the bowsers. The poor ground control chaps were rushing about with their yellow flags, firing red Verey lights in all directions, trying to park aircraft from each flight all together.

We came across a few of our mates. Fifi had stood his Spitfire on its nose properly and it looked pretty comic, with its tail in the air and its propeller buried in the ground.

We counted heads-only ten. Commandant Mouchotte and Sergt. Chef Magrot were missing. We hung on the telephone. Biggin Hill had no information, the controller had lost all traces of Mouchotte, and none of the emergency fields had reported his arrival. Not much hope now, for his tanks must have been empty for the last quarter of an hour at least. It was a tragic blow, and the world no longer seemed the same.

THE NUREMBERG RAID by Martin Middlebrook 61 Squadron Lancasters 1944

Against a strong head wind with two engines out we made only about 80 knots over the ground so we set course for Woodbridge. We opened the rear door and threw out everything we could move - guns, ammunition, parachutes - but we continued to lose height and I thought we would have to ditch. Then, over on the port side, we saw the lights of Manston. The pilot simply said 'Going straight in' and put her down first time.

We were a bit shocked and had a couple of stiff brandies before going to bed. Next morning I woke up and looked out of the window. It was like a grave-yard. There were aircraft all over the place, some smashed up, some burnt out.

With victory achieved in Europe it was decided that Manston would be a full strength peace time station. The western powers demobilised almost completely and airfields across Britain emptied virtually overnight. The aircraft which had used Manston in their hundreds were no longer needed, the R.A.F. squadrons were mostly disbanded while the American groups returned to the U.S.A. to be deactivated.

By the end of 1945 most of Manston's squadrons had gone although the R.A.F.'s High Speed Flight, flying Meteors, had been based on the airfield in November to recapture the world air speed record. The station transferred to R.A.F. Transport Command and became a Staging Post, the resident squadron using Dakotas. Manston was designated an 'R.A.F. and Civil Customs Aerodrome', a feature that has been so significant in the airfield's post war operations.

As Britain under her new Labour Government struggled through the years of austerity fresh storm clouds were already appearing over the horizon. The U.S.S.R. had not demobilised after the war; having suffered twenty million casualties this was perhaps understandable, but her aggressive attitude was causing grave concern to her wartime allies as well as former enemies. For at least two years after WWII the Red Army could have overrun mainland Europe, and Berlin quickly became a flashpoint. While the Americans and

TO SET THE SCENE

British were exploring ways to rebuild Europe, the Russians blockaded Berlin and for a year the city was supplied from the air in an epic operation by the U.S.A.F., the R.A.F., and a collection of British airlines. Some of the independents involved, such as Eagle, later became household names.

Russia continued to make technological advances, her Mig 15 jet fighter rendered the U.S.A.F. and R.A.F. front line equipment obsolescent and, by 1949, the Soviet Union had exploded a nuclear device. In June 1950, having been given tacit approval by Moscow, North Korea attacked her southern neighbour and the Korean war began. In the air the U.S.A.F. B29 bombers suffered badly at the hands of the new Migs.

Across the world from this conflict, the deficiencies of British equipment and the laborious development of new types for the R.A.F. had been causing concern for some time and this contributed to the decision to accept help from the Americans in the defence of the United Kingdom. Bombers of America's Strategic Air Command had been using British airfields on temporary deployments since 1948, a practice that was to continue with variations for many years, but now some R.A.F. airfields were nominated for use by U.S.A.F. fighters.

Within weeks of the start of the Korean war U.S.A.F. F84 Thunderjets landed at Manston, an American presence that was to last for eight years. The distinctive iron cross shape of the Thunderjet quickly became a familiar feature in the Kentish skies; if the B29 bombers had gone into action over a European battlefield, Manston's F84s would have been used for escort duties.

In September 1950 an F84 involved in the development of in-flight refuelling flew from Manston to Maine in the U.S.A., a distance of 3,300 miles. The pilot was Colonel Dave Schilling, leader of the wartime 56th Fighter Group of the Eighth Air Force, who sadly died later in a car crash back in England.

In 1953 the coronation of the Queen was the cause of many celebrations and Ramsgate at night will be long remembered by those who saw the town's illuminations. In November there was excitement of a different kind at Manston when the F84s were replaced by the F86 Sabre, surely one of the most beautiful aircraft ever designed. By the middle of that year the Korean war ended, Stalin had died, but East-West tension remained high. Dean Rusk, U.S. Secretary of State to Presidents Kennedy and Johnson, talking in later years about the grim, chilling days of the cold war, said the West carried much of the responsibility; the post war demobilisation had subjected Stalin to intolerable temptation.

New aircraft were now entering R.A.F. service, the Hunter, Javelin and the Valiant, the first of the V bombers; all would be visitors during the Air Ferry days. In April 1956 Manston became a Master Diversion Airfield and, in December, the station was formally transferred to the Americans as U.S.A.F. Manston. Relations between London and Washington were under considerable strain at this point as Britain, France and Israel had carried out the Suez operation which the Americans, at the height of a presidential election campaign, had not supported. Tempers ran high and the Russians, although busy with the brutal suppression of the Hungarian uprising, were threatening to become involved. A Hungarian airlift, on a much smaller scale than Berlin, gave some support and one U.S. transport aircraft used on this by General Airways was N56006, later to be Yankee Kilo of Air Ferry.

By 1957 the new R.A.F. fighters made the American contribution to our air defence unnecessary and, in June 1958, the Stars and Stripes were lowered for the last time in front of the station headquarters with Manston reverting to Air Ministry control. Gone were the red baseball caps and colourful jets, the familiar sonorous drone of the Albatross air sea rescue amphibians, and a great deal of the trade in Thanet. In August the airfield was put under 'Care and Maintenance', a depressing classification which has foretold the demise of many a famous airfield as closure and disposal usually follow.

Tension continued unabated between the N.A.T.O. powers and the Communist Bloc. The U.S.S.R. had put an earth satellite into orbit and the development of the launcher rocket as a missile made the R.A.F.'s V Force vulnerable as it was still building up. One solution was for the V Force to adopt a scatter policy with aircraft, usually in fours, using stations away from the main bases to provide greater protection on the ground. Manston was one of the dispersal airfields and the V bombers visited quite frequently. The Valiants, Vulcans and Victors were an impressive sight in their white anti-flash paint schemes and made an eerie spectacle if they landed in the dark and taxied round the perimeter track between the blue marker lights.

The international crises in the early 1960s were as dramatic as they were dangerous. One highly secret aspect of the cold war was the operation of strategic reconnaissance flights across the U.S.S.R. by U.S.A.F. and R.A.F. aircraft, and the destruction of one of these by a new generation missile caused the Soviet leader,

TWILIGHT OF THE PISTONS

Nikita Khruschev, to angrily berate the N.A.T.O. powers. He gave an ultimatum over Berlin at a meeting in Vienna which brought the superpowers near to war and the following year brought them even closer by causing the Cuban Missile Crisis of October 1962.

By this time America was already providing air support missions in a far off Asian country that was to dominate so much of her thinking in the coming years - Vietnam. This then, in that same autumn, was the world background to the formation of Britain's newest independent civil airline.

We left Manston under Care and Maintenance, a state which continued until March 1959, when the airfield reopened under R.A.F. Fighter Command. Before continuing the story let us briefly go back to 1945 and trace some of the milestones in U.K. civil aviation in the intervening years; some of them would later influence the future of Air Ferry.

* * * *

The British Overseas Airways Corporation had carried out diplomatic flights during the war on a number of routes; now, with the end of hostilities, it was possible for conventional civil operations to recommence in Europe. There was no shortage of aircraft as, although thousands had been scrapped, many ex-bombers and transports were readily available.

B.O.A.C. flew from the newly opened London Airport while B.E.A. was based for eight years at R.A.F. Northolt. Equipment for the state airlines, as for the emerging independent operators, included Halifaxes, Yorks and DC3s although new aircraft, such as the Viking, were leaving the production lines and would later become the workhorses of the independents. These airlines flew a variety of passenger and freight charters until the Berlin Airlift which then provided as much work as hours could be flown. There were then some ninety independents but time and chance would drastically prune these numbers

In America military aircraft were also being released for civilian use. The U.S., with her vast production capability, and an eye for the post war civil market, had manufactured transport aircraft in very large numbers. For a time, before turning to new types, the factories continued to produce new aircraft or refurbished transports to airline standards. This led to different descriptions being applied to basically the same aircraft, the military C47 or Dakota became a DC3 in civil guise while the C54, used on the U.S.A.A.F. Air Transport Command's long range flights, became the DC4; for simplicity only the civil designations have been used in this work.

After the Berlin Airlift many operators closed down and those remaining faced stringent times. The independents' share in the airlift had underlined their potential as a military transport reserve and this now led to some government orders to boost the revenue earned from civil passenger and freight charters.

In the 1950s Britain still had extensive overseas possessions with service garrisons to be maintained. The economics and convenience of air travel resulted in trooping contracts to move military personnel and their dependents. Trooping became one of the main sources of income, reaching a peak in the mid 1950s, when it provided some two thirds of the passenger miles flown by the independents.

From 1956 the Government wished the independents to have a larger share of the aviation cake. It was already rationalising the aircraft industry by encouraging the formation of two large groups, the British Aircraft Corporation and Hawker Siddeley, and it was felt that a similar formula applied to the independent airlines would be beneficial. It would also reduce the competition for the trooping work, a reversal of the usual divide and rule philosophy practised by the men from the ministry.

Competition between the independents was fierce, and a Committee of Enquiry was held in 1957 to consider the implications of the low returns from this work and how they affected factors such as safety and the economic viability of the participants.

By 1960 Britain was withdrawing from the Middle East and bases east of Suez, leaving West Germany as the main trooping destination.

Colonial Coach flights provided another source of revenue for the independents, these were the routes serving Britain's colonial possessions in Africa in the years before those countries gained independence. It was permitted to charge fares below the scheduled rates and these services were very popular; two airlines, Airwork and Hunting, flying a successful partnership for some years.

TO SET THE SCENE

Inclusive Tour work also built up during the 1950s, Starways from Liverpool and Air Kruise from Lympne being two pioneers in what has become a large industry. In 1956 Air Kruise, by then at Lydd, had the most extensive holiday flight programme of any U.K. airline.

Much of the traditional work was seasonally based and of an unpredictable nature; many of the operators sought licences to enable them to fly scheduled services on domestic routes and to Europe. As the state corporations had a monopoly on the issue of licences, any routes flown were awarded only with their agreement. Nevertheless some scheduled networks were built up to supplement other work.

The 1960 Civil Aviation Act abolished the state airlines monopoly for scheduled services and the Air Transport Licencing Board was created to award routes. Even after this change, however, it was still very hard to obtain routes. When advances were made at the British end, foreign governments frequently prevaricated and blocked progress to protect their own state companies.

One of the main post-war developments started at Lympne in 1948, when Silver City opened their car ferry route to Le Touquet. With little competition from the ships of the time business expanded rapidly. Silver City transferred its operations to its own airfield at Lydd in 1954 and the following year claimed to be the non-communist world's largest air cargo carrier. Competition from Channel Air Bridge at Southend started the same year and, by 1957, Silver City had completed its 100,000th. crossing of the Channel.

With slightly longer routes than Silver City, Channel Air Bridge had been making steady and profitable progress under the leadership of Douglas Whybrow. Douglas had been sought out by Freddie Laker for the position of General Manager; he started in November 1955 and joined the Air Bridge board five years later.

Life for the independents was never easy, those companies which survived through the 1950s were generally backed by the large shipping companies which invested in civil aviation as it built up after the war. In 1958 the changes required by the government began to take shape. Gatwick reopened after its modernisation and, with Croydon due to close, some operators moved into Gatwick. Airwork acquired Transair, Morton and Bristow and, at the end of the year, bought out Freddie Laker's operations. Based at Southend these comprised Air Charter, Channel Air Bridge and Aviation Traders.

In March 1960 the enlarged Airwork merged with Hunting to form British United Airways. The Chairman was Sir Miles Wyatt and Freddie Laker emerged from the changes as Managing Director. The new airline soon demonstrated that it was taking the lead expected of it, in 1961 orders were given for two new types of jet airliner, the BAC1-11 and the VC10, an unprecedented step. B.U.A. gained the contract as the sole trooping carrier to West Germany and was energetically seeking scheduled route licences.

Many independents had failed since 1945, but the 1961 season saw the sudden and highly publicised collapse of one of their fraternity, Overseas Aviation. Holidaymakers were stranded abroad, holidays not yet taken were cancelled and much money lost. Overseas was second in size to B.U.A. and the timing, in August, and the manner of the failure caused great concern. It would not be the last event of this type.

In January 1962 British Air Services, which included Silver City amongst its operators, became part of B.U.A. with a new holding company, Air Holdings, being formed to administer the group. This merger made B.U.A. almost half the size of B.E.A. and it was probably the largest independent airline outside the U.S.A.

The car ferry business peaked in 1962 with the carriage of 137,000 cars at some 27% of the market. Although Channel Air Bridge was introducing the Carvair, a DC4 conversion which was able to carry five cars, by this time new sea ferries had been introduced and the mainstay of the work, the Bristol Freighters, were ageing.

At Gatwick B.U.A. were encountering problems with the unions and in 1962 all the engineers were dismissed following a dispute. Trooping accounted now for just over half of B.U.A.'s revenue and buying Silver City had left Eagle as the only competitor. With the shrinking of the defence responsibilities and with R.A.F. Transport Command's capabilities building up, the future income from trooping was uncertain. This, with the beginning of the decline in the car ferry operation, underlined the need for diversification into scheduled routes and inclusive tour work.

Silver City was involved in two other ventures, both of which concerned Manston. From 1955 Skyways flew their Coach-Air services between Lympne and Beauvais and the following year Silver City introduced their Silver Arrow service from Lydd in competition. With the cutback in trooping, Silver City's parent operator, Britavia, had surplus Hermes aircraft and these were made available for the Coach-Air service although runway restrictions at Lydd led to the transfer of the service to Manston. Silver City arrived at Manston in April 1959 and remained until 1962 when, following their integration into B.U.A., the service moved to Gatwick.

During the winter of 1960/61 the Silver City Hermes were used on a trooping contract between Manston and West Germany, a diversion from ordinary routine which attracted critical comment in Freddie Laker's biography.

A further stage in the consolidation of the Air Holdings business occurred on 1 November 1962 when the regional scheduled service and other networks of Silver City and Jersey Airlines, both already part of the group, were merged to form B.U.(C.I.) Airways.

Back in use, Manston saw more activity, and the Central Training Establishment of the Air Ministry Fire Service was formed in 1960. B.E.A. used the airfield for crew training on Vanguards and, in July 1961, No. 22 Squadron's Whirlwind Air Sea Rescue helicopters moved in. The following year B17 Fortresses were seen in the circuit again for the filming of John Hersey's fine novel '*The War Lover*', the station was transferred from Fighter to Bomber Command, and plans were taking shape for the new operator on the eastern, or civilian, side of the airfield.

Post-war Aerial View   (Roy Doherty Collection)

CHAPTER 2
STARTING UP

The man who opened up Manston for civil operations in April 1959 was Wing Commander H.C. Kennard. He was involved, at one time or another, with virtually all of the famous Kent airfields and his exploits through the years are worthy of a book of their own.

He learnt to fly at Prestwick in 1937 and by the following year was a Pilot Officer on No. 66 Squadron when they were the second R.A.F. unit, after No. 19 their sister squadron at Duxford, to receive Spitfires. During the evacuation of Dunkirk, in May 1940, Hugh flew covering patrols; this operation, and the French campaign it ended, inflicting very serious losses on Fighter Command. No. 66 Squadron was at Coltishall, as part of 12 Group, during the Battle of Britain and Hugh fought in this historic struggle over the southern counties. At the end of August he was posted, as a flight commander, to assist in forming No. 306, a Polish squadron with Hurricanes, this unit becoming operational towards the end of the battle.

Hugh's organisational abilities must have been notable because in May 1941 he was transferred again, this time to help form No. 121 Squadron, one of the three famous American 'Eagle' squadrons that flew in the R.A.F. In early 1942 Hugh took command of No. 121 and, that summer, led them on offensive sweeps over occupied France. He shot down several German aircraft, and on one very eventful sortie, following an attack by three FW190s, he was injured. Just making the coast, he crash landed in a potato field close to where Lydd Airport was later constructed.

Hugh at North Weald, 1942, with 121 Squadron   (Cecil Beaton)

Hugh was taken to hospital and put to bed; whereupon a doctor said that the injuries to his arm made an operation necessary. As one

TWILIGHT OF THE PISTONS

who did not like the clinical atmosphere, Hugh replied that he was not going to have this treatment. The situation was neatly resolved by the American pilots of No. 121, who held Squadron Leader Kennard in some regard, by 'kidnapping' their commanding officer and staging a tactical withdrawal back to their airfield in Essex.

In September, Hugh left the squadron which was handed over to the U.S.A.A.F. and became part of the 4th. Fighter Group of the Eighth Air Force. Hugh received a DFC and was taken off operations; in May 1945 he returned to fighters when he was given command of one of the famous units, 74 Squadron.

By September 1945 Hugh had been appointed Commanding Officer of R.A.F. Hawkinge and it was while he was there that he received a signal notifying him of an impending posting to Malaya. Not wishing at that stage to go east, the Wing Commander flew his personal Hawker Tempest to see the Commander in Chief of Fighter Command, Sir Sholto Douglas. As a result of this meeting Hugh Kennard left the R.A.F. three days later and immediately turned his attention to the field of civil aviation.

Following its active role during the war Lympne was also reverting to civilian use and Hugh Kennard acquired a single hut from the large selection available, invested some of his gratuity in a brand new Miles Messenger, and began to look for business.

In the early postwar years it was often necessary to fly to Croydon Airport to seek charter work. Against a European backcloth of destruction and massive shortages the credentials of some of those chartering light aircraft to go there were sometimes less than impeccable. Flying aircraft such as the Messenger, Hawk and Consul and assisted by his wife Audry, who ran the Traffic side of the business, Hugh Kennard built up his company, Air Kruise. Audry's father farmed at Alkham and at one time owned his own aircraft. As a pilot he became friendly with Hugh, who was also from a farming background, and from this acquaintance Hugh and Audry first met. As more work came in for Air Kruise they acquired some Dragon Rapides and started to carry passengers whose journeys, and stay abroad, had been organised as a package; the beginning of Inclusive Tours.

As mentioned earlier, Silver City was also developing their business at Lympne, the well known pre-war airfield once again well in the limelight.

As a member of the Royal Auxiliary Air Force, Hugh Kennard kept closely in touch with military flying and on one occasion flew a Meteor F3 into Lympne, an event which must have caused some heads to turn on the grass airfield and from which the local aircraft spotters have probably never recovered.

Hugh Kennnard's fertile mind was receptive to many entreprenerial opportunities; he had taken a twenty one year lease on Ramsgate Airport, often referred to locally as 'Pysons Road'. This was a typical pre-war municipal airport built when any town worth its salt wanted to be part of the developing aviation scene. Ramsgate Airport would feature again and again in the following years of Hugh's life. In 1953 he advertised for a flying instructor to act as manager and, after a meeting, Ron Pullinger was appointed. For Eileen Pullinger this was the beginning of a close acquaintance with Hugh Kennard that would last over forty years.

The operation at Ramsgate was by Air Kruise at this time and a two-tone painted hangar adjoined the control/administration block which had been completely refurbished. As C.F.I., Ron looked after the training although other work for the Austers, Messenger and other light aircraft of the day was pleasure flying and some aerial photography.

Needing some help from a photographic shop in Hythe one time, Hugh became very involved in a discussion which resulted in the formation of Sky Photos at Lympne, an aerial photographic company which used light aircraft such as the Auster and was a familiar part of the Kent scene for many years. Flying back from some chore one day along the south coast they passed above a ferry heading for Dover; Hugh bade the reluctant photographer to take a few shots and they sold the result as framed pictures for the cabins and company offices and as a print for postcards to sell to passengers using the ferries.

Silver City and Air Kruise worked closely together at Lympne, Silver City carrying out a number of services, including engineering, for the Kennards' company. This collaboration eventually resulted in Silver City taking over Air Kruise and Hugh Kennard became the joint managing director of the enlarged company. Air Kruise aircraft continued to operate under that name, the faithful Rapides being replaced by DC3s.

By this time Silver City had taken the brave decision to build their own airport at Lydd and the companies

STARTING UP

moved there in 1954; Air Kruise finally lost it's separate identity four years later. When an opportunity arose Hugh was still quick to see the potential; there was a need for the gearboxes of the hard worked Bristols and the Hermes to be overhauled and this led him to form a company called Aircraft Engineering and Maintenance at Ramsgate Airport to carry out the work.

Eileen joined Ron at Pysons Road and looked after the books of A.E.M. although her duties at the airport were somewhat broad, being involved in most of the activities such as charging landing fees and bar stocktaking. One day Hugh said to her: 'You had better take a first aid course,' and this was nearly needed in earnest later on when a pilot landed a light aircraft upside down in a tree on the edge of the airport. Eileen trotted over with her little case to be greeted by the inverted aviator calling down: 'By jove am I glad to see you.'

Although sometimes a stern looking figure, Hugh was a considerate employer and on one occasion lent his Messenger to Ron and Eileen to take two friends over to Paris. There was a friendly club atmosphere at Pysons Road and occasionally a small group would stay around the bar without too much heed as to how quickly time was passing. One night the jealous landlord of the pub up the road tipped off the police who raided the airport and interviewed all concerned, except the company solicitor who had baled out through a convenient window, as to what they had been drinking.

A court case followed and Hugh asked Eileen: 'Are you going to be alright?' They were not sure, so Hugh arranged for a Q.C. to represent the airport, successfully, as the case was eventually thrown out. In their zeal the police had entered five minutes the wrong side of midnight and their contention that the brown liquid they had seen poured, while they were looking in through a window, was alcoholic was contested as being Coca Cola!

One of the many enthusiasts who visited Ramsgate Airport at this time was Brian McAvoy, a general practitioner and a friend of Hugh's.

Later on, after a spell flying oil prospectors round North Africa in DC3s, Ron Pullinger joined Silver City flying the Wayfarers and the pleasure flying at Ramsgate was let out as a concession.

Once the Silver Arrow service was established, Hugh spent some time away from Manston, usually in London seeking new business. The Kennards lived at Linton, near Maidstone, and it was common practice when he was away for Audry to make a daily round trip, driving Linton-Lydd-Manston-Linton to keep everything running, in addition to a days work at Manston. On one occasion there had also been a visit over to the Paris Air Show and back, on top of this tiring routine and, next day, Audry went to sleep while driving through New Romney and collided with a tree.

After some eighteen months at Manston, Hugh resigned from Silver City in November 1960. The break was mostly due to the differing personalities of Hugh and Eion Mekie, the chairman of Silver City. Hugh was probably keen to follow through some of his entrepreneurial ideas while the remainder of the Silver City management were becoming somewhat beleaguered through continuing unprofitability, compared with Channel Air Bridge.

There was an eighteen month restraint of trade clause in his contract so he moved to Ramsgate Airport to lay plans for the day that he could re-enter the airline business. The clause was almost mathematically adhered to as Air Ferry began to take physical shape at Manston in the summer of 1962. While at Pysons Road they built up Aviation Engineering and Maintenance as, for a time, the Kennards' income had to come from this company.

Hugh felt some rancour against his former colleagues who called themselves 'The Air Ferry', operated from an airport called 'Ferryfield' and used the telex callsign 'Air Ferry'. Airline names beginning with 'Air' have always been popular but the decision by Hugh Kennard to call his new airline 'Air Ferry' was bound to be provocative and seen as a way to get back at Silver City.

The actual registration that notified the business world of the new company's name must have occurred about May or June 1961 and it was not long before Freddie Laker, Managing Director of B.U.A., was on the telephone to Ramsgate Airport. It seems unlikely that the registration alone of a new company was a material enough threat to the B.U.A. group for it to be seriously concerned. It is perhaps more likely, given the fiercely independent record of the two individuals concerned, that there was a touch of pique due to Hugh Kennard's previous success.

TWILIGHT OF THE PISTONS

Freddie Laker said: 'You can't do this,' whereupon Hugh Kennard said that he had and a lively debate ensued. It was obvious that Laker was determined to obtain the name and he made an offer to acquire it. The figure mentioned was substantial and it is interesting to consider what the effect upon the future course of events would have been had the offer been accepted. It is almost certain that the suggestion was placed before the B.U.A. board but, for whatever reason, Hugh Kennard heard no more of the matter.

At this time the B.U.A. drive to lead the independents was in full flood and it is possible discussions had commenced with P. & O. for the takeover of British Air Services, which included Silver City. According to Douglas Whybrow's book, the Chairman of P. & O. and Sir Miles Wyatt reached the agreement some months later for the sale of P. & O.'s 51% holding, without Laker being consulted. Following this upheaval most of the remaining Silver City directors resigned.

Within a few months of this change the Silver City operation at Manston ended. Freddie Laker came down to give the staff a 'pep' talk in the hangar which resulted in a few of the engineers being offered jobs at B.U.A. The Hermes went to Gatwick, the remainder of the staff were made redundant and the civilian side of the airfield closed until Air Ferry opened some months later.

Another telephone call received when Hugh Kennard was in his 'bolt hole' at Ramsgate Airport was from a previous First Officer on the Hermes, Adam Thomson. He said he was planning to start operations with a DC7 leased from Sabena and wondered if Hugh would like to be involved. Hugh Kennard decided to continue with his own plans for Air Ferry while later on, in November 1962, Thomson's company, Caledonian Airways took to the skies.

A '*Flight*' article of 2 August 1962 provides some interesting details of the significant contribution to aviation made by Hugh Kennard and about the inception of his latest venture.

> *'A well known name in British independent air transport, Wg Cdr Hugh Kennard, is behind the new company Air Ferry Ltd, which makes its first application for licences in the July 25 issue of ATLB Civil Aviation Licensing Notices. The company was actually registered more than a year ago, when Wg Cdr Kennard first said that he was returning to the operating side of the aviation business. His wife, Audry, is also a director of Air Ferry. By coincidence, the name Air Ferry made its debut on almost the same day as did the name - more recently registered - British United Air Ferries. Some confusion of identity seems likely to occur, though the two companies are quite unconnected.*
>
> *Air Ferry Ltd have applied with LeRoy Tours for more than a score of B licences to operate inclusive-tour services with DC4 and DC6 equipment from Manston to the popular holiday resorts of Europe. A large volume of business is involved, perhaps of the order of 100,000 passengers, and the new company is clearly not "just another small operator."*
>
> *Wg Cdr Kennard's experience of the air tour business is considerable; it was actually his company, Air Kruise, which pioneered inclusive-tour operations in the early fifties, probably at one time carrying more I.T. passengers than the rest of the independents put together. When Air Kruise, which he formed in 1946, was taken over by Silver City in 1953, Wg Cdr Kennard became joint managing director of that company, resigning in November 1960. Since then he has been negotiating for a suitable base, and also for finance.*
>
> *So far as finance is concerned it is believed that travel-industry interests have a substantial investment in the company. If correct, this is the second instance of travel interests participating in the formation of an airline run by professionals - the other example being Universal Sky Tours and Euravia.*
>
> *For some time Wg Cdr Kennard negotiated with the Rochester authorities with a view to basing his operations from the aerodrome there, and he is believed to have come close to choosing Rochester. But because of the grass runway, which would have limited operations by the DC4s and DC6s that he hoped to use, he decided against it. Also, at about the same time (April this year) it became known that the Silver City base at Manston was to be vacated. The excellent long runway and the Silver City terminal, office and hangar accommodation prompted the opening up of negotiations with the Air Ministry. These have now been completed and Air Ferry Ltd. will be moving in to Manston during the autumn. The recruiting of staff has already started and it*

STARTING UP

seems likely that many of the ex-Silver City employees who are still at Manston will find jobs with the new company. Indeed, in many ways Air Ferry looks rather like a rejuvenation of Silver City.'

The supposition that travel interests were involved was correct. Hugh Kennard worked closely with Mr. Lewis Leroy in the days of Air Kruise and Silver City and now he had reached agreement on the formation of Air Ferry. The airline would be a subsidiary company to Leroy Tours Ltd. with Wg Cdr Kennard and Mrs. Kennard as directors and Mr. Leroy as Chairman.

In 1924 the Leroy organisation consisted of two people with a capital of £100. In those days independent holidays abroad were the prerogative of the wealthy but even then the Leroy family was able to arrange reasonably priced inclusive holidays on the continent. The organisation was quick to see that, although some people enjoyed touring, others preferred to reach a sunny location as quickly as possible and spend their holidays basking in the sun.

Lewis Leroy

Lewis Leroy, habitually seen wearing the black beret which he had made his personal trademark, had built over the years before and after the second world war a business with a solid reputation for good value and personal service. By 1962 Leroys was a substantial touring and holiday business, owned a fleet of coaches and now held the controlling interest in an independent airline.

Without detracting anything from Hugh Kennard's vast skill and experience there is no doubt that Audry, an attractive and able business woman, was a strong partner and two comments made during the compilation of this work referred to her as a power behind the throne. Even at Lympne, one recalled, she would be up in the cockpit of a departing aircraft saying: 'Shouldn't we be going now?'

Setting up Air Ferry, a brand new airline, was a complicated business. 'It was a terrific struggle,' Audry recalled recently: 'We were feeling our way.'

The setting up or, in some ways as *Flight* indicated, re-opening of the various departments continued through the autumn of 1962. The writer applied to Manston at this time hoping to be involved at an early stage and received a courteous but negative reply; it was to be another seven months before the much sought after vacancy arose.

Air Ferry occupied what, at that time, was all of the area given over to civil use on a roughly rectangular site. This adjoined the large concrete apron, constructed by the U.S.A.F. for their F84s, on which the civil aircraft were parked and manoeuvred for loading and unloading.

A line of buildings faced onto the apron, a fascinating microcosm of airfield architecture as can be found on airfields dating back to the first world war. The line was dominated at one end by the large hangar, constructed in 1918, where Engineering was established; made up of the traditional sections for Airframe, Engines, Instruments, Radio, Tyre Bay, Trimshop and Technical Records. The Refuellers and Aircraft Cleaners also came under the Chief Engineer, the former with their tankers and oilers parked next to the hangar.

There was also a smaller hangar, brought over long ago from Westgate and not used by Air Ferry, the Bonded Store which housed the stocks of duty free goods sold on the aircraft and a more modern brick building for Customs use. This contained the emigration and imigration hall, with the landing officer at one end, through which the passengers filed on their way to and from the aircraft.

Next came a long single storey wooden building, probably R.A.F. built, and utilised for the Silver City trooping flights. It was used at one end as offices for Management, Commercial and Accounts and at the other end by Operations. A small, unpretentious wooden hut, usually equipped with the best piece of carpet on the airfield, was sited out on the apron. This was the domain of the Tarmac staff, responsible for marshalling the aircraft and carrying out the loading and unloading of baggage, bonded goods and catering.

Immediately behind the offices was a staff car park and a nissen hut used by Operations, the Chief Air Hostess and as a uniform store. A service road ran along behind the line of buildings with the second part of Air Ferry's accommodation on the other side of the road.

Opposite the nissen hut were some huts used by Flight Catering and which adjoined the passenger terminal. Originally built in the 1920s as an R.A.F. workshop, the terminal was of brick construction with an unusual, but attractive rounded roof, rather like a very large nissen hut. In the fifties the American Air Force used the building for the overhaul of jet engines from the Thunderjets and Sabres and oil residue in the concrete floor caused recurring difficulties in making carpet tiles stick during the following decade. Now, with its white walls and woodwork painted in 'Air Ferry blue', it presented a smart appearance for the coming season. In addition to the departure lounge the terminal accommodated the Traffic section, a small shop, the kitchen and the staff canteen.

Next to the terminal were several WWI wooden huts, into one of which Accounts would be banished during 1964, and then a large open space used as a car park for passengers arriving independently to join their tours.

Manston received some publicity in the local papers, although not all of this was positive as a short article in the 13 July '*Isle of Thanet Gazette*' was devoted to a complaint about the noise of jet aircraft flying over Ramsgate which the Ramsgate Hotel, Guest and Boarding Association had addressed to the town council.

Air Ferry was the subject of a lead article on 17 August which featured an interview with Wg Cdr Kennard and included details about the formation similar to that published in '*Flight*'. A further headline article 'Day Air Trips to Ostend' in the '*Gazette*' on 21 September featured another interview with Hugh Kennard who explained that the company was quietly and gradually settling in at Manston. It was anticipated that day trips during the summer season with flights on a regular basis to Ostend and to Le Touquet would have a big appeal for holidaymakers in the area.

Hugh and Audry Kennard

The 5 October '*Gazette*' reported that Minster's ten year footpath war had flared up again with repeated requests for better access from Alland Grange along past the loop hangar entry to the Acol road. Part of the villagers' ire was directed at the bus company whose charge for a necessary, but circuitous, diversion was resented. The following weeks issue featured the marriage of Ingrid Challis, ex-Silver City and now Senior Traffic Assistant for Air Ferry, to John Osborne, a Customs & Excise officer based at Manston.

Air Ferry's applications to the Air Transport Licensing Board for scheduled flights, including day return trips, to Ostend and Le Touquet, were covered in the last news item in the '*Gazette*' that year. Objections to the applications predictably came from British United, Silver City and also Channel Airways. It was stated on Air Ferry's behalf that the permanent Thanet population of some 85,000 increased with the summer influx to something like 3,500,000 with a consequent demand for day trips.

Ron Illsley

Preparations continued through the winter of 1962/63, the snow which arrived on Boxing Day heralding the worst conditions since 1947. Snow fell in huge quantities and the sea froze in places around the south coast.

The management at this time comprised Hugh Kennard as Managing Director; Audry Kennard as Traffic Director; Captain W.H.B. Wood, Chief Pilot; R.H. Illsley, Chief Engineer; P. Wannop, Commercial Manager and J.Russell as Traffic Superintendent. T.R. Leigh, the son of Hugh Kennard's Commanding Officer back in 1940, was Chief Accountant. Peter Wannop and Joe Russell were both ex Silver City. Joe was also ex-Royal Navy; he had been injured in the Battle of the River Plate and later in the war was on the Arctic convoys to Russia.

STARTING UP

Ron Illsley had been in aviation since 1934 when he began work with the Boulton & Paul Aircraft Company. His career took him to Saunders-Roe, Imperial Airways and Flight Refuelling Ltd. In 1954 he joined Silver City as Engineering Superintendent at Blackbushe and in 1959 was transferred to Manston as Engineering Manager - Silver City Airways.

HB-AAN of Balair, later Victor Foxtrot   (Eddie Fuller collection)

HB-ILC of Balair, later Foxtrot Yankee   (Air Britain)

Flight catering was under the supervision of Jeremy Kennard while the Kitchen and Staff Canteen were run by Gwen Laycock.

By this time suitable aircraft had been located and arrangements were being made for their delivery to Manston. Balair, a subsidiary of the Swiss national airline, Swissair, operated DC6, DC4 and Viking aircraft and Air Ferry purchased one DC4 and their two Vikings which were up for sale. Hugh kept the DC6s in mind for the future. Starways, based at Liverpool, was one of the DC4 operators in the U.K., and an aircraft from them was also acquired.

Captain W.H.B. (Bill) Wood had been appointed Chief Pilot on 1 October 1962 and made a very significant contribution to getting Air Ferry off the ground. He wrote the operations manuals which proved their worth when in use and were highly regarded. Another key area was his design work on the DC4 to enable it to carry 84 passengers - safely. On the ground the aircraft was tail heavy and the first act by the ground crew, as the engines were shutting down, was to place a tail post beneath the rear fuselage, the post being held in place by a pin on a chain.

To carry more passengers it was necessary to move some weight forward and Bill thought out several modifications to achieve this. The water tanks for the toilet and the galley were re-sited from the back of the fuselage to a more forward position, this work naturally included some re-running of the piping, and following these changes the galley box was also re-located further forward. Another modification he required was the re-siting of the oil tank from a flat position amidships to a more forward location and placed on end. When these changes were made they found that they had added 10 knots to the top speed of the DC4 and the pilots were occasionally asked: 'Are you a DC6?' All this, of course, was in addition to the task of interviewing and engaging pilots in time for the start of operations.

Ron Blake and Tony 'Spike' O'Reilly were the first two engineers appointed and their first job was to partition off a section of the great echoing hangar, which could be exceptionally draughty in a Thanet winter, to work in. After R.A.F. service in Hong Kong, Ron had joined Silver City at their formative stage at London Airport when they operated some Lancastrians and two DC3s. This was long before car ferry operations were thought of and he moved with Silver City to Blackbushe, Lympne, Lydd and finally to Manston. Following Freddie Laker's talk earlier in the year he was one of those who went to B.U.A. at Gatwick when the civil side of Manston closed. Ron would be the inspector in charge of the radio section.

Another ex-Silver City Manston employee starting at this time was Frank Strainge, as Electrical Inspector, and another early joiner was Robbie Thomson as Hangar Foreman. After working for Newcastle Flying Club, Robbie had joined the R.A.F. in February 1940 and, by the Battle of Britain, was working on Hurricanes and Spitfires at two key sector stations, Kenley and Tangmere. He was at North Coates in Lincolnshire when the Beaufighter Strike Wing operated from this exposed coastal airfield and post war, was in Berlin at the time of the famous air lift to the beleaguered city.

In the beginning ..... (Ron Blake)

An early photograph taken in front of the hangar shows Robbie, Gordon Spires, (? Stores), Len Mees, engines; Reg Hampton, stores; Doug Twyman, tyre bay; Sid Walker (in cap), refueller, John Verrion, refueller; Jim Jones, airframe; Eddie Edgar, engines; Don Baigent, technical records; Harry Burgess, Instrument Inspector; Ron, Frank and Spike. Not on the photograph, but an important member of the team, was Ken Barker, a senior man on engines and airframes. Although many of the engineers were ex-R.A.F., Ken came from an aircraft industry background and had once worked up at Wymeswold on DC3s.

Don Brooker

The Chief Air Hostess was Maureen Pople, usually known as 'Pop'. Maureen had started her working life in farming, as a herdswoman, and later worked in a hotel near Maidstone. Occasionally one of the Skyways Coach-Air staff called in, very smart in her uniform, and Maureen decided to make a move into aviation. She eventually gained an interview with Audry Kennard at Lydd. Pop was labouring under a heavy cold and felt ghastly; she had the awful feeling that the interview might be in the balance and stressed to Audry: 'I'm very good with animals.' Audry thought this was the funniest thing she had heard for a long time and, for whatever reason, Pop was in.

STARTING UP

The air hostesses were required to fly on the air ferries in addition to the charters and later on Maureen flew for two companies out of Gatwick. She recalls those early days fondly; one day, with early enthusiasm, she helped to unload baggage at Basle until the crew pointed out this was not quite the thing; another time on a Palma night flight she found there were only eight sets of plastic cutlery for thirty two passengers. Then there was the hostess who returned from Paris having left the inner, but vital, part of the Elsan over there and whose absence was not noticed by the passengers using the facility, although it was noticed by the horror struck staff back at base; and the very rough flight for one of her colleagues when, after many used sick bags had been piled into the toilet, one passenger urgently required that a search be made for some missing dentures.

Early aircrew appointments, on 1 February 1963, were Captains P.J. Souster, H. Tubman and D. Brooker, followed two weeks later by R. McNay. Captain Stimpson joined at this time and, on 1 March, Captain J Gibson arrived. The First Officers at this stage were W. Steel, from 1 January and, in February, K. Winyard, V. Kellard, D. Laker and D. Hendley; John Hazel and P. Thomas joined on 1 March.

Hugh Tubman had joined the R.A.F. in July 1940, gained his wings in February 1941, and from April of that year was with

Hugh Tubman (Rosemary Wood)

AIR FERRY

Manston Ramsgate Kent

With Compliments

THE R.F.D. TYPE 50C Mk. 2a
LIFEJACKET

A.R.B. APPROVAL No. E 1296

This lifejacket is a most efficient item of personal lifesaving equipment and can be used on an unconscious person. It is self-righting and designed to maintain the head well above water.

GODALMING · SURREY · ENGLAND
(A member of R.F.D. Group Limited)

Also in N. Ireland, Australia, Denmark, Germany, Holland, Italy, New Zealand, Norway, South Africa, Sweden, U.S.A.

on receiving emergency warning, loosen clothing at the neck and remove shoes

your lifejacket is stowed close to hand

do not inflate lifejacket until after leaving aircraft or until instructed by a crew member

The instructions for putting on your lifejacket are given overleaf.

Hugh Kennard   (Jane Kennard)

No. 57 Squadron flying Wellingtons in Bomber Command. By September he had flown on twenty one operations and then had a 'rest' at an O.T.U. After a time with No. 115 Squadron he joined 420 (R.C.A.F.) Squadron in January 1943 for more war operations, being awarded the DFC and was Mentioned in Despatches. Post war he remained in the R.A.F., flying Yorks in Transport Command until 1949, when he left the service but continued to fly Yorks, although now for Skyways. He also flew Constellations and DC3s with Skyways before joining Silver City at Lydd, again with DC3s and also the Bristol Freighters.

Audry and Maureen Pople spent much time writing the cabin attendants' manual, a comprehensive list of procedures which, when finished, filled a thick binder and had a serviceable cover in 'Air Ferry' blue. There were also safety leaflets to organise and life jacket instructions, Maureen being the model used for the latter. Then they turned their attention to advertising for hostesses and going through the initial selection process for interviews. After that Pop was busy working up her establishment of hostesses and arranging training, survival exercises and, most important, the provision of well tailored uniforms. The air and ground crew uniforms were standard navy blue although the hostesses' headwear was a fetching, new style bowler; this and the AF winged crest used as the company logo were designed by Audry.

Even at this stage Hugh Kennard was alert for new opportunities. About this time serious consideration was given to acquiring the civil side of Manston to reduce the dependency of the civilian operations on military requirements. The Ministry, however, was not receptive to these overtures.

Meanwhile, the aerial activity had already started.

CHAPTER 3
1963 THE FRANTIC SUMMER

THE AIRCRAFT

Douglas DC4   G-APYK   G-ASFY

Vickers Viking   G-AIVF   G-AIVD

It could be said that Air Ferry came alive on 9 January 1963 when Bill Wood started the four engines of G-APYK and taxied out to the end of the runway at Liverpool Airport for the short flight to Wymeswold in Leicestershire, an airfield Bill had been based on for a time in the war.

An early production model, Yankee Kilo had flown for at least three airlines in America prior to coming onto the U.K. register in 1960. Her career with Starways had not been an auspicious one as she suffered a wheels up landing at Elizabethville in the Congo and later, in an accident at Liverpool in May 1962, landed short after a training flight, only being returned to service five months later following repairs at Wymeswold.

Now, arriving back at Wymeswold for pre-delivery work prior to joining Air Ferry, Yankee Kilo taxied round the perimeter track of the old Bomber Command training airfield to the T2 hangars used by Field Aircraft Services. The ferry flight had been long enough for Bill to decide he was not satisfied with the quality of the overhaul Yankee Kilo had undergone at Liverpool, and Starways were made to send a maintenance crew across to Wymeswold to carry out the Check 4 again, this time under supervision. At this time the aircraft had flown 36,672 hours.

On 5 February the distinctive shape of the Vickers Viking joined the circuit at Manston as HB-AAN and HB-AAR completed their delivery flights from Basle, still in their red and white paint schemes. Both Vikings began their careers in 1947 with British European Airways and had later been sold to German companies before being reunited at Balair. While at Basle both had been used for a time on United Nations flights, a type of charter work that had sometimes proved hazardous and would do so again.

The Vikings now reverted to their original U.K. registrations of G-AIVF and G-AIVD; before leaving Basle they had recorded 16,761 and 18,269 flying hours respectively. The Viking between Victor Foxtrot and Victor Delta on the production line at Brooklands, number 218, was registered as G-AIVE. The career of this aircraft, 'Victor Easy' in the old phonetic alphabet, was cut short when it collided with high ground in Scotland in 1948. Miraculously, all the occupants survived.

On 18 February Peter Souster and Hugh Tubman ferried Victor Delta to Air Couriers at Gatwick for work prior to use by Air Ferry on inclusive tours; later that day Peter Souster repeated the flight, this time with Victor Foxtrot.

The new colour scheme for the fleet had been outlined by Ron Illsley to his son Geoffrey, then at university, who applied the ideas to side drawings of the aircraft. The scheme ended up with a medium blue cheat line along the fuselage with 'Air Ferry' in blue on the cabin top. The fin and rudder were blue with a white central band on which the letters AF were entwined and coloured red.

On 6 March Bill Wood flew HB-ILC from Basle, in full Balair colours, and ferried her the following day, now as G-ASFY, to join Yankee Kilo at Wymeswold. A veteran with 44,435 hours in the skies on leaving Basle, Foxtrot Yankee had also served with the wartime U.S.A.A.F. As mentioned earlier, most of these ex-military transports had been constructed as 'C54s' while only the late production aircraft, far fewer in number, had been built to airline standards as 'DC4s'. In practice, down the years, most were called DC4s when in civil use but some of the wartime aircraft were subjected to a conversion process to bring them to full DC4 standard and, of the four of these aircraft Air Ferry operated, Foxtrot Yankee was the only one to undergo this process. Following conversion at El Segundo in June 1946 she had been delivered to Pan American World

Airways. One of the names carried by the aircraft at this time was 'Clipper Dusseldorf', a city she would visit frequently with Air Ferry, and she remained with Pan-Am until sold to Balair in 1960.

To many of the staff at Manston this aircraft, with her length of service, almost came to personify Air Ferry, even after the advent of the more modern types. Unique among the three DC4s operated in the early years, Foxtrot Yankee had the orange strobe light fitted to the top of the fin and was always easily recognisable.

Bill Wood carried out an air test for Yankee Kilo at Wymeswold on Friday 8 March with Peter Souster and Hugh Tubman, and after this was satisfactorily completed, they brought Air Ferry's first operational aircraft to Manston during the afternoon. Most of the remainder of March was taken up by crew familiarisation on Yankee Kilo. The aircraft next flew on Wednesday 13th., on Thursday and twice on Monday 18th., all recorded as Manston-Manston with a total time of 8 hours 35 minutes. Hugh Tubman recorded for the flight on the 14th.: 'Six take-offs and landings, stalls clean and with undercarriage and flaps down. Stalls and circuit work.' On Tuesday 19th., after a local flight, the DC4 went to Gatwick and returned. The following day Gatwick was visited again for several landings there, a night stop, and return on Thursday. Friday saw another local flight and a visit to Basle. There were then no movements for a week.

THE YEAR

On Saturday 30 March the first coaches of Leroy voyageurs arrived at Manston for the inaugural passenger flight. At 1037 Yankee Kilo departed from the apron and piloted by Bill Wood set off for Perpignan with 48 passengers. At Perpignan 27 people disembarked and Yankee Kilo continued on to Palma and then Ibiza, the Palma stop probably because there were no customs facilities on Ibiza The aircraft night stopped at Ibiza, strangely the only occasion an Air Ferry aircraft used this airport, although there was a government requirement that, usually, only Spanish aircraft should carry passengers across to the smaller island. The aircraft returned on Sunday via Palma to Manston. '*Flight*' marked the event with a photograph on 18 April and the shot was reused many times for publicity purposes.

G-APYK, the inaugural flight, 30 March, 1963

The heroes and heroines at Air Ferry, of course, were the aircrews who entrusted their lives to the air and the engineers whose skill and care, often working in cramped conditions and poor weather, were centred on the safety of the aircraft. Without in any way detracting from this statement, it is the aircraft that occupy centre stage in this narrative for most of the time, they were machines with character and almost as well known as individuals.

April There was no movement on Monday 1st. and over the next two days Yankee Kilo carried out more local flying. Peter Souster and Hugh Tubman shared some of this with critical speed work and engine failures on take-off. The next 'movement' was at Gatwick on Friday 5th. when Victor Delta had an air test prior to returning to Manston the next day. On Sunday 7th. the Viking made her first revenue flight, to Dijon, taking the first of these tours and piloted by Captain Gibson while Yankee Kilo took the first 28 of what would be many passengers by Air Ferry to Ostend.

Yankee Kilo flew locally again on Monday and Tuesday and next day made the first revenue flight to Basle. Fully loaded the DC4s would work in 84 seat configuration and the Vikings 42, this would give some flexibility to interchange and was also compatible with the coach seating used. Both types of aircraft were flown by two pilots, with the DC4s carrying two cabin crew and the Vikings one.

Thursday 11th. was busier, Yankee Kilo flew a Dusseldorf charter, made a short local flight and carried passengers to Le Bourget. During the day Victor Foxtrot had an air test at Gatwick while Victor Delta flew Manston-Southend-Ostend-Southend with passengers. Next morning Victor Foxtrot flew into Manston at 0915 on delivery from Gatwick, Victor Delta continued Southend-Ostend-Beauvais-Manston and later went to Le Bourget and Ostend. Yankee Kilo meanwhile also went to Ostend and operated the first tour to Naples.

On the second weekend Victor Delta took the first of the Saturday morning Basle tours on the 13th. although the DC4s would fly this later on. Yankee Kilo went to Perpignan during the afternoon, flown by Peter Souster and Hugh Tubman, and set off for Palma at 2105; both these flights being the first of the main tours to these destinations. After take-off for the journey home Yankee Kilo made a return to Palma although the reason is not known. Both the Perpignan and Palma tours started as one flight per week although these would increase in frequency during May. On Sunday there were just two flights, both by Victor Delta to Ostend.

The first departure on Monday 15th. was by Victor Foxtrot, making her first revenue flight, to Ostend, with John Gibson in command. Later that day, and into the 16th., the aircraft flew Manston-Ostend-Southend-Ostend-Southend-Manston. That week Victor Delta went to Le Bourget and to Dijon, returning from there via Ostend. Yankee Kilo went to Dusseldorf twice, flew a Manston-Ostend-Birmingham-Manston and made two local flights.

On Saturday 20th. Yankee Kilo flew Manston-Palma-Perpignan-Manston, combining these tours; next day Victor Delta took the first 0830 weekly tour to Dijon and later made the first visit to Le Touquet. During the afternoon Yankee Kilo operated the first Sunday Basle.

Up at Wymeswold Foxtrot Yankee made an air test on Tuesday 23rd. after which some further adjustments were required. The following day Victor Delta flew Manston-Ostend-Gatwick-Manston. After another air test on Thursday Captain Souster flew Foxtrot Yankee back to Manston and the 1963 fleet was complete. The next day, again with Peter Souster in command, she flew her first revenue flight to Le Bourget.

The tours continued to build up over the weekend 26th./28th. Yankee Kilo took the second Naples on Friday, a fortnightly tour at 1400, and the first of the weekly 0845 tours to Pisa on

The 1963 Fleet (Skyfotos Ltd.)

Saturday while Foxtrot Yankee flew to Perpignan and to Palma. Victor Foxtrot made the first two visits to Rotterdam, always a popular short distance destination in the spring. On Sunday Yankee Kilo operated the first DC4 Dijon, taking over from the Vikings. The last flight of the month, flown by Victor Foxtrot, was Manston-Luton-Rotterdam-Luton-Manston.

Leroy Tours, of course, provided a significant part of the programme and other licences to fly inclusive tours were held for Blue Cars, Excelsior European Travel, Hards, Clarksons, Friendship, Lumbs, Lyons, Raymond Cook, Herman's European Luxury Tours and Page & Moy. Some flights that year were also made for John Bloom's company, Rolls Razor.

Although the inclusive tour licences were the primary concern, applications were also made to the Air Transport Licensing Board for permission to fly scheduled services for passengers and vehicle ferry operations. The 11 April issue of the 'Gazette' reported on the appeal before the Commissioner appointed by the Minister of Aviation against the granting by the A.T.L.B. of two applications by Air Ferry for the services to Ostend and Le Touquet. The three airlines objecting were all Air Holdings companies, B.U.A., B.U.A.F. and Silver City

TWILIGHT OF THE PISTONS

who sought to limit the frequency and to exclude Le Touquet from the licences granted.

It was early July before the '*Gazette*' was able to print that Air Ferry had won the battle to operate scheduled passenger services to Ostend and Le Touquet although, because the result of the appeal had only just been made known, no schedule for the cross channel flights had been worked out. In the end, these in fact were the only scheduled services ever operated by Air Ferry. There were few passengers and they were invariably placed on programmed inclusive tour flights, the return and day return prices being £7-1-0 and £4-12-0 to Ostend and £6-10-0 and £3-10-0 to Le Touquet. Passenger licences were granted for Manston to Verona and Belfast to Le Touquet but these were never used.

THE CREWS

Other aircrew came and left during the season, Captain Salmon joined in May, while Captain Stimpson left, and Captain Frank Hargreaves flew the Vikings from June until the end of November. Basil Salmon, the son of a Margate garage owner, had been at school with Hugh Kennard and later was an apprentice with him at Rootes. First Officer John Page joined in May followed by Tony Ahmad on the 29th of that month. John was not a newcomer to Thanet, having spent the 1960 season joy-riding from Ramsgate Airport in a Prentice. He later flew as a co-pilot on Viscounts for Maitland Drewery Aviation, including a wet-lease to Austrian Airlines. One of the captains he flew with was Bill Wood. John also operated DC4s for B.U.A. and took part as a test pilot in the flight trials of the A.T.L. Carvair. Tony Ahmad, by the end, would be equal with Bill Wood as the longest serving operational pilot at Air Ferry, both flying for sixty one months of the sixty nine that Air Ferry was operational. The last appointment, starting on 1 August, was W (Bill) Isaacs.

Air Hostesses for the first season, in addition to Maureen Pople, included Jill Bell, Jill Bentham, Margo Hathaway, Judy Leete, Jane Mills, Gillian Starr-Gosling and Liz Tapp. There were some additional freelance cabin crew that season, who flew as required by operations.

THE YEAR CONTINUED

May The month opened quietly and to schedule. Victor Delta departed on Wednesday 1st. for Basle at 1400 and Victor Foxtrot carried out a Manston-Southend-Dinard charter, returning via Southend the next day. There were eleven flights over the first weekend 3rd./5th. including Air Ferry's first visit to Luxembourg, flown by Victor Delta. There was just one flight on Monday 6th., to Ostend and a Basle on Wednesday, no flights were made on Tuesday and Thursday.

With the weekend round again, there were another eleven flights, Foxtrot Yankee to Naples, Pisa, Dijon and the first Verona, while Yankee Kilo went to Perpignan and Palma, having to make a return there again early on Sunday morning. The remaining flights were to Ostend and Basle by the Vikings. On Wednesday 15th. Victor Foxtrot and Foxtrot Yankee flew Manston-Southend-Rotterdam-Southend-Manston, Victor Delta went to Ostend and Yankee Kilo flew a round trip Manston-Basle-Rotterdam-Gatwick-Manston, the latter captained by Don Brooker with John Page making his first Air Ferry flight as co-pilot.

An early photo, Maureen Pople (left), Bill Wood (right)   (Roy Doherty Collection)

There were no flights on Friday 17th., next day Yankee Kilo flew the first DC4 Saturday morning Basle and with

1963 THE FRANTIC SUMMER

Foxtrot Yankee off to Pisa thirty five minutes later one of the seasons pressure points was highlighted. The third Saturday morning flight, to Perpignan, presumably being sub-chartered. Victor Foxtrot flew a Luxembourg and in the evening both DC4s went to Palma, a routine from now on.

Obtaining enough work, but not too much, was a delicate balance to achieve and Hugh Kennard was reluctant to decline any hours. He needed a bank of customers, especially with an eye for 1964 and good aircraft utilisation; he knew there was capacity available to carry out sub-charters if they were required.

Inevitably, to fit in with the usual holiday pattern, the major movements occurred over the period from midday Friday until Sunday evening. As a result the DC4 programme was highly stressed at this time and there was a substantial reliance on sub-charters. The flights at the beginning of the weekend, during Friday, naturally had the best chance of keeping to schedule. Conversely, it was at this point that the programme was most vulnerable, weather or technical problems could make delays escalate quickly and lead to a ripple effect through the weekend.

The main weekend departures for the DC4s, with programmed times estimated as closely as possible, illustrate that there was not a great margin for the turnrounds at the destinations and back at Manston.

Day	Time	Destination	Frequency	Average block time hours/minutes
Friday	1400	Naples	two weekly	11.30
	2230	Perpignan	weekly	7.00
	2300	Perpignan	weekly from July	7.00
Saturday	0830	Basle	weekly	4.40
	0830	Pisa	weekly	8.41
	1000	Perpignan	weekly	7.00
	1930	Palma	weekly	9.30
	2000	Palma	weekly	9.30
Sunday	0830	Dijon	weekly	4.05
	0930	Verona	two weekly	9.11
	1000	Basle	two weekly	4.40
	1330	Basle	weekly	4.40

Victor Delta
30 May 1963

Victor Foxtrot
4 June, 1963

TWILIGHT OF THE PISTONS

The Naples and Verona tours operated on the Friday and Sunday of the same week and were accorded some priority as, throughout the season, they avoided any lengthy delays. Flight times were subject to some variation, particularly those to Basle. From early June the Basle tours on Sunday were operated by a Viking and a DC4 one week, with a Viking and two DC4s the next.

Operating more of the shorter legs the Vikings were less sensitive to delays. Their main work, in addition to the Ostends, was primarily daytime flights such as Le Touquet every Friday morning and at 1230 on alternate Sundays throughout the season. There was a series of flights to Copenhagen at 1100 on alternate Fridays and the aircraft went to Luxembourg each Saturday morning to the end of August when there was a substantial increase for September and October, assisted by the DC4s. As mentioned, there were also regular Viking Sunday flights to Basle and fortnightly ones to Dijon as part of the weekend programme

The four aircraft visited Ostend most days of the week with Basle as the other main destination midweek with DC4 and Viking flights leaving at 1400 hours on Wednesdays for most of the season. After Ostend and Basle the most frequent destination in 1963 was Dusseldorf with flights to that airport largely confined to the weekdays with Friday being most popular, there being two days when the Vikings and DC4s made seven trips there. The Vikings made a regular Friday afternoon flight from June to October although the number of aircraft used on these charters varied considerably.

The Dusseldorf flights were carried out for a West Country firm who quickly achieved some notoriety with their cash flow problems. It became a weekly feature to ensure that cheques would be honoured by the bank before the aircraft were permitted to depart from Manston and on some fraught occasions Tim Leigh collected a bundle of notes from the courier before the engines of the Viking started up.

There was one flight on Monday 20th., by Victor Foxtrot to Ostend, no flights on Tuesday while next day Victor Foxtrot operated Manston-Le Touquet-Gatwick-Le Touquet-Manston, her sister aircraft went to Amsterdam while the DC4s flew an Ostend and a Basle.

Friday 24 May saw a historic departure when Foxtrot Yankee made the first night flight to Perpignan, leaving Manston at 2254 and returning via Basle. It is possible that the Saturday Basle was sub-chartered and that Lloyd International's DC4 G-ARWK positioned into Manston for this as she was parked on a hardstand on the Monday morning.

During May there were no flights from Manston on any of the Tuesdays and Thursdays in the month. On Friday 31st. Victor Foxtrot left slightly late on the first Copenhagen tour and Yankee Kilo closed the month with a departure at 2317 to Perpignan.

June   There were more flights in June, 161, than in all the previous months together, with a considerable increase over the weekends and to Ostend. The first big delay occurred on Saturday 1 June when Yankee Kilo left the apron at 0810 with 75 passengers for Basle and returned with technical difficulties 43 minutes later; she was towed away from the flight line and did not fly again until she had an air test on Wednesday. With Foxtrot Yankee booked for Perpignan, the Basle, Pisa and second Palma flights had to be sub-chartered. Lloyd International's other DC4, G-ARWI, Whisky India, undoubtedly did some of these as she was at Manston that weekend; she and her sister aircraft Whisky Kilo would be frequent visitors during the season. Help is also likely to have been given by Caledonian on Sunday 2nd. as their beautiful DC7C, G-ASIV, was at Manston that day.

G-ARWI of Lloyd International

(Air Britain)

1963 THE FRANTIC SUMMER

On Sunday morning the Basle gremlins struck again as Foxtrot Yankee departed at 1042 and aborted her take-off. After a brief air test at 1640 she finally left for Basle at 1800 although it is not known whether this was the first or second programmed departure, the other being sub-chartered. It is likely that Foxtrot Yankee had more trouble on the return leg as the *Gazette* reported an 'Alert at Manston' which listed the DC4 as being: 'Bound from Basle to Manston when one of its four engines was put out of action. County ambulances stood by but were not needed as the plane made a perfect landing.' With DC4s thin on the flight line, Victor Delta took the DC4 flight to Dijon and it is likely the second coach was diverted to another airport for a sub-charter. During the next week Foxtrot Yankee carried out two charters, one to Cherbourg and the other to Aalborg in Denmark.

> *Leroy Tours, who used Ostend a great deal, actually had an agent based there, a smartly uniformed young ambassador called Richard Grist, and it was decided he would also represent Air Ferry. With the high frequency of operations Richard was a frequent visitor at Manston and recalls that, enjoyable as the advent of the Air Ferry involvement was, it was an opportunity to double his work without increasing his pay!*

Air Ferry's handling agent in Ostend was Herfurth Air Services, and a close association between the two companies quickly built up.

On Friday 7th, Yankee Kilo departed early for Naples at 1345 but lost this time later on having to make a technical return after leaving there. The Saturday mornings Basle and Perpignan must have been sub-chartered although the aircraft was back on the line for the second of the nights Palmas.

June continued, the long bright days busy with many short range flights and quick turn rounds. It was not surprising that there were some delays, the 1000 flight to Perpignan on Saturday 15th. suffered one of over three hours and the tour there on Saturday 29th. was sub-chartered, almost certainly to one of Balair's sleek red and white DC4s, HB-ILU, which was at Manston that day.

From Sunday 16th. the 0830 DC4 to Dijon had a Viking added on alternate weeks, the Viking leaving first.

Balair's HB-ILU, 29 June 1963

Although virtually all of the flights were out of Manston there were occasional variations as on the 21st. when Victor Delta flew Manston-Le Touquet-Gatwick-Le Touquet-Manston while her sister aircraft combined an Ostend with a Le Touquet that day. On Saturday 22nd. no Basle operated and this must have been sub-chartered.

Unplanned night stops were costly affairs and the captains could come under some pressure from Hugh Kennard to avoid them if at all possible. One time a senior engineer was working at Basle and joined a departing Viking to come home for the weekend. A Hercules engine failed soon after take-off and, the Viking being somewhat marginal on one, the captain quickly put the aircraft down again at Basle. Although by now this was after seven p.m., Hugh did not like it that the passengers would have to be accomodated at a hotel and the engineer recalls the captain smoking his pipe while pacing perplexedly up and down in the operations room. This occurrence was likely to be Victor Foxtrot's flight of Wednesday 26 June that returned to Manston the next day although Victor Delta replicated the incident on the Wednesday flight eight weeks later on 21st. August.

> *Pop and two other hostesses had installed themselves in a flat in Thanet called 'North Sea Lodge'. The bathroom was in need of redecoration and with a leave day coming up, Pop said: 'We'll have a working bee, let's organise some help and we can have a party afterwards.' A willing crowd turned up with more bottles than brushes and a show of individualism by some of the painters meant that they ended up with a fresh, but multi-hued, bathroom.*

News of another licensing appeal was reported by the *'Gazette'* on 14 June, this time by B.E.A. and B.U.A. against the A.T.L.B. decision to allow Air Ferry to run a summer service to Verona, looked on as the gateway to Northern Italy. By the time the appeal was heard Air Ferry was operating inclusive tour flights to this destination with the scheduled service planned for the future.

July By mid July the heat was telling. Some passengers reacted philosophically to delays and waited patiently while others were more assertive and required a large measure of tact from the Traffic staff. Because the coaches were required to arrive in good time for checking in and baggage handling it was a common sight to see families, couples and little groups seated outside in the sunshine during that summer, when the delays built up the grass areas took on the appearance of a picnic site.

Everyone worked long hours, especially the engineers and refuellers, with the overtime calculations producing some impressive results. The engineers were expert at working out their gross pay with extreme accuracy; these were the days of pounds, shillings and pence and well before pocket calculators were invented. Cash was still delivered to the hangar in packets by the Wages Clerk and it was sometimes a hunted looking Olly Hagerty who came panting back to the offices.

The month started, as June had ended, with an Ostend, and tour flying continued to Basle, Perpignan, Palma, Dijon, Dusseldorf, Naples, Le Touquet, Pisa, Luxembourg, Verona and Copenhagen. There was still a great deal of pressure, the Saturday morning Perpignan did not operate on the 6th., but there was also the opportunity for an extra charter and Victor Foxtrot made Air Ferry's first visit to Hanover on 8 July, her sister aircraft making the return journey to collect the passengers on the 11th.

Yankee Kilo left for Perpignan close to schedule on Friday 12th. although Foxtrot Yankee, due to follow thirty minutes later, went unserviceable. The aircraft recorded a Manston-Manston of 1 hour 20 minutes at 2324 and finally departed at 0257, returning to take the Saturday morning Perpignan just an hour late. This weekend marked the start of three Perpignans a weekend, a venture which lasted a month before variations were introduced. The Saturday Pisa was sub-chartered, Balair's HB-ILB being used for this. The return leg of Monday's Ostend was used for training, with John Page making a take-off with engine failure and a three-engine landing.

One recurring impression of the DC4s, not only in 1963, was the defect these American aircraft threw up prior to takeoff, the magneto (mag.) drop; a disease caused by faulty sparking plugs or their harnesses. Mag. drops would frequently introduce two hour delays and cause great inconvenience, especially at the weekends when the planners had worked to minimum turn round times. (Paul Noller).

The following weekend proved to be an even more traumatic one. Friday 19 July was notable for the two DC4s and Victor Foxtrot flying seven Dusseldorfs, one of these making Yankee Kilo leave slightly late for Naples. Foxtrot Yankee left 30 minutes late at 2300 for Perpignan but, undouebdly due to the weather over the Pyrenees, was diverted to Barcelona. She returned well behind time to leave again for Perpignan, the second Friday night flight leaving at 1015 on Saturday. Yankee Kilo meanwhile had set off for Pisa on time, flown by Bob McNay and John Page, but this gain was quickly dissipated as she had a port outer tyre burst on take-off for the return journey, and the programme came under more strain. Foxtrot Yankee returned to Manston from Perpignan and after a quick turnround left on the first of the Saturday night Palmas, the second being sub-chartered. The hapless 1000 Perpignan passengers left at 2115 and 2155 respectively, the load split between the two Vikings. Yankee Kilo was back on the line by Sunday morning to take the Verona flight, albeit two hours late. The Saturday morning Basle was another tour to be sub-chartered.

Although officially joining in August, Bill Isaacs went to Basle on Yankee Kilo as supernumary F/O with Hugh Tubman and John Page on the 24th. The weekend of 26th./28th. July was relatively quiet but there is a gap in the flight log for the Saturday morning Perpignan and as Balair's DC6 was at Manston the likelihood is that that particular tour travelled in style.

The Kennards' of course, had total authority and responsibility, and were always on call when not on the airfield. If there was an operational issue to be discussed, Peter Souster would ring them at Linton, although there were many occasions when they worked at Manston overnight or right through a weekend. In terms of personal satisfaction, these months were a high water mark for Hugh and Audry, perhaps even more than the Air Kruise days, with Air Ferry on course and enjoying a busy and vibrant time.

1963 THE FRANTIC SUMMER

August The weather intervened again on Friday 2nd. with Foxtrot Yankee once more being diverted to Barcelona although on this occasion she flew back to Perpignan to collect the returning passengers, thus saving them a long coach trip to meet the aircraft. Back at Manston Foxtrot Yankee was turned straight round leaving again for Perpignan at 1355 and returned to leave for the third time to that airport within twenty four hours at 2230 on Saturday night, the passengers having endured a delay of over twelve hours. In the small hours of Sunday morning, Foxtrot Yankee had to make a technical return to Perpignan with engine failure. Two hours later Captain Tubman and F/O Page gave the aircraft an air test, and at 0630GMT the DC4 finally climbed out into the French airways en route for Manston with a cabin containing some very tired and anxious passengers. With Yankee Kilo making the long haul to Pisa, there was no Saturday Basle and only one Palma that night.

Jeremy Kennard was in charge of flight catering, a specialised activity that required a production line of operatives preparing sandwiches and packing trays. The quantity in the pack was not considered too significant as, on the shorter trips, the aircraft was often nearing the destination by the time the passengers had managed to open the sealed packets. Occasionally, when time was short, or there were delays, Jeremy had the meals served on the coaches.

One time, due to a protracted delay, there was a need to set up an improvised production line to make sandwiches and Ronnie Cox was borrowed from Traffic to help. Jeremy, ever cost conscious, required one operative to mash the corned beef on the grounds that the product would go further by this method than by being sliced, whereupon Ronnie exclaimed: 'You can put me anywhere else on the line, but I will not be a corned beef masher!'

Another occasion, vividly remembered by those present, was when Gillian Starr-Gosling inspected the 'tiffin' trays at the aircraft and threw them across the tarmac with the withering criticism: 'These cups are not clean.'

Foxtrot Yankee's run of snags recurred the next weekend, the 9th./11th., and resulted in the programme being frantically reshuffled. The DC4 flew to Dusseldorf twice and then went unserviceable. Yankee Kilo flew two Perpignans, the second Friday night flight departing at 0901 on Saturday. One of these was flown by Hugh Tubman and Bill Isaacs; other pilots who flew frequently with Hugh that year were F/Os Kellard, Laker, Hendley, Page and Winyard. Both of the Balair DC4s, HB-ILU and HB-ILB, were pressed into service, their flights naturally including the Saturday Basle carried out in reverse as Balair was based at the Swiss airport, one to Pisa and probably the DC4 Sunday Dijon. HB-ILU, incidentally, has a niche in aviation history as the first aircraft to carry out a scheduled transatlantic freight service, in February 1955, while operating with Swissair.

One of the ground hostesses recalls loading an aircraft five times due to hold ups for various technical snags and thinking: 'If I was a passenger I wouldn't go.' On another occasion she was standing with Hugh Kennard beneath a DC4 from which fuel was dripping and he remarked: 'We'll have to get some chewing gum.'

The morning Perpignan departed late on Saturday afternoon split between the Vikings. Order was sufficiently restored for Yankee Kilo to depart for Palma on the first of the Saturday evening flights on time and Foxtrot Yankee was back on the line to take the second Palma, leaving some six and a half hours late early on Sunday morning. Victor Foxtrot alone went to Dijon, whether this was part cover for a DC4 or only one coach load was planned is not known.

On 14 August a stranger appeared when a Viking with a very worn paint scheme landed and taxied over to a hardstand away from the main activity. This was D-BABY, late of Luftransport Unternehmen, on delivery to Air Ferry from Dusseldorf. The aircraft had originally been delivered to the R.A.F. and flown with the Empire Test Pilots School; she later flew with the Royal Australian Air Force and before delivery to Manston had accumulated only 8,006 flying hours.

TWILIGHT OF THE PISTONS

Charlie Hotel arrives from Germany

The hectic pace continued on the third weekend, 16th./18th. August, with delays to the Perpignan flights and sub-charters for the Saturday morning Basle and Sundays Dijon.

Manston was an invigorating place to be that summer, Traffic girls leading crocodiles of passengers over the road, through Customs and across the apron; snakes of tarmac trolleys weaving towards the roller conveyor, brightly coloured coaches arriving and departing. The smart uniforms of the Traffic staff and of the pilots and air hostesses; in the rain or wind the girls wore neat white scarves to keep their Air Ferry bowlers from taking off. After a flight or at the end of their duty the hostesses would bring their bar takings, usually in a sick bag, into Accounts. Quite often the complications of shortage of time on the flight, different currencies and a few breakages to account for, necessitated some help from the Cashier and the bar would be spread out for a recount.

The Terminal   (Roy Doherty Collection)

The hostesses' pay, which at that time was £7.10.0 per week, with the chief hostess on just £10.0.0, was supplemented by their bar commission. It was not unusual for the girls, including Pop, to find on final reckoning after a hectic flight that the cash was short and they had to put in some of their own money to balance.

Delays struck at most destinations on the programme and did not mostly affect Perpignan and Palma as might appear from this narrative. Thirty years on, without the programme as a guide, the flights to the more distant destinations are more easily charted from the flight logs. In August, for example, of the 182 flights made, 88 were to Ostend and 19 to Basle. In the event of a long delay accruing to an Ostend tour, at either end, it was sometimes expedient to send the coaches to Ostend or to Dover and make the Channel crossing by boat. Very long delays sometimes necessitated an overnight stop in a hotel, although this was very much an action of last resort in view of the cost involved. It was not always the fault of the airlines, coaches occasionally broke down in which case the tour operator would pay for the accomodation or this would be shared.

> *The season was punctuated by occasional parties at which a combination of high and potent spirits combined to provide welcome relaxation, the success measured on at least one occasion when doubts were expressed as to the whereabouts of missing pyjamas. As with all dynamic organisations containing both sexes, romances blossomed and there were cases of unrequited love, especially of one hostess for a captain. While seeking to portray an accurate picture, warts and all, in a narrative of this sort, some recollections have been toned down or omitted altogether in order not to cause embarrassment or distress to any individuals.*

On Wednesday 21st. both Yankee Kilo and Victor Delta made returns to Basle, the reasons not being known although Yankee Kilo's was probably technical as later on she made a local flight back at Manston.

The weekend of 23rd./25th. passed in a well regulated manner and both of the DC4s left on Friday night within half an hour for Perpignan. It was not the weekend for Naples and Verona and Balair's HB-ILB was again at Manston in support. The next weekend also went quite well with the Saturday morning Perpignan departing close to schedule although two main flights, the Saturday Basle and the Sunday Dijon, on 1st. September, were sub-chartered.

September

> *Manston, in its heyday, was a large grass airfield and the wartime emergency runway was built at the highest, southern extremity, of the station, running parallel to the Ramsgate-Canterbury road. The view from the civil side across the grass airfield to the T2 hangar on the R.A.F. side was virtually identical to how it was during September 1940, with sleek Spitfires awaiting the next scramble. During the summer the heat haze caused distant objects to shimmer and dance, especially difficult if you were using binoculars to try and read military serials, and there would be a soporific hum from the tractor busy with the periodic grasscutting. In places on the airfield the grass still showed 'fairy rings' where circular impressions remained thirty three years after bomb craters were filled in while the Battle of Britain raged overhead.*

On Saturday 7th. the Pisa tour had its longest delay of the season when Foxtrot Yankee left four and a half hours late. One of the DC4 flights that morning encountered difficulties which required one propeller to be feathered and the radio call reporting engine trouble resulted in Thanet's fire and ambulance services being on alert for thirty minutes until the aircraft landed safely. Next day Victor Delta departed for Dijon early and events ran well to plan.

People were wilting now after a long hot summer and would wilt some more with the last disruptions over the weekend of 13th./15th. September. Foxtrot Yankee left reasonably promptly to Naples on Friday lunchtime, Captain Tubman and John Page returning via Ostend, a diversion due to fog over the U.K., in the small hours of Saturday. Yankee Kilo, already very late for Perpignan, started up at 0325 and recorded only five minutes block time before the passengers were disembarked. She finally left at 0551 and the flight was routed to Toulouse. The aircraft returned to fly the Saturday Basle before taking another Perpignan tour, this flight also being routed to Toulouse. The use of Toulouse on both occasions could have been a change of flight plan rather than weather diversions. A Viking of the French company Airnautic had crashed in the vicinity of Perpignan on Thursday 12th. and it is possible that Perpignan was temporarily restricted. The Viking involved, F-BJER, had once flown as G-AIVC and had preceded Victor Delta on the production line.

As a result of these difficulties the second Palma was sub-chartered and the Sunday Verona, which had somehow kept close to schedule all season, experienced a delay of four hours.

> *Many years on the impressions remain vivid and no doubt will be recalled differently by all those who worked so long and unstintingly to put Air Ferry on the map. The engineers toiling in the*

sun over the Pratt & Whitney motor of a DC4, with the engine covers laying on the grass; some engineers, particularly Sid and John the refuellers, clocking in on Friday morning, working all weekend and disappearing homewards on Monday; quite a few of the staff would have hesitated if questioned as to which day of the week it was.

Through the season, as mentioned, DC4 and Viking flights had operated at 1400 hours on Wednesdays to Basle. For some reason, a puzzle in retrospect, the Viking flight did not take place on the 11th. but left at 0535 on Thursday morning. A similar event took place the following week when Foxtrot Yankee left at 0541 on Thursday and flew to Strasbourg, almost certainly a Basle diversion. After this the programme began to wind down, although not without difficulties. Victor Foxtrot operated the last Copenhagen on Friday 20th although Yankee Kilo suffered an oleo collapse at Basle on the night of Sunday 15th., causing Hugh Tubman and John Page to abandon the take-off. The aircraft came back next day but did not fly again until the second Saturday Palma, at 0420 on Sunday 22nd. This resulted in the Vikings operating one of the Perpignans on the 20th, carrying just 57 passengers between them. In addition, the Saturday Pisa did not operate and must have been sub-chartered.

Delays in the season occasionally put great pressure on short tempers and one time a frustrated Lumb's Tours passenger hit a member of the Traffic Staff over the head with an umbrella; folklore has it that Audry was the victim but this was not so.

The last weekend in September, 27th./29th., saw three Perpignan flights by DC4, all by Foxtrot Yankee, leaving Victor Delta and Victor Foxtrot to go to Basle on Saturday morning. On Sunday Yankee Kilo flew the last Verona tour.

As mentioned, one destination increased while others reduced, this being Luxembourg; the tours which had averaged seven a month until August increased substantially in September and October with autumn visits to the Ardennes.

At the time the seasonal staff were ending their contracts and leaving, Mike Harradine joined the Commercial Department. Mike was already involved in Air Ferry work; some of the early charters from Southend had been booked by him. Lewis Leroy, with whom Mike had worked before, was very keen for him to come to Manston and in the ensuing months and years Mike and Hugh Kennard spent much of their time together finding new business. In Commercial, Jenny Nias, nominally the secretary, but who was also used to helping out in Operations and Traffic, now had someone else to look after.

October There were some charters interspersed with the closing tour flights, especially for the Vikings. On Saturday 5th. Victor Delta flew Manston-Jersey-Basle-Manston and over the 11th./12th. a Manston-Frankfurt-Jersey-Manston. On Sunday 13th. the aircraft carried out a flight Manston-Lille-Dusseldorf-Lille-Luxembourg-Manston. For the DC4s, Foxtrot Yankee made Air Ferry's first visit to Berlin on the 6th.

Of the tour flying, Sunday 6th. saw the last Basle, by Yankee Kilo, and the last Sunday Le Touquet, by Victor Foxtrot. The following Friday Yankee Kilo ended the Naples visits with Foxtrot Yankee closing the Dijons on Sunday 13th.

Victor Delta operated the last tours to Le Touquet on Friday 18th. and to Perpignan, making two flights there, on Saturday 19th. Foxtrot Yankee flew the last Luxembourg the following day and was then handed over to the engineers for a check. There were no flights on Monday, Tuesday or Wednesday; Yankee Kilo flew an Ostend on Thursday while Victor Delta went to Dusseldorf twice on Friday 25th. The next day Yankee Kilo flew out empty on both occasions to bring the last tour passengers of that frantic summer back from Pisa and then from Palma. Victor Foxtrot had been undergoing maintenance since a Le Touquet flight on 7th. October, and this aircraft made the only other flight in the month, a 30 minute Manston-Manston, on Wednesday 30th.

D-BABY, now back to being G-AOCH, had departed in the hands of John Gibson on 15 October to Air Couriers for an overhaul, cabin refurbishment and a repaint. Captain Gibson did not seem over impressed with the pre-check condition of the new acquisition when he came in to claim his expenses on his return from Gatwick.

As the season drew to a close the aircraft appeared more often, and stayed longer, in the hangar. There, grounded and often looking little like flying machines, with components removed and panels taken off, it was possible to stand and reflect on the miracle of flight. Although well maintained and in smart livery, the noses of the aircraft were marked with numerous small impressions which were a silent testimony of ice and hail encountered during thousands of hours in the air.

November November was very quiet with just twenty flights and no flying on fifteen days. Victor Delta flew a charter with 40 passengers to Le Bourget on Saturday 2nd., returning next morning, and this was the only movement in the first thirteen days. On Thursday 14th. Victor Delta made the first in a series of freight flights to Le Touquet and next day made a short local flight while her sister Viking went to Ostend, as described below.

Victor Delta flew five more Le Touquets between the 16th. and the 23rd. and on Friday 22nd. Victor Foxtrot went to Dusseldorf with passengers. On Monday Victor Delta reverted to passenger flying with a Manston-Southend-Amsterdam-Manston while Victor Foxtrot looked after the Le Touquet freight.

On Tuesday 26th. Victor Delta flew passengers to Ostend while Victor Foxtrot took freight twice to Le Touquet and once the following day. There were three passenger flights on the 28th., Yankee Kilo left for Madrid at 0505 while the two Vikings went to Le Touquet. Foxtrot Yankee made a 43 minute local flight on Friday for an air test and a six monthly check flight by Peter Souster for John Page. Victor Foxtrot made the last cargo journey to Le Touquet on Saturday 30th.

One of the mechanics at this time was a young Spaniard who broke his leg in a motor cycle accident in one of the first frosts of the approaching winter. After treatment in one of the local hospitals his parents were keen for him to return to the Continent to recuperate and the Kennards kindly allowed one of the Vikings to take him over to Ostend. The young man was carefully loaded aboard on a stretcher and lashed to the floor, managing to put up with this indignity under the ministrations of his personal and gorgeous air hostess. As there were only two 'empty' Viking flights to Ostend over the winter period, on 15 November and 31 January, this was almost certainly the former.

December Freight flights to Le Touquet ran throughout December and, up to the 12th., those made by Victor Foxtrot were the only movements apart from a passenger flight by Victor Delta to Dusseldorf on Friday 6th. In all there were nineteen Le Touquets, Victor Foxtrot made fifteen and Yankee Kilo four, the latter carrying eight 'passengers', for some reason, on her Christmas Eve flight. There was no flying at Manston on eleven days of the month.

A broad grass runway was maintained at Manston on a northeast/southwest heading for use by light aircraft and was most frequently used by the R.A.F. Chipmunks. During the winter months, when the prevailing wind whipped in from the sea, the Vikings occasionally used the grass runway. The road across the airfield would be closed while the aircraft taxied up to the north-east corner, near to 'The Drome' garage. After a while, with a roar from it's two Bristol Hercules engines, a Viking would lumber down into the dip and accelerate up the incline to lift away and quickly disappear into the scudding clouds.

On Friday 13th. there was a training or calibration flight by Foxtrot Yankee at Stanstead and there was another Friday Viking Dusseldorf; this charter and the remaining flights in the month, apart from Le Touquet, all being for passengers. Over the 19th/20th. Victor Delta flew Manston-Southend-Bremen-Southend-Manston while on the 20th. Foxtrot Yankee operated to Dusseldorf and Victor Foxtrot flew Manston-Dusseldorf-Manston-Manchester-Manston.

Some of the charters were for ships crews and, on the whole, the passengers behaved well although on one occasion a burly seaman was not prepared to extinguish his cigarette, at Pop's request, before entering the toilet. 'I'm not going to be told what to do by a young woman,' he maintained, but he did when two equally burly colleagues appeared, one on either side of him.

'They all used to make out they didn't know how to do up the seat belts. I used to go along absolutely poker faced, not amused; they'd try it on a bit but I just ignored it, never had any trouble at all.' (Maureen Pople)

TWILIGHT OF THE PISTONS

On the contrary, Pop had started collecting letters of appreciation sent in to her by grateful passengers at her previous companies and the practice continued at Air Ferry. She did have one brush with Customs, as probably many of the crews did. One day she had somehow left two cartons of cigarettes among the opened boxes and bottles and Customs peremptorily called over the tannoy for her to report to them immediately. Whether they thought she was smuggling or this was an opportunity to frighten the life out of her, which they did, is not known.

Audry (right) with Gwen Laycock   (Audry Kennard)

There was quite a flurry of activity in the last part of the month. On Saturday 21st. Victor Delta flew a Geneva, two Dusseldorfs and started a Manston-Southend-Dusseldorf-Southend-Dusseldorf-Manston, while Victor Foxtrot went to Palma, a 9 hour 21 minute block time. This aircraft went to Dusseldorf on Sunday and on Monday.

After Christmas Victor Delta flew Manston-Zurich-Manchester on the 27th. and returned to Manston on the 30th while Foxtrot Yankee flew two more Dusseldorfs, on the 28th. and 29th. Next day, Monday 30th., Yankee Kilo carried out the final Basle of the year before going into the hangar on check while Victor Foxtrot operated the last two Le Touquet freight flights of 1963. It fell to Victor Delta, (not 'VD' as the writer was once gently reminded in those far off days), to close the year with a flight, perhaps appropriately, to Dusseldorf.

STATISTICS

By the end of 1963 Victor Delta and Victor Foxtrot had flown 554 and 539 hours respectively, while Yankee Kilo had amassed the most with 1,050 to Foxtrot Yankee's 950. Charlie Hotel's delivery and transfer to Gatwick added a further 2 to make a total of 3,095. During the year 70,598 passengers had been carried, and some freight. Victor Delta had carried most passengers for the Vikings and Foxtrot Yankee most for the DC4s.

August had been the busiest month in terms of passengers carried and of flying hours for both types of aircraft. During the first year 41 different airfields had been visited in 940 flights, the latter figure excluding repetitive training flights and technical returns. In compiling the details the rule followed throughout has been to treat delivery flights and their flying hours as being for Air Ferry while flights away from Manston, on the departure of an aircraft to new users, have been excluded.

The local newspapers provided some publicity in recognition of the first seasons results and of Air Ferry's contribution to reducing the high unemployment prevalent in the eastern corner of Kent. An article and three photographs appeared on 17 January 1964 highlighting the success to date and giving an optimistic view of the future. In an interview for the article Wing Commander Kennard outlined four factors working for the benefit of Manston. These were the position of the airfield being closer to the Continent than any other; the reduction in journey time for coaches now that the M2 motorway, leading on to the Thanet Way, had been constructed; the fact that Manston was outside the London air control zone and lastly, that Air Ferry was a self contained unit and benefited from being the only civil operator on the airfield.

This article perpetuated, or possibly began, the myth that Air Ferry carried 120,000 passengers in 1963. Without retracting anything from the achievement of that first successful year the actual total, as given above, fell substantially short of this figure. The writer's data was drawn, at the time, from the Flight Operational Returns completed by the pilots, a copy of which went to Technical Records for their entries in the aircraft log

1963 THE FRANTIC SUMMER

books. The Flight Operational Returns provided the key information, not only for confirming charges to customers, but for the agreement of the duty content on the Petrol Drawback claims with Customs. Details from these were subsequently checked by the writer not only to the hours listed by Technical Records but also to the R.A.F. Landing Sheets which were the basis for the Ministry charges of landing fees each month to Air Ferry.

MANSTON

The R.A.F. side of the airfield had also been busy in 1963. During March No. 618 Gliding School formed to encourage activities for A.T.C. cadets and in the summer the winch launched gliders began to soar into the air. April saw No. 1 Air Experience Flight transfer from White Waltham with their Chipmunks, used to initiate Air Training Corps and Combined Cadet Force cadets to flying. The Pyrene Runway Foamer began development trials at Manston in June. This was a device that pumped out a carpet of foam on which an aircraft with undercarriage trouble could land, with a much reduced risk of sparks causing a fire.

Partly due to its position and also to having Customs facilities, Manston attracted a steady flow of visiting aircraft. Civil visitors included light aircraft, sometimes handled by Air Ferry, and a few owners protested vigorously at being subjected to a small handling charge. There were the sub-charters by Air Ferry such as Balair's immaculate DC4s and DC6 HB-IBZ. There were also some flights by companies using Manston independently, two extreme examples were visits by a smart DC3 of Fairways of Rotterdam and a series of flights carried out during the summer by a Spanish company called Tassa.

Tassa operated two rather shabby DC6s, one of which rejoiced in the name of 'Princessa Lynne.' Air Ferry carried out the airfield handling for these flights and this led to some informed discussion afterwards. The pilots had no aspirations for sartorial elegance, being usually dressed in T shirts, jeans and baseball caps, but it was the engine problems which held the fascinated attention of the night staff. If an engine would not start the DC6 taxied back up to the runway on three motors, took off and air-started the fourth. The aircraft then landed, taxied back and loaded the passengers while keeping the recalcitrant engine idling. Sadly Tassa experienced a crash in the sea later on and the Spanish authorities closed them down.

EC-AUC of Tassa 13 July 1963

The military visitors were a kaleidoscope of types then in service, for the R.A.F. there were Lightnings, Javelins and Hunters, V bombers flew in or carried out roller landings and Canberras were a familiar sight. Transports were represented by Beverlies, Hastings, Argosies and Valettas and the training variant, the Varsity. This was probably the most frequent R.A.F. type, often remaining on the airfield to drone around on night training flights. Foreign air forces appeared too, Magisters, Fiat G91s and Noratlases of the Luftwaffe, a German Navy Albatross and frequently a Royal Canadian Air Force T33, the very successful trainer version of the Shooting Star. From France there were visits by an Armee de L'Air C47 and a Bretagne, plus a Navy Flamant. One day a Messerschmitt 108 appeared in wartime Luftwaffe camouflage.

On Saturday 16 November the Air Experience Flight suffered a sad accident when a Chipmunk, which was doing aerobatics at the time, dived straight into the sea. The pilot and his fourteen-year-old A.T.C. cadet passenger both lost their lives.

R.A.F.

1963 saw much activity in the R.A.F., particularly the V Force which, in a bid to outwit Soviet radar and the ever increasing number of ground to air missiles, switched to low level operations. The white anti-flash paint scheme with pale roundels changed to green and grey camouflage on the big aircraft. In February the Vulcans of 617 Squadron increased their capability substantially by equipping with Blue Steel stand-off missiles and in April No.139 became the first Victor squadron to take this weapon. Following these changes the last Thor ground launched missile squadron disbanded at the end of July.

Although designed and created against a background of austerity, the V bombers possessed excellent technical qualities and compared well with their U.S.S.R. and U.S. counterparts. These features were usually demonstrated by participation in U.S. bombing competitions, but there were other occasions. 'V Force' included one tale: 'There was a wonderful story of a private wager between a Vulcan crew and a steely American fighter pilot to see who could climb the fastest to 50,000 feet out of Goose Bay, Labrador. The American took off 30 seconds ahead of the Vulcan, yet when he got to height he found the Vulcan already there waiting for him.'

There was especial rivalry with the American B52s which, with their very long take-off run, were considered by the V Force crews only to become airborne due to the curvature of the earth.

CIVIL

The annual airline edition of '*Flight*', published in April of each year, gave a fascinating summary of the commercial scene of the day. There were occasional inaccuracies in the number of aircraft listed as some double counting easily occurred when one airline leased an aircraft to another. The rising stars were shown, other companies on the decline to closure or a take over, and those stalwart organisations which seemed to be a permanent feature of the independent scene.

In 1963 Autair, Caledonian and Euravia were in the ascendant while Starways would soon be absorbed by British Eagle. Although still operating under its old name, Skyways, as distinct from Skyways Coach-Air, had become a subsidiary of Euravia during 1962.

A variety of types were in service, DC4s being operated by Air Ferry, B.U.A., Channel, Lloyd International and Starways together with a new company, Transmeridian, which commenced operations during the year with two of the type. In addition to Air Ferry, Vikings also flew for Autair, Channel and Eros, a company formed at Gatwick in April 1962. Derby Airways flew Argonauts and other types which equipped the independents were DC3s, Ambassadors, Yorks and Heralds together with newer aircraft such as the Viscount and Britannia.

AIR HOLDINGS

Air Holdings rationalisation of operating companies continued when on the first day of 1963 two large parts of the group, Silver City and Channel Air Bridge, were fully merged to form British United Air Ferries, with Douglas Whybrow as General Manager. The dominance of B.U.A. in the group dictated the new title while those who put a value on the goodwill of the two well known names now being discarded were overruled. It was indicative of how the group would work. The main operating components of the group now being B.U.A., B.U.A.F. and B.U.(C.I.)A. Freddie Laker's biography: 'Fly Me, I'm Freddie,' quotes 'B.U.A.' with 94 aircraft carrying 1.8 million passengers, 130,000 cars and nearly 90,000 tons of freight a year at this stage.

The signs now firmly pointed to a car ferry decline although August 1963 was actually the record traffic month and the summer also saw the introduction of the 'deep penetration' routes by the Carvairs to Basle, Geneva and Strasbourg.

About half of B.U.A.'s revenue was being generated by trooping flights and it was experiencing an uphill path in introducing its European scheduled services which finally started in the late spring, but only to a few seasonal destinations. Matters were not helped by mid year clashes with the state airlines regarding the air transport industry's joint negotiating body with the unions.

On 22 October an unexpected shock came when the prototype BAC1-11, which had made its first flight in August and on which so many hopes rested, crashed while on a test flight. The aircraft, testing conditions at the extreme aft position of the centre of gravity, had entered a deep stall condition, a difficult and dangerous area of experimentation on high tailed jet aircraft.

Towards the end of the year Douglas Whybrow at B.U.A.F. came under pressure from Miles Wyatt and Freddie Laker to join B.U.A. on the commercial side, with some input to B.U.A.F., but in other respects virtually leaving the vehicle ferry operation to run itself. On 31 December Douglas left 'the Ferrymen' with much regret and became Chief Commercial Executive of B.U.A.

SAFETY
Safety was a continuing cause of concern for civil aviation. The 1950s had seen a series of crashes with fatal consequences involving both the independents and the state corporations. British European Airways had experienced four such accidents in just over eighteen months.

1961 and 1962 saw three fatal crashes to aircraft of the British independents resulting from collisions with high ground, a Viking of Cunard-Eagle and DC3s of Derby and Channel. The Derby Airways aircraft hit ground 7,500 feet up in the Perpignan area while 20 miles from the expected route, killing all 34 on board.

In 1963 there were two more accidents in the vicinity of Perpignan; in January a French Constellation crashed while in September, as mentioned earlier, the Airnautic Viking crashed, sadly while carrying a charter for Lyons Tours, all forty occupants being killed.

OTHER EVENTS
Snow had fallen widely on Boxing Day 1962 and Britain experienced blizzard conditions during January with the highest snowfalls since the bad winter of 1947.

The Queen made a Royal Tour of New Zealand in February and in the spring Sir Winston Churchill was made an honorary citizen of the U.S.A.

A historic meeting took place in Britain in June between the Prime Minister, Harold Macmillan, and the President of the U.S.A., John F. Kennedy; the American contingent coming to West Sussex for this. Only four months later Mr. Macmillan was forced to resign through ill health and was succeeded as the Conservative leader, after days of speculation, by Lord Hume.

In the autumn the Melody Maker awards proclaimed the Beatles as the top vocal group with Cliff Richard and Susan Maughan as the top male and female singers. Mary Quant took the award for Britain in an international fashion show.

On the world scene, President Castro, the catalyst of the Cuban Missile Crisis of the previous year, visited Moscow in May and the following month Pope John died.

U.S.S.R. space exploration continued with the flights of Vostock 5 and 6, the latter containing Valentina Tereshkova, the first woman to fly in space. The U.S.A. made significant advances in rocket technology; the U.S.A.F. deployed its Atlas intercontinental ballistic missiles and the satellite reconnaissance system became operational. It was undoubedly due to the awareness of such advances by both sides that a nuclear test treaty was signed by the two big powers and Britain in Moscow during August.

October saw the retirement in Germany of Chancellor Adenaur, a man who had contributed a great deal to the post war reconstruction, materially and politically, of his country.

In America, nearly three years had passed since President Kennedy's historic inauguration. Much of the legislation needed to make changes was making very slow progress through Congress and the military mission to Vietnam had grown until there were now 16,000 U.S. advisors attempting to hold together a fragile and corrupt government in the never ending struggle against communism. On 22 November the president was assassinated in Dallas, a startling event which cast a chill over the free world. There was an eerie feeling that a superpower, the one relied on by so many, was suddenly leaderless and there was anxious speculation as to who had instigated the deed. Days later, on Thanksgiving Eve the new president, Lyndon Johnson, rallied the nation with an impassioned address to the joint session of Congress.

TWILIGHT OF THE PISTONS

AIR FERRY

Safety instructions

PLEASE READ BEFORE TAKE-OFF AND REPLACE IN SEAT POCKET

AIR FERRY

SICHERHEITS ANWEISUNGEN

BITTE VOR ABFLUG LESEN UND ZURUCKLEGEN

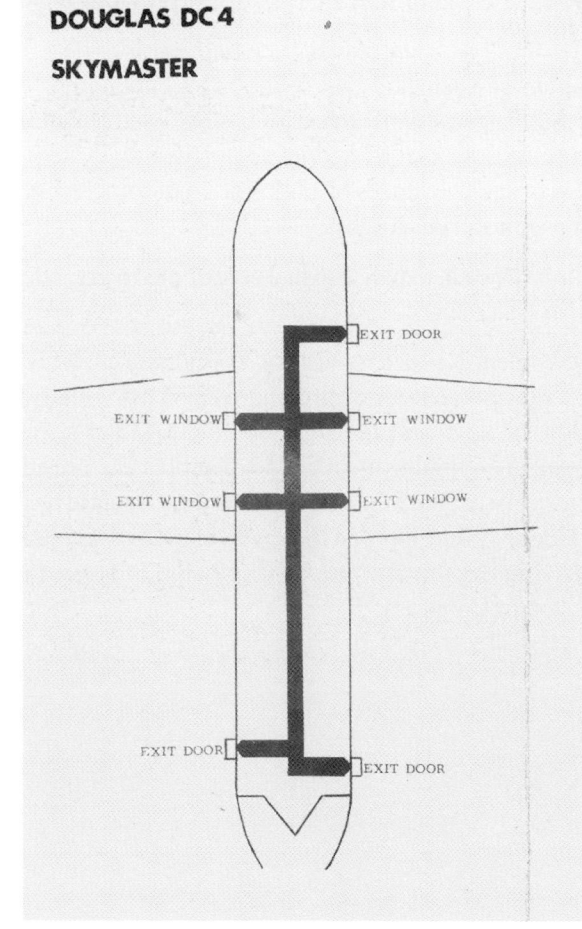

DOUGLAS DC 4 SKYMASTER

VICKERS VIKING

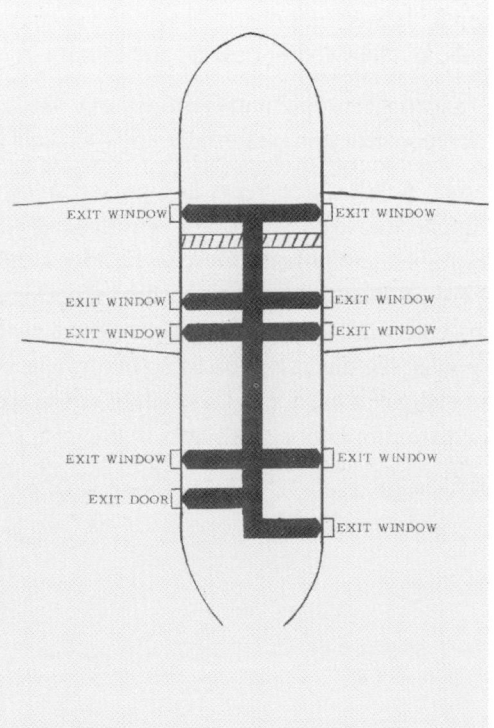

DC4 in the hangar

Len Mees at left

Jill Bell - a deer-like elegance

Douglas DC4 at Manston

CHAPTER 4
1964   SECOND WIND AND A TAKEOVER

THE AIRCRAFT

Douglas DC4   G-APYK   G-ASFY   G-ASOG

Vickers Viking   G-AIVF   G-AIVD   G-AOCH   G-AHOW   G-AJBX

Bristol Freighter G-AMLL

THE CREWS

The tour companies were indicating a buoyant season, deposits were flowing in, and Air Ferry increased the aircrew establishment to meet the additional demand. First Officer Laker transferred to Captain on 10 February, Captain A Nicol joined in March followed by P Ashpitel and R Wigley, complete with their aircraft, on 6 April. Bill Steel rejoined in May for the season and other Captains that year were J Mason, intense, enthusiastic and a navigator like Viv Kellard, and Reg Eames, the latter from June until October. Basil Salmon left in July although he returned occasionally to carry out some freelance work.

Andy Nicol at the controls of a Bristol Freighter   (Andy Nicol)

TWILIGHT OF THE PISTONS

His 1963 appointment having been seasonal until the end of October, Tony Ahmad rejoined as permanent staff on 1 February. Another 1963 seasonal pilot who reappeared in March, rather like a migrational swallow from his home in Palma Nova, was Bill Isaacs. Invariably smiling, he was always appreciative of the small help we in Accounts were able to provide. A connoisseur of cars, like Hugh Kennard, whose maroon Bristol was a familiar sight, he owned a 120 Mercedes.

The new First and Second Officers included some who would be stalwarts from this time on, Peter Johnston and Jeep Jackson, Vic Surrage started on 1 April, followed by Peter Gutteridge a fortnight later. Two others who would be long servers were Patrick Hope on 11 May and Paul Horsting on 19 August. There were some leavers too, Viv Kellard in January who would return later; K Winyard in April, P Thomas in July, John Page in November and John Hazel at the end of the year.

For the cabin crew, 'Pop' and Jane Mills continued as permanent staff and were joined by Jill Firkin, Terry Heffernan and Maggie Studt who, by the end, would easily be Air Ferry's longest serving air hostess.

THE YEAR

January There were no movements on New Years Day and flying began on the 2nd. with Victor Foxtrot making the first two in a series of freight flights to Le Touquet, twenty in all during the month by the Vikings and four by Foxtrot Yankee. Also on Thursday 2nd., Victor Delta carried the first passengers of the year, to Dusseldorf.

To enable him to concentrate on the more strategic work, Tim Leigh appointed Mike Austin as Assistant Accountant in late 1963. Mike, a young married man with two small children, was awaiting the results of his professional examination when he joined. He travelled to the airfield on a motor cycle and with his quiet thoughtful style soon settled in.

There were just three aircraft in service as Yankee Kilo, which had last flown to Basle on 30 December, was on a check at Manston and would not fly again until March. The side opening hangar having been built long before nosewheel undercarriages were a standard design, it took some careful manoeuvring to get the DC4s inside. As mentioned, on the ground and unloaded the DC4s had a tail post fitted underneath to prevent them tipping over backwards, and it was necessary for the engineers to carefully move the aircraft into the hangar in a very tail down position to ensure that the top of the fin did not hit the sliding door mechanism. Once inside, the DC4 was allowed to regain its normal position.

Victor Delta carried out all the Viking passenger flights in January and flew to Zurich on Friday 3rd. while Foxtrot Yankee went to Dusseldorf. There was just one flight on Saturday 4th., by Victor Delta with 25 passengers to Palma, a block time of 9 hours 38 minutes. Foxtrot Yankee went to Dusseldorf again on Sunday.

The next week saw more Le Touquets by both Vikings, there were no flights on the 7th. and 8th., and Victor Delta went to Dusseldorf and Zurich. Foxtrot Yankee, meanwhile, had been put into freight trim in order to carry out Air Ferry's first long range freight charter, to Baghdad. The outward journey from Manston on Friday 10th. was via Damascus with the return flight through Damascus and Brindisi, arriving back at Manston on Friday 17th. A Saudi Arabian Airlines Convair 440, HZ-AAY, had been involved in an incident and suffered damage; the charter was to collect the two engines from this aircraft and bring them to the U.K. for repair.

For the new season Audry and Pop had advertised for seasonal flight attendants who would need to be engaged and trained well before the spring tours. One applicant, who had a name that could be misconstrued, also came from an address on Sandy Balls Estate and, looking through the letters together, Audry exclaimed: 'We must have her.'

The Commercial Department was strengthened about this time by the appointment of Charles Carroll, a man with considerable experience of the travel industry. On leaving the army he had worked in the United Nations transport division based in Geneva and then spent twelve years as the Continental Manager of a well known European coach company.

Monday 13th. saw the Le Touquet freight flights resumed, there was no flying next day and more Le Touquets

1964 SECOND WIND AND A TAKEOVER

on Wednesday and Saturday, while Victor Delta took passengers to Dusseldorf on Friday 17th. There were only three flights from Sunday 19th. to Monday 27th., all to Le Touquet, the first by Victor Foxtrot and the others by Foxtrot Yankee.

Tuesday 28 January was an exciting day, one that still stands out clearly thirty two years later. Captain Wood flew Air Ferry's new DC4 in from Basle shortly before two o'clock. Last seen at Manston in Balair's red and white livery as HB-ILB, she was now in full Air Ferry colours although still bearing her Swiss registration. Peter Wannop explained that ILB would become G-ASOG as everyone went out for a look over the new acquisition. The aircraft had flown for several U.S. airlines, including one that had owned Yankee Kilo, prior to coming to Europe. She had the lowest hours of the DC4s with 30,695 before delivery.

Oscar Golf 29 January, 1964 (above & right)

Balair were held in some respect at Air Ferry, the aircraft purchased from them, especially the DC4s, were considered to be in impeccable condition. During 1963 Yankee Kilo, the ex-Starways aircraft, did not compare well to this standard; it was recently described as 'a sod' at that time by one senior engineer, and Hugh Kennard asked that, on the current check, she be brought up to Oscar Golf's standard as far as possible. Balair was something of a league of nations as regards staff, with Swiss nationals, French and German employees but the chief engineer at that time was an Englishman.

There were two more Le Touquets, on Wednesday and Thursday, both by Foxtrot Yankee, and the DC4 completed the second with a series of landings at Manston. Victor Delta completed the months flying on Friday 31st. with a flight to Ostend.

The '*Gazette*' reported that, at a buffet lunch at the Royal Aero Club in London on 21 January, Hugh Kennard outlined future plans for the commencement of scheduled services to Ostend and Le Touquet for 1964 and the probability of car ferry operations in 1965. Planning was well advanced for this additional work but the licence application was unlikely to be through in time for the coming season. The staff at this time was quoted as being 150.

February There had been 38 flights in January, and February would have even less, with 25 and no aerial movement at all on thirteen days of the month. The only flight on Saturday 1 February, by Foxtrot Yankee, was the first in a series of weekly charters to Geneva for winter sports holidays.

There were just two flights during the next week, Le Touquet freight trips by both Vikings on Wednesday 5th. Foxtrot Yankee operated the second Geneva on Saturday 8th., flown by Bob McNay, John Page and with Guy Clapshaw as supernumary F/O. The writer and his wife went on this flight, it was a clear day with an incredibly smooth journey over the snow covered mountains. Victor Delta also flew that day and went over to Le Touquet.

One of the early bookings, covered by the '*Gazette*' that week, was for a trip by air, on 3 May, for a one day tour of the tulip fields and the famous Keukenhof Park in Holland by members of the Birchington Horticultural Society.

The next flight was by Foxtrot Yankee to Ostend on Wednesday 12th. and the following day Bill Wood flew

TWILIGHT OF THE PISTONS

Oscar Golf up to Field's at Wymeswold for some work which would include the removal of the rest bunk behind the cockpit, once used on long range flights. One of the inspectors would sometimes travel up to Wymeswold to check on the work being carried out, Frank Strainge being one of these. Foxtrot Yankee went to Ostend on Friday and next day operated another Geneva, following this with a 35 minute local flight on return to Manston.

After this the DC4 flew, on both the 19th. and 20th., to Marseilles with cargo and on the latter day Victor Delta took passengers to Antwerp. Over the weekend 21st./23rd. Victor Foxtrot went to Ostend and the remaining flights were for passengers. Foxtrot Yankee flew Manston-Southend-Le Bourget-Manston on Friday and returned the passengers Le Bourget-Southend on Sunday, having flown the fourth Geneva in between, while Victor Delta went to Beauvais on Friday, had two night stops and came back on Sunday.

The next movement was by Foxtrot Yankee on Wednesday 26th. and this was a positioning flight up to Prestwick for a check by Scottish Aviation. At this point all three DC4s were off the line for a few days as Yankee Kilo was still in the hangar and because of this the Saturday tour to Geneva had to be rearranged.

Victor Foxtrot completed the flying for February with Le Touquets on Thursday and Friday. Also that day the aircraft flew Manston-Ostend-Southend, possibly due to weather, and at 1730 on Saturday 29th. flew Southend-Geneva-Beauvais-Manston.

March Victor Delta took the second half of the Saturday Geneva tour at 1009 on the morning of Sunday 1st. from Manston. Yankee Kilo returned to the air 50 minutes later with a 2 hour local flight and made a longer one the following day. Back in service she went to Geneva on the 7th., Ostend on Monday 9th., then switched to freight configuration for two flights to Marseilles. The aircraft flew the last Geneva tour on the 14th., routing back via Gatwick on the 16th. Yankee Kilo then reverted to freight for four more flights to Marseilles, the charter on Thursday 19th. included additional legs Marseilles-Lyons-Marseilles. After this the tour work built up, Yankee Kilo flying the first inclusive tours to Basle on the 26th. and to Perpignan on Saturday 28th., this tour being fortnightly until the end of April.

Victor Delta had gone into the hangar for work which would last for much of the month while Victor Foxtrot began her March flying with passengers to Beauvais on the 6th. On the same date Captain Salmon flew Charlie Hotel back from its winter overhaul at Gatwick and he was in command the following day for the first revenue flight to Ostend.

The main inclusive tour season started with many similarities to 1963 but also some contrasts. Victor Foxtrot had opened the tours by going to Palma on Saturday 21 March, the Viking calling at Lyons outbound, as a refuelling stop outwards or on the return was needed if the load factor was high enough. The aircraft also went to Dusseldorf and took the first Rotterdam tour before concentrating on the Ostend work. Charlie Hotel flew to Beauvais, Antwerp and Dusseldorf while Victor Delta, after a long local flight on Wednesday 25th., flew Manston-Dusseldorf-Berlin-Dusseldorf-Manston next day.

> *During the return of one Dusseldorf flight that year, a German lady passenger gestured to Maggie Studt and asked: 'Vy is there all this vater in Belgium?' Maggie replied: 'Why, that is the English Channel, madam,' and the passenger retorted: 'But I only vish to travel from Dusseldorf to Brussels.'*

If errant passengers were unusual, errant suitcases were not in that second season, and there were several instances of passengers reaching their destination only to find that their luggage had gone to Basle or Perpignan or Dijon.

A new type was added to the fleet on 11 March when Bristol Freighter G-AMLL, crewed by Captain Salmon and F/O Page, flew from Lasham to Gatwick and then to Manston. Lima Lima was specifically for freight use and was on a year lease from its owners Handley Page. The Bristol arrived still painted in the basic red livery of Dan-Air, the previous users, although without the name, and was quickly repainted by the engineers at Manston into Air Ferry colours. The aircraft went to Stanstead on the 18th., this was Andy Nicol's first flight in Lima Lima, before making the first revenue flight to Le Touquet on Monday 23rd, piloted by Basil Salmon.

On 26 March Lima Lima went to Le Touquet three times with pigs and to Ostend with sheep, all flown by Andy Nicol and John Page. These were Jeep Jackson's first flights with Air Ferry, and his only ones in the

1964 SECOND WIND AND A TAKEOVER

Bristol Freighter; his duties on this occasion being restricted to poking pigs. During her time with Air Ferry, Lima Lima was operated almost exclusively for the carriage of live animals to the Continent. These flights were mostly with sheep, although some were for pigs, with the animals invariably being taken to Ostend or to Le Touquet. Other freight was carried from time to time, including Ford Motor Company parts to Germany. The usual crew of the Bristol was Andy Nicol and Peter Johnston.

Being so close to Ostend it was viable to load the Bristol Freighter with one hundred live sheep and sometimes make three sorties a day. In order that no animal should sink to its knees and suffocate under the pressure of the others, a volunteer, safely clad in oilskins and wellington boots, moved amongst them in flight ready to haul any unfortunate animal upright again. One of the qualifications for this job was to have a poor sense of smell. (Paul Noller)

Foxtrot Yankee returned from the check at Prestwick on 21 March. She went to Dusseldorf, flew the first Naples on the 27th., and a Manston-Palma-Lyons-Palma-Manston over the 28th./29th. Over the last two days the DC4 flew Manston-Dusseldorf-Berlin-Zurich-Hanover-Berlin, where she night stopped. Poor weather caused Hugh Tubman and John Page to divert to Zurich instead of Basle and to Hanover due to conditions at Berlin.

Oscar Golf   (Eddie Fuller Collection)

Peter Souster and John Page gave Oscar Golf her C of A air test at Wymeswold on the 23rd. before bringing her back to Manston the following day. Bob McNay flew Oscar Golf on her first revenue flight to Ostend on 26 March. The aircraft took the first Pisa tour on Saturday 28th. and also the first Sunday Rotterdam next day. As they built up, the Pisa tours were fortnightly until the end of April.

The years operations would exceed 1963 on most statistical measurements by about 100% but one particular feature was the volume of flying to Ostend; in all 1326 visits were made, a 274% increase. As an example, even so early in the season, there were 13 flights to Ostend on Friday 27th. and 21 on Monday 30th if the last one, squeezed in by Yankee Kilo and departing at 0021 on the Tuesday morning, is counted in.

Dusseldorf would be a frequent destination again in 1964, sometimes linked with onward flights to Berlin although some went there direct if the numbers justified this. Victor Delta made the first of these as already mentioned.

Lyons itself was a new destination for tours, used regularly in 1964 but very little in the other years of the airline's life. Victor Delta and Yankee Kilo both took tours to Lyons on the 28th., it is not known whether, on Foxtrot Yankee's Palma flight that day, the Lyons legs were a separate charter or for travel agents' use. Victor Delta's flight was the first in a series of Viking 0830 Saturday morning departures, commencing fortnightly, that would operate all season.

On the last day of March Lima Lima made a local flight before making a revenue flight to Ostend and Victor Foxtrot went into the hangar on a check.

TWILIGHT OF THE PISTONS

Leroy Voyageurs were offered a comprehensive selection of holidays from which to chose in the 1964 brochure, an attractively presented little booklet. The tour details were sprinkled with 'Mr. Leroy's Comment' and 'Independent Opinion' from previous, satisfied, customers.

The prices ranged from a day in the Dutch Bulb Fields, London to London, including the return flight Manston-Rotterdam, for eight guineas, to a 'Stay Put Holiday' in the Bay of Naples which could cost eighty three guineas. Le Touquet was used for three main holidays: 'Seven Countries and Paris,' 'The Road to Rome' and a 'Costa Brava' tour. Ostend was similarly a starting point for many coach touring holidays including Austria and Scandinavia.

Leroys used Luxembourg at that time for a 'Highlight of Yugoslavia' tour, fifteen days at forty seven guineas; and Perpignan for the 'Grand Tour of Spain' or for 'Stay Put' holidays on the Costa Brava. Basle was the destination involving the most varied choices with 'Highlight Tours' of Switzerland, Austria and Italy, lasting twelve days at an average of forty guineas; 'Leisure Tours' and Two or Three Centre Holidays which lasted for twelve or fifteen days and usually cost from thirty six to sixty guineas. One intriguing Pisa option was a fifteen day 'Mediterranean Yacht Cruise'.

> *Various methods were used to maximise duty free bar sales, sometimes the captain would be told by the hostesses when the bar sales were complete. Lyons Tours, ever keen for a bargain, agreed to ten shillings off per seat for Air Ferry to route the passengers straight past the duty free shop and onto the aircraft! (Mike Harradine)*

As in 1963 the scheduled service operation was at a fairly low key and only flown on the Manston to Ostend and Le Touquet routes. During their stay at Manston, Silver City had spent a lot of money on the facilities, particularly the terminal, but also with the intention of commencing vehicle ferry operations. Hugh Kennard considered that as the facilities were there it was a shame not to use them and licence applications were filed for various vehicle routes. A car ferry operation would also have hit at B.U.A.F., something that Hugh would have liked, and if profitable would have been a useful contribution, although Audry had reservations about going into this work.

1964 SECOND WIND AND A TAKEOVER

Vehicle licences were granted for both Manston and Belfast to Ostend and Le Touquet but they were never used. Plans were also made for Glasgow and Leeds to Le Touquet, and from Manston and Leeds to Luxembourg but, again, nothing came of these. Some reputable publications have erroneously printed that there was a far higher level of scheduled service activity than actually happened, and also some considerable vehicle ferry work, but the Bristol Freighters were only operated by Air Ferry for fourteen months and never, to the writer's knowledge, carried a car.

By this time, Hugh and Audry were aware of a potential threat that would cause them much anxiety throughout the season, and lead to some dramatic scenes later in the year.

Lima Lima, 7 April, 1964

April Foxtrot Yankee returned Berlin-Dusseldorf-Manston on Wednesday 1st. while Victor Delta went to Rotterdam, Charlie Hotel to Basle and Oscar Golf to Ostend. Next day both Oscar Golf and Lima Lima flew Ostends, while Victor Delta carried out some training at Manston and Le Touquet. On Friday Foxtrot Yankee went to Ostend, crewed by Bill Wood, John Page and Captain Salmon, for type training by Basil.

The first weekend of April was relatively quiet with Victor Delta going to Palma and stopping at Lyons in both directions. The fact that 150 passengers were carried, instead of the out and return maximum of 84, indicates that passengers were disembarked at Lyons and others carried to Palma and back; an unusual charter and perhaps connected with Foxtrot Yankee's similar flight the previous Saturday.

Mention has been made of Eros Airlines. It was only in May 1962 that *'Flight'* introduced the new U.K. independent company which inaugurated operations in April of that year with three Vikings and

In from Eros 7 April 1964

included a picture of one of them, G-AJBX. After barely two years Eros had closed in early 1964 and Mr. Kennard acquired two of their aircraft, which arrived at Manston from Gatwick on Monday 6th. Still in Eros colours, Captain Wigley brought G-AHOW to Manston while Captain Ashpitel flew G-AJBX. Oscar Whisky had flown 14,536 hours at this time, Bravo Xray probably more.

The oldest of the Vikings used by Air Ferry, Oscar Whisky had received her certificate of airworthiness in October 1946 and operated with BEA, Crewsair and Eagle before going to Trek Airways in South Africa where, as ZS-DKI, she made an emergency landing in the Transvaal. Back on the U.K. register, Oscar Whisky flew with African Air Safaris and Air Safaris before joining Eros.

Bravo Xray, conversely, was the youngest of the Vikings and had also flown with BEA and with Eagle. After that she had three owners in Germany and three more in the UK before meeting up again with Oscar Whisky at Air Safaris.

The 1964 fleet was now complete with Air Ferry having increased from two DC4s and two Vikings in 1963 to three DC4s, five Vikings and a Bristol Freighter for the current season. With new aircraft and crews, April was a month of training in addition to the revenue work. During the month all of the nine aircraft, with the exception of Charlie Hotel, made local flights from Manston, mostly for training and Yankee Kilo had her C. of A. test, carried out by Bill Wood and Hugh Tubman.

TWILIGHT OF THE PISTONS

Phil Townsend was a Licensed Aircraft Radio Maintenance Engineer who joined during the year from Silver City at Lydd. Phil started in aviation as a policeman at Gatwick in 1946 and some months later, when radio mechanics were required to maintain the ground equipment on the field, he became the first man to be employed in that capacity. When Gatwick was closed down, Phil was posted to Lympne where he joined Silver City, achieved a lifetime ambition of working on aircraft, and made the acquaintance of Hugh Kennard.

The activity increased over the weekend of 10/12 April. A weekly Viking flight that would operate all season began on Friday 10th., a 1300 departure to Dusseldorf, operated by Charlie Hotel, while Oscar Golf took the first Friday afternoon flight to Palma, one that would operate fortnightly through the season. This flight was crewed by Bill Wood, John Page flying the outward leg as P1(S), Jane Mills and Terry Heffernan. Hugh and Audry Kennard went on this trip, the DC4 coming back on Sunday. Foxtrot Yankee took the second Naples, a tour that also operated fortnightly as it had the previous year. On Saturday, after an incredibly quick transition to Air Ferry colours, Bravo Xray left, exactly at 0830 on the weekly Lyons tour, and her own first revenue flight, piloted by Paul Ashpitel. Two other Saturday flights, as in 1963 although with different departure times, were DC4s going to Perpignan and Pisa. The Perpignan now left an hour earlier at 0900 while the Pisa departure was about an hour after this. Foxtrot Yankee flew the Perpignan on the 11th. and later that day flew an evening Palma that was a fortnightly departure as the tours built up. Yankee Kilo took the Pisa tour, unusually late, at 1535. Victor Delta operated the regular Sunday Viking flight to Basle and there were trips to Rotterdam which lasted until the end of May.

Foxtrot Yankee was particularly busy with training work, on Wednesday 15th. going over to Le Touquet for six landings and returning to Manston for another eight; she continued with another local flight, lasting an hour, the following day. Yankee Kilo's Rotterdam on the 23rd was flown by Bill Wood, John Page and Tony Ahmad as supernumary F/O, Tony now transferring to the larger aircraft. On first joining, the previous year, John had been accommodated in the officers' mess, kindly arranged by Hugh Kennard; and later sharing a flat with Tony Ahmad. John had an unpleasant experience in the centre of Margate one day, when someone who had parked badly first threatened to damage John's car and then, incredibly, to press charges against him; this was another occasion when Hugh Kennard found time to sort out a situation on behalf of one of his employees.

The last weekend saw some variations to the patterns building up. There was no Naples flight on Friday 24th. and no Palma on the Saturday. Starting that day, the Perpignan and Pisa flights would now operate on a weekly basis.

In all Rotterdam was visited on 34 occasions in April for tours of the Dutch bulb fields. In addition to the IT work the Vikings flew numerous charters. Victor Delta flew Manston-Gatwick-Frankfurt-Manston on the 7th./8th., to Brussels on the 10th., while on Friday 24th. she flew Manston-Hurn-Bordeaux with 34 passengers, made three night stops and returned, with 35 on board, Bordeaux-Hurn-Manston on Monday 27th. The aircraft went to Beauvais on the 29th. and next day had a technical return to Rotterdam.

Following her overhaul Victor Foxtrot returned to her natural element on 25 April with an early morning air test before going to Rotterdam. An Ostend followed before she flew to Frankfurt over the 28th./29th. Bravo Xray

1964 SECOND WIND AND A TAKEOVER

also went to Frankfurt, on the 21st., while Charlie Hotel flew to Zurich on the 11th. and to Rheims on the 26th.

Bravo Xray had an unusual charter, leaving Manston on Monday 27th. to take a cargo of live chickens and turkeys to Moscow for the British Agricultural Exhibition due to open in Moscow in May. Two weeks later '*Flight*' printed a photograph of the aircraft preparing to leave. Bravo Xray flew via Copenhagen where she was required to uplift a Russian navigator, and returned the same way to drop him off again. In view of the incredible strictness surounding any sort of contact with the Soviet Union then, it was the source of some amusement that Air Ferry was never charged for the fuel uplift in Moscow. With flights such as Bravo Xray's charter to Moscow, which attracted some media attention, Air Ferry was now becoming better known outside the local area of Kent.

May   With five weekends, May was busy with virtually three quarters of the activity involving four destinations, Ostend, Rotterdam, Le Touquet and Basle. On Saturday 2nd. Bill Steel took Oscar Whisky on her first revenue flight to Rotterdam and the same day Bravo Xray started the Luxembourg tour, a fortnightly one in May, with a departure at 1135. Victor Delta operated the Saturday Palma on 2nd./3rd., flying out via Lyons, although after this the DC4s took over. Yankee Kilo had taken the first flight out on Sunday to Rotterdam, and came back to Manston at 1930 that evening. On touchdown Hugh Tubman and John Page were amazed to see the starboard outer mainwheel, which came off on landing, bouncing up the runway ahead of them, having somehow passed through the propellers untouched.

An hour before midnight on Sunday, Oscar Golf departed on another Damascus-Baghdad flight, returning Baghdad-Manston direct on Wednsday morning, this leg being an incredible block time of 14 hours 3 minutes. The cargo was to collect some more components from the Saudi Convair whose engines had been brought back in January. To the groundlings at Manston the DC4s apppeared to have seven league boots in carrying out flights of this length.

> *Captain Steel was one aircraft commander the new second officers flew with. Jeep Jackson had been taught, early on, that in radio communications one should inhale deeply and not break the transmission; on one trip which needed a longer than usual response Jeep was at gasping point and Bill Steel retorted: 'For goodness sake Jeep, take a breath.' (Jeep Jackson)*

The weekend of 8th./10th. May was busy, and noteworthy for Victor Delta taking the Saturday morning Perpignan, presumably due to the numbers involved, as all the DC4s were operating. That evening Oscar Golf took the Palma, a weekly tour from this point on. Yankee Kilo started the weekly Sunday Dijon tour, programmed for 0800, and the Sunday Basles built up.

Brian Koering joined the Operations Department in May; Peter Souster was Operations Manager now, and had probably stopped flying at this time.

The next weekend Foxtrot Yankee left at 0223 on Saturday 16th. for Lyons, a weekly tour of the Costa Brava by Leroys, lasting eight days and costing twenty three guineas. This aircraft operated two of these and then the Vikings flew it again for some weeks. Yankee Kilo left at 0938 to operate the first Verona flight and within the next twelve minutes two Vikings had departed on the morning Perpignan. The Verona tours would be weekly and, with two morning exceptions, departed close to 1315. Oscar Golf, flown by Hugh Tubman, had a number 2 engine failure on the midday Sunday Basle tour, the aircraft making a short local flight the next day before going to Rotterdam. Bravo Xray went to Perpignan again on Monday 18th., flying from there to Malaga and Jersey, returning direct to Manston the following day. On Tuesday Bill Wood and John Page with 43 passengers had No.2 engine overspeed en route to Ostend, and came home on a 3-engine ferry.

On the fourth weekend, 22nd./24th., Lima Lima varied her usual routes on Friday 22nd. by making two trips to Calais; that day Patrick Hope made his first Air Ferry flight and the Palma tour frequency increased to two flights, at 1700 and 2000. From Saturday 23rd. the 0830 Viking to Lyons left weekly so there were now two departures there each Saturday morning, at approximately 0200 and 0830. Through Saturday and Sunday the Basles continued to increase in number. During the week Oscar Golf changed over to freight for a flight to Geneva on Wednesday 27th.

On the 30 May the Saturday evening Palma flights increased to two although Oscar Golf departed somewhat late, at 0100 on the Sunday morning. By the last day in May the Sunday Basles were up to five, usually operated by two DC4s and three Vikings, a frequency that would carry on through the high summer.

TWILIGHT OF THE PISTONS

There was also more local flying training in May and Victor Foxtrot went to Stanstead twice. Andy Nicol converted onto the Viking at this time, checked out by John Gibson and Paul Ashpitel. During the month John Page carried out some intensive P1(S) flying training on Vikings with Paul Ashpitel, on Oscar Golf with Bill Wood and had a F/O competency check with Don Brooker, including a 3-engine overshoot and a flapless landing. Although the tour work was brisk there was still capacity for numerous additional charters and the two ex-Eros Vikings in particular ranged further afield from the usual destinations. In addition to Lima Lima's cargo work, Oscar Golf carried out a freight flight to Salzburg on Friday 29th.

> *One day the lorry due to collect the sheep from the lairage and deliver them to the Bristol Freighter did not arrive. The Tarmac staff decided to use the Operations Morris and loaded twelve sheep at a time; on one journey as the van went past Operations there was a sheep in the passenger seat. (Brian Koering).*

Victor Delta flew to Frankfurt and Jersey in the month while Victor Foxtrot visited Munich over the 14th./15th., crewed by Paul Ashpitel and Jeep Jackson. This was an auspicious occasion, as recorded in Jeep's log book, in that he made the take-off on the return flight, flew the sector and landed the Viking. The aircraft also flew an Ostend-Hamburg on the 25th., the return of a charter being made Hamburg-Ostend by Charlie Hotel on the 21st. Oscar Whisky flew Manston-Nice on Friday 8th. and returned Nice-Lyons-Manston on Monday, and also went to Jersey, to Munich over 18th./19th. and to Frankfurt later that day. Over the 27th./29th. she operated Manston-Brussels-Vienna-Brussels-Lydd-Manston.

Bravo Xray flew Manston-Newcastle-Dinard-Manston on Friday 8th., to Frankfurt, to Malaga as mentioned, to Amsterdam on the 24th. and Cologne over the 30th./31st.

June   Monday 1st. started off with more Ostends, followed by Oscar Golf operating the beginning of a fortnightly series of DC4 daytime tours to Malaga that would continue until October. These tours to the Costa del Sol were fifteen days from sixty five guineas and departed from Victoria Coach Station on Sunday, with an overnight stay in a Ramsgate hotel prior to the flight. The peak monthly totals to Le Touquet and Basle for 1964 were achieved with 45 and 44 flights respectively.

The average block times to Basle that year were 4 hours 42 minutes for the DC4s and 10 minutes longer for the Vikings. The Vikings took 6 hours 40 minutes for Copenhagen while for the DC4 journeys: Pisa was 8 hours 35 minutes, the flight to Verona took 9 hours, Naples 10 hours 11 minutes and Malaga 11 hours 31 minutes.

> *One pilot who joined at this time flew as supernumary crew for some weeks but then decided to leave. On a flight to Copenhagen, together with a young second officer, this pilot was having some difficulty with the radio whereupon the crusty captain retorted: 'When you two clowns have finished sorting this out, let me know,' then promptly left the cockpit and disappeared to the rear of the Viking!*

Bravo Xray started the first weekend, 5th./7th. June, with a charter flown by Paul Ashpitel and Patrick Hope, Manston-Jonkoping-Hamburg-Manston; Oscar Whisky repeating this journey two weeks later. Also on Friday 5th., Victor Foxtrot flew the first of a fortnightly 1030 Viking tour to Copenhagen that would run through until mid September although, on this occasion, the aircraft returned via Ostend. The weekend ran well with the Friday flights departing on time; two Vikings went to Dusseldorf, Oscar Golf went to Naples while the other DC4s carried out the nights Palmas.

All nine aircraft flew on the Saturday, Victor Delta left on the 0200 for Lyons exactly to time, and for some reason called into Dijon on the way. During the morning Oscar Golf went to Verona, Yankee Kilo to Pisa, while Foxtrot Yankee took the Perpignan; and that day Lima Lima went to Le Touquet four times. The Vikings covered the Lyons, Basle and Luxembourg tours. The Viking flights to Luxembourg left weekly from this point. On Sunday there were five Basles again with the usual allocation of two DC4s and three Vikings, although this route saw the most interchangeability to meet operational needs.

The Basle turnrounds allowed a relatively short while on the ground and did not leave much time in the middle of the day for the crew to get some lunch. After several rushed meals a crisis was reached when Pop had to leave a dish of fresh strawberries. They considered radioing ahead with their choices of menu, but Pop found that if she made out a sheet with their selection on, and gave this to the handling agent the moment the door

1964 SECOND WIND AND A TAKEOVER

was opened, they would find their lunch waiting in the restaurant when they finally arrived.

On Friday 12th. Victor Delta started a series of Dusseldorf-Berlin flights that would be repeated for some weeks and Oscar Whisky flew the first Friday night Perpignan of the season, operated fortnightly in June.

It was about this time that it was necessary to call on the standby captain to take a flight one Saturday afternoon. Unfortunately the captain in question was attending a family wedding that day and was called from the celebrations as they were becoming enjoyable. Slight concern was expressed by those preparing the aircraft for departure at the general air of affability shown by the captain but the Viking, with Peter Gutteridge as second officer, climbed safely away and disappeared out to sea.

(Sunbeam Photo Limited)

TWILIGHT OF THE PISTONS

Two Vikings operated the Saturday Perpignan on the 20th., the reason almost certainly low load factors as all the DC4s were operating. On the last weekend 26th./28th. June neither of the Lyons tours operated for some reason. Yankee Kilo made a flight Manston-Manston at 1945 on Saturday evening, making her late leaving for Palma, while Oscar Golf did not take the second Palma until 0100 Sunday, but these were small issues set against the background of another busy and successful month.

Some other charters were flown in the month. On Friday 5th. Yankee Kilo flew Manston-Deauville-Ostend-Manston while Foxtrot Yankee operated Manston-Deauville-Manston. On Tuesday 9th. both Yankee Kilo and Charlie Hotel flew Manston-Ostend-Deauville-Manston. Oscar Whisky went to Liege on Sunday 14th., and flew a Manston-Ostend-Gatwick-Orleans-Gatwick-Ostend-Manston over the 15th./18th. Bravo Xray went to Geneva on the 27th.

> *The impressions of that year come back in a kaleidoscope of activity, one of the pilots remarking that he had a uniform, parts of which had been contributed by several airlines, and he had come to Air Ferry to get a new cap; how the delays affected peoples' duty hours and could easily put the aircrew beyond their limits; a captain mentioning how he had difficulty sleeping after night duty, with all the daytime sounds of grass mowing or children playing going on to distract him.*

July   The season built up with 428 flights of which 330 were to Ostend, Basle and Le Touquet, and 21 to Dusseldorf, although there were some technical problems as a result of the high activity. Oscar Golf left at 1345 on Wednesday 1st. for Basle and, on taking off for the journey back, had to make a technical return to the Swiss airport, not arriving at Manston until early the next day.

Two features contrasted with 1963 and Naples was a good illustration of this. The departures were not so evenly timed and the tours did not always operate to a consistent pattern with occasional weeks omitted. The number of flights on usual days varied too, especially to Perpignan. With eight passenger aircraft available it is unlikely that delays or sub-charters were a significant cause and it is probable that uneven booking patterns accounted for the variations.

Commencing with Friday 3rd. when Charlie Hotel flew Manston-Dusseldorf-Berlin-Dusseldorf-Manston, there were four Friday Dusseldorf-Berlins, while on the 31st. Victor Delta flew there direct. The weekend 3rd./5th. marked several changes to tours that had operated regularly until this point. Foxtrot Yankee went to Naples as usual on Friday but this tour then had a large gap until 28 August. Yankee Kilo left late for the second Palma, at 0125 on Saturday morning, and returned after 50 minutes. It is likely this tour was sub-chartered as Yankee Kilo then left for Lyons at 0310, the DC4s taking this early flight over from the Vikings. After this she went to Pisa, the last of this tours weekly departures, henceforth they would be fortnightly.

After two weeks of the Vikings taking the Saturday morning Perpignan, Oscar Golf went there on the 4th., signalling another variation in that there was no Verona, this tour now changing from weekly to fortnightly frequency. There was a further variation on Saturday evening as the DC4 Palmas increased to three so, just after 2130, all the DC4s were airborne heading for this airport.

On Monday 6th. Oscar Whisky started a small series of Viking day flights to Perpignan. Victor Foxtrot had an internal flight up to Birmingham next day and on Wednesday 8th. Foxtrot Yankee made a return after take-off from Basle.

> *One pilot, then an inexperienced second officer, recalls a night return to Manston. Captain Wigley called out: 'Point me at the runway old boy,' whereupon the second officer lined the Viking up on the brightest row of sodium lights he could see. These unfortunately marked the Dover Road but the situation was 'recovered.'*

The following weekend of 10th./12th. July there were two DC4 flights to Perpignan on Friday night while Oscar Whisky and Bravo Xray went there on Saturday. The Friday night Perpignans were the subject of many variations and occasionally these were operated by just one Viking. Yankee Kilo left for Verona slightly late and when she got back to Manston the delays lengthened even more as she had a problem prior to leaving on the third Palma, finally getting away at 0342, over five hours late. The five Sunday Basles were, as usual, flown by two DC4s and three Vikings.

> *One time, it was necessary for Frank Strainge to go out to Perpignan on an electrical problem and he came back in the jump seat of the DC4. After take-off Hugh Tubman gestured he would*

1964 SECOND WIND AND A TAKEOVER

make a left turn while the co-pilot, who must be nameless, indicated a right hand turn was necessary. Frank sat peering through the windscreen hoping they would continue straight ahead, in case of error, but fortunately Hugh was correct.

It was Oscar Golf's turn for a delay on the 13th as she left over two hours late for Malaga and Hugh Tubman then had to make a return to the Spanish airport with engine failure, recording a block time of 12 hours 18 minutes, and not reappearing at Manston until early on Tuesday.

There was just one Palma flight on Friday 17 although the usual three tours operated on Saturday. Next weekend there were just two night flights on Saturday 25; it is not known if these were sub-charters or due to insufficient numbers. All the usual tours to Basle, Dijon, Verona, Luxembourg, Copenhagen and Dusseldorf in those weekends departed well to time.

On Sunday 26th. the writer and his wife, having left their dog in the care of some friends, went to Basle on a Viking, intending to spend a few hours there and return on the last DC4. Oscar Golf duly arrived, but Traffic said that Manston was fogged in and the aircraft would have to return the next morning. A telex went pelting to Manston, advising them that a dog was alone in the bungalow, and shortly afterwards Peter Wannop arrived at the friends' house in Minster, complete with a tin of dog food. Bob McNay, Pop and the rest of the crew were most kind and the writer retains an impression of Pop, shoes off, relaxing on a bed and exclaiming: 'My poor feet, I've walked across Europe today.'

During the season Audry mentioned that a local Womens' Institute had approached her and asked that they be given a talk on the life of an air hostess and 'suggested' that Pop might like to do it. In spite of acute pre-performance nerves, not having done any public speaking before, Pop's talk went down very well.

On top of all this work there were still some Rotterdam flights, Oscar Whisky went to Brussels on the 30th. and during the month three of the Vikings made the short trip to Calais.

Ron Blake used to make periodic flights to check that the radio equipment performed satisfactorily and recalls a flight to Dusseldorf with Don Brooker who was the Training Captain. The DC4 was droning across Belgium when Don said to the first officer: 'We've just lost an engine, what are you going to do?' The first officer was thinking what action he should take when Don rapped out: 'We've just lost another one, what are you going to do?' The first officer said he would call Brussels, indicate a problem, and ask for an alternate. Don remarked: 'How about looking out of the window, there is a military airfield down there you must have flown over many times, you would go into that.'

August The season peaked in August; the flights for Saturday 1st. started on time with Foxtrot Yankee departing for Lyons at 0140 and the Ostends under way by seven o'clock. There was no hint at this point that Air Ferry's most celebrated technical diversion was about to take place, one which resulted in five aircraft descending at different times on one French airport.

The ex-Eros Vikings shared the Perpignan tour leaving within five minutes of one another. Bravo Xray was on the way back to Manston in the early afternoon when excessive vibration and falling oil pressure made Captain Steel feather the port engine. The remainder of the crew, Jeep as Second Officer and the hostess, were both relatively inexperienced. With the fully laden Viking steadily losing height Jeep was busy writing out a 'Mayday' while the hostess was asking her charges, a tour mainly of senior citizens, to remove their dentures.

'Find me somewhere to go,' Bill asked Jeep, and over the R.T. someone said: 'Why don't you try Clermont Ferrand.' At the height of the activity Jeep upset a cup of coffee, with the resulting trickle of brown liquid into the cabin hardly likely to have inspired confidence into the passengers. They managed the approach and landing into the joint civil and military airfield and, on trying to clear the runway, found that taxiing a Viking on one engine was not a practical proposition.

Oscar Golf, taking the third Palma tour, diverted into Clermont Ferrand soon after midnight, almost certainly with some engineers, as Len Mees went out to work on Bravo Xray, the DC4 then continuing on to Palma. The shortage of a Viking caused some pressures and made Victor Foxtrot late for the Saturday evening Basle. At 0625 on Sunday Oscar Whisky, piloted by Captain Wigley and Peter Gutteridge, left Manston to collect the stranded passengers from Clermont Ferrand, who had had to night stop in a hotel, and the aircraft returned just before midday. The Sunday seven 'Air Ferry loads' to Basle, as these were described at the time, were carried by three DC4s and Victor Delta.

Meanwhile the engineers had decided that the fault was serious enough to require an engine change and early on Tuesday morning Captain Nicol flew Lima Lima out, via Bordeaux, to Clermont Ferrand with a spare Hercules and flew back direct to Manston the next day. On Wednesday morning, the 5th., it was Oscar Whisky's turn for technical problems as she flew Manston-Perpignan-Perpignan-Perpignan and did not return to Manston until Saturday. The engineers began to think that Vikings were dropping like flies, with two aircraft grounded in France. Early on Thursday, Charlie Hotel flew to Perpignan, calling in to Clermont Ferrand en route; later in the afternoon Lima Lima went to Clermont to collect the engine that had been removed. Andy Nicol then flew on to Perpignan, presumably with spares, or another engine for Oscar Whisky, before returning direct to Manston from there on Friday. While all this was going on, Bravo Xray had at last returned to Manston during the Thursday.

The next weekend 7th./9th. was calmer, Victor Foxtrot flew an extra Perpignan on Friday at 0525 in the morning and there was brisk activity to Dusseldorf; Bravo Xray taking the Dusseldorf-Berlin schedule. Charlie Hotel had a charter to Munich on Saturday night and the Basle variation on Sunday 9th. for the seven 'Air Ferry loads' this time was two DC4s and four Vikings.

Bravo Xray had more problems on Tuesday 11th., with Jeep aboard again, aborting a flight to Ostend due to a generator overcharging and was replaced by Oscar Whisky. On Thursday it was Victor Foxtrot's turn to go unserviceable prior to departing to Le Touquet and Bravo Xray replaced her. All five Palma flights operated to plan over the weekend 14th./16th. although the Perpignan tours seemed to be erratic with Victor Foxtrot making one of the Friday trips and Oscar Golf carrying out the second at 0330 on Saturday morning. Foxtrot Yankee flew the usual Saturday morning tour there and, on Sunday, Victor Delta operated Manston-Ostend-Perpignan-Manston.

During the season Andy Nicol's mother died and he had to go up to Scotland for the funeral. With Basil Salmon having left there was no other captain available for the Bristol just then, and Bob McNay took a hasty conversion course so that he could keep the freight flights running.

On Tuesday 18th. Lima Lima flew a different freight route, Manston-Southend-Antwerp-Manston, the same day that Oscar Golf positioned up to Wymeswold for some work to be carried out; she returned to Manston three days later, at teatime on Friday, and was back in service with flights on Saturday 22nd. to Ostend, Perpignan and Palma.

Yankee Kilo (Eddie Fuller Collection)

Yankee Kilo switched briefly to freight work on Wednesday 26th. with a flight to Lille, one of the few occasions Air Ferry went to this airfield.

The Naples tours resumed briefly on a fortnightly basis on Friday 28th. and Oscar Whisky left at 2249 with the Perpignan tour. On Saturday morning Charlie Hotel left at 0659 for Lyons, calling into Ostend en route, and Victor Delta and Oscar Whisky shared the Perpignan. This last weekend, 28th./30th. August, now saw some delays and substitutions due to Yankee Kilo which left Manston at 1000 on Saturday for Pisa, but Captain Tubman and Bill Isaacs had to divert into Marseilles with a fire warning on the number 4 engine.

Frank Strainge, who had certainly worked all of Saturday, and possible some of Friday night as well, was sent off home for a quick wash and brush up before leaving for France. At 2158, after a short local flight an hour earlier, Charlie Hotel departed on the Palma tour and stopped at Marseilles on the way out, to let Frank off.

1964 SECOND WIND AND A TAKEOVER

Frank traced the problem to the fire extinguisher circuits and, very tired, went into the restaurant shortly after eight for some breakfast, only to be greeted with the information: 'Sorry, we closed at eight!' After an air test, the aircraft continued onto Pisa, but it was Sunday before she returned and flew the afternoon Basle.

Some malfunction must have struck Foxtrot Yankee during or after the first Palma on Saturday night as she did not fly again until the next Thursday afternoon and this was undoubtedly the cause of the Sunday Dijon being split between two Vikings.

In this month, particularly, the porpoise shape of the Vikings always seemed to be in the circuit, often a wide one out above Acol and round over the marshes at Minster. On one of the longer Viking flights everything that could go wrong seemed to have done so and on his return Captain Wigley was heard to remark: 'They should not send an old man so far!'

The Vikings continued with additional charters, both Bravo Xray and Oscar Whisky flew to Jersey, Oscar Whisky and Victor Delta went to Frankfurt, Victor Foxtrot visited Beauvais on the 10th. and Charlie Hotel flew to Calais on the 28th.

When Yankee Kilo returned from Basle early in the evening on Monday 31st. the curtain rang down on a most remarkable month in which there had been 487 flights with 291 of these to Ostend. Never again would these numbers of flights be made and it is difficult to convey now the kaleidoscopic activity that summer made by the eight passenger carrying aircraft.

September The pace eased in September although the daily and weekly programmes were still well filled. The weekly programme was a black stencilled document, foolscap size of course, while the daily programme, delivered from Traffic by Ronnie Cox or one of the others, was blue roneoed print with the paper still damp and smelling of the fluid used when it arrived.

Oscar Golf made a return to Basle on the 2nd. and came back to Manston the next day. She made a two hour local flight on the 4th. before going to Dusseldorf. Foxtrot Yankee went to Ostend twice in the week, entered by John Page as flying with Captain Palmer, a name not listed anywhere in the writer's records. Oscar Whisky took one of the Friday night Perpignans that day, stopping at Marseilles on the way out, probably due to weather, and on Saturday Oscar Golf stopped at Munich on the way to Verona. The Luxembourg tours built up that weekend, 4th./6th. September, with 5 flights and this month saw the peak reached of 27 Luxembourg flights.

The following weekend Bravo Xray took the last of the weekly Copenhagen tours on Friday 11th. and Yankee Kilo went unserviceable that evening as she was leaving for Palma with 63 passengers and Foxtrot Yankee substituted two hours later. The gremlins attacked Oscar Golf next as she went U/S at 0235 prior to departing to Lyons, Bill Steel and John Page experiencing No.1 engine failure on take-off, and again Foxtrot Yankee stepped into the breach, although five hours late on this occasion. Oscar Golf caught up some of the lost time by combining a Basle with the Pisa tour. On Sunday 13th., while Yankee Kilo was on the way to Dijon, Foxtrot Yankee became the third of the DC4s to abort a take-off, this time for Basle. The passengers left on Yankee Kilo four hours later. The next day Oscar Whisky made the last visit to Copenhagen of the season and did not return until Friday.

Like many small charter firms then, Air Ferry had few specialised pieces of ground equipment, ground power for the aircraft was supplied by ex-R.A.F. trolley-accs, a universal provider of 24 volts. Tugs were of either the large farm tractor variety or, again, ancient survivors from the R.A.F. One bright idea was in the acquisition of two electric milk floats which were stripped down to flat-backs that were able to carry toolboxes, components and personnel, and also tow trolleys. They were quite exciting to drive as the brake and 'go' pedals were reversed relative to car controls. (Paul Noller)

September was the peak month for the Bristol Freighters operations at Air Ferry with 75 hours being flown. Lima Lima made a rare Sunday flight on the 20th. with a charter Manston-Southend-Cologne-Manston and the Bristol Freighter positioned Manston-Dublin on Friday 25th with Captain Nicol in command. She then carried out five Dublin-Cambridge-Dublin flights and returned Dublin-Cambridge-Manston on the 28th. These flights were to carry young Irish horses over to the yearling sales at Newmarket. One frightened horse broke a window of the Bristol, severing an artery in the process, and sadly died. The final weekend of 25th./27th.

saw five Palmas depart to schedule, the last Naples and the Vikings operating the Saturday Perpignan, with Bravo Xray stopping at Lyons on the return journey.

As mentioned most of Lima Lima's flights were for the export of live animals, usually sheep and pigs, and still an emotive subject at the time of writing. The cargoes were rarely kept waiting long at Manston and were always accompanied in the Bristol Freighter by one or two of the Tarmac men. The handling staff on the Continent did not always treat the livestock with the respect they had received under British control and the Tarmac men were sometimes upset and angry when they returned; the writer recalls Ted Friend saying one day that perhaps he would not go again.

There were extra charters the last week, Yankee Kilo flew Manston-Gatwick-Munich-Tarbes on Monday 28th., night stopped, and returned Tarbes-Gatwick-Manston next day. On Tuesday 29th. Charlie Hotel flew Manston-Liverpool-Dusseldorf-Manston while Bravo Xray set off Manston-Gatwick-Frankfurt, night stopped, and flew to Munich on Wednesday where the aircraft remained until it returned Munich-Gatwick-Manston on Friday 2 October.

We are familiar these days with the difficulty in discerning who actually makes decisions in a large organisation. In contrast Air Ferry, under Hugh Kennard, was like a family concern, or even an active monarchy, and there was never any ambiguity as to where the power lay, he was on the spot and radiated authority, whether you met him in the corridor or in the wash room.

In writing any historical work there is a responsibility to portray events fairly but sensitively, without dramatising at one extreme or being unduly inhibited at commenting on the leading players on the other. Those who have worked at a senior level with a strong willed and highly motivated person will know there is a fine line, between what is a clear requirement for a professional to deliver if possible, and a threat of some sanction for non compliance. Hugh Kennard was not the most patient of men and there is no doubt that he occasionally crossed this line. The possible displeasure resulting from a night stop has been mentioned earlier, but sometimes there were similar debates as to whether a flight should take place at all; Don Brooker had several rows with the managing director over issues such as this.

One such issue concerned whether a Viking should go to Amsterdam, the captain involved giving his opinion that, due to the weather, it shouldn't. Captain Wood, as Chief Pilot, was appealed to to make this request an order, which he declined to do on the ground that this had to be the captain's decision. Following a colossal row with the Managing Director, Bill abruptly left Air Ferry on 30 September and went off to Kuwait. In view of what happened to the company during the following month, there is no doubt that at this time Hugh Kennard must have been under a considerable strain.

October The inclusive tours ran down during October, on Saturday 3rd. Victor Foxtrot flew the last Lyons while Foxtrot Yankee carried out the last of the Verona tours. Next day the same aircraft made the last visit of the year to Basle. Also that weekend Oscar Whisky flew to Antwerp, returning via Ostend, and Charlie Hotel went to Jersey, also coming back through Ostend.

One of the hangar staff, who frequented the 'Jolly Farmer' too much, built up such an amount of credit that, when he received his wage packet, he took it down to the 'Jolly' to help redress the balance outstanding.

On Friday 9th. Victor Delta went to Maastricht, night stopped and flew Maastricht-Gatwick-Maastricht-Manston over the 10th./11th. On Saturday Yankee Kilo took the last Pisa tour and on Sunday Foxtrot Yankee closed the Dijons, returning via Ostend. Also that day Oscar Golf flew Manston-Exeter-Palma-Exeter-Manston. The next day, Monday 12th., Foxtrot Yankee positioned to Gatwick for a Gatwick-Palma-Gatwick charter and did not return to Manston until Friday.

Oscar Golf made only one further revenue flight, to Jersey over the 16th./18th., before positioning up to Prestwick on Monday 19th. for a check that would last two months. On Saturday 17th., Oscar Whisky made the last flight to Perpignan after which she went into the hangar at Manston for an overhaul and would not fly again in 1964. Yankee Kilo on the first Palma that night returned, for some reason, via Ostend.

One time when they had stripped down a Viking on check, and it was probably Oscar Whisky, they found one of the control cables almost worn through by friction with other metal.

1964 SECOND WIND AND A TAKEO

Foxtrot Yankee closed the Luxembourgs on Wednesday 21st. and on the weekend 23rd./25th. there were the last three flights into Palma. Foxtrot Yankee flew the last Friday trip at 1645 and Bravo Xray left Manston at 1735 on Saturday, the aircraft flying there direct. The Viking, with Captain Mason in command, came back via Lyons; a significant flight as on her return to Manston early on 25th. October, Bravo Xray touched down for the last time after a long and distinguished career. An interesting feature was that her first and last flights with Air Ferry had been through Lyons. The other Palma flight, over the 25th./26th., was by Yankee Kilo and another Manston-Exeter-Palma-Exeter-Manston.

Victor Foxtrot closed the Dusseldorfs on Friday 30th. and the only flight on the last day of the month was by Foxtrot Yankee positioning to London Heathrow for a freight charter.

> *The Bristol Freighter continued her work during the month, the engineers nicknamed her 'Leaping Lena' partly because once, returning from Ostend empty and trying to land in a gale on Manston's runway 27, it had to make three attempts to persuade it to settle solidly as the big wings had so much lift. In the end Captain Nicol had to fly it into the runway until the last second. (Paul Noller)*

THE TAKE OVER

At the end of October, everything seemed suspiciously quiet on arrival at work. Someone said: 'The Kennards' have gone, we've been taken over.' The security had been complete and the staff were very surprised and shocked.

During the year the B.U.A. Board had entered discussions with Mr. Leroy with a view to the acquisition of Leroy Tours Ltd. and, of course, Air Ferry. Mr. Kennard's view is that Freddie Laker was always set on eliminating Air Ferry and eventually made Lewis Leroy a generous offer for his shares on condition that his, Mr. Kennard's, would also be included. Mr. Leroy, being overwhelmed by the offer, accepted and as he had the major shareholding it was impossible for Hugh Kennard not to follow suit.

The exact negotiations took place between Laker/Air Holdings and Leroy without Hugh Kennard's knowledge and the result must have been a crushing blow to him and his wife after all the work that they had put in. The management of the airline was a very onerous responsibility alone, without having to try and fend off such an attack, most of which had been in secret. An additional cause of anxiety to the Directors' during the year had been a brief strike by the pilots. Although this lasted only for two days or so it resulted in a visit to Manston by a prominent Trade Union official.

Subsequent to the final meeting at Portland House, Mr. Kennard and Audry returned immediately to Manston, cleared their offices, and moved the short distance to Ramsgate Airport. The senior staff most closely identified with the Kennards' were treated by the Air Holdings directors rather like cold war spies in America, as if they were infectious, especially Mike Harradine with his commercial knowledge. Incredibly, Mike was confined to his office at the critical time by Ken Sheppardson and locked in, while his car was temporarily put out of action!

Back in the 'bolt hole', the terminal and tower building at Ramsgate Airport; the Kennards made plans to form Invicta Airways in order to start their operations again. Whether or not there had been another restraint of trade clause in the contract was almost immaterial in the highly charged and emotional atmosphere; Hugh Kennard was in no mood for history to repeat itself.

If Air Holdings had deprived Air Ferry of an exceptional Managing Director they now put in a man of

Our air ferry is taken over, he says

Nov 3.

Express Staff Reporter

FORMER Battle of Britain pilot Hugh Kennard, stood in a hall at Manston, Kent, airfield last night and told 150 of his employees that his company, Air Ferry Ltd., had been taken over.

Mr. Kennard, who was the managing director, explained that he had "no alternative" than to sell his shares in the company to Air Holdings Ltd., the parent company of British United Airways.

Mr. Kennard said that he had fought for eight months to keep the company which in two years he and his wife Audrey, the traffic director, have built to a prosperous business.

BITTER

He started in 1962 with no planes and little equipment. Last year Air Ferry flew 160,000 people to the Continent for holidays.

Mr. Kennard, aged 47, told his employees: "I intend to start up again and I will not make the same mistake again. This is not goodbye but au revoir."

One after another the employees shook hands with Mr. and Mrs. Kennard and thanked them. Mr. Kennard said that he hoped the new owners would continue to employ them.

"I'm embittered, but I must be careful what I say," he said. "I intend to start up again somewhere in the Home Counties in six months' time.

"Unfortunately I was a minority shareholder. My wife and I were told to resign."

considerable managerial ability to replace him. K.J. Sheppardson arrived to take up his appointment as General Manager in what was an electric atmosphere. He started off by meeting the senior staff and seeking as much information as he could obtain on the results of the first two seasons.

Sheppardson's first priority at this stage was to hold Air Ferry together. It was now well known that Hugh Kennard had set up his battle headquarters at Ramsgate Airport with the intention of flying out of Manston in the spring.

On 20 November a Cessna 210 of B.U.A. flew into Manston with Freddie Laker on board, he had arrived to give everyone a pep talk and was in high good humour. For some reason he required everyone to group around him out on the grass by the apron; why the meeting was not held in a more conventional location, such as the terminal, has puzzled the writer since that occasion. Laker commenced by saying that, taxiing in past the parked aircraft, he had recognised the Vikings which he had bought several times before, a comment which drew some nervous laughter. He enthused about the size and security of a large group and said that Air Ferry had a future. There was no intention at Air Holdings of closing the company down.

There were then some very curious weeks, rather like the build up to a civil war. Who would be invited over to Ramsgate for an interview? Who had already been, and had they kept quiet about the visit, or received an offer and accepted? Tim Leigh, who had been closely identified with the resistance to the takeover, had left with the Kennards.

Mike Austin, now Chief Accountant, confided that he had received an invitation to see Mr. Kennard and departed one bitterly cold night on his motorbike in the direction of Ramsgate. Following this meeting, the writer received a written invitation for a discussion and also departed, by now with a carpet of snow covering Thanet, on a push bike through the dark and icy lanes. Mr. Kennard was installed in a small panelled room in the control tower at the airport and ended the conversation with the firm conviction: 'They will never last.'

Then followed the most appalling indecision the writer, and no doubt many others, has ever experienced. Loyalty to Mr. and Mrs. Kennard was weighed against the still felt shock that the takeover had happened; many people had put an awful lot of effort into Air Ferry, leaving now was akin to throwing that away; yet Hugh Kennard had done that and, like General MacArthur, had said: 'I will return.' How could he obtain aircraft, crews, engineers, let alone inclusive tour operators; on top of all that, he didn't even have a hangar.

From this distance of time what the Kennards' set out to do looks, if anything, even more impossible now than it did then. If news of the intended takeover had leaked in some way, as no doubt in this day and age it probably would have been, it is quite likely that most, if not all, of the staff would have defected to Invicta. Mr. Kennard took the honourable course, fought as long as he could, spat on his hands and started again from

Charlie Hotel 20 November 1964　　　　　Bravo Xray 4 November 1964

nothing. Gradually news percolated round that so and so was staying, then someone else who was respected had decided to remain and, in the end, most of the staff stayed with Air Ferry.

After wartime service Ken Sheppardson joined B.E.A. in 1946 and had been on the same course at Aldermaston that year as Bill Wood. Twelve years later he was employed by Fison Airwork which based him in Nigeria and after that he worked in Freetown for Sierra Leone Airways before joining Air Ferry. Now, in the months after the takeover, he exercised a steadying hand on the organisation; it was known that he had flown on

1964 SECOND WIND AND A TAKEOVER

Bomber Command's raid on Nuremberg in March 1944 which had resulted in that organisation's worst losses of the war, ninety six bombers. Now he regularly travelled to Manston from his home in a village next to Cromer in Norfolk in four hours, a respectable time even now with vastly improved roads.

With Bill Wood gone, Captain Don Brooker now took over responsibility for the crews. After flying with the R.A.F. he joined Airwork's overseas division in 1948. He flew with the company in the Sudan operating with Sudan Airways where he was appointed Deputy Chief Pilot. In 1954 he was transferred to the U.K. Airwork Air Transport Division at Blackbushe and flew as a captain on Hermes, Vikings and DC3s. Captain Brooker later transferred to long range operations flying DC4s and Constellations. Of a more serious disposition than some of his colleagues, Don Brooker, with his piercing blue eyes, gave an impression of great coolness and decisiveness.

November   Returning to the operational side, there was still some of 1964 left! After the upheaval of the previous month, November was very quiet with 41 flights of which 25 were to Ostend by Lima Lima.

> *In the vicinity of Ostend there was some restricted airspace which, of course, incoming aircraft were expected to avoid. There were occasions when, with her usual Captain, the Bristol Freighter would often take a short cut across this area while the tower could be heard saying: 'Lima Lima you are crossing the danger area,' and on the ground they would expect something to happen, but it never did. (Richard Grist)*

Foxtrot Yankee carried cargo Heathrow-Amsterdam-Heathrow on Sunday 1st. and returned to Manston on Tuesday. Her only other flight was to Lille, also with freight, on the 10th., after which she went into the hangar for a check. Yankee Kilo flew only once, a Manston-Amsterdam-Oslo-Amsterdam-Manston passenger charter on the 18th./19th.

There were five Viking flights, all with passengers. Victor Foxtrot flew to Le Touquet with a full load both ways on Thursday 5th. and to Ostend on Saturday. Over the 18th./19th. she flew Manston-Bristol-Gatwick-Manston and completed the month Manston-Ostend-Liverpool-Ostend-Manston on the 25th./26th. Charlie Hotel's contribution was Manston-Southend-Le Bourget on Wednesday 25th. with a return via Southend on Sunday 29th. There were no movements on nine days and Lima Lima made the last flight on the Monday morning, the 30th., to Ostend.

December   Captain Souster, another senior man closely identified with Hugh Kennard, left on 9 December for a position at Invicta.

Invicta's formation was the feature of an article in the '*Gazette*' on 11 December with applications for 1965 operations already having been submitted to the A.T.L.B. and the company was reported as currently negotiating further contracts through its London-based commercial department.

The last month was busier, although Lima Lima was the only aircraft used for the first twelve days. The Bristol went to Ostend on Tuesday 1st., there were no flights for three days then Lima Lima went to Ostend three times on Saturday 5th., three more on Sunday and two on Monday.

> *In November and December the weather was very severe and there were many days when Lima Lima departed in frosts so hard they almost crackled. On one occasion the taxiways and runway were so icy the Tower expressed genuine concern for Captain Nicol as the bulbous Bristol cautiously tiptoed away from the apron.*

There were no flights on Tuesday 8th. and Wednesday 9th. Two more Ostends followed on Thursday, no flight on Friday and Ostend again on Saturday, the Freighter striking technical or weather problems as she did not return until the next day. In addition to more Ostends, Lima Lima went to Rotterdam twice on Monday 21st. and made Air Ferry's final flight of the year, to Ostend, on the afternoon of Thursday 31st.

The first DC4 movement was Oscar Golf's return from Prestwick on the 17th. The next day Foxtrot Yankee departed on a marathon tour of the Holy Land and ancient civilisation with 82 passengers, possibly an American group. The flight started Manston-Frankfurt-Athens and on Tuesday 22nd. continued Athens-Heraklion-Istanbul-Beirut where the aircraft remained until early on Saturday 26th., when it flew Beirut-Damascus-Jerusalem. On the 29th. the DC4 went to Cairo and next day flew Cairo-Luxor-Cairo where she remained over the new year.

TWILIGHT OF THE PISTONS

The Jerusalem leg caused some anger and consternation, 'accidentally' contrived by a ground hostess, with a well known flower as a sobriquet, who would have left to join Invicta by the time the aircraft returned. At this time Jerusalem was part of Jordan and the aircraft papers in the concertina file were carefully labelled as 'Jerusalem-Israel;' almost sufficient to cause an international incident in those days.

This flight was probably Pop's swansong, part of the crew captained by Hugh Tubman. At Cairo some of them joined the passengers for a ride on a camel, Pop revelling in the warm weather, so unlike an English winter.

> *'I always liked flying with Hugh Tubman; the crews were such gentlemen, they always looked after us.' (Maureen Pople)*

Yankee Kilo left Manston on Tuesday 29th. and made a Manston-Prestwick-Toulouse-Prestwick cargo flight, the aircraft then remained in Scotland on the 31st. for a check from which she would not return for two months.

Victor Foxtrot carried passengers to Ostend on the 13th. and to Le Bourget on the 15th. The Viking then had a freight charter to Bordeaux on the 22nd. that necessitated a return to that airport. Victor Delta, operating on 15 December for the first time since 23 October, made only passenger flights and that day flew to Rotterdam, recorded a Rotterdam-Rotterdam the next day, and came back to Manston on the 17th.

After a short local flight on Monday 14th. Charlie Hotel had two longer passenger charters, with an Ostend in between. The first was Manston-Edinburgh-Rotterdam-Edinburgh-Manston over the 15th./17th., followed on Wednesday 23rd. by one Manston-Bordeaux-Bilbao-Manchester-Manston. Bilbao being a Spanish port in the Bay of Biscay, it is likely that both of these charters carried ships crews being returned to the U.K. for Christmas.

There was a flurry of passenger activity over the festive period. Victor Delta and Oscar Golf went to Brussels on Christmas Eve, the latter aircraft then due to take another group to Ostend. On landing an air hostess went sick and, with no replacement available, Ronnie Cox was pressed into service to replace her. The Chief Pilot gave Ronnie an individual training course and took her out to the aircraft to demonstrate the emergency procedures.

Meanwhile snow at Ostend closed the airport and when it became apparent the flight was not going to leave, Traffic telephoned round to see if they could disperse the passengers in the local hotels for a night stop. With the exception of the San Clu who took in a husband, wife and their little girl in a staff room, the hotels were full and unable to assist. The remainder of the passengers spent the night in the terminal and Joe Russell stayed on with them.

On Christmas morning they set out, Ronnie accompanied by Alan Wood who doubled up his Tarmac duties with some flights as a steward. It was a very bumpy ride and poor Ronnie set a record, which may still stand, of being sick five times between Manston and Ostend. There was not much time to serve duty free goods and even the approach into Ostend was rough. At one point Ronnie saw the ground beneath, then they climbed away and only the sea could be seen from the window. 'Quick,' said Alan: 'Get up the front and make some more sales.'

Later in the morning Victor Foxtrot and Victor Delta also went to Ostend and it is likely the crews of two aircraft returned on Victor Foxtrot as Victor Delta came back to Manston on Sunday 27th. and Oscar Golf on Tuesday 29th. On Sunday 27th. there were six other flights to Ostend, five by the Vikings and one by Yankee Kilo. Victor Delta made the last passenger flight to Ostend on the 28th.

STATISTICS

In statistical terms the year had been an outstanding success with 153,057 passengers carried and 6,516 hours flown. August was the peak month in total and for each type of aircraft; Charlie Hotel carried most Viking passengers that month with Victor Delta flying most hours. Foxtrot Yankee took both totals for the DC4s.

1964, in retrospect, was the peak year of the three in which the Vikings operated with Charlie Hotel taking both passenger and flying hour record totals. In all, 77 destinations were visited in 2,520 flights, nearly three times those of the previous year. The top ten destinations, in numbers of flights, made interesting reading:

1964 SECOND WIND AND A TAKEOVER

1963		1964	
Ostend	355	Ostend	1326
Basle	111	Le Touquet	204
Dusseldorf	78	Basle	198
Le Touquet	73	Rotterdam	102
Perpignan	51	Dusseldorf	97
Luxembourg	51	Palma	91
Palma	50	Perpignan	67
Dijon	30	Luxembourg	58
Pisa	23	Lyons	53
Naples	14	Dijon	25

	Hours flown	Passengers carried	Flights made	Airports visited	Passenger aircraft	Seating available	Ostend flights
1963	3095	70598	940	41	4	252	355
1964	6516	153057	2520	77	8	462	1326
% increase	111	117	168	88	100	83	274

MANSTON

One quiet, late afternoon in May, the word suddenly went round: 'They are foaming the runway.' Nothing for a while, then the next message was relayed from the tower: 'A Valiant is in trouble, nosewheel problem.' People slowly drifted out onto the apron and looked searchingly to the west. At last a speck appeared, already very low down and grew slowly into a white Valiant, dragging in from miles out in one single, flat, approach. The pilot eased the big bomber, WZ396 of 543 Squadron at Wyton, down on the runway without a tremor and the first of the live foam landings was safely accomplished. Only a day or so later another Valiant almost repeated the drama but this fortunately proved a false alarm and the bomber left on 3 June.

There were many other visitors during the year although none quite so dramatic. Civil visitors included a Dan-Air Ambassador, a British Eagle Viscount on a weather diversion, two French registered Bristol Freighters from Compagnie Air Transport and Carvair G-ASDC of B.U.A.F. In April, two Euravia Constellations flew in and, on two days running, PH-MAE, a smart DC4 of Martin's Air Charter appeared. A rare type for Manston in August was G-ALHT, an Argonaut of Air Links, and the last recorded civil visitor of the year in December was yet another aircraft with undercarriage trouble, this time a VC10. The military types were as fascinating as ever, including a Royal Navy Dragonfly; on 9 March three Meteor NF14s, and on 9 April a Canberra bearing the winged tin-opener badge of No. 6 Squadron. The two resident Air Sea Rescue Whirlwinds of No. 22 Squadron were both replaced, presumably on rotation for overhaul. During June one of the air display teams of the time, the 'Red Pelicans', arrived with their Jet Provosts and in October a clutch of four Victors flew in on one of their dispersal exercises, what a sight!

Caledonian's G-ASHL, 30 March, 1964

The R.A.F. suffered another loss on Saturday 12 December when a Whirlwind crashed into a ploughed field at Westgate, but the crew of three managed to scramble out unhurt. The helicopter had just taken off on a training flight when it probably had engine failure, causing the aircraft to fall on soft ground but with sufficient force to snap off the tail assembly.

Varsity WP329, 8 April, 1964

TWILIGHT OF THE PISTONS

One item in the local press that year brought some unwanted attention. A service wife on the camp, who also worked for the airline, had gone off the rails to an extent that resulted in a divorce case. The paper reported on this, including the list of twelve co-respondents read out and, as most of these were familiar names, there were some red faces for a while.

Left:
Valiant WZ396 after her eventful landing.

Below:
Whirlwind of 22 Squadron, 26 June, 1964

R.A.F.
The military scene during the year saw the Ballistic Missile Early Warning System become operational. The distinguishing features above ground were the huge white spheres housing the radar, and the British site at Fylingales in Yorkshire was linked to others in Greenland and Alaska to provide Britain with a three minute warning in the event of a Soviet missile attack. With British capability now at an acceptable level, the U.S.A.F. Strategic Air Command bases here were closed.

An R.A.F. instructor, F/Lt. Lee Jones, who had previously flown with the famous team of black Hunters of 'Trebble One' squadron, conceived the idea of using the new advanced trainer, the Folland Gnat, for formation aerobatics. Permission was given and the new team, painted yellow overall and called the 'Yellowjacks' after their radio call sign, started their displays in 1964.

CIVIL
As mentioned, the season had seen the beginning of a period of spectacular growth in inclusive tour business and so had been a good one for other airlines.

Autair, expanding with Euravia at Luton, had doubled the size of their fleet. Caledonian had increased from one DC7 to three of the type, while B.K.S. had added a Britannia to their inventory. Across at Southend, Channel had the same aircraft as in 1963 but supplemented by the acquisition of no less than eight Viscounts.

British Eagle were expanding their scheduled service network and had increased from six aircraft to fifteen while Lloyd International had acquired a DC6, G-ASTW, to join Whisky India and Whisky Kilo. Other items of interest included ACE Freighters which had started up in March with a single Constellation; Air Links were operating the last Hermes, and the Yorks were almost gone with Dan-Air and Skyways using the last examples.

The state airlines were also adding new types to their route networks, B.E.A. introducing the DeHavilland Trident in April and with B.O.A.C. adding the VC10 to their fleet.

Two name changes took place; in August in recognition of the fleet re-equipment with eight Bristol Britannias, Euravia became Britannia Airways. Soon after this Derby Aviation, which had flown since 1959 as Derby Airways, was renamed British Midland Airways.

AIR HOLDINGS
Within Air Holdings the operating parts of the group experienced mixed fortunes. B.U.A.F. opened a new vehicle ferry service, to Liege, but this and other measures taken was not sufficient to stop the decline in this work.

1964 SECOND WIND AND A TAKEOVER

On 1 October the last B.U.A. Britannia trooping service left from Stanstead, replaced from this time on by VC10s from Gatwick. B.U.A. had spent much time planning their takeover of the B.O.A.C. South American service which was due to start later that month. The General Election result of a Labour victory gave the management some concern; it was felt that a private initiative bent on succeeding, where a state corporation had produced only indifferent results, would not receive much sympathy or support. The service was allowed to proceed, however, and began on 5 November.

B.U.A.'s Managing Director, in spite of his bullish words at Manston, was becoming disillusioned with his position within the Air Holdings Group. Although outwardly a successful organisation, B.U.A. had not proved easy to knit harmoniously together and Laker's relationship with Miles Wyatt had often been a difficult one. As a result Laker was already considering breaking away and forming his own airline.

Douglas Whybrow's misgivings as to the influence he would be able to bring to bear on B.U.A. were born out in practice and by the end of the year he decided a change was necessary. After some discussion, two appointments were offered to him and for personal reasons he chose the Leroy Group, joining as Managing Director at Tunbridge Wells in early 1965.

SAFETY

On the safety front 1964 saw just one serious accident to a British airliner, unfortunately another case of a terrain strike. On 29 February a British Eagle Britannia hit ground 8,535 feet up while flying in cloud near Innsbruck, killing all 83 aboard.

OTHER EVENTS

Away from the aviation scene, in January Pope Paul made a pilgrimage of the Holy Land and in Panama there were strident demands for an end to the sixty one year old canal treaty with the United States.

The mediterranean island of Cyprus was another troubled area where the Greek Cypriots did not want to have N.A.T.O. for an international garrison and sought instead a U.N.-Canadian peace keeping force; this against a background of protests for the U.K. to leave the island. An earthquake in Alaska severely damaged the town of Anchorage and the Indian Premier Nehru died in April having been a Chief Minister since independence in 1947.

A new sound was heard on British radios from the first commercial pirate radio station, a ship anchored off the east coast. *Radio Caroline* evoked strong feelings both for and against her brand of broadcasting.

As mentioned, the British General Election ended in a Labour victory, a cliffhanger result with a majority of just four for the new Prime Minister Harold Wilson.

In America the biggest issue, demanding attention, was that of civil rights. In 1964 segregation still ruled the south and President Johnson resolved to complete what President Lincoln had started during the civil war a hundred years earlier. With the passing of the 1964 Civil Rights Bill a milestone was reached which enabled blacks and whites to at last use the same buses, restaurants and toilets. The immediate result however, after decades of frustration, was an outpouring of bitterness and civil unrest that shook the country to its foundations.

An incident occurred one dark night in August and, as a result of a naval skirmish between Vietnamese gunboats and U.S. destroyers, a fundamental turning point was reached in this struggle. Lyndon Johnson sought to cut himself off from congressional control and the Gulf of Tonkin resolution, enabling him to expand the war without further authority, was passed virtually without dissent. The war that Johnson really wanted to fight, however, was that of poverty, and the election in November resulted in a landslide in his favour.

While travelling abroad during the summer, the Soviet leader Khruschev was overthrown and succeeded by Mr. Breznev and Mr. Kosygin. Nikita Khruschev had risen from peasant stock to astounding power and historians will probably consider that his greatest achievment was to bring the U.S.S.R. out of the era of Stalinist terror.

TWILIGHT OF THE PISTONS

NEWS ABOUT AIR FERRY

CHAPTER 5
1965   NEW MANAGEMENT

THE AIRCRAFT

Douglas DC4	G-APYK	G-ASFY	G-ASOG
Vickers Viking	G-AIVF	G-AOCH	G-AHOW
Bristol Freighter	G-AMLL	G-ANVR	G-AMLP

For passenger flying Air Ferry had progressed from four aircraft in 1963 to eight the following year now, for 1965, it would be six, the three DC4s and only three of the Vikings. Bravo Xray's last flight had been back in October and her Certificate of Airworthiness expired on 9 May 1965. Victor Delta made just two flights in 1965, on the 2nd and 6th January, the latter commanded by Don Brooker and her C of A expired on 3 April.

On the freight side, Lima Lima was nearing the end of the years lease. Her very presence at Manston was an offence to Air Holdings / B.U.A.F. who had Superfreighters standing idle at Lydd and Southend. Two B.U.A.F. machines were provided, one being G-ANVR from 14 January until 26 March which overlapped with Lima Lima for some weeks as the latter was returned on 11 March. There were no Bristols at Manston for some days until G-AMLP arrived for a seven week stay until she too left, signalling the end of Bristol Freighters with Air Ferry.

The year started, of course, with Yankee Kilo away at Prestwick and Oscar Whisky on a major check in the hangar.

Captain Ken Sheppardson, General Manager

THE CREWS

On the aircrew side, Bill Wood, who had received a message in Kuwait from Ken Sheppardson saying: 'Your job is available,' returned on 8 February. The Captains for the third season were Brooker, Wood, Tubman, Gibson, Laker, Nicol, Ashpitel and Mason, while Bob McNay left on 7 March to rejoin Hugh Kennard, as Chief Pilot for Invicta. In addition to Bill Wood's return, there were three joiners during the year, Captains C Gwyther, S Hunnable who had been with Don Brooker in Sudan Airways, and R Honeyman.

The First Officers for the season included Tony Ahmad, Peter Johnston, Jeep Jackson, Bill Surrage, Peter Gutteridge, Patrick 'Bob' Hope, Paul Horsting and Norman Armstrong. Two joiners were F Simpson and H Chang. A senior man who had kept his licence current was also pressed into service later on, but for an unusual reason, that was Ken Sheppardson.

The Cabin Crew for the season included Gillian Appleby, as Chief Hostess, and Air Hostesses Bowery, Heather Britton, Brown, Desmond, Krebstarkies, Lemm, Masters, Jane Mills, Molli, Morgan, Rendall, Rolls, Setchel, Maggie Studt, Pat Willcox, and Woods. Gone now were the Air Ferry bowlers worn for the first two years. For the new season the hostesses wore

Stan Hunnable   (Maura Hunnable)

63

a more conventional pill box type of headwear which, nevertheless, looked very attractive.

There had been an embarrassing hitch to the employment of the hostesses for the new season which caused some chuckles at the time, at the expense of the person who inadvertently caused it. It was decided that, now Air Ferry was part of a large group, the quality facilities of the London offices should be used for the interviews of the hostesses. It so happened that the letters arranging interviews at the spacious Air Holdings building in Portland House, Stag Place were despatched requesting attendance at Stag House, Portland Place with the result that there were many howls of protest from baffled young women unable to keep their appointments.

IT AND CHARTER OPERATIONS

In January the '*Aeroplane*,' in those days the other highly respected weekly aviation journal with '*Flight*,' included a special supplement devoted to Air Holdings Ltd. The cover was a pictorial representation of the group as a pot plant with the constituent companies shown as leaves. The acquisition of Leroy Tours was given good coverage together with that of another tour company, Whitehall Travel. Hugh Kennard's efforts were damned with faint praise with the comment: 'Although as a business this venture (Air Ferry) was successful, it became obvious that the volume of traffic could not suffice to sustain the jet aircraft which would be needed if Leroy Tours was to maintain its position. By joining forces with Air Holdings, Leroy is now able to offer his Voyageurs air travel of the high quality with which his name is associated.' It must be said that one of the policies followed by Whitehall Travel was that of always flying British and choosing the latest aircraft available. B.U.A. in particular were now in a position to offer this.

The year saw new publicity material, particularly in the provision of A4 sheets advertising the airline and used for mailshots and other distributions. These usually used photographs of the aircraft and hostesses but one day there was a need for some cabin shots and most of the office staff were rounded up and loaded onto a DC4 to substitute for passengers. The publicity handouts

1965 NEW MANAGEMENT

paid attention to the freight characteristics of the aircraft, noting that the cargo doors of the DC4s when fully opened were 9' 6" wide and 6' 6" high with a capacity of 7.8 tons. The Vikings, in turn, could carry almost 4 tons.

On 1 January the '*Gazette*' reported that the A.T.L.B. had announced the withdrawal of an inclusive tour application by Air Ferry for a service between Manston and Salzburg, an application which B.E.A. had opposed. The next week Lima Lima featured in a large group photograph, following a Christmas party held in the terminal for the children of employees and also some from the Manston Cottage Homes. The party was organised by catering officer Gwen Laycock and Captain Gibson took the part of Father Christmas.

The Traffic department, already depleted when the seasonal staff departed, virtually ceased to exist as the permanent ones melted away to rejoin Audry Kennard. Ronnie, Sue Cooper and then Joe Russell left to join Invicta. Phil Dalton was appointed as the new Traffic Superintendent; always dapper, Phil was slightly built in contrast to Joe's rather burly appearance. Peter Everingham joined later as Phil's deputy.

Over the winter period the hearings were heard of the applications by Invicta to operate inclusive tours from Manston with the same companies previously booked by Hugh for Air Ferry. The hearings were conducted in an accrimonious atmosphere with the applications fiercely opposed by Air Holdings; this was a life or death struggle, touched at times with comedy. The learned representative for Air Holdings naturally made much of the facts that Hugh Kennard did not have an airline, not even any key staff. It would be at this point, or one like it, that Peter Souster, who had joined Invicta as Operations Manager, or someone else, was produced by Hugh to disprove the statement. Joe Russell was similarly 'produced' at a key point and the Air Holdings man was heard to mutter: 'But he was at Air Ferry yesterday.'

1965 would be a very different year to the preceding ones. The loyalty expressed by many of the Inclusive Tour Operators to Hugh Kennard was strong and most of those which had flown with him before now transferred business to Invicta. The amount of this work carried out by Air Ferry suffered accordingly, and the top ten destinations for the year, in comparison with those in Chapter 4, now included positioning flights and freight charter stopovers and destinations:

1965
Ostend   692
Basle   202
Perpignan   188
Gatwick   139
Le Touquet 118
Rotterdam   78
Southend   41
Brindisi   33
Lyneham   32
Gutersloh   28

The change over to more freighting work meant that planning the daily and weekly programmes became more difficult as charters were sometimes obtained without much notice and the duration of the flights varied considerably.

There were clear signs, too, that the times were changing. Other airlines were able to offer newer types for inclusive tour work. On one occasion during the season a group of passengers at Rotterdam refused to board an Air Ferry Viking on the grounds that it had a tail wheel undercarriage and was too old. After some discussion, a DC4 was sent over which they boarded quite happily, although unaware that it was some three years older that the Viking.

Ken Sheppardson was convinced that the flying hours should not only be significantly increased but that the monthly profile should move away from the seasonal peaks and troughs, and he had set about this with some vigour, working initially to increase the off peak freight work as much as possible. The three months to March, for example, produced 626 flying hours to 1964's 432, a 45% increase.

As a result of this policy, 1965 saw a considerable increase in freight charters, some made available through the group and others successfully quoted for by the Commercial Section. Assistance from the group showed through in the amount of work flown from Gatwick, Southend and, to a lesser extent, Lydd. Gatwick, as

TWILIGHT OF THE PISTONS

Mike Austin, Chief Accountant

Dick Sanders, Sales Manager

Charles Carroll, Commercial Manager

shown above, being the fourth most used airport, much of this work being service related with the movement of dependents to airfields used by R.A.F. Germany.

Much more work came through Ministry freighting carried out from R.A.F. Transport Command's base at Lyneham, with the DC4s carrying out the type of long range work for which they were designed.

THE YEAR

January There were no flights on New Years day and only five by the Vikings in January, all with passengers; the year getting underway ten minutes into Saturday 2nd. with Victor Delta departing to Ostend. The aircraft closed her career four days later with another Ostend, commanded by Don Brooker. The other Viking flights were an Ostend by Victor Foxtrot on 3rd., after which she joined Oscar Whisky in the hangar and two by Charlie Hotel. These were a Manston-Gatwick-Dusseldorf-Gatwick-Manston charter over the 6th./11th. during which the aircraft stopped for five nights at her old German base, and another Ostend on Wednesday 13th.

Foxtrot Yankee returned from her epic journey on 3 January, routing back from Cairo via Athens and Frankfurt. For her next flight, the DC4 went to Ostend on the 14th. There was a positioning flight to Gatwick next day for a charter Gatwick-Gutersloh-Manston and Foxtrot Yankee made the last DC4 flight of the month with freight over the 21st./22nd., Manston-Le Bourget-Heathrow-Manston.

Oscar Golf did not fly until Tuesday 12th. and all flights were for passengers. She positioned to Gatwick for a Hanover that day, night stopped at Gatwick and on Wednesday flew Gatwick-Zurich and night stopped again. The DC4 came back Zurich-Gatwick-Hanover-Manston on Thursday. The aircraft went back to Gatwick on Tuesday 19th., flew a Gutersloh from there, night stopped and flew another Gutersloh before returning to Manston on Wednesday evening. These were service related flights, Gutersloh being an R.A.F. base in Germany. Oscar Golf did not fly again in January and that month, in addition to the 1st., there were no flights at all on Monday 4th., three Sundays running from the 10th., Monday 25th. and the last three days.

Lima Lima continued to ply backwards and forwards to Ostend, often in the most bitter weather. She was complemented by G-ANVR which arrived from Southend on 14 January. Victor Romeo spent part of her time with 'British United' lettering but, at a time of great sensitivity regarding names, this title was replaced by 'Air Ferry' in pale blue although the remainder of the scheme was the darker blue of B.U.A.F. The first revenue flight was on the 18th., piloted by Andy Nicol. On the 21st. Victor Romeo went across to Lydd and returned next day. Ostend was the only destination towards the end of January, flown by both freighters.

Hugh Tubman took Victor Romeo there with pigs on the 26th and it fell to this aircraft to make the final flights of the month, to Ostend, on Thursday 28th.

> *One recollection, it could have been 1964 or 1965, concerned the poor condition of some of the Viking components as one entry on a defect sheet after a survey in the hanger stated: 'Replace wooden window finishers - suffering from woodworm.' (Paul Noller)*

February Viking activity continued at a low level during February. Following the check, Oscar Whisky flew an air test on 5th. which was probably combined with training as she was aloft for three and a quarter hours, and made just one more flight in the month, with passengers to Ostend on 20th.

1965 NEW MANAGEMENT

Victor Foxtrot emerged from her overhaul on 26 February with a 40 minute local flight as her only movement in the month. Charlie Hotel made two local and four revenue flights before becoming the last of the airworthy Vikings to go on check, the latter being a Manston-Gatwick-Lyons-Genoa-Manston with freight on the 10th., and with passengers to Le Touquet on the 5th., Amsterdam on the 19th./21st. and Ostend on the last day of the month.

Jeep Jackson and Patrick Hope were two of the pilots who started their DC4 training at this time. With Invicta actively recruiting aircrew, there was a risk of pilots transferring to Hugh Kennard, with the opportunity to fly the DC4s he was intending to operate. After being made up to first officer, and commencing the DC4 conversion course, Jeep did not pursue the Invicta option.

Foxtrot Yankee started off with a freight trip Manston-Bremen on the 3rd., flew Bremen-Heathrow the next night and came back to Manston at midday on Friday 5th. There were also passenger charters, Manston-Liverpool-Cologne-Liverpool-Manston over the 10th./12th., two Luxembourgs and on the 23rd., a Manston-Gatwick-Dusseldorf-Gatwick-Manston. Foxtrot Yankee was also in demand for training and familiarisation. Over the 16th./18th. in flying locally and at Le Touquet she clocked up at least fifty five landings in three days with a further nine landings on a local flight the following week. On Friday 26th. there was a return to freight with a Manston-Manchester-Bremen-Manston and next day Foxtrot Yankee positioned to Lyneham, on what would become a well trodden aerial route to the R.A.F. Transport Command base in Wiltshire, to carry out the first M.O.D. freight flight. By the end of the month she had flown out via Brindisi and was at Damascus on the way to the Far East.

Oscar Golf went to Frankfurt with freight on 3rd./5th. February and next flew on the 20th., with passengers Liverpool-Rotterdam. This was followed on Tuesday 23rd. by a Manston-Gatwick-Gutersloh-Gatwick, the aircraft coming back to Manston at five minutes after midnight and no doubt once more having carried service personnel and their dependents. With the trooping connections it is likely the work to the bases in Germany was provided by or facilitated from within the group. The aircraft went to Gatwick again on 26th. to take passengers to Le Touquet and completed the month with a local flight on Sunday 28th., followed by one positioning to Gatwick for passengers to Genoa, returning from there direct to Manston.

Lima Lima operated only once in February with a flight on Friday 19th. Manston-Lydd-Ostend-Manston, this being her last revenue flight, piloted by Hugh Tubman. Victor Romeo flew twenty Ostends, and made four journeys to Rotterdam. There was no flying on three days in February, the three Sundays from the 7th.

On 19 February, Thanet Civic Heads visited Manston and the '*Gazette*' printed a photo of Ken Sheppardson with the group under the wing of an aircraft. The same edition carried an item reporting that Invicta had taken delivery of its first aircraft and would be ready for the coming season. It was anticipated that work on the new terminal and administration building would be completed well within the original schedule and the majority of staff should be re-housed at Manston by the end of the month.

> *As part of the winter activity there were usually a few winter holiday flights and passengers who had boarded the aircraft in an athletic manner fourteen days previously would often return with arms and legs encased in large white plaster casts; still, it must be said, looking amazingly cheerful.*

March The way that Air Ferry operations had changed was most noticeable in March with passengers 49% down but flying hours 39% up compared with 1964. The increase in hours for the three months to March was even higher, as mentioned, and this activity tended to mask the dramatic switch of inclusive tour work to Invicta by the companies that expressed their loyalty to Hugh Kennard.

> *The main impression of 1965 of course, was the presence of Invicta somehow, incredibly, putting together an airline with all its attendant facilities with realistically not enough time to accomplish this. There were not many spare buildings on the eastern side, suitable or not, and Hugh Kennard had to improvise every day. They used the old parachute building, some huts and the old loop hangar, which had been used only for storage since the U.S.A.F. moved out, was pressed into service. In some ways though, having been through the formation process for Air Ferry, Invicta was easier to set up and the Kennards had the necessary and vital contacts with the tour companies. The Station Commander at this time was Wing Commander W. Hoy, DFC, AFC, and*

TWILIGHT OF THE PISTONS

he helped in many ways to smooth the path of the emerging airline. As Audry recalled recently, 'William Hoy was a good friend to us.'

Normally by March a range of inclusive tour work was underway, but 1965 would be very different. Over the whole season the number of tours to Lyons, Luxembourg, Copenhagen, Naples and Verona totalled just twenty six, with none at all to Palma and Dijon. The work this March was predominately freighting with passenger hours accounting for only 27% of the hours flown.

Foxtrot Yankee staged on from Damascus through Karachi and Calcutta to Changi airfield in Singapore, returning the same way to Damascus and then via Lyons to Manston on Monday 8th. Oscar Golf followed on the 1st. with a second cargo making two extra stops, at Bahrein and Delhi, before reaching Singapore on the morning of Saturday 6th. The aircraft did not leave there until Saturday 13th. and coming home flew Damascus-

Invicta's Papa Mike

Manston direct on the 17th., this last leg taking 11 hours 35 minutes.

Jeep Jackson went on the first Changi flight. He had taken his DC4 base check at Le Touquet on 16 February, carried out his competency check on the Manston-Lyneham leg prior to loading, and the route check was made en route to Karachi!

Foxtrot Yankee positioned to Gatwick on Friday 12th., flew a Gatwick-Zurich-Gatwick freight charter next day and came back to Manston on Sunday afternoon. A Manchester-Bremen with freight on the 15th./16th. followed and, later on the 16th., the DC4 positioned up to Prestwick for an overhaul.

Oscar Golf continued with freight, flying Manston-Salzburg-Basle-Manston on the 19th., Manston-Coventry-Bremen-Manston over the 20th./21st., and then switched to passenger work. The aircraft went to Gatwick on the 22nd., flew to Wildenwrath, another R.A.F. Station in Germany, and to Gutersloh with a return to Manston on the evening of Tuesday 23rd. Four cargo journeys completed the months work, two Manchester-Bremens and two Madrids from Manston.

After an air test on 4 March, Yankee Kilo returned from Prestwick the following day and spent most of the month operating passenger charters out of Gatwick. Between the 6th. and the 30th. the DC4 used Gatwick on six occasions, flew two or three charters, and came back to Manston. The flights were to Geneva, Zurich, Gutersloh, Wildenwrath and Hanover. There was a variation over the 8th./10th. when Hugh Tubman and Tony Ahmad in Yankee Kilo flew Manston-Dusseldorf-Gatwick-Hanover-Dusseldorf-Gatwick-Manston, the Dusseldorfs being diversions from Wildenwrath. There was another variation on Wednesday 17th. when the aircraft diverted into Manston from Gatwick with 64 passengers, stayed an hour and then continued on to Wildenwrath. Back at Manston the aircraft went to Le Bourget on the 27th./28th. and then flew Manston-Gatwick-Geneva-Gatwick-Manston. The DC4 was then changed over to freight trim and next day went to Pori in Finland.

Viking activity was low. Victor Foxtrot went to Brussels over the 4th./6th. flying Brussels-Brussels for some reason that day, to Bordeaux on the 12th./14th. and to Beauvais on 26th./29th., all with passengers. The aircraft also carried out a training flight on 29 March to Stanstead although she probably did not land there.

Oscar Whisky made two revenue flights, with passengers Stanstead-Rotterdam-Stanstead over the 5th./7th.,

1965 NEW MANAGEMENT

to Le Bourget over the 12th./14th., and either a training sortie or a freight charter to Le Touquet on the 22nd. Two training sorties closed the month, a four hour trip to Stanstead and a local flight of one hour.

Both Bristol Freighters departed during the month, the first was on March 11 when Captain Nicol delivered Lima Lima to Radlett, Handley Page's airfield in Hertfordshire. Victor Romeo flew all seventeen trips by Air Ferry to Ostend, one on the 16th. being a route check by Hugh Tubman on Andy Nicol, and went to Rotterdam on the 12th. The aircraft made her last revenue flight, Manston-Bordeaux-Madrid-Manston on 25th./26th. March and was then returned that evening to B.U.A.F. at Southend, both of these flights being commanded by Captain Tubman.

Victor Romeo, 26 March, 1965

April There were no flights on All Fools Day and this was the first month that the flying hours fell below the 1964 comparative figure. The weekend 2/4 April comprised just three passenger flights by Yankee Kilo out of Gatwick, to Wildenwrath, Gutersloh and Geneva and four flights to Ostend from Manston. Oscar Whisky and Oscar Golf took passengers out on Friday and returned on Sunday while Victor Foxtrot flew on Friday with ten passengers recorded and Sunday with four!

Before the Invicta facilities were completed their traffic person responsible for shepherding the passengers between customs and the aircraft was located some distance away, somewhere behind the new hangar site. The ground hostess concerned was often Marilyn Wilson, now Lyn Povey, who used to cycle backwards and forwards across the apron to meet them.

Ostend was visited more frequently than in any other month, on 115 occasions, but still considerably down on the previous year. On Thursday 15th. and Good Friday there were 32 flights to the Belgian airport and 28 on the Monday to return the Easter holiday makers to Manston. All six aircraft participated, with Foxtrot Yankee crossing the channel seven times on Monday. Flights to Rotterdam and the bulb fields built up with 25 flights there in April.

Foxtrot Yankee had had an air test at Prestwick on 5 April and came back to Manston the following day. The DC4 flew Manston-Gutersloh-Gatwick-Birmingham-Ostend-Manston on the 9th., the years first Perpignan the following day and the first Basle IT on Sunday 11th. Towards the end of April, Foxtrot Yankee flew the second tours to Perpignan and Basle, a Manston-Southend-Ostend-Southend-Rotterdam-Manston and a Manston-Southend-Rotterdam-Southend-Manston, before changing to freight trim over 29th./30th. for Manston-Heathrow-Copenhagen-Heathrow-Goteborg-Manston.

Yankee Kilo positioned back to Gatwick on the 5th. flying to Hanover, Dusseldorf, Wildenwrath, Le Touquet and Gutersloh before returning to Manston on the 9th., and did not fly again until the 15th. In addition to the Manston tours, on Thursday 22nd. there was a Manston-Ostend-Southend-Gatwick-Le Touquet-Gatwick-Manston and another Gatwick-Wildenwrath-Gatwick on the 28th.

Oscar Golf took freight to Le Bourget on the 9th. and then resumed IT work from Manston. On the 14th. the DC4 flew Manston-Wildenwrath-Gatwick-Manston and on the 24th. Manston-Ostend-Southend-Amsterdam-Southend-Manston. There was another Gatwick on the 28th. flying to Rotterdam, Le Touquet and Gutersloh, the aircraft coming back direct from Gutersloh to Manston next day.

Following her check, Charlie Hotel had made two local flights on 8 April before resuming revenue flying. In addition to the tour work the Vikings also carried out some charters, Victor Foxtrot went to Tirstrup over the 6th./8th., and to Lyons and Bremen on the 17th. Charlie Hotel made two visits to Hanover, on the 15th. and 19th.

Training flights were made in April by Oscar Golf; by Charlie Hotel, with the aircraft making seven landings in one session on 14 April, and by Foxtrot Yankee.

TWILIGHT OF THE PISTONS

The last of the Bristols arrived on 8 April, G-AMLP being brought from Southend by B.U.A.F. Captain Langley; she flew in that company's colours with 'British United' on each side throughout her stay at Manston. The aircraft was airborne locally for a short time the next day followed by the first revenue flight to Rotterdam, commanded by Andy Nicol; she made five other flights in April, all to Ostend.

Lima Papa, 15 April, 1965

One day Brian McAvoy, the company doctor, was driving past Ramsgate Airport and stopped to watch a Tri Pacer coming in on its final approach, his interest in flying had been kindled during a time he provided medical cover in Canada. He stood by the fence as the little aircraft rolled to a stop and Paul Horsting climbed out. 'Would you like a try?' he asked. They flew some circuits and from then on Brian started working for his licence, flying from Pysons Road and Biggin Hill. In collaboration with Paul and Tim Leigh, he later started the first Thanet Flying Club.

May The new pattern of flying continued in May with a mix of tour and charter flying from Manston and other bases plus some long range flights. There were 98 Ostends in the month, the bulb field excursions through Rotterdam and Amsterdam reached their peak, and tours on the main routes to Basle and Perpignan quickly built up.

Yankee Kilo made the first flight, to Calais with a block time of under an hour, and that weekend 1/2 May all six passenger aircraft went to Rotterdam. During the month Gatwick was visited on 32 occasions for charters to Rotterdam, Le Touquet, Gutersloh and Wildenwrath. Yankee Kilo positioned to Gatwick for one of these on Wednesday 5th., made three passenger journeys and was de-seated there for a Gatwick-Dusseldorf-Hanover-Gatwick freight flight early on the 7th. The aircraft was back in passenger trim that afternoon to go to Wildenwrath and returned to Manston via Rotterdam on Saturday.

There were also numerous flights into Southend, mainly from Ostend. On Thursday 6th Oscar Whisky made an internal flight from Gatwick to the R.A.F. training base at Valley in Wales. On return to Gatwick the Viking flew to Manston via Rotterdam.

Rosemary Wood (then Tubman), recalls an amusing incident from that season. She had gone to Amsterdam for four nights with some friends and boarded a Viking for the flight back to Manston. The air hostess, a foreign girl, went forward to give her little safety talk and started by saying: 'Captain Tubman welcomes you aboard and hopes you have a pleasant flight.' Rosemary was pleased that she had coincided with one of Hugh's flights and asked the hostess if she would let him know they were aboard so he could perhaps come back into the cabin or she could briefly visit the cockpit. There was no response from the pilots and they duly landed and taxied in, Rosemary feeling somewhat chastened. She finally asked if there was any reason and the hostess said: 'Well, actually the pilot is Captain Hunnable, but the way I say his name it sounds rude, so whenever I fly with him I say it is Captain Tubman!'

At 2137 on Sunday 2nd. Foxtrot Yankee left Manston for Lyneham followed by Oscar Golf three hours later, and between that day and 9th May both aircraft journeyed to Aden routing out via Brindisi, Damascus and Bahrein. Foxtrot Yankee came back Cairo-Manston direct while Oscar Golf returned by the outward route, getting to Lyneham on Saturday morning and Manston at midday on Sunday.

Foxtrot Yankee was back on tour duties for Saturday morning and next day the work included a Manston-Lydd-Calais-Southend-Ostend-Southend-Ostend-Calais-Lydd-Manston. Early on Monday Yankee Kilo went to Gatwick and then returned, presumably for some fault to be corrected, and went back the following day to continue the Gutersloh flights.

On Friday 14th, Yankee Kilo flew the first Friday evening Basle and the next night the weather intervened. The aircraft flew the 1500 Perpignan to schedule but Foxtrot Yankee on the later one, piloted by David Laker

1965 NEW MANAGEMENT

and Jeep Jackson, was diverted from overhead Perpignan to Marseilles and Yankee Kilo, operating the first of the early Sunday morning flights, left at 0200 and was diverted to Toulouse.

On Saturday, Oscar Golf flew Manston-Cologne-Southend-Ostend-Southend-Ostend-Manston and made a return trip direct to Cologne on Monday 17th. Next day the aircraft flew a Gatwick-Hanover-Rheims-Gatwick charter. Both Oscar Golf and Foxtrot Yankee flew early on Wednesday Manston-Munich-Gatwick and returned the passengers Gatwick-Munich soon after 0100 on Thursday. Charlie Hotel showed that the Vikings were still in the market place with a freight flight on the 20th./21st. Manston-Luton-Vienna-Bucharest-Munich-Manston.

The great 'find' during the compilation of this story was of two foolscap books kept by the engineers which covered the period from May 1965 until the end. The first of these records was entitled 'Maintenance Handover Book' while the second rejoiced in the name of 'Robbie's Record Book for Naughty Engineers.' The majority of entries were signed off by Ken Barker, Eddie Edgar and Les Dray, with others by Robbie Thomson, Bob Jack, Dave Jennings, Bill Simpson and Tony O'Reilly; needless to say they were invaluable.

Over the weekend 21/23 May the Perpignan flights increased, there were now departures at 2100 every night of the week. In addition there was a Saturday afternoon departure at 1600 and a 2200 flight on alternate weeks, plus an early 0130 flight each Sunday. Foxtrot Yankee flying the middle tour on Saturday 22nd. had to return to the French airport, and the telex message back at Manston reported the DC4 was U/S with the elevator trimmer jammed, a birds nest being suspected! A note by Bob Jack said: 'Jim Jones going down to investigate.' Meanwhile the Basles also increased with three or four flights on Saturdays and similar numbers on Sundays.

One more snag involving Foxtrot Yankee on the Perpignan route occurred on the night of Thursday 27th. when she returned from the end of the runway with a mag. drop on No. 2 engine and Oscar Golf took over the flight. Foxtrot Yankee was back on the line for the Friday night Perpignan although Oscar Golf's Basle ran nearly four hours late.

Lima Papa made flights from Rotterdam-Southend on the 3rd., Gatwick-Le Bourget on the 17th. and three Ostends before closing the score sheet on Bristol operations with a Manston-Gatwick-Antwerp-Manston charter by Captain Nicol on 28 May. The aircraft was returned to B.U.A.F. at Lydd by one of their crews on the following day.

Ken Barker (Joan Barker)

On Sunday 30th. Yankee Kilo took the first of a small number of Naples tours in 1965 with 45 passengers and took a block time of 11 hours 16 minutes. On the outward leg the DC4, flown by Bill Wood and Jeep Jackson, was struck by lightning. Oscar Golf ended the month in Damascus on the way out to Aden once more.

June Oscar Golf continued on to Aden flying the 'usual' route but returning to Manston via Rome very early on Friday 4th., the Aden-Rome leg taking 15 hours 20 minutes. Yankee Kilo had positioned off to Gatwick on Tuesday 1st., flew to Gutersloh, Dusseldorf, Le Touquet and Hanover, and came back to Manston via Le Touquet on Friday. For the next three weeks a DC4 positioned into Gatwick each Monday. Problems arose on Wednesday 2nd. and that night's Perpignan did not depart until 0740 on Thursday, with both of the other DC4s away there was no backup for Foxtrot Yankee at this point. After Thursdays Perpignan the aircraft took the first of a small series of Copenhagen day tours on Friday.

Oscar Golf was changed to passenger trim for the Friday evening Perpignan, which departed late and then returned from an hour out with CSU trouble; the 78 passengers finally left at 0111 on Yankee Kilo. Charlie

TWILIGHT OF THE PISTONS

Hotel flew an internal charter that day, Saturday 5th., from Renfrew, at this time still Glasgow's airport, to Heathrow. The rest of the weekend, including nine Basles, operated close to schedule although Oscar Golf, crewed by Charlie Gwyther and Jeep Jackson, suffered a lightning strike. Foxtrot Yankee flew Manston-Akrotiri-Manston over 6th./8th. June with just 20 passengers, no doubt a service related flight.

The second week in June went well, all the Perpignans and nine Basles over the weekend running to time. Yankee Kilo had gone to Gatwick on Monday 7th. and returned from there via Jersey on the 9th.; on Sunday she went to Naples again, the aircraft being converted to a 60 seater configuration for this long haul. The Vikings operated some late night freight flights to Le Bourget during the week, possibly with newspapers; Charlie Hotel operating alone one night and with Victor Foxtrot the next. Oscar Golf left for Lyneham on Sunday night, the 13th., en route for Aden and did not get back until 0220 the following Saturday morning. The return journey this time being via Malta-Tangier-Gibralter to Lyneham, the Aden-Malta leg taking 13 hours 13 minutes.

The most ill-advised charter made by the company was to Africa to collect a DC4 load of wild boars. They made such a smell that Oscar Golf was out of service for a week for 'neutralising.' Even after that, when the cabin was warm, the passengers would wrinkle their noses and enquire what the unpleasant odour was. (Paul Noller). From the log it seems likely that this was when the aircraft called into Tangier on the way back from Aden.

In the third week Yankee Kilo worked again from Gatwick, and on Monday 14th. Charlie Hotel operated a meat cargo flight to Rotterdam. Foxtrot Yankee was late going to Basle on Wednesday morning, the same day that Oscar Whisky took passengers to Hamburg. On Friday 18th. Yankee Kilo went to Copenhagen and Victor Foxtrot to Cologne but it was Foxtrot Yankee which had a thoroughly bad weekend.

The aircraft, already behind time for the Friday Perpignan, left the apron at 0105 and Hugh Tubman brought her back 45 minutes later. The fault was an engine snag that could not be reproduced on the ground and, with the other DC4s on the way back from Lyneham and Basle, this tour must have been sub-chartered. Foxtrot Yankee was serviceable at 0600, but instead of going to Perpignan flew to Lydd and Le Touquet; the DC4 was due to have an air test on the Manston-Lydd leg. Among other evils, the refuellers had accidentally dropped a filler cap screw into one of Oscar Whisky's tanks and Ken Barker's closing comment that Saturday morning was: 'It's been murder, even the tractor big wheel had a flat.'

After this Foxtrot Yankee set off on time for the 1600 Saturday Perpignan and again returned, Yankee Kilo taking the flight at 1940. Fortunately this was a week with only two Perpignans on the Saturday but the Basles were also affected, with two Vikings taking over one of the DC4 tours and with a possible sub-charter. At 0112 on Sunday morning Foxtrot Yankee made a 48 minute flight which was either an air test or another return and the aircraft finally left for Perpignan at 0240. Also that day Oscar Whisky combined an Ostend with the second Viking visit in June to Cologne.

On Monday 21st. there were six Le Touquet flights and all the DC4s went to Deauville. Foxtrot Yankee flew Manston-Deauville-Lydd-Deauville-Manston while Oscar Golf operated Manston-Deauville-Lydd-Gatwick to carry out a flight Gatwick-Hanover-Gatwick. Yankee Kilo flew Manston-Lydd-Deauville-Manston to return the second group of passengers.

The letter regarding this work printed by 'Flight' in late 1994 brought in a response from a Monsieur Ferry from Bour-La-Reine in France, who still remembers the DC4s operating into Le Touquet and sent a copy of the Air Ferry section of a book on British Independent Airlines which the writer had been seeking for years.

Over the 22nd./23rd., Foxtrot Yankee took freight Manston-Madrid-Valencia-Manston. The rest of the week and the weekend of 25/27 June, including a Naples tour, passed fairly uneventfully although Yankee Kilo's oil consumption on the Saturday afternoon Perpignan caused concern, especially to Vic Surrage. On Sunday Oscar Golf positioned to Lyneham for another Aden, coming back through Dubai to Damascus at the end of June; a technical return being required at Damascus.

Tuesday 29 June was notable for 14 Le Touquet flights, part of the months total of 34 which was the maximum for 1965. There was an extra DC4 day flight to Perpignan the next day which resulted in two Vikings taking the Wednesday DC4 flight to Basle. The night flights to Perpignan on both the 29th. and 30th. were delayed with Foxtrot Yankee having the rotating beacon go U/S one night and instrument trouble on the next.

1965 NEW MANAGEMENT

During the summer an international incident had been building up which would affect Air Ferry during the winter months. This concerned Southern Rhodesia and her reluctance to bow to the 'Winds of Change' which had swept, and were still sweeping, through Africa. The entrenched governing white minority saw the demands being made by the majority black nationalists as a threat to all that they had built up, while the latter now scented an opportunity to be involved in the management of their country.

The Commonwealth Prime Ministers' conference in June included some tough discussion as to how the situation might be resolved. Prime Minister Harold Wilson had a difficult time in drafting a communique that would encapsulate the discussions in a way satisfactory to all the participants; a feat not achieved as President Nyerere of Tanzania disassociated himself from the document.

Another disagreement, which would affect Air Ferry considerably sooner, concerned relationships within the Air Holdings Group, particularly B.U.A., with the British Airline Pilots' Association. In the event of the dispute resulting in a strike it was likely that this would affect the younger pilots, leaving Air Ferry very exposed to a potential loss of business at a crucial

Victor Foxtrot, 30 June, 1965

time. Ken Sheppardson, who had kept his licence current, now went onto the duty roster and flew Vikings with Don Brooker to ensure at least one more pilot was available.

July In July the strike accordingly took place and was not one of the most glorious episodes in Air Ferry's history. There were token pickets at one stage and much hard work by Operations, and the pilots who remained on duty, before the situation returned to normal. Tour work continued through July, keeping quite well to time considering the interruptions caused by the staff unrest and more freight work.

Oscar Golf returned from the Aden flight via Brindisi on the first day and Yankee Kilo went to Gatwick for a charter to Tarbes. With two hitches, a late departure for Copenhagen on Friday and a technical return by Oscar Whisky at Basle on Saturday afternoon, the weekend 2nd./4th. went well. Oscar Golf departed to Lyneham Sunday evening and operated two Akrotiri's from the Wiltshire base before returning to Manston on the 8th.

Foxtrot Yankee's Perpignan on Wednesday 7th. was delayed leaving due to an unserviceable fuel pump and the baggage hold key being taken home by the loaders! On Thursday the seats came out for a Renfrew-Madrid cargo charter. The week continued reasonably smoothly until Saturday night. This was a three flights to Perpignan Saturday with departures due at 1600, 2100 and 2200, plus 0130 and 2100 on Sunday. The aircraft that operated the 1600 should also have taken the 0130 but Yankee Kilo was delayed at Basle for a fuel pump to be changed by the B.U.A.F. engineers. This resulted in Foxtrot Yankee making the second flight, Oscar Golf taking the first and third, and Yankee Kilo the fourth, both of the latter two somewhat late. Yankee Kilo's departure was further held up with a hydraulic leak, generators out of balance and the mixture on one engine being too rich.

The Sunday night flight was also delayed to end a tiring weekend; this time it was Oscar Golf delayed by crew hours and then returning from the end of the runway with an RPM drop which blew out the magneto. With all this, the Ostends and eight Basles were operated to time and the Vikings had some extra charters, on Saturday Victor Foxtrot flew a Manston-Rheims-Ostend-Manston, reversing this on Sunday, while Charlie Hotel had an internal charter to Manchester.

TWILIGHT OF THE PISTONS

1965

Tuesday July 6th 22.00hrs YK two P/P Bay men staying on to complete fitting exhaust system. Generator #1 Engine to be finish in the morning. #2 just slung in bolts torque loaded. #3 needs cleaning down & cowling up. #1 Engine needs control check. FY taxied out at 22.00hrs. T/O time 22:40hrs no tec delay. Will be en Day as soon as possible in the morning.

Wed. 7th July ++ Pass. late departure -23.30-
#4 fuel pump u/s. Baggage hold key taken home by loader, further delay.

THURS. 8-7-65. Y/K TOOK OFF 22.20 NO TECH DELAY.
OC LANDED 22.30.

July 9/65. FRI.
FY. In at 20.00 HRS.
Re leased and Cleared for Passengers
23.25 HRS - Durban 00.05 HRS. (SAT)

KB.

July 10/11. YK. tech delay — hydraulic leak, generators out of balance. #4 engine SR mixture a too rich. Departed 03.30 (Sunday morn.)
(#3 eng. fuel pump changed at Bable BOAF engineer)

1965 NEW MANAGEMENT

AIR FERRY LIMITED

ALL TIMES G.M.T.

DAILY PROGRAMME FOR SATURDAY 17th JULY

MOVE NO	A/C	STD	STA	SECTOR		LOAD	FLT. NO	A/CREW	C/CREW
1	VF	0030	0100	OST	MSE	NIL	MT	MASON GUTTERIDGE	BRITTON
2	DC6		0100	BSL	MSE	PAX	BB2600	BALAIR CREW	
		0200		MSE	BSL	PAX	BB2601		
3	YK	0001	0215	BSL	MSE	25	LK540/100	LAKER JOHNSTON	BOWERY DESMOND
4	FY		0340	BDS	MSE	MT		NICOL HORSTING F/E WHITE	
5	OG	0125	0450	PGF	MSE	75	LK545	ASHPITEL SIMPSON	MASTERS RENDALL
6	CH	0710	0740	MSE	OST	40	LK551/561-2	BROOKER SHEPPARDSON	WILLCOX
		0810	0840	OST	MSE	NIL	MT		
7	YK	0720	0750	MSE	OST	80	LK551/561-2	GIBSON JACKSON	ROLLS MOLLI
		0820	0850	OST	MSE	NIL	MT		
8	OG	0730	0800	MSE	OST	80	LK545/6-9	GWYTHER SURRAGE	APPLEBY LEMM
		0830	0900	OST	MSE	NIL	MT		
9	VF	0740	0810	MSE	OST	21/8	LK551/573 + 8 LYONS	MASON GUTTERIDGE	BRITTON
		0840	0910	OST	MSE	NIL	MT		
10	YK	0910	1125	MSE	BSL	79	LK509/C12-13	GIBSON JACKSON	ROLLS MOLLI
		1230	1445	BSL	MSE	80	LK509		
11	CH	0920	0950	MSE	OST	37	LK539/1	BROOKER SHEPPARDSON	WILLCOX
		1010	1040	OST	MSE	NIL	MT		
12	OW	0930	1000	MSE	OST	37	LK539/3	HUNNABLE HOPE	MILLS
		1130	1200	OST	MSE	34	LK540/710		
13	OG	0940	1155	MSE	BSL	80	LK509/C20-40	GWYTHER SURRAGE	APPLEBY LEMM
		1300	1515	BSL	MSE	80	LK509		
14	FY	1000	1215	MSE	BSL	67	LK540/220	WOOD CHANG CLAPSHAW	SETCHELL MORGAN
		1315	1530	BSL	MSE	79	LK540/220		
15	VF	1010	1040	MSE	OST	37	LK540/710	MASON GUTTERIDGE	BRITTON
		1230	1300	OST	MSE	26	LK544/2		
16	CH	1120	1150	MSE	OST	29	LK544/1	BROOKER SHEPPARDSON	WILLCOX
		1300	1330	OST	MSE	25	LK540/630		
17	OW	1300	1515	MSE	BSL	25	LK540/500	HUNNABLE HOPE	MILLS
		1600	1815	BSL	MSE	30	LK540/500		
18	VF	1330	1545	MSE	BSL	33	LK540/530	EAMES AHMAD	BROWN
		1630	1845	BSL	MSE	23	LK540/530		
19	CH	1400	1430	MSE	OST	40	LK583/1	BROOKER SHEPPARDSON	WILLCOX
		1530	1600	OST	MSE	40	LK551/561-2		
20	YK	1520	1845	MSE	PGF	78	LK545/50	LAKER JOHNSTON	BOWERY DESMOND
		2000	2325	PGF	MSE	80	LK545		
21	CH	1630	1700	MSE	OST	NIL	MT	GIBSON JACKSON	ROLLS
		1730	1800	OST	MSE	40	LK551/561-2		
22	DC6		1630	BSL	MSE	PAX	BB5600	BALAIR CREW	
		1730		MSE	BSL	PAX	BB5601		
23	OG	2100	0025	MSE	PGF	80	LK545/38	ASHPITEL SIMPSON	WOODS KREBSTARKIES
		0125	0450	PGF	MSE	74	LK545		

75

TWILIGHT OF THE PISTONS

The number of freight flights in mid season now began to cause pressures to the DC4 programme. Foxtrot Yankee left for Aden on Monday 12th., Len Mees and Bill Ayres coming in early to see her off. The aircraft had to make a technical return to Bahrein on the way out, and was not back in passenger use until Saturday morning. The Vikings went to Hanover and Amsterdam during the week and Oscar Golf took cargo to Madrid. Yankee Kilo flew to Copenhagen on time on Friday 16th. but went unserviceable on leaving for the nights Basle, finally departing at 0040 on Saturday. The aircraft returned from the runway twice, with the number 2 feathering switch U/S and then with a mag. drop on number 4 engine. Oscar Golf's departure for Perpignan was also delayed with a return from the runway as a hold fire warning switch had been tripped by the baggage loaders.

> *With two operators to approach, there were now many people keen to earn some pin money from casual labour work. The most obvious areas were for baggage handling to meet the heavier demands of the peak times and many of the servicemen stationed on the airfield saw this as an interesting and profitable way to spend their off duty time. This activity escalated until the management began to have serious concerns as to the legality of the situation and what the views of the Inland Revenue and the Auditors might be. On closer inspection, it was apparent that many of the signatures of the casual workers on their pay chits bore some unusual names, such as D.Duck, M.Mouse, R Hood, M (Merrie) England, S. Forest and so on.*

The programme for Saturday 17th. included two Basle-Manston-Basles by a Balair DC6 and crew, but as the flight numbers were 'BB' rather than Air Ferry's 'LK,' these could have been handling flights rather than sub-charters; HB-IBR was at Manston again the following weekend. There were nine Basles over Saturday and Sunday with the Vikings taking four of these, it was at times like this that the substitutions worked well. On Sunday evening, the 18th., Oscar Golf left for Aden flown by John Gibson and Jeep Jackson who took the aircraft to Damascus and then handed it over to another crew. John and Jeep were told to go to Beirut by taxi over the mountains and eventually reached a plush hotel which, at a very late hour, was devoid of any service. Captain Gibson had a tin of corned beef but unfortunately neither possessed an opener. They then travelled on to Cairo in a Middle East Comet. At Cairo, although they were to take over Oscar Golf and were in uniform, they were treated with some suspicion and actually confined for a while in a detention room - Middle East politics were sensitive at this time. The situation was resolved and they flew back into Manston on Thursday.

One of the other DC4s was in the hangar on the 19th., probably Yankee Kilo, and an inspection of one engine revealed 'another' cracked cylinder which left the duty engineer suggesting the other three engines should be checked as: 'This aircraft must have taken a right thrashing from someone.' Foxtrot Yankee had a local flight on 21 July, probably for training at 1 hour 40 minutes; her Perpignan departure that night being delayed as there was no transport for the crew. Yankee Kilo made a short local flight the following day, most likely an air test. As the engines on the DC4s suffered from dampness, engine covers were sometimes used when an aircraft stood on a pan for any length of time and Oscar Golf appeared on the flightline that week wearing a smart red set of covers that she had brought from Balair.

Oscar Golf, with red engine covers, 23 July, 1965

Ironically, with all six aircraft on the line, the next weekend of 23/25 July proved to be a very fraught one. Both Yankee Kilo and Oscar Golf flew Manston-Manston on Friday evening, the latter flown by Hugh Tubman and was due to a runaway propeller, when flights to Verona, Basle and Perpignan were all due off, so these short flights were tests or returns and set off a chain reaction that affected the whole weekend; Oscar Golf did not fly again until Wednesday. Oscar Whisky and Charlie Hotel shared the Basle without much delay, Yankee Kilo went to Verona while the 2100 to Perpignan passengers left on Foxtrot Yankee at 0150 on Saturday, although this delay was due to weather conditions at the destination.

> *In addition to serving the catering and making duty free sales, the air hostesses needed to keep an eye on the passengers. Elderly and overweight lady tourists were prone to take off their shoes and in unpressurised aircraft the result was that their feet and ankles became swollen. Other holidaymakers sometimes took out their teeth to eat the packaged meals so that a careful check*

1965 NEW MANAGEMENT

was needed when packing up the trays afterwards to prevent a holiday being spoilt through lack of dentures. (Gillian Appleby)

The Saturday Basles were operated with two Vikings substituted but it was the Perpignans, a three flight week again, that suffered. The first left 50 minutes late, Foxtrot Yankee took another at 0135 but the third must have been sub-chartered. These days this was usually done by re-directing the coaches to another airport en-route rather than have an aircraft fly in to Manston. After a quick turn round Yankee Kilo got away with the Sunday 0130 some 45 minutes late, this departure being recorded by Les Dray as: 'Airborne for Perpignan 0322 (local) and going like a good one should.' On Sunday it was the turn of the Vikings to have trouble as Oscar Whisky had to make a technical return to Basle for the second time in the month and did not get back to Manston until Thursday 29th.

Although Oscar Golf was not available for part of it, the last week went quite well. On Tuesday 27th. there were thirteen Le Touquets, Foxtrot Yankee arriving back from one after 1530 hours, yet was converted to freight trim and off on a Lyneham-Akrotiri by 1910. On Wednesday Charlie Hotel went to Bremen; although the object of this flight is unknown the Vikings, as mentioned, were useful for transporting ships crews as shown by the number of ports in their destinations lists. On Thursday Yankee Kilo operated three Le Touquet charters from Gatwick and with the departure of this aircraft to Perpignan on Saturday night the busiest month of the year, in terms of hours flown, had ended.

August Although there were more flights than in any other month, including the most to Perpignan, there was also the largest shortfall in flying hours, 300 down, on the 1964 figure. Destinations such as Copenhagen and Verona contributed just two flights each, while Ostend, Basle and Perpignan accounted for 189 of the 293 flights.

The weather on 1 August was not very seasonal, the night's comment by Les Dray was that Foxtrot Yankee was parked in the hangar to keep the engines dry and all the Vikings were 'S' (serviceable).

It was another very mixed month with flights again using Gatwick and Southend. Foxtrot Yankee had an engine change on the 4th., sharing the hangar with Charlie Hotel on a check, then carried out some training later that day and making eight landings. There was cargo work as well, with five Lyneham-Akrotiris by the DC4s before Foxtrot Yankee left for Aden on Sunday 29 August, this flight delayed leaving because two engines had high cylinder head temperatures.

Inevitably there were some delays and incidents. Yankee Kilo was delayed leaving on the night of Thursday 5th., returning from the runway with a hydraulic gauge pointer sticking and then diverted into Marseilles soon after midnight, returning via Perpignan to Manston in the early afternoon. Two Vikings substituted on that days Basle. On Saturday Foxtrot Yankee was en route to Basle when an engine gave trouble. When there is an indication of a problem it is usual to watch the gauges when pressing the feathering button, but Hugh Tubman looked out of the window in time to see a gush of oil spew out of the motor. The DC4 put down at Calais where the fault was rectified and Hugh and Jeep Jackson continued the flight.

The Sunday morning Perpignan on the 8th. was also delayed leaving when Captain Nicol returned from the runway with an unserviceable generator on Yankee Kilo, finally getting away at 0500.

The only aircraft which went to Perpignan on Monday 9th. was Charlie Hotel, presumably an extra charter, and returned via Exeter. With Foxtrot Yankee at Akrotiri and Oscar Golf being worked on by a servicing crew comprised of Messrs. O'Reilly, Mees, Hopkins, Nurthen, Graveney and Wickens, Yankee Kilo went U/S with a cracked cylinder. With no replacement available a driver set off for an AOG spare from Lydd, and the nights Perpignan was sub-chartered to Air Links.

One of the permanent staff, a young lady in the Canteen, had an extraordinary escape during the summer. The road past the terminal was now very busy at times and the catering assistant came out of the terminal bearing a tray of afternoon tea, presumably destined for Ken Sheppardson. The assistant omitted to look both ways and was literally scooped onto the bonnet of a car travelling towards the hangar, fortunately with no harm done and she was able to reappear shortly afterwards with her tray and some replacement china.

Yankee Kilo left on schedule for the Thursday 12th. Perpignan and then went U/S there with an engine defect, not getting back to Manston until Friday night. Oscar Golf left Manston at 0756 on Friday as the relief aircraft to collect the waiting passengers. After a technical delay on the morning's Basle of Wednesday 18th., Yankee Kilo featured in the engineers notes again for that nights Perpignan when Captain Wood was recorded as: 'Not being very happy to take it,' but Oscar Golf was unusable with a suspect cylinder. There was a query over the 2000 DC4 to Basle on Friday 20th., which was apparently operated by Victor Foxtrot at 1930 on Friday and at 0810 on Saturday morning via Ostend.

A catalogue of delays afflicted the Perpignan tours in the last week of the month, of the six night flights from Sunday 22nd. to Friday 27th., five were delayed on departure. Foxtrot Yankee flew the first four, she returned to the tarmac with a jump lead and mag. blown through on the first, then had an RPM drop and needed a mag. change on the second. Although the aircraft departed at 2100 precisely the next night she was late again on the fourth when a landing light failed. Oscar Golf on the 26th. was delayed twice over, the passengers were late and she then returned to the tarmac with an engine snag. The next night Foxtrot Yankee went U/S on the pre-departure run and Oscar Golf substituted. Oscar Whisky recorded another unserviceability with a Manston-Manston en-route to Basle the following weekend, the 28th.

Of the DC4 charters, there was a Manston-Dublin-Ostend-Manston on the 1st., reversed two weeks later; one to Munich and the only seasonal flight to Luxembourg on the 4th. Oscar Golf visited the Channel Islands, on the 12th. flying Manston-Gatwick-Jersey-Guernsey-Gatwick-Manston and on the 18th. Gatwick-Guernsey-Jersey-Gatwick and Gatwick-Jersey-Guernsey-Gatwick. There was a Hamburg flight on the 20th.

Charlie Hotel operated most for the Vikings and went to Maastricht on the 3rd., flew a Luton-Dusseldorf-Luton on the 6th., a Munich on the 13th. and on two Saturday evenings, Manston-Liverpool-Dublin-Manston with freight. On the 30th. Charlie Hotel flew Manston-Ostend-Lydd-Ostend-Cologne-Manston. Victor Foxtrot and Oscar Whisky both flew an Ostend-Lydd-Ostend and Oscar Whisky went to Hamburg on the 9th.

Jodi (right)   (Jodi Hope)

September The tour flying began its autumn decline although there were enough cargo hours flown to make the month the ninth busiest in Air Ferry's history to date. The first week ran close to schedule although the Perpignan on the night of Thursday 2nd was a noted exception. Yankee Kilo departed but returned to the tarmac with an incorrect ASI reading, departed once more and returned again with the same defect. Oscar Golf was refuelled, departed and returned with a mag. drop before finally leaving. The poignant footnote by Eddie Edgar said it all: 'It's still raining, I've got two shoes full of water.'

Foxtrot Yankee returned from Aden while Oscar Golf flew passengers Gatwick-Wildenwrath-Gatwick and Yankee Kilo freight Heathrow-Orly-Heathrow-Orly-Heathrow. The programme on Saturday 4th. recalls that year very clearly, all three DC4s going to Basle within an hour in the morning and all three off to Perpignan in the evening. Oscar Whisky took freight from Gatwick to Dublin, the first of four consecutive Saturday visits to the Irish capital by different aircraft. Oscar Whisky had replaced Charlie Hotel on the 4th., this aircraft having had a mishap at Ostend during the morning. The Viking had aborted the take-off having struck a wooden stake after veering off the runway, the starboard propeller striking the stake. Ken Barker and Jim Jones left to effect temporary repairs at Ostend and the aircraft returned that night. There was one more delay that Saturday when Yankee Kilo, late back from Ostend, had a generator problem before going to Perpignan.

Foxtrot Yankee went to the Transport Command base at Abingdon to uplift cargo for Wildenwrath on Monday 6th., returning direct to Manston. That evening the aircraft flew a Manston-Manston; it is not known if this

1965 NEW MANAGEMENT

was technical but Yankee Kilo took the Perpignan tour and Foxtrot Yankee set off on a cargo journey at 0313 on Tuesday 7th. for Manston-Basle-Zurich-Geneva, and returned via Abingdon and Wildenwrath to Manston on Thursday. After an Ostend-Lydd-Ostend, Victor Foxtrot flew Manston-Bordeaux-Luton on Monday 6th., night stopped and continued Luton-Dusseldorf-Luton-Manston.

Bordeaux was visited again on Friday 10th., this time by Charlie Hotel. The Copenhagen tour that day was operated by Victor Foxtrot which had an engine problem soon after take off and returned to Manston, being quickly replaced by Oscar Whisky. Mike Austin was greatly amused that the writer, who went on these flights, returned with only aerial photographs of Manston from a day trip to Copenhagen. Also that day Oscar Golf went to Hamburg and next day another Saturday freight journey, Manston-Gatwick-Dublin-Manston was flown by Charlie Hotel.

The third week was hampered by weather and technical problems. Yankee Kilo flew up to the R.A.F. fighter airfield at Leconfield in Yorkshire and back on Monday 13th., the first of many visits in September. On Thursday 16th. Foxtrot Yankee had a Manston-Prestwick-Toulouse-Manston freight charter while Oscar Whisky flew Manston-Exeter-Brussels-Ostend-Manston. The Vikings suffered another rare technical delay on departure when Oscar Whisky returned from the runway on her next flight with a suspected oil leak before leaving for Le Touquet. Oscar Golf followed this with a delay for the nights Perpignan when the ground crew could not close the passenger door; Ken Barker was called in and, after the removal of the door and the repair of the locking gear, the DC4 left at 2342, only to be diverted into Toulouse in the early hours of Friday 17th. During the morning Charlie Hotel flew to Maastricht and came home via Ostend.

Cyril Nurthen and Les Dray   (John Somerville)

That Friday night all three DC4 flights, to Perpignan, Verona and Basle were delayed leaving. The Verona delay was Oscar Golf again when number 3 would not start and blew out the magnetoes, she then returned

Foxtrot Yankee, 14 September, 1965

from the runway with the number 3 generator unserviceable. The next flight by this aircraft, to Basle on Saturday afternoon, was also delayed leaving with a mag. drop while Yankee Kilo took the first Saturday Perpignan at 1555 and came home with nearly a full load and the number 3 engine stopped and the propeller feathered. The engineers found metal in the filter and she did not fly again until Wednesday night. Charlie Hotel made another visit to Dublin, this time from Ostend. To round off a bad day Phil Townsend fell from the crew steps and was taken to Ramsgate Hospital.

Foxtrot Yankee left for the early Sunday Perpignan four and a half hours late and went to Naples in the afternoon on the last of that city's seasonal tours. The Vikings helped with the Basles, but as Oscar Golf had positioned off to Leconfield on Sunday evening, after a delay with water in a magneto, the nights Perpignan was sub-chartered to Air Links.

TWILIGHT OF THE PISTONS

There was an unusual problem when the Perpignan flight departed on Monday night, the 20th., as Foxtrot Yankee had to return because Dave Laker and Jeep were unable to get the undercarriage to stay retracted. On the DC4 when the undercarriage was fully up the hydraulic latches engaged to offload the hydraulics and on this occasion there was a latch failure. Bob Jack was called in and the aircraft left again at 0035.

Military duties dominated that week with Oscar Golf making six Leconfield-Gutersloh-Leconfield flights and Foxtrot Yankee one. Victor Foxtrot also went to the Yorkshire base on Wednesday 22nd. with crews, engineers or both, before the DC4s completed this work with flights Leconfield-Gutersloh-Bodo. Both aircraft should have flown Bodo-West Raynham, an R.A.F. station in Norfolk, on Friday 24th.; Foxtrot Yankee did this but Oscar Golf diverted into Manston with suspected complete brake failure. The brakes were bled and found O.K. although the cargo, of course, was still aboard. Oscar Golf flew up to Norfolk on Saturday morning to be unloaded. These flights were almost certainly connected with a N.A.T.O. exercise in the protection of Norway as Bodo was also a military airfield.

As a result of the military work the Vikings operated the Wednesday Basle on the 22nd., John Mason and Jeep bringing Charlie Hotel briefly back to Manston at the company's request to change the navigation charts. For the first time in many weeks there was no Friday Basle, this probably being due to Victor Foxtrot adding to that day's drama by coming in from Ostend with a boost defect and a rough running engine. On Saturday Foxtrot Yankee made the last visit to Ireland again flying Ostend-Dublin. Yankee Kilo kept the Perpignan tours running and had to divert into Toulouse on the night of Saturday 25th., although Oscar Golf, three hours behind, did not have to. The early Sunday morning Perpignan on the 26th. was delayed leaving when Foxtrot Yankee had a mag. drop and there was some concern over the number 4 engine which was, in fact, changed that day.

On Sunday evening Oscar Golf positioned off to Lyneham en route to Aden while at 0110 on Monday Foxtrot Yankee also left for Lyneham, loaded at the Wiltshire base, and set off for Brindisi and Akrotiri. The DC4 turned back over Paris and came into Manston with the number 4 engine feathered. The engineers found the CSU pulley spindle sheared and the aircraft set off once more for Brindisi at midday on Tuesday.

During the last few days of September Yankee Kilo again operated the Perpignans, returning via Lydd early on Tuesday 28th. and coming back from an hour out on Wednesday night when Captain Gwyther and Jeep Jackson had both ADFs fail, before leaving again at 0325 on Thursday.

> *As the summer wound down there was more opportunity for free time and the thoughts of many householders turned to catching up on some home maintenance work. It was not long before the story went round of one abode in Thanet attractively redecorated in 'Air Ferry blue' paint.*

October   October saw the last trickle of tours which was just as well as a drama, if anything on a grander scale than the Clermont Ferrand epic of the previous season, was about to unfold. On Friday night Yankee Kilo went to Verona and the number 2 engine failed and had to be feathered on the return flight next morning. Foxtrot Yankee left Manston for Lyneham an hour after Yankee Kilo left for Verona, arriving in Brindisi at 1745 on Saturday 2nd with technical difficulties and would not leave that airport for over a week before resuming the journey to Akrotiri. Just about twenty four hours after Foxtrot Yankee's arrival, at 1435 on Sunday 3rd, Oscar Golf returning from Aden via Cairo also arrived at Brindisi; she in turn also had to make a stay of some days. On Monday 4th Charlie Hotel, with five engineers, flew out to Brindisi via Nice arriving early on Tuesday morning.

> *Roy Doherty recalls that a DC4 engine was carefully inched aboard the Viking, the only one with freight doors, and that following take-off the navigation lights all went out, although the aircraft continued on its journey.*

When Yankee Kilo, pressed into freight service for another Aden, passed through Brindisi later on Tuesday morning, there were four Air Ferry aircraft on the airfield. Oscar Golf took off on the Thursday for Manston with Charlie Hotel following an hour later and stopping again at Nice. Foxtrot Yankee finally departed Italy for Cyprus on Sunday 10th.

> *The engineers, of course, were prone to emergency callouts in the event of aircraft unserviceability. 'Many times, he would be sent for in the early hours to fly off to some place overseas with a crew*

Sun 26-9-65 Cont'd.
F.Y. Cont'd. A/c cleared 01.45 (27/9/65) Ops informed.
  Airborn at 02.25.

V.F. Prop Deicer Snag in Tech Log. — defect dis
  covered at Pump assy. New pipe/Nipple assy
  herewith ready for fitment.
                                    K Barker

Mon. 27-9-65.
  YK. — depart Perp. 22-00 — no tech delay.

  F-Y — returned to base from Paris. (freight flight
  (Lyn Club.) #4 eng feathered — CSU pulley
  spindle found sheared. — New CSU fitted.
                                    R?

Tues. F-Y. depart for Brindisi at 13-30.
  YK. depart Perp. at 22-05 — no tech delay
                                    R?

Wed Sept 29/65
  YK. depart to Perpignan Airborn 22.10. No
    tech delay.
  Thurs. 22-00 Perp YK. departed on time.
                                    K?

Fri YK depart on time.
  FY run at 20-00 dead cut No 2 RH
  departed 23-00.
                                    [signature]

of maintenance workers to repair an aircraft and fly home with it,' Rose Edgar recalls of Eddie. 'I never knew when he would be gone and when he would return. We got so used to it that we would carry on regardless as they say. He'd come back one day and shout: 'The boy's home,' and I would set another place at the table!' There is no doubt that Eddie was held in extremely high regard and it was said that the pilots had such faith in his opinions that they remarked: 'If Eddie says its OK, I'll fly it.'

The Aden by Yankee Kilo over the 4th./8th. was the fastest one to date at 41 hours although this was reduced later in the month. Oscar Golf flew another, staging through the outward journey according to plan, arriving in Aden at 0910 on the 12th. October. On the 14th. she had to return to Aden twice and Captain Nicol's request for an engineer to be sent out was finally answered. The aircraft remained there until the 18th. when she did a 15 minute local flight and finally left the next day for Brindisi, returning to Manston at 1120 on Wednesday. Foxtrot Yankee looked after the other three Adens, routing home once through Turin, and was homeward bound at Dubai on another at the end of the month, the crew on this occasion being Captains Tubman and Honeyman, F/O Horsting and E/O Nurthen.

Cyril Nurthen had spent ten years in the R.A.F., five and a half of them in Singapore during the emergency, before coming to Air Ferry. In addition to being sent out to IT and charter destinations at times of breakdown, he went on several DC4 long range flights as Engineer Officer. It was usual to draw a uniform, as civilian clothes attracted more attention, and to fly in the jump seat as Flight Engineer.

On the ground, if there was a problem, the aircrew would tend to walk off and leave the E/O to it while he tried to evaluate what was wrong. Faults did not necessarily relate to the engineer's particular speciality, of course, and they sometimes found themselves dealing with a manual written before the snag was invented.

At Cairo one time, one of many occasions of tension in the Middle East, a snag on the fire warning system caused the DC4 to be stationary for two days. Things were not helped by two guards armed with rifles following me everywhere. (Cyril Nurthen)

Oscar Golf (John Somerville)

Apart from the excitement of the long distance trips there were many other flights. As the only DC4 to carry passengers, Yankee Kilo flew the last Verona on the 1st., the last Basle IT on the 3rd., went to Perpignan via Jersey on the 9th. and flew Manston-Dusseldorf-Gatwick-Jersey-Manston next day. Saturday 16th. saw the last visit to Perpignan for the season, for some reason via Liege. There was a Jersey and a Maastricht next day and a Gatwick-Dusseldorf on the 19th. Over the 29th./30th. the aircraft flew freight Heathrow-Milan-Heathrow, before changing to passenger trim for an Amsterdam, and then freight to Basle as the last flight of the month.

After the long range journey, Oscar Golf flew freight Manston-Prestwick-Toulouse-Manston over the 25th./27th., then Manston-Heathrow-Milan-Heathrow-Manston and on Sunday 31st. a Geneva to complete October.

1965 NEW MANAGEMENT

For the Vikings, in addition to the Ostends, Victor Foxtrot went twice to Le Bourget, to Maastricht on the 10th. and took the last Copenhagen next day. Oscar Whisky went to Amsterdam and to Bremen on the 2nd., flew Manston-Maastricht-Ostend on the 4th, where she night stopped and returned to Manston. The aircraft operated to Dusseldorf on the 8th. and twice more to Maastricht next day.

Charlie Hotel flew a Manston-Le Bourget-Southend, night stopped and returned Southend-Ostend-Manston; there was a Manston-Ostend-Amsterdam-Manston on the 3rd., Rotterdam with freight on the 20th. and to Marseilles with 30 passengers on the 23rd.

On 20 October Bravo Xray was finally broken up, her wings and tail leaving Manston on a 'Queen Mary' transporter with the fuselage being removed on 29th./30th. This load was followed by the writer who, with the help of two companions from Accounts and a stout hacksaw, was able to obtain the control column for posterity.

FLIGHT International, 28 October 1965

EXPERIENCED FITTERS

Both engineer and airframe fitters required. Experienced with either Viking, DC-4 or Bristol 170 is preferable, although applications are welcomed from other fitters with R.A.F. or other suitable experience.

Please apply in writing to:
Chief Engineer, Air Ferry Ltd.,
Manston Airport, Ramsgate

**AIR FERRY LIMITED,
MANSTON AIRPORT, KENT**

Require for 1966 operations
FLIGHT ENGINEERS
Qualified in DC-6 aircraft. Candidates with suitable experience will also be accepted for training. Salary will be by negotiation within approved scales.

Require for 1966
CAPTAINS AND FIRST OFFICERS
for DC-4 operations. Permanent or contract terms will be available. Also required co-pilots for training on DC-4 aircraft.

Contact:—Mr. D. Froud c/o Air Ferry Ltd.
or Captain D. Brooker-Manston 333

At one time Maura Hunnable had to undergo some medical treatment and, while he was away on a trip, Stan asked Jeep Jackson if he would keep an eye on his wife. Mrs. Hunnable was unable to start the car one day, in spite of all her efforts, and eventually telephoned Jeep who arrived and proceeded to fire up the engine on his first turn of the key!

November Yankee Kilo carried out a freight charter over the 2nd./4th. Manston-Heathrow-Milan-Heathrow-Manston and then went into the hangar for an overhaul that would last the better part of three months. Foxtrot Yankee returned from Aden on the 2nd. and was on freight all month, apart from the 12th., when she flew to Stanstead for training or calibration but did not land at the Essex airfield. On the 17th. there was a 30 minute local flight before departing next day on a Manston-Tripoli-Brindisi-Manston followed by three Manston-Southend-Antwerp-Manstons. The first was delayed when the aircraft returned from the runway with a weak starboard brake, this being a wintry day and Oscar Golf, due for some work, was left outside the hangar due to the strong wind blowing. Over the 26th./27th. Foxtrot Yankee went to Genoa, the Captain pointing out that the heater was not working! At the end of the month the DC4 was at Bahrein where she was being unloaded. Before leaving Manston the crew bunks on this long flight had been criticised by Captain Gwyther as it was considered that portable bunks were not suitable and there should be correct ones set on the seat rails.

Oscar Golf also went to Heathrow, over the 4th./6th., and flew Heathrow-Milan-Rome-Milan-Heathrow-Manston. From the 15th./22nd. the aircraft went to Doha and Dubai, via Brindisi and Damascus, and on the 26th. flew the last Manston-Southend-Antwerp-Manston; this departure delayed with the number 1 starter having to be changed and the replacement removed from Yankee Kilo. There was then another delay due to lack of hydraulic fluid and there was an angry footnote in the book: 'When are we getting some spares in the stores!'

> *At Dubai on one freight journey we were in the terminal and asked a local worker if he could go aboard the DC4 and bring us the box containing the ship's papers. The Gulf State was very officially 'dry' with no alcohol allowed at all and soon afterwards we were horrified to see the man coming towards us, accompanied by the very obvious clinking of spirit bottles. He had picked up the bar box usually carried aboard and everyone cringed at the thought of disclosure!*
> (Cyril Nurthen)

Earlier in the year the holding of a session of the West German parliament in Berlin caused obstruction of land access by the Russians and their jet fighters flew continuously over the city. All was quiet, however, over the 26th./28th. when Oscar Golf went there, after a slight delay, with the only DC4 passengers that month and who had arrived late at Manston.

Oscar Whisky went to Brussels over the 9th./10th. and flew a training sortie on Friday 12th. On the 18th. there was a flight Manston-Gatwick-Geneva with 29 passengers, a night stop and a return the next day.

Victor Foxtrot flew just once and carried out a freight flight over 12th./14th. which routed Manston-Tours-Rome-Athens-Rome-Lyons-Manston; this was almost her swansong as time for the Vikings was now running out at Air Ferry. This flight, captained by Andy Nicol, took live partridges to Athens for a Greek shipping magnate. Charlie Hotel also made just one flight, to Brussels with passengers on the 24th., remained for two night stops and returned them on Friday 26th. There were just 40 flights in all, the lowest in the year.

The debates and arguments about Rhodesia had continued throughout the autumn but, on Armistice Day, the Rhodesian leader Ian Smith firmly took the initiative by making a Unilateral Declaration of Independence. Michael Stewart, the U.K. Foreign Secretary, promptly left for New York to place the British views before the United Nations.

Late in November the Security Council finally agreed a compromise solution calling on all member states to cease trading with Rhodesia, including the supply of oil and petroleum, but stopped short of demanding that military force should be used. On 30 November Mr. Bottomley, the Commonwealth Relations Minister, flew to see President Kaunda in Zambia to explain the conditions under which the U.K. would send forces for the protection of his country. The next day it was announced that a detachment of the R.A.F. Regiment and a squadron of all weather fighters would be sent to Zambia.

December The Javelins of No. 29 Squadron arrived at Ndola on 3rd. December with the R.A.F. Regiment following the next day. No. 29 Squadron's detachment in Zambia would last for nine months. On 19th. December the U.K. began an organised air lift of oil for Zambia and, back at Manston, Air Ferry preparations were continuing apace for her contribution to the lift as soon as the aircraft could be made available. Before this there was other work to do.

Foxtrot Yankee came back from Bahrein on the 3rd. Next day in preparation for the oil lift, she flew out to Livingstone in Zambia. This long journey was via Lyneham-Tripoli-Kano and Leopoldville with Hugh Tubman, Paul Ashpital, Pete Gutteridge, Doug Erswell and E/O Evans. The DC4 returned Entebbe-Jeddah-Benghazi-Milan-Manston on 13th December, a block time of 3 minutes under 62 hours. The DC4 did not fly again until she took freight to Zurich on Wednesday 22nd.

At 0325 on Wednesday 1st., Oscar Golf left on a Manston-Southend-Antwerp-Southend, flew on to Antwerp again the next day and returned to Manston via Southend on Friday. Next day there was a 2 hour local flight over to Ostend, although the DC4 did not land there, before leaving Manston for Lyneham and Aden. The Aden-Brindisi leg coming back took 14 hours 10 minutes. Between the 13th./15th. there was a flight Manston-Heathrow-Rome-Milan-Manston followed over the 15th./17th. by one Manston-Heathrow-Milan-Heathrow-Manston.

1965 NEW MANAGEMENT

The two Vikings in service were busy carrying all the December passengers, plus some freight. Charlie Hotel took freight to Zurich and on the 11th. flew Manston-Marseilles-Naples to collect 27 passengers, returning by the same route on the 13th. Her next flight was Manston-Lydd-Lyons-Southend-Manston, again for passengers. The aircraft then changed to freight with visits to Basle on the 22nd. and 23rd. Victor Foxtrot flew passengers to Rotterdam on the 8th. and next flew with freight to Basle on the 23rd.

Both aircraft participated in eight Ostend passenger flights over Christmas, Charlie Hotel remaining in Belgium for four nights although almost certainly with the crew returning to Manston on Victor Foxtrot. The last Viking flight of the month, by Victor Foxtrot, was to Hamburg on Wednesday 29th. with 30 passengers and return the following day. This was her final Air Ferry flight, piloted by John Gibson.

Returning to the oil lift, Oscar Golf left Manston at 0928 on Wednesday 29 December bound for Tanzania. She flew via Benghazi, Khartoum and Entebbe, arriving at Dar-es-Salaam on the last day of the year. Foxtrot Yankee, leaving 36 hours later, missed out the stop at Entebbe and arrived at Dar-es-Salaam on the 1 January.

STATISTICS

No year total records were broken in 1965, although Oscar Golf notched up a monthly record to date by flying 267 hours in August. The flying hours for the year ended with a total of 6,238; only 278 short of the previous year. Charlie Hotel flew most hours for the Vikings with Foxtrot Yankee flying most for the DC4s.

The passenger total was down to 108,956 with Victor Foxtrot taking the Viking total and Yankee Kilo easily achieving the one for the DC4s.

It was the long distance work which had seen an amazing increase; in 1963 there had been one long flight of 16 hours. In 1964 there were three long flights with a total time of 98 hours but for 1965 thirty four flights contributed 1,319 hours to the year total. There had been two trips to Singapore, fifteen to Aden and eleven to Akrotiri. With varying routes to and from Aden the times reflected this, the quickest return time was by Foxtrot Yankee with one trip of 40 hours 45 minutes.

With the end of the Vikings it was possible to evaluate their contribution in numerical terms. They had flown 5,472 hours and carried 122,252 passengers. Victor Foxtrot, being the only one in service through each of the three seasons, had accumulated the highest figures with 1,637 hours flown and 40,137 passengers carried.

The twin engined workhorses had done their work well and with a high degree of reliability. Because of the competition now present at Manston they would still be in demand....

Air Ferry did not suffer unduly from engine problems apart from one time when the quality control of the overhaul contractor caused concern and the supplier was changed.

The transition from using the British Bristol Hercules engines on the Viking to the American Pratt & Whitney R2000 motors on the DC4 must have been similar to the changes at B.U.A.F. when their crews converted from the Bristol Freighters onto the Carvairs. Douglas Whybrow includes a good description in his book of the causes of some of their engine failures, although there were other reasons, the R2000 having a life of only 1500 hours between overhauls. Part of this description, by A.T.Ls' Director and Chief Engineer Bob Blatt, was as follows:

> *'The Pratt & Whitney engines were quite elderly and were never designed for such short hauls. Apart from the frequent use of take-off power the descent needed careful handling, just closing the throttles caused the propeller to drive the engine and with minimum boost pressure small ends, big ends and piston rings suffered from centrifugal loads unbalanced by boost, piston ring flutter in grooves was a bad sign. Also reduction gears were not intended to drive the engine from the propeller! Undoubtedly a contributory factor was pilot handling of American engines. British engines had boost pressure and mixture automatically controlled by the throttle - American engines had separate mixture controls that could cause trouble if mishandled. Pilots who had converted from Bristols were suddenly confronted with a lot more levers: 4 throttles, 4 propeller pitch levers, 4 Gill levers and 4 mixture levers (something of a problem with 3 positions: 'Idle cut-off' 'Auto-weak' and 'Auto-rich'). It was not all that easy for the pilots, they were used to the simple Bristol Hercules engine and when presented with fourteen or more levers on the Pratt and Whitney they were liable to go the whole hog and try and play Bach's Fugue!'*

TWILIGHT OF THE PISTONS

MANSTON

The activity at Manston during the year was as fascinating and varied as ever; regrettably it is possible to mention only a fraction. No. 22 Squadron and 1 A.E.F. continued their work although the third R.A.F. unit, 618 Gliding Flight left in June to transfer to West Malling, considered by some to be one of the most beautiful airfields in the country.

G-AHOY of Invicta 25 March 1965

Civilian light aircraft were represented by older types such as the Rapide, Proctor, Gemini, Auster and even a Hornet Moth. More modern ones included an Aero 145, Debonair and an L200 Morava, the first of these Czech machines purchased in Britain.

Airline movements started in earnest in February with the delivery of the first of Invicta's DC4s, G-ASPM, followed within a few days by G-ASPN. In March Viking G-AHOY joined the Manston residents with Viking G-AHPL arriving in April. The Invicta livery was a dark shade of red with white, the prancing white horse of Kent being prominently displayed in a black circle on the fin. The shade of red was probably influenced by the acquisition of SPM and SPN from British Eagle as photographs of these DC4s in Eagle colours appear to have the same cheat line and fin and rudder marking so that only the airline name and the tail insignia had to be repainted.

Invicta's Oscar Yankee suffered a taxiing accident on 15 April which necessitated some repairs, the incident occurring the same day that an Andover of the Queen's Flight positioned into Manston to collect the Queen, who had been on a visit to Canterbury. The Andover, piloted by S/L Jackson, used the call sign of 'Kitty Hawk'.

There were visits in March and June by two Doves in Morton Air Services livery, the company retaining its identity following the formation of B.U.A., while July saw visits by two Argonauts of Air Links.

On 2 August Invicta Viking Papa Lima nosed over on the runway causing a buzz saw like noise to reverberate momentarily across the airfield as the whirling propellers bit into the tarmac. Papa Lima was running again just over a week later.

The latter months of the year saw visits from Britannias in a colourful selection of liveries; those of Transglobe, the new name for Air Links, R.A.F. Transport Command, Caledonian, British Eagle and Lloyd. Another Morton aircraft, this time a DC3, appeared in December.

Military visitors included a Magister of the Belgian Air Force and three U.S. helicopters, 2 Marine S58s and an Army Mojave. Two rare birds passed through the airfield on 10 June, an HP115 aerodynamic research aircraft and a BAC126 jet flap research vehicle, both types en route to the Paris Air Show; they returned on the 23rd.

August provided a stand off bomb carrying Vulcan and four Luftwaffe Noratlas transports, while the following month saw Merlin engines over Kent again as a Spitfire and Hurricane of the Battle of Britain Memorial Flight positioned into the airfield.

There were two unusual Dutch visitors in October, a Konmarine Neptune and a C8 Troopship bearing the formidable title in large letters on the side of 'Koninkluke Luchtmacht.'

Towards the end of the year Invicta advertised for crews for the 1966 season and the details, which provide a glimpse of the pay rates at the time, were:

			Minimum Qualifications
DC4	Captain	£2900 - £3875	ALTP plus 4 engine command experience
Viking	Captain	£2345 - £3375	SCPL

1965 NEW MANAGEMENT

DC4	First Officer	£2065 - £2265	CPL and Instrument Rating
		- £2625	if ALTP held
Viking	First Officer	£1640 - £1840	CPL and Instrument Rating
		- £2100	if ALTP held

R.A.F.

The R.A.F. had an early set back to the year with the shock withdrawal of all the Vickers Valiants from flying. In the last weeks of 1964 the inspection of an aircraft on check had revealed advanced fatigue in the wing spar and this diagnosis was confirmed in other bombers. The switch to low level operations had resulted in more stress than expected and, with the cost of replacements prohibitive, there was no alternative but to prematurely retire the bombers in January.

Continuing a traumatic year, the intended new aircraft for the R.A.F., the TSR2, was axed by the new Labour Government, although not before there had been an unprecedented march through London in protest at the threatened cancellation by 10,000 workers from the aircraft industry. Then, in July, a Hastings transport crashed in Oxfordshire on a routine flight with the loss of many lives.

On the positive side the new Gnat display team of the previous year had been judged a success and were now established as the premier one for 1965. Resplendent in a new colour scheme, the Red Arrows gave their first public show at the Biggin Hill Air Fair in May.

No. 53 Squadron was re-formed in November in preparation for the introduction of a new type in Transport Command - the mighty Belfast while, as a sign of things to come, one of the Victor bomber squadrons, No. 55, converted over to tanker operations during the year.

CIVIL

Civil aviation during the year reflected many of the enduring problems caused by governments and their regulations. Scheduled Service expansion was still very difficult with the independents largely limited to the U.K. routes. The new Labour Minister of Aviation banned further development of the independents on British routes, causing British Eagle to respond angrily by announcing its withdrawal from all its main internal routes and deferring an order placed earlier for six BAC1-11s.

The state corporations tended to chip away at any profitable market laboriously built up by the independents; the price advantage held by the Coach-Air services, notably Skyways Coach-Air, now being eroded by B.E.A. working in conjunction with Air France.

There was a technical advance in June with the successful use of the B.E.A. Autoland system when a Trident became the first airliner in the world to land by automatic control on a normal passenger service.

AIR HOLDINGS

The January '*Aeroplane*' supplement included details of the share structure of the group, 80% of which was held by the shipping companies which inherited their shares via Airwork, Hunting-Clan and Silver City.

The Air Holdings Group worked to consolidate its position. B.U.A. were flying the South American routes taken over from B.O.A.C. although any expectation of profit was some way off. Industrial relations were still proving a problematic issue to the group as there were difficulties early in the year with the pilots' union, B.A.L.P.A.

B.U.A., with their trooping contracts, scheduled services, charter and inclusive tour flying were now the second force to B.E.A. and were offering Britannias for inclusive tour work. The introduction, in April, of the world's first commercial service with the BAC1-11 raised morale still further.

The car ferries continued to see their trade melt away however, and by the end of the year total movements were down to 101,000.

Freddie Laker, by now disenchanted with B.U.A., had suffered the sad loss of his son Kevin in a car crash in July and resigned abruptly and accrimoniously from the group in October.

TWILIGHT OF THE PISTONS

SAFETY

The B.U.A. safety record was unfortunately broken on 14 April, when a DC3 hit the approach lights, in fog, threequarters of a mile short of the threshold to the runway at Jersey. Of the 23 passengers and 4 crew only the hostess survived, severely injured, although the young lady returned to work in the Paris traffic section the following year. Skyways Coach-Air suffered a rare and almost miraculous accident three months later when an Avro 748 flying into the wet grass airfield at Lympne crashed onto one wing, somersaulted and landed upside down. Incredibly there were no severe injuries to the 52 persons on board.

It was B.E.A.s turn to feature in the statistics in October with a terrible Vanguard crash at London Heathrow following an internal flight from Edinburgh. The accident occurred in fog and resulted in the complete disintegration of the airliner along the runway.

OTHER EVENTS

The year started in Britain with blizzards raging over most of the country while, across the world, our forces in the Far East were being strengthened to meet growing aggression by Indonesia against Malaysia.

Domestic issues caused concern and controversy in the early months of the year. Family Doctors, incensed at the pay award offered by the government, threatened to leave the N.H.S., while the second stage of the Beeching Plan for the future of British Railways unveiled cuts to the network on a considerable scale. A credit squeeze on consumers was intensified by orders given to the banks regarding the restrictions on the provision of loans.

The country lost two of its respected elder figures, Sir Winston Churchill died in January at the age of 90 and his funeral reflected the respect of the nation. In May the great British pioneer in aircraft design, Sir Geoffrey De Havilland died.

The Conservatives, still coming to terms with being the unaccustomed opposition party, elected Mr.Edward Heath as their new leader in July.

There was anti British rioting in Aden in October following the suspension of the constitution and the year ended as it began with severe weather and heavy snow; November 16 being recorded as the coldest November day for a hundred years.

In America civil rights disorders marred much of the year while, abroad, the coming months saw the continuation of the slow, inexorable slide into the quagmire that was Vietnam. In February the U.S. began the bombing of North Vietnam, moving from an advisory role to active participation. Mr. Kosygin, the Soviet Premier, met his Chinese counterpart, Chou En-Lai, at Peking while en-route for a four day visit to North Vietnam's capital, Hanoi and both the U.S.S.R. and China warned of possible consequences to American actions. For the U.S. decision makers the choice in Vietnam was a stark one, escalate or withdraw; they chose the former and the year saw the introduction and build up of fighting troops, a development which had been promised would not happen. The domino theory was very real in those days, based on the assumption that as each country under communist pressure fell within their orbit, the adjoining country was susceptible to the same fate.

A notable achievement was made by the spaceprobe Mariner 4 which sent pictures back to earth of the planet Mars through 134 million miles of space.

America too lost some highly respected figures including Nat 'King' Cole the popular singer at only 45, and the internationally famous radio and TV reporter, Ed Murrow, an honorary Knight of the British Empire following his wartime broadcasts from a beleaguered Britain.

Looking back through records of years gone by highlights how, in a world of considerable stability for most, the recurring natural disasters of earthquakes, tornadoes, hurricanes and typhoons cause enormous suffering where they do strike.

CHAPTER 6
1966 OIL LIFT AND A NEW LIVERY

THE AIRCRAFT

Douglas DC4   G-APYK   G-ASFY   G-ASOG

Douglas DC6   G-APNO   G-APNP

For 1966 Air Ferry would essentially operate five aircraft. During 1965 it became known that, when B.U.A.'s Britannias were fitted with a freight door, they would take over the Africargo service currently operated by two DC6s which would then be available for other use. Mainly through Douglas Whybrow's endeavours these were obtained for use by Air Ferry. The aircraft in question, G-APNO and G-APNP, had been purchased new by Hunting-Clan for the African routes and were near to the end of the DC6 production run. These, together with the three DC4s, would provide Air Ferry with a strong mixed passenger and freight fleet capable of long distance work.

The DC6s were first seen at Manston in February for crew training but it was not until late April that one was delivered and November Papa had the distinction of carrying out her first revenue flight before official delivery to Manston.

November Oscar with Hunting-Clan at London Heathrow
(Air Britain J.J. Halley)

The year would see the departure of the rest of the Vikings with Charlie Hotel and Oscar Whisky flying just 32 hours 40 minutes in January. Ken Sheppardson received a request for some details from Hugh Kennard and a deal was put together for three aircraft to be sold to Invicta. The names were deleted from the cabin tops, contracts and bankers drafts organised and, on 23 March, Victor Delta, Victor Foxtrot and Charlie Hotel were handed over to their new owners. Oscar Whisky was similarly sold to Hugh Kennard on 28 October and of the four aircraft only Victor Delta did not fly again after leaving Air Ferry.

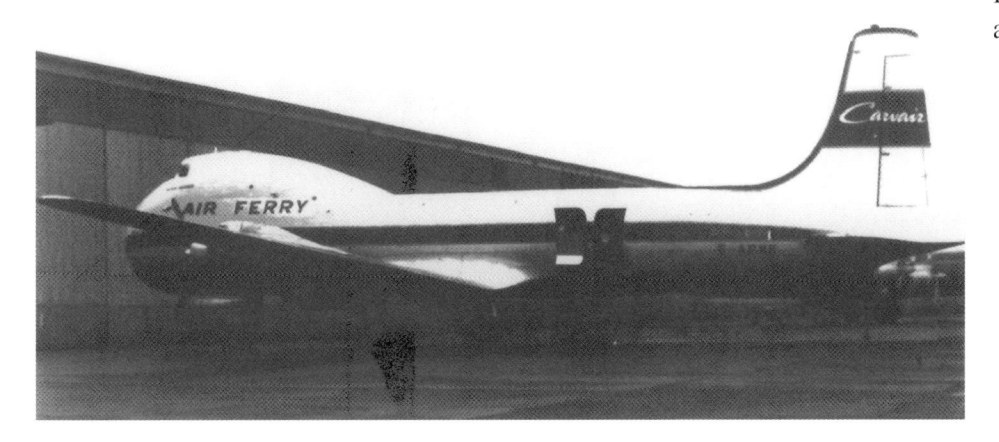

B.U.A.F.'s G-APNH used on the Oil Lift ('Propliner' - 'Military Aircraft Photographs')

89

TWILIGHT OF THE PISTONS

The year started with Yankee Kilo on check at Manston and, in addition to the overhaul, she was being repainted in the new livery. Geoffrey Illsley was again involved and this time was given a freer hand in the design. The result was 'Air Ferry' in a very dark blue with the cheat line also dark blue, edged in gold, and curving down more at the nose, which emphasised the larger white area between the cheat line and the black anti-glare panel in front of the windscreens. The fin and rudder were now white with the AF enlarged and also in dark blue edged in gold. The scheme did not look its best when Yankee Kilo was pushed from the hangar on a grey and cheerless January day as the greater area of white made the aircraft blend into the sky but, on brighter days, and with a solid background, the scheme looked very stylish.

Oscar Golf and Foxtrot Yankee had arrived at Dar es Salaam on 31 December 1965 and 1 January 1966 respectively. There were two other aircraft bearing the Air Ferry name on the oil lift, B.U.A.F. had contracted to send two Carvairs and these operated, with B.U.A.F. crews, in B.U.A.F. colours but with 'Air Ferry' in light blue on the sides. G-ASKG left Southend on 28 December, arriving at Dar es Salaam on 1 January, with G-APNH following two days later.

B.U.A.F.'s G-ASKG used on the Oil Lift
('Propliner' Tony Merton Jones / Peter R. Keating)

THE CREWS

To meet the expected demand for work, the crews would need to be increased during the year. Of the captains, Bill Wood, Hugh Tubman, David Laker, Andy Nicol, Paul Ashpitel, Stan Hunnable and Captain Honeyman would fly all year. During this time Don Brooker came off flying duties and concentrated on Operations, John Gibson left at the end of July and John Mason went in December. Harry Chang transferred from First Officer, and Captain Eames, who had flown in 1964, rejoined. Two other senior men who joined in 1966 and flew as captain within a short time were John Cropp and Keith Sissons, the only pilot current in Britain with a floatplane licence.

Keith Sissons learnt to fly at Southend Municipal Flying School, did some pleasure flying from the airport and joined the R.A.F.V.R., at that time still at Hornchurch. He also became a helicopter pilot and spent three years flying Whirlwinds in the Antartic where he came to know Alan Bristow; later on he spent time in Nigeria where he was the helicopter pilot for the Prime Minister, at that time, Sir Alahaja Aboubaker Tafawa Balewa. Before joining Air Ferry he was with Morton's at Gatwick where he flew as a captain on the Herons and DC3s

Other joiners were Captains Ross, Brown and Vines. Adrian Ross had been involved in the management of Transeuropean Airways at Southend some years before. In September Viv Kellard returned, a captain now, in addition to being a specialist navigator.

Flying with them were First Officers Ahmad, Johnston, Jackson, Surrage, Gutteridge, Hope, Horsting and Simpson, who left in September. Bill Isaacs reappeared in April, having spent the previous season with Hugh Kennard at Invicta, and another wave of long staying pilots joined at varying times, F/Os Champneys, Phillp, Waddingham, Watson and Gilson. Norman Watson and George Gilson had learnt to fly together and both were sponsored by Air Ferry for their instrument rating courses.

At the end of August, for example, the establishment was approximately fifteen crews. The acquisition of the DC6s also led to the appointment of Flight Engineers as part of the crew complement and these included Des Froud and Brian Dunlop.

The air hostesses, again led by Gillian Appleby, included A/H Barnett, Bird, Byrne, Catherine Dunn, Ereckson, Jill Firkin, Hoffman, Huckle, Liz Johnson, Manning, Molli, Margaret Norton, Anna Oates, Odile Parsons, Rees, Setchel and Pat Willcox.

THE YEAR

The 'Top Ten' airfields for 1966 again made fascinating reading and portrayed how the emphasis had changed towards freighting while still keeping a high volume of IT work to selected destinations.

1966 OIL LIFT AND A NEW LIVERY

Airports	Visits
Basle	641
Perpignan	253
Dar-es-Salaam	110
London Heathrow	91
Ostend	79
Lusaka	61
Manchester	49
Ndola	48
Dusseldorf	47
Copenhagen	46

January The only flight recorded on New Years Day was the last leg of Foxtrot Yankee's journey from Khartoum to Dar es Salaam. On 2 January Oscar Golf made Air Ferry's first flight of the airlift with a cargo of oil drums to Lusaka, Foxtrot Yankee joined her the following day.

The bulk of the 483 hours flown in the month were by the two DC4s working the oil lift with 36 flights to Lusaka and 11 to Ndola. One of the Ndola's, by Andy Nicol in Oscar Golf on the 18th., was a diversion from Lusaka due to bad visibility. There were four local flights from Dar es Salaam, the nature of these, apart from a return by Hugh Tubman in Oscar Golf on the 26th. with the number 2 U/S, is not known.

The base for the oil lift, Dar es Salaam lies in the east of Tanzania on the Indian Ocean coast. The name means 'a haven of peace' and the port is home to a mixed African, Arabic and Indian population. For the DC4s the haul to Ndola, in northern Zambia near to the Congo border, was a round trip of 8 hours 45 minutes. The return flight to Lusaka, virtually due south of Ndola, took, on average, an hour longer.

Oscar Whisky in the snow, 17 January, 1966

Back at Manston the Viking days were drawing to a close. Charlie Hotel made a freight flight to Beauvais on Tuesday 4th while Oscar Whisky had a local flight of 25 minutes on Thursday. Over that day and the next Charlie Hotel operated Manston-Cambridge-Le Bourget-Cambridge, night stopped and flew Cambridge-Le Bourget-Manston. Later on the 7th. both Vikings made cargo journeys to Metz and for Oscar Whisky this was her last revenue flight, taken by John Gibson. Charlie Hotel went to Le Bourget on the 11th. and made an exact repeat of the Cambridge-Le Bourget work over the 13th./14th. Then, on Tuesday 18th., a Le Bourget from Manston was the last Air Ferry flight by Charlie Hotel, piloted by Captain Mason. Finally, on the 26th, David Laker took Oscar Whisky over to Ostend on the last Air Ferry Viking flight of all. It was the end of an Act, the pause at Manston like a half way interval in the Air Ferry story.

Three days later a new Scene began when Yankee Kilo flew an airtest in the new paint scheme after her check.

Air Ferry's promotional material in 1966 stressed the versatility of the two types available for charter work. In freight trim the DC6s had a payload of 11,500 kg with access through forward and aft doors, the larger measuring 10'4" x 6'6". The DC4s appeared to have shrunk during the previous year as, in variance to the 1965 publicity material, the rear fuselage access was now given as 7'10" x 5'6".

Yankee Kilo being repainted (Steve Pigg)

TWILIGHT OF THE PISTONS

Sometimes when the work was up to date the engineers would turn their creative abilities into other channels. Roger Pearce recalls making some of the tools he needed, and that someone in the trim shop lent the final touch to the Triumph motorcycle he had restored to mechanical serviceability by professionally recovering the saddle.

February The oil lift continued into February for the two Air Ferry DC4s and the two B.U.A.F. Carvairs. The deliveries by the DC4s were more even with 24 trips each to Lusaka and to Ndola during the month. On Wednesday 2nd. Captain Nicol, in Oscar Golf, took off from Dar and returned after an hour with an oil leak.

On 4 February Yankee Kilo left Manston and flew out to Africa, via Benghazi and Khartoum, arriving in Dar es Salaam on Sunday 6th. She made a local flight the following day and started in earnest on the lift on Tuesday with a departure to Ndola. Virtually as Yankee Kilo arrived there, Oscar Golf was leaving Lusaka on her final leg of the oil lift back to Dar es Salaam; with Foxtrot Yankee also on an Ndola run this was the only day that the three DC4s operated together.

On the 9th. Oscar Golf set out for home via Khartoum and Malta arriving back after lunch on Friday 11th. The aircraft carried out a local flight of 2 hours 45 minutes the next day before being manoeuvred into the hangar for a check which would last nearly eight weeks.

As mentioned earlier, Air Ferry's new DC6s made their first appearances during the month, both of course still in full B.U.A. livery. On 3 February November Papa flew Southend-Southend-Manston-Ostend-Manston for the first visit with an Air Ferry crew, and indeed this was the first Air Ferry movement at Manston in February; the aircraft returned to Southend the following day. On 14th. it was November Oscar's turn; she flew Southend-Manston-Southend-Manston, staying until the 16th. before returning, via Ostend, to Southend. The last training sortie, again by November Oscar, and captained by Bill Wood, was on 24th./25th. of the month with a return, once more, to Southend.

Oscar Golf taxies in, home from the Oil Lift, 11 February, 1966

Hugh Tubman, Jeep and Patrick all had DC6 training at this time, the former two also made flights on B.U.A. operations as supernumaries.

March The two DC4s on detachment continued the oil lift into March, primarily now to Ndola with 13 journeys before the Air Ferry participation ended. On the 7th. Foxtrot Yankee made the final flight to Lusaka, a round trip of nine hours. While Foxtrot Yankee was still on the outward leg, Yankee Kilo left Dar es Salaam bound for Khartoum, Malta and Manston. The aircraft arrived back in the early afternoon of Wednesday 9th., the first Air Ferry movement at Manston for nearly a fortnight.

November Papa with B.U.A. (Air Britain)

The next to leave Dar was Carvair G-ASKG which arrived back in the U.K. at about the time that Foxtrot Yankee was carrying out the last flight to Ndola on Friday 11 March. On Sunday, Foxtrot Yankee also set out for home returning the 'usual' route and leaving Carvair G-APNH to ply backwards and forwards on the lift for almost three more months.

1966 OIL LIFT AND A NEW LIVERY

Not all of the aircrew returned on the Air Ferry aircraft, Captain Nicol came back in a Britannia of British Caledonian.

While Foxtrot Yankee was airborne between Khartoum and Malta on the Monday, November Papa arrived from Southend for two days of familiarisation work at Manston and Ostend, the DC6 returning to Southend on Wednesday 16th. That day, with Oscar Golf still on check, Yankee Kilo flew up to Prestwick for work by Scottish Aviation a company which, apart from it's air transport operations, had diversified into aircraft manufacturing in addition to engineering and maintenance work. There were then no movements by Air Ferry aircraft for a week until November Papa flew in again on Thursday 24th; after more training it was back to Essex the next day.

Andy Nicol had flown all of the Vikings, DC4s and Freighters up to this time. As an Instrument Rating Examiner he carried out many of the test checks for his fellow pilots, including Ken Sheppardson's. Andy was one of those taking the DC6 conversion under Bill Wood and made his first flight in the new type on the 15th.

> *The DC6s carried a Flight Engineer on the flight deck and an analyser that would pin-point the faulty sparking plug in the now rare event of a mag. drop. This helped greatly to reduce technical delays. (Paul Noller)*

After months of freight work Foxtrot Yankee carried the first passengers of the year on Friday 25 March to Ostend, fitted in a training flight on Saturday, and returned with the passengers on Sunday. Foxtrot Yankee closed the months revenue work for the DC4s with more freight work, flying Manston-Edinburgh-Basle-Edinburgh-Basle, where she arrived at 2350 on Tuesday 29th. The DC4 left the tarmac at 0200 but recorded a Basle-Basle of 25 minutes and returned to Manston early on Wednesday evening. There was a short local flight next day, either an air test or training.

In March some of the staff, led by Sylvia Clark from Commercial, decided to start a company news sheet. The first edition came out in April and reported that an Inter-Airline social evening had taken place at the Roman Galley on the Thanet Way; the Air Ferry contingent being considerably outnumbered by the Invicta staff.

Gillian Appleby told the editor that she and her new air hostesses went to the swimming pool at Butlins one afternoon to practice ditching. After this rather dampening exercise had taken place they duly returned to a somewhat drier instruction course. The next morning the Chief Hostess received a card and drawing from Mr. Gus Britton, the Swimming Instructor at Butlins:

> *"Dear Top Bird,*
>
> *............I think that is what you said you were!*
>
> *Please thank your class for the gifts they left behind,*
>
> *three bathing caps, one pair of white shoes*
>
> *and a dress but, unfortunately, none of these things*
>
> *fit me. What, pray shall I do with them? Oops!"*
>
> *Mr. Britton was what is known as 'extremely well built.'*

The second edition covered May/June and is the last that the writer has. It contained several articles and some very good cartoons. Odile Parsons contributed an article on 'Fashion' which gives an interesting insight into the 'swinging sixties.'

> *'On Wednesday, 18th May, Sarre Court transformed itself into a Fashion House when local ship-broker, Peter Holmes, instigated the presentation of some of the clothes now on sale at his shop, 'The Mermaid'. Obviously, Martha Hill, who designed the clothes, had some idea as to how to introduce the trend of the mid-sixties to the Isle of Thanet.*
>
> *Mid-thigh-length shifts, striped, checked and plain, with matching tights and caps, various and vivid shades of red and black and white predominating. At the time during the presentation when I, and many with me (according to whispered comments from all around) were beginning*

to wonder, with perplexity, whether we would find an occasion to wear what looked like a pyjama top with knee-length socks and buckle shoes, we had the pleasant surprise of a modern version of anybody's dream evening gown. A simplified 'Empire' looking dress in a non-crease, hazy blue material. At six guineas, definitely my choice. I hear that each dress comes in one model only. You will not have the ghastly misfortune of finding yourself, and the rest of your cabin crew, wearing yet another uniform - you may be assured to be exclusive! I feel that I cannot end this little article without a word of criticism on the London photographic models who presented the collection and who certainly attracted sarcasm from the assistants. One who, with her boyish socks and cap, reminded me of David Copperfield and seemed to have stepped out of a picture book. Half a dozen needed grooming very badly - even the least critical eye would have noticed the dirty toe-nails, the laddered stocks and the split pants! Hilarity came upon the public when one of the models walked in as if she was at the end of a marathon, panting and stamping the floor as she tore frantically along the platform. She was in such a hurry that I cannot remember what she was wearing!

We left Sarre Court with mixed feelings. It had been a pleasant interlude but we had our moment of sadness for one could not help wondering whether, in one's early twenties, one was old already. We did not know, perhaps, how to appreciate pop-art and its geometrical patterns? But I like to think that what is sad, is that some girls should want to be so unsophisticated and do away with their greatest and most natural asset - femininity.'

Another article concerned what appeared to be a family letter left over from when the U.S. Forces were at Manston, 'found' by Sally Maycock.

'Dear Son,

You Pa has a good job now, the foist he has had for forty-eight years. We are agrate deal better off now than we were.

Your Pa gets 44-55 dollars every Thursday so we thought we would do a little fixing up. We sent to MontyWards for one of they new fangled things they call bathrooms you hear tell about in some houses.

Its put in by a man called a plumber. On one side of the room is a big long thing like the pigs drink out of, only you get in that and wash allover. On the other side is a little think they call a sink, thats for light washing such as your hands and face.

But over in the corner, my son, now I'll tell you; we've really got something there. This little contraption you put one foot in and wash it clean, then you pull the chain and get fresh water for the other foot! Two lids came with the durned think, and we ain't had any use for them in the bathroom, so I'm using one for the bread board and the other had a round hole in it and we took and framed Grandfather's picture with it. They are awful nice people to deal with, they sent us a great big roll of writing paper with it.

Take keer of yourself my son. Mother.'

April   The activities at Manston that April seemed very much in tune with spring, things seemed to be bursting open in all directions. During most of the first week Foxtrot Yankee was the sole revenue earner, starting on 1 April with passengers flying Manston-Heathrow-Le Bourget-Manston. Later that day the aircraft started a circuitous flight, including two night stops, and travelled Manston-Ostend-Stanstead-Hanover-Le Bourget-Heathrow-Ostend-Manston. After this came an Ostend, a Hanover-Stanstead charter and a Basle without passengers, although whether this was for cargo or familiarisation is not known. Foxtrot Yankee carried out local flying on the 5th. and 6th. before taking the first passengers to Basle later on Wednesday 6th. By then Oscar Golf had emerged from the hangar, the second aircraft to be painted in the new livery, and had a short test flight.

The passenger flying was building up rapidly; there were 35 visits to Ostend in April, including training; a small number by comparison to other years but the largest monthly total for 1966. The two DC4s in service went to Ostend a total of eight times on the 7th. and 8th. where they were both fog bound at one point that day; then over the 8th./9th. Foxtrot Yankee flew Manston-Ostend-Southend-Ostend-Birmingham-Beauvais-Manston, while Oscar Golf varied this slightly with Manston-Ostend-Southend-Ostend-Coventry-Ostend-Beauvais-Manston. Some tours to Beauvais and Rotterdam followed and on the 11th. Oscar Golf flew Manston-Beauvais-Castle Donington-Ostend-Manston.

Yankee Kilo had positioned from Prestwick to Wymeswold on 3 April for work by Fields, finally returning to Manston on the 12th. After a Basle IT on 13 April it was Foxtrot Yankee's turn to be handed over to the engineers for a check.

Oscar Golf continued with tour flights to Ostend, flew a Manston-Geneva-Ostend-Coventry-Manston on the 12th. and went to Venice on the 14th./15th., an out and back haul of 10 hours. She then flew two charters from Gatwick, to Le Bourget and Rotterdam, flew more training and went back to Geneva on the 22nd. There were two visits to Dusseldorf; these flights were now government work primarily carrying the relations of service personnel stationed in Germany. More training followed and then a change to freight configuration for Basle on the 26th., and Manston-Stuttgart-Basle-Manston over the 26th./27th., the first Air Ferry visit to the German town.

Also on the 27th., Oscar Golf took passengers to Ostend, then returned there on training, making six landings, and went to Venice again on Thursday 28th. Oscar Golf then changed again from passenger to freight trim, the engineers were expert at removing the 84 seats from their rails and then protecting these from the rigours of moving freight along the cabin. The next flight that day at 2330 was Manston-Manchester for loading, then at 0300, the aircraft continued Manchester-Berlin-Manston. Another training flight followed and then more passengers with a Manston-Gatwick-Rotterdam-Gatwick for a night stop at the end of the month.

Yankee Kilo flew two training sorties and two Rotterdam tours and then changed to freight trim, leaving for Lyneham on Sunday 17th. and routed out to Aden through Rome and Cairo and returned on the 21st April. The aircraft changed to passenger trim for several flights including a Gatwick-Wildenwrath-Gatwick charter, and on the 24th. left for Aden again. On the return journey the aircraft stayed in Brindisi from Thursday 28th until it positioned directly back to Manston on the Saturday evening, as the final movement of the month; a note in the Engineer's book read: 'Dave, things went a little adrift last night. Ken and Jim have gone to Gatwick - OG has hydraulic troubles. YK still has freight on board. Rob.'

There were not many DC6 movements, but they were significant ones. On Friday 29 April, Bill Wood brought November Oscar from Southend on delivery, the aircraft resplendent with 'Air Ferry' on the fuselage sides although still with the Union Jack on the tail; this would not be changed for some time. The following morning, at 0905, the first DC6 revenue flight took place, to Rotterdam, again commanded by Bill Wood. Later that day the aircraft went to Rotterdam once more and then positioned across to Gatwick. Air Ferry would operate the DC6s with two pilots, a flight engineer and, for passenger work, three cabin crew. The maximum passenger load was normally 104.

While on the ground the DC4s had a strap that fell vertically from the roof which was used to hold the controls in place. In lighter moments Adrian Ross would stand on one of the seats and do a magnificent chimp impression while holding on to the strap.

May May started with a series of passenger charters through Gatwick by November Oscar, Yankee Kilo and Oscar Golf, the latter, as mentioned, having hydraulic trouble early on 1 May which necessitated Ken Barker and Jim Jones going across to Gatwick. Later in the week Oscar Golf made a varied flight Manston-Dusseldorf-Glasgow-Dusseldorf-Gatwick-Rotterdam-Manston that included two night stops. From Manston inclusive tours continued to Rotterdam and built up to Perpignan and Basle, flights to the Swiss airport dwarfing all other movements throughout the summer.

From: 'Murphy,' an article in K.A.H.R.S.:

At one time the airline operated a series of charter flights from Gatwick. On one occasion the aircraft returned as usual; coming to a stop at the ramp, the waiting ground party had it ready for unloading in about two minutes. Chocks were placed around the wheels, a ground power unit already running was plugged in and switched on. Next, steps were positioned up to the cabin entrance and the passengers began to disembark. Underneath, the baggage handlers were offloading cases from the freight hold onto a small train of trollies. When the last of the

TWILIGHT OF THE PISTONS

passengers had departed, a Customs officer searched the plane, finally checking the contents of the 'Duty Free' containers which he then sealed; they were then returned to the Bonded Store by the cabin staff. All quite routine, except for the fact that on this occasion, for some reason, the crew had not followed the usual practice of switching off the radio as soon as the aircraft came to a stop, they just sat in their seats completing their paper work; when they had finished the aircraft was now deserted, and the captain simply switched off the main power switch, plunging the DC4 into darkness and silence.

Shortly after, there appeared a couple of airport staff with a tractor, a DC4 towbar and a small ladder, their job was to take the plane to a parking bay for the night. The towbar was attached to the nosewheel and the steering link disconnected. While the driver removed the chocks, his mate climbed up to the flight deck, pulling the ladder up after him. His job was to operate the brakes, to do this he would have to pump up the hydraulic pressure with a large hand pump; to do this he would need to be able to read the gauge, and so of course switched on the main switch. At once the aircraft was flooded with light and noise; this was the era of valve equipment, to obtain the HT needed, each unit contained a rotary transformer, a small 24 volt motor with a 250/350 volt generator on the same shaft, there was something like eight of these motors running, including two invertors, quite a racket. Any tarmac crew back at Manston would have at once switched off and called upon the nearest Radio or Electrical engineer to put the switches in the correct alignment. But this was not the home base and these were not company employees; so there he sat, quite happy with everything. By the time they reached the dispersal the accumulators would already be severely discharged, but not irretrievably so. But now came the final blow, having put the parking brake on, the two characters hopped onto their tractor and sped off into the night, having left the DC4 still switched on. So there it was, all through the night the batteries got lower and lower, till come the morning they were completely flat, the aircraft dark and silent.

The aircraft was now returned to the ramp, being daylight the cleaners did not require lights, so the situation was not noticed. In the terminal building the passengers were arriving, booking in they handed over their baggage and collected their boarding cards, they were then free to roam the waiting area until such time as they would be called forward, crocodiled and fed into the departure complex. Meanwhile the crew had booked into the crew rooom. The captain first inspected the technical log, noting with satisfaction the previous evening's entry: 'Nil defects.' Having collected the Met information and filed their flight plan, they made their way out to the tarmac to the waiting plane, only to find that it was completely unserviceable. A panic message to Manston initiated a flurry of activity. A replacement plane was readied, the biggest problem being to bring in a crew, the Gatwick one would not now have enough hours left for the round trip. With a spare set of batteries and one or two engineers to check over the U/S aircraft, they set off for Gatwick; in about one and a half hours the passengers were on their way at last, no doubt they quite rightly grumbled, but considering what was involved, quite a creditable performance. As the defect was discovered before departure time, the real delay was under one hour, but it should not have happened. (Phil Townsend)

All the DC4s and November Oscar participated in local flying, for training and familiarisation during the month, Oscar Golf's sortie on Wednesday 18th including eight landings.

Back in the hangar, and near to the end of her check, Foxtrot Yankee's nosewheel hub was found to be badly scored and bruised. The Goodyear representative was called in, but for the time being there was no spare DC4 nosewheel at hand. On Saturday 7th Yankee Kilo took the first Perpignan tour of the season and on Sunday evening Oscar Golf turned back from a Rotterdam flight with a backfire that caused the engine to be feathered. Back on the ground it was decided the engine would have to be changed and Yankee Kilo was substituted. There was a further delay when this aircraft returned to the tarmac with generator and relay trouble and the passengers finally left at 0030, five and a quarter hours after the original departure.

Yankee Kilo arrived back at 0300 and by 0500 the DC4 had been changed to freight trim and was awaiting its crew for positioning to Lyneham on an M.O.D. flight. On leaving, however, it returned from the runway with the number 4 engine U/S and this had to be changed. The Maintenance entry read: ' Two engines in one night Rob, sorry Ken.' The aircraft finally left at 2230 on Monday and from Lyneham flew via Rome to Nicosia in Cyprus, returning direct to Manston in 11 hours 11 minutes.

HOLIDAY CHARTER

FOR GROUP TRAVEL ORGANISERS ALL OVER BRITAIN AIR FERRY WILL REDUCE COSTS IMPROVE SERVICE

Everyone knows chartering aircraft is cheaper, but AIR FERRY make it convenient and easy and provide unbeatable personal service into the bargain.

AIR FERRY 3 POINT SERVICE

① FROM ANYWHERE

Our own airport is at Manston, Kent, but we will quote for series charter flights and give discounts on quantity business from any airport in Britain.

② FINE AIRCRAFT

Our DC6's and DC4's can carry economically tour numbers between 40 and 100.

③ TO ANYWHERE

Charters can be arranged to anywhere in the world. Specially advantageous rates are available for holiday flights mid-week and off-season to Europe.

Better Charter Air Ferry

Whether you want single flights for private parties and special group tours or series flights for inclusive tours AIR FERRY LTD will give value for money.

FOR FURTHER DETAILS CONTACT YOUR TRAVEL AGENT

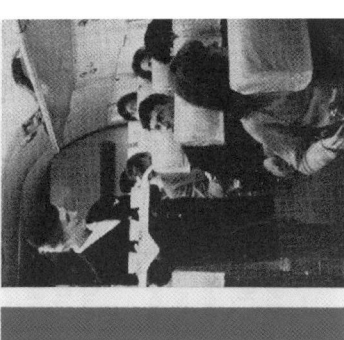

TWILIGHT OF THE PISTONS

1966 OIL LIFT AND A NEW LIVERY

Foxtrot Yankee had by now emerged from the hangar looking extremely smart in dark blue and gold and needed only a 15 minute air test on Friday 13 May before taking the 0830 to Basle the following morning. After two Perpignans and another Basle it was back to freight trim, and back to Africa, as Foxtrot Yankee left Manston on Monday 16th. bound via Tripoli and Kano to Port Harcourt in Nigeria, returning through Tripoli and Gatwick to Manston on Thursday 19th. with another 36 hours to record.

Also on 13 May, and just before Foxtrot Yankee's air test, November Oscar took the first passengers to Genoa on what would be an all-DC6 tour. The next day a Balair aircraft was used for a sub-charter although the route is not known. November Oscar flew a Manston-Basle-Gatwick on that Saturday and must have been de-seated there as the next flight on Sunday 15th. was freight, Gatwick-Dusseldorf-Hanover-Manston.

The third week of the month included a Manston-Manchester-Amsterdam-Manston passenger charter on the 16th by Yankee Kilo with a return journey the following day, and the carriage of freight to Jersey by Oscar Golf. The DC6s took over the remainder of the Venice tours for the season with November Oscar operating there on 20/21 May and linking two Italian destinations by flying Genoa-Venice and brought back 33 passengers from the latter. Over the 22/23 the DC6 flew freight Heathrow-Copenhagen-Heathrow.

The Inclusive Tours to Perpignan were now programmed for 2100 hours every night of the week. There were additional flights each Saturday afternoon, at 0100 on Sunday morning, at 0015 on Monday morning and two more on Wednesday evenings, at 2200 and 2245. When running to schedule on Wednesday nights, all three DC4s departed for Perpignan within two hours.

In the last week Oscar Golf made the short trip to Calais while Yankee Kilo took freight from Heathrow to Dusseldorf. The aircraft had mag. trouble on number 3 and was called into Manston on the Dusseldorf-LAP leg; an engine change was required and Yankee Kilo flew to Heathrow and back on Saturday 28th., presumably to unload her cargo.

November Oscar's Basle on the evening of the 25th. was delayed when the number 3 engine would not run in weak or rich mixture or anything below 1200 RPM but the defect was cleared and Bill Wood finally left at 2200. November Oscar also operated to Genoa, Venice and took the first Copenhagen on Saturday morning. The weather intervened on that last Sunday, Yankee Kilo left at 0300 for Basle but was diverted to Zurich, while Foxtrot Yankee on the first of the Sunday night flights to Perpignan was diverted to Toulouse. To coincide with the new equipment, there was a series of day flights by the DC6s to Perpignan on Mondays and Wednesdays, November Oscar making the first DC6 visit on Monday 30th before switching to freight the next day for a journey to Charleroi in Belgium.

November Oscar, 1966

Following the writer's letter in 'Flight' requesting anyone interested in the project to contact him, two of the first replies were from people who did not work for Air Ferry but who still have pleasant memories of the company at that time.

Steve Pigg, who later went on to work for Invicta, was at school at the time and earned pocket money by cleaning cars for the engineers. He recalls being allowed to progress to carrying out some basic jobs in the hangar, such as cleaning engine components and remembers Ron Illsley's surprise at first seeing him there. He recalls also a certain refueller whose car ran creditably on 100 octane fuel and of occasions when he was able to scrounge a ride on Oscar Golf and November Papa.

June November Oscar returned to Charleroi on 1st and 2nd June; these visits and the one on 31 May being the only occasions that Air Ferry aircraft would visit Gossilies Airport. Although not strictly an Air Ferry movement, Carvair G-APNH finally returned to the U.K. on 2 June from its long stay on the oil lift.

Inclusive Tours continued to the two main destinations of Basle and Perpignan with some increases to the DC6 tours. With just one DC6 for most of the month it would be July before these settled into their usual patterns. For Genoa and Venice this would be two departures per week each; those to Genoa were on Friday evening at 1900 hours and at 0100 on Saturday morning, while the Venice flights were Saturday evening at 2100 hours and at 0100 on Sunday morning.

From 1963 to 1965 it had sometimes been necessary to go to an alternate on the Perpignan flights; Toulouse was the logical choice with five visits during that time although Marseilles was used on two occasions and Barcelona, over the border and the mountains, was also used twice. In 1966 however, Barcelona was used as an Inclusive Tour destination in its own right, primarily by the DC6s, although the DC4s went on three occasions.

November Oscar had a delay on the Wednesday evening Basle on the 1st., for the second week running, with a repeated fuel pump problem. The DC6 went to Southend on Thursday 2nd., and left that airport at five minutes after midnight on Saturday, to return to Manston in time to take the Genoa flight and went on to Venice after that. With the fleet not complete and some technical and weather complications thrown in, June was not the most straightforward month. Yankee Kilo caused difficulties the first weekend with a Manston-Manston carrying 51 passengers on Friday afternoon but departed for Basle 45 minutes later.

At this point it is perhaps useful to chart the arrival of November Papa as she lived a rather itinerant existance for the first two weeks. The aircraft arrived from Southend at Manston at 2250 on the evening of Friday 3rd., technically still on loan, and left on her first revenue flight 71 minutes later to Genoa. The aircraft also flew a

1966 OIL LIFT AND A NEW LIVERY

Copenhagen tour before departing to Heathrow on the Saturday evening. She returned from Heathrow in the small hours of the 9th and flew Manston-Genoa-Gatwick-Verona-Gatwick early on the 11th and somehow fitted in the last B.U.A. Africargo service before her actual delivery to Manston from Heathrow on Wednesday 15 June. Although slightly academic at this point, the aircraft's first revenue flight after this was on the 17th./18th. to Genoa and Venice and commanded by Captain Laker. The aircraft was still in B.U.A. colours: 'Air Ferry' on the sides was added after delivery. At last the five aircraft fleet for 1966 was now complete.

Yankee Kilo with small tail marking, 15 June, 1966

Bill Wood made some changes to the training practices on the DC6 that had been followed at B.U.A. with a resultant saving in both time and money. He arranged for the training loads to be palletised for speed of loading and unloading, as the aircraft were required to be at 90% of maximum landing weight for some sorties. Where possible training flights were made over to Ostend so that the drawback on petrol duty could be claimed, and again reduce costs.

On the 6 June Yankee Kilo came back from Basle with radio interference. While being moved towards the hangar the tow bar broke owing to the dip in the tarmac in front of the hangar and the aircraft overran the tractor, fortunately without damage. In the second week there was no Thursday night Perpignan for some reason and the weekend flights to that destination did not go according to plan. The Friday night flight on the 10th. was delayed when Yankee Kilo had another radio defect, and an hour later Foxtrot Yankee returned to the tarmac with a dead cut on number 2 engine before finally leaving for Basle.

November Oscar took the Saturday afternoon DC4 flight to Perpignan while the early Sunday morning tour departed four hours late. November Oscar operated the first DC6 Barcelona on Sunday evening and, half an hour later, the gremlins struck Oscar Golf as she had to make a return from Dieppe while bound for Perpignan with 80 passengers some 70 minutes into her flight, the aircraft was airborne again at 0240.

Twenty four hours later, bad weather over Southern England caused its own chaos with Foxtrot Yankee on Monday night's Perpignan being diverted into Southend, and with a feathered number 1 engine, piloted by Andy Nicol and Pete Johnston. She remained there on Tuesday 14th. and flew back, via Ostend, to Manston on Wednesday. Yankee Kilo returning from Basle was also obliged to go to Southend. The aircraft arrived back at Manston at 0920 on Tuesday, and later that day took the evening flight to Basle. On Saturday 18th Foxtrot Yankee went to Basle via Geneva, whether this was a chartered leg or a diversion is not known.

On the 22 June November Papa carried freight to Dublin, the first of cargo visits three days running by that aircraft to the Irish capital. June's problems accelerated as the month drew to a close. Taking off from Manston late on Tuesday afternoon of the 21st. Yankee Kilo's shear bolt broke on the nose undercarriage. This was repaired at Basle but broke again on retraction out of Basle. The engineers suspected the latch gear but a full retraction test back at Manston found no fault. November Oscar was next with a U/S engine at Basle; Balair investigated the fault as an 'AOG' and Eddie Edgar's note said: 'Sounds like engine failure.' It was, and the engine was changed on return to Manston, the DC6 also being 'AOG'd' for a nose wheel strut. Meanwhile, one of Yankee Kilo's motors was also giving trouble which led to a cylinder change then, after returning from her second Basle on Saturday 25th., a different engine had to be changed!

On the weekend of 24th./26th., which included 19 Basles and also a Gatwick-Verona-Gatwick by November Oscar, there were several delays which averaged three hours including Friday's Genoa and Saturday's Copenhagen, while all four Perpignans between Saturday night and Monday morning were late. Oscar Golf was delayed in Basle on one of her visits on Sunday 26th. with a mag. board and jump lead defect.

Foxtrot Yankee with small tail marking, 24 June, 1966

On Tuesday 28th Yankee Kilo made an early passenger flight to Barcelona, followed by a sortie for local circuit training by Paul Ashpitel and Mike Waddingham. Later that day November Papa took freight to Lyons. At 0115 on Wednesday Foxtrot Yankee, coming back from Perpignan with 74 passengers, had to make a technical return there when Reg Eames and Jeep had a fire in number 3 engine after take off. It was 0523 before Yankee Kilo got away from Manston to collect the tired and dishevelled passengers as Foxtrot Yankee had to return home empty. On Wednesday night the first two Perpignans went according to plan but Oscar Golf on the third had a technical delay there with a hydraulic leak when the pressure regulator adaptor cracked. The aircraft returned late to Manston via Basle and Foxtrot Yankee made an unscheduled visit to Perpignan on Thursday morning, presumably as the relief aircraft as she carried passengers one way. So ended a hectic month, incredibly one with just three visits to Ostend, all of them most probably for training.

> *At Manston Air Ferry employed a number of ladies as cabin cleaners, their housewifely skills admirably suited to the task of maintaining the cabins, seats and furnishings in pristine condition. One day we were engaged in a routine Check 2 on a DC4. Suddenly the relative tranquility of the cabin was shattered by a piercing shriek; we looked up to see one of the ladies standing transfixed, staring aghast at something in her hand. It was quickly established that the something was a packet of those photographs, obviously purchased by one of our customers abroad who, on the journey home had had second thoughts, possibly contemplating discovery by H.M. Customs and had unloaded the packet into the back of the seat in front of him, (well, it wouldn't be a her, would it?) Our cleaning lady had been checking the pockets for the correct sick bag and safety leaflets etc., at the same time removing any sweet papers or empty cigarette packets when she made her unwelcome find. Needless to say, she was quickly relieved of the unappreciated burden, in fact you might say, she was almost killed in the rush!...(Phil Townsend)*

July   It was not surprising there were some delays; the aircraft utilisation was high and July saw the peak hours ever flown in one month by Air Ferry, together with the most movements of any month in 1966. Yankee Kilo took the fortnightly DC4 tour to Copenhagen on Friday 1st, followed by November Papa with passengers to Lyons, the first weekend going well, although for some reason with no Sunday Barcelona. This tour operated regularly for the rest of July, once by Yankee Kilo and the remainder by the DC6s.

The week commencing 4 July was a bad one for problems. On Tuesday 5th. Yankee Kilo went U/S on the pre departure check for Perpignan and Oscar Golf was used. This aircraft then returned to the tarmac with an instrument defect, although she left half an hour afterwards. The closing comment in the book was: 'My name's Goff and I'm *!*?**! off.' Yankee Kilo had trouble the next night, rostered for the third Wednesday Perpignan, when she returned from the runway with a mag. drop and flat batteries. After that her number 1 was very troublesome to start and, on top of all that, the towing arm broke again.

Thursday night was no better, November Papa was delayed leaving for Basle with the port main undercarriage extension below limits, and the R.A.F. came to the rescue with compressed air. Ken Sheppardson was obviously concerned as an embattled Les Dray commented that it was bad enough not being able to find an air bottle without having the General Manager on his neck. Then Yankee Kilo returned from the runway with another mag. drop, the third night in a row this engine had played up, and Oscar Golf substituted, Foxtrot Yankee taking her Basle. The agony continued on Friday night when Oscar Golf went U/S at Perpignan and came back empty on a three engine ferry. Yankee Kilo flew from Basle to the French airport to collect the passengers. Oscar Golf was back on the line by midday Saturday however, to load a tour for Basle. Also that week, on the 6th., November Oscar had a Glasgow-Ostend charter, the return flight ten days later operated by her sister aircraft.

It was pouring with rain on the 11 July when November Oscar was being readied in the hangar for a cargo flight. November Papa was waiting to come inside as she had had an engine feathered in flight, and the engineers were so perplexed at the lack of any damage they wondered if the crew had feathered the wrong engine. The first DC6 M.O.D. charter through Lyneham occurred on 12 July when November Oscar uplifted cargo for Bahrein and returned Thursday evening. Yankee Kilo on the 2000 Basle on Friday 15th had to make a return there, which impacted on the programme, and Oscar Golf did not depart to Perpignan until early Saturday morning. She had been held up with a hydraulic pressure loss and was listed as airborne at 0100 (local) then: 'Not quite airborne, turned back, mag. drop, left.' To round off the night the main wheel of the big tractor punctured and one was borrowed from Invicta. There was an extra Perpignan by DC6 that day and also a Palma tour, a rarity now, with the only other visit in 1966 also by November Oscar later in the month.

1966 OIL LIFT AND A NEW LIVERY

On Monday 18th July, November Papa went to Glasgow for a tour to Tarbes, the airport used for pilgrimages to Lourdes; the same aircraft reversing the journey for the returning passengers a week later. Next day two Basle flights returned into Southend due to weather; November Papa took another Basle flight from the Essex airfield while Oscar Golf returned empty to Manston. The diversion by Oscar Golf was compounded by pitch control problems on the approach that caused some anxiety to John Mason and Jeep Jackson before John was able to put her down safely. Afterwards they took up part of the flooring and it was found that an extraneous object, which should not have been there, was entangled in the elevator cables.

The morning was a little fraught early on Wednesday 20th., Yankee Kilo was delayed leaving for Basle, getting away at 0400 after numbers 3 and 1 refused to start, and Ken Barker and Jim Jones were fetched out to go to Southend to assist Oscar Golf. There was a rather world weary comment in the book that night after more tribulations: 'The same old story, mag. drops, dead mags and finger trouble.' Yankee Kilo flew over to Ostend in the week, presumably for training, as the flight duration was over two hours.

While under line training at Air Ferry, Keith Sissons had, in fact, continued flying for Morton's and made use of two different uniforms. On 20 July he had a command check with David Laker and flew as captain from then on.

> *During that summer Oscar Whisky was parked at Manston and there was talk of it being sold for use in Biafra. (Keith Sissons)*

Difficulties continued over the weekend 22nd./24th. when metal in a filter meant a Saturday engine change on Yankee Kilo which had an air test next day. The engineers felt even more oppressed that Sunday, some disgusting passenger used November Papa's handbasin as a toilet, and they were trying to clear the pipes. Oscar Golf was causing concern with a persistent water leak in the cockpit: 'Another gyro filled with water,' but the crowning incident happened at 2349 when Catering shut up shop and there were no suppers available for the hangar staff. There was a near walkout but Invicta obliged; it was then discovered that the Invicta canteen not only served real food, but it was 6d. cheaper!

On Monday 25th's night Perpignan departure, Oscar Golf returned from the runway with a cockpit window defect, then returned again with an engine fire warning, this problem duplicated the next night on leaving for Basle. Two other night delays in the week were caused by a hostess arriving late and by the pilots overpriming a DC4's engines. A DC6 operated the third Wednesday Perpignan in the final week, one DC4 being serviced, and there were additional passenger flights by DC6 to Munich and Lyons. There were some delays that last Saturday and Sunday, the Venice tours in particular seemed prone to them as both were delayed making these tours late on three weekends out of the five. Considering that 186 hours were flown in the final weekend of July it was incredible what was achieved.

> *Subject to some health problems, Don Brooker had come off flying and taken over responsibilities as Operations Manager. Thunderstorms over France could be a serious problem at the heights the DC4s flew and he gave some wise advice in that sometimes, if the weather was bad, it may be best not to take-off at all, and sensible not to have to make a diversion. (Keith Sissons)*

During that amazing month Basle was visited on 160 occasions, a minimum of three times daily every day and with a much higher frequency at the weekends. This was the highest activity to the Swiss airport in Air Ferry's history.

DATE	TIME	
26/7/66	21:00	NO departed ½ late due to small hole in tip of rudder.
	22:00	FY departed.
	23:15	YK departed.
	23:30	OG departed returned 23:40 fire warning No 4 eng. Rectified departed 00:10.
	03:15	NO departed.
	03:30	Edgar departed.
27th	10:40	OG - 15 minutes late - crew unable to start #3 & 4 engines - (over priming)
	10:50	YK. - 20 minutes late - owing to movements of aircraft with tractor
27.7.66	05:00	FY. Oil leak cured by changing Vacuum pump no 3. No 4 Standing OK. Finish 0500.
	21:30	NO. Late - owing to ship's batteries being flattened by use of blue "Houchin". - Yellow Houchin being serviced - fan belt u/s.
28.7.66	19:15	NP departed air test.
	19:50	Returned NP satisfactory
	20:40	NO departed.
	21:55	YK departed.
	22:35	FY departed.

1966 OIL LIFT AND A NEW LIVERY

August   This was another very busy month and, in contrast to June especially, the programme ran smoothly. With two exceptions the tours to Venice, Genoa, Barcelona and Copenhagen ran like clockwork. There was no Copenhagen on Saturday 13th for some reason and there was a weather diversion into Ostend on the return Venice flight a week later. Almost as a finale to July's difficulties, Oscar Golf already late for the 0010 Perpignan on the 1st., had a snag soon after 0340 and had to be replaced by Foxtrot Yankee on her return from the 2100 flight; the passengers finally leaving at 0605. The night flight that day was taken by Yankee Kilo and an extension to her Check 1 was applied for, and granted, against the probability of bad weather at Perpignan.

There were three main DC4 delays that week, two Perpignans by a hydraulic leak and a mag. change and a Basle when an engine would not start. The Maintenance Book reflected the lighter mood from the slackening of serious faults when Bill Simpson signed off one night with:

> 'And so, once again the night throughout,
>
> A pleasant night without a doubt,
>
> May all the snags you have today,
>
> Be passed on to Sidi Ben Dray.'

The cabin heaters of both the DC4s and DC6s gave trouble from time to time and a note on Sunday 7th. said: 'FY cabin heater inoperative again, must be brought into hangar and ground tested.'

In general tours to Basle and Perpignan ran well and with some additional charters fitted in. In the second week November Oscar went up to R.A.F. Leconfield in Yorkshire and flew to Goteborg and Copenhagen before returning to Manston, while November Papa went to Dusseldorf on consecutive days. Early on Saturday 13th. Foxtrot Yankee had to divert into Southend coming back from Perpignan, undoubedly due to weather. There had been a series of DC6 flights to Perpignan at approximately 0345 on Saturday morning for some weeks, and the last one that day was a DC4 substitution with Oscar Golf carrying just 25 passengers on the flight.

The third week, 15/21 August, saw three more Leconfields, on these occasions the aircraft returned home direct from Goteborg. November Papa had some work done on Thursday 18th. prior to going to Leconfield next day but, when this was completed and ready for an air test, it was found Air Traffic Control would not allow one after 2200 hours, so it had to be carried out on the way up to Yorkshire next morning. The weather clamped down at Manston between 0400 and 0500 on Sunday 21st., catching out both Yankee Kilo on her return from Perpignan which diverted into Southend, and November Papa coming back from Venice, which stopped for a time at Ostend. Balair's HB-IBU was at Manston that day on an Invicta sub-charter and the Air Ferry engineers gave some assistance to the DC6.

November Oscar made an intriguing daytime trip to Perpignan on Tuesday 23rd., no passengers were carried so perhaps this was for freight. There was also an interesting note in the Maintenance Book which said: 'YK - Harry the Clock wanted a rudder check for excessive play. Rudder checked with locks in, locks out and external lock; no excessive play found, trim tabs operate satisfactorily.' Next day Yankee Kilo had to make a quick visit up to Wymeswold, it is not known if there was any connection, and returned to Manston two days later, leaving November Papa to carry out the first of the Wednesday night three Perpignans. Also in that week, Oscar Golf went to Maastricht, November Oscar to Lyons and Yankee Kilo made an early morning stop at Zurich en route to Basle, almost certainly a diversion on the last Sunday in the month.

There were two last delays near the end of August, on Monday 29th. Oscar Golf was late going to Basle due to an instrument defect and next night Foxtrot Yankee had all sorts of trouble getting away to the same destination. There was a ground run at midnight, the mag. board changed, HT lead checked, the jump lead changed, and finally the sparking plugs were changed after a 'cold pot' check. The aircraft finally taxied away up to the runway at 0255.

There was some training by both types, locally and at Ostend; November Oscar making one flight of six hours and another of four. On Monday 29th. both DC6s went to Leconfield once more, night stopped at Goteborg, and returned via Teesside Airport, once better known as R.A.F. Middleton St. George.

TWILIGHT OF THE PISTONS

September   The Inclusive Tours continued through September although scaling down a little. With autumn approaching there was more prospect of weather diversions and these did occur.

Both DC6s went to Dusseldorf in the first week, November Papa had a Basle-Gatwick-Basle flight, and Foxtrot Yankee took the first of three consecutive Sunday Luxembourgs by DC4, surprisingly the only occasions this airport was visited in 1966. The tours to Barcelona, which had operated weekly, increased in September with a DC6 flight each Saturday and an extra flight on Sunday 4th. Balair's HB-IBR was in early on Saturday 3rd., perhaps on a Basle sub-charter, and the aircraft was turned round and away again within 45 minutes. Captain Mason meanwhile was delayed leaving for Basle, with Foxtrot Yankee's cockpit heater U/S and a top beacon that would not revolve; the latter responded to being thumped hard and was declared O.K. During that afternoon's Perpignan the Captain reported that the de-icer boot on Foxtrot Yankee had inflated during the climb, but was alright afterwards, and the defect was rectified on return to Manston.

There was a different problem a day later, Monday 5th., when a message came back that Yankee Kilo was coming in with a virus aboard and Doctor McAvoy was sent for. Oscar Golf did some training at Ostend, coming back with an engine snagged because the pilots said it was slow to recover from feathering. The engineers found all four CSU levers locked incorrectly, the aircraft apparently having landed like that, and the propeller then feathered and unfeathered normally. The DC6 Basle that Monday was delayed, according to a droll comment in the handover book, due to the captain wanting personal refuelling before leaving.

November Papa left Manston with freight for Gibralter on Thursday 8th and that night bad weather over the Pyrenees caused Yankee Kilo to divert into Toulouse. The next night was also one of chaos and snags with aircraft fogbound, the engineers reported: '5 Machines and 1 Houchin, everybody with ****** ache!' At the weekend both Venice flights ran late and, to show the weather in Italy could also be bad, November Papa on the second one was diverted into Milan on the outward leg. Upon her return to Manston the aircraft was put into freight trim and left on Sunday night for Lyneham and another M.O.D. cargo to Aden. Oscar Golf returned to the tarmac late that night with a dead cut mag. before leaving for Basle but Yankee Kilo, on the Perpignan route, was held back for bad visibility and finally departed at 0240 on Monday 12th.

November Papa returned Aden-Rome, this leg taking 11 hours 40 minutes, to Lyneham and came back to Manston on the afternoon of Thursday 15th; within a few hours she had departed on another cargo journey, this time to Luton and Warsaw. November Oscar meanwhile was engaged on a freight flight Manston-Manchester-Stuttgart-Manston.

The Thursday Perpignan continued to be subject to incident, this time a very unexpected event. Yankee Kilo, flown by Keith Sissons and Bill Isaacs, operated the flight out according to schedule. In the early hours of Friday 16th. they set off for the return journey and there was soon an air of peaceful contentment in the cockpit as the DC4 droned back across France. Keith and Bill were suddenly brought out of their reverie by the door opening and a passenger's head appearing. They immediately sat up straight, carefully adjusted their ties, and were informed that one of the stewardesses was very ill. The hostess was foreign, possibly French, and her colleague was Maggie Studt.

Keith asked Bill to assess the situation and shortly after he reappeared to report: 'She is flat out, we have tried oxygen and loosening her clothes, but all to no effect'. At this point they declared an emergency and French Air Traffic Control responded very positively. They were diverted to Clermont Ferrand where they requested that a doctor and ambulance meet the aircraft. On landing Keith taxied quickly in and within a short while the hostess had been driven away to hospital.

It was only then that they realised that it would not be permissable to continue with just one stewardess and Keith asked if any of the passengers had any nursing or relevant experience. One lady had, and Maggie gave her a short introductory safety course after which they returned to Manston.

Early on Saturday morning 17th., with the programme running late due to weather, November Papa stopped at Basle en route to Genoa. Technical difficulties now added to the seasonal weather problems, Foxtrot Yankee reported a bang in flight and needed a new jump lead and board on return. For the DC6s, November Papa had returned with a pressurisation defect and was late out on Saturday's Barcelona due to crew hours. She was then late going to Venice, flew a Basle and was late again for Sunday nights Barcelona due to a booster pump change. Her sister aircraft, meanwhile, came back from Basle on Saturday with radio and instrument defects and was also late going to Venice. By Sunday evening the DC6 had been converted to freight trim and made the 1 hour positioning flight to Lyneham for an Aden.

1966 OIL LIFT AND A NEW LIVERY

AIR FERRY LIMITED

DAILY PROGRAMME FOR WEDNESDAY 21ST SEPTEMBER

ALL TIMES G.M.T.

MOVE	A/C	STD-STA	SECTOR	LOAD	FLT NO:	A/CREW	C/CREW
1	FY	- 0410	BSL - ~~MSE~~ STH	79	LK40/22 (COSMOS)	ASHPITEL CHAMPNEYS GILSON	MOLLI HOFFMAN
2	YK	- 0420	BSL - ~~MSE~~ STH	83	LK40/50	NICOL ISAACS	WILLCOX BYRNE
3	OG	- ~~0450~~ 1000	PGF - MSE	81+2	LK42/52 (LYONS)	TUBMAN JOHNSTON	SETCHELL ERECKSON
4	OG	0930 - 1150 1250 - ~~1510~~ 2000	MSE - BSL BSL - ~~MSE~~ LGW	NIL 78	MT LK40/24	BROWN WADDINGHAM	BIRD REES
5	~~YK~~	0940 - 1200 1300 - 1520	MSE - BSL BSL - MSE	NIL 72	MT LK40/54	SISSONS GUTTERIDGE*	NORTON JOHNSON
			G1 EX BASLE BY GLOBE AIR				
6	NP	1030 - 1310 1410 - 1650	MSE - PGF PGF - ~~MSE~~ LGW	76 98	LK1006 LK1006	WOOD* ROSS AHMAD F/E DUNLOP	HUCKLE* PARSONS
		NP AT LGW. PAX AT STH !!					
7	~~FY~~ NP	0730 22/9 STH ~~1930~~ - 2125 2255 - ~~0100~~ 1500 21/9	MSE - BSL BSL - MSE	66 63	LK41/310 LK41/210 (LEROY)	NICOL* HOPE F/E TOGHILL	MOLLI (1) BARNETT
8	~~YK~~ OG	0730 22/9 STH ~~2100~~ - 0030 0130 - 0450	~~MSE~~ - PGF PGF - MSE	NIL 75+1	MT LK42/53	ASHPITEL ISAACS	SETCHELL ERECKSON
9	~~OG~~ YK	0830 22/9 LGW ~~2230~~ - 0150 0300 - 0620	~~MSE~~ - PGF PGF - MSE	81 80	LK40/25 LK40/26	TUBMAN* JOHNSTON	WILLCOX FIRKIN
10	~~NP~~ FY	0830 22/9 LGW 2240 - 0200 0310 - 0630	~~MSE~~ - PGF PGF - MSE	83 80	LK40/53 LK40/54	CROPP WATSON	DUNN MANNING
	NO	0600 - 1215	ADE - CAI	FRT	LK302/39	LOCKHART SURRAGE F/E TILLEY	

AMENDMENT TO MONTHLY PROGRAMME WEEKS 37 - 42

MONDAY 26TH SEPTEMBER ADD

DC6/1	1415 - 1530	MSE - DUS	LK1098
	1630 - 1810	DUS - BSL	POSN
	1910 - 2105	BSL - MSE	LK40/18

THE DC4/1 DEPARTING AT 1600 IS NOW CANX.

TWILIGHT OF THE PISTONS

The day flights on Wednesday 21st, three Basles and a Perpignan, were all disrupted by the weather and diverted; Foxtrot Yankee and Yankee Kilo to Southend, the latter flown by Captain Brown and Mike Waddingham, with November Papa and Oscar Golf going to Gatwick. The Wednesday night Perpignans were operated between 0750 and 0925 on Thursday morning, from Southend by Yankee Kilo, and from Gatwick by Oscar Golf and November Papa. Foxtrot Yankee took another tour to Basle from the Essex airfield.

November Oscar came back from Aden that day, having missed the weather problems, but encountered some of her own as the Maintenance Book recorded:

1) fork lift had a fight with port flap, fork lift not hurt thank goodness, port flap lost. Damaged section removed, hope Jack can manufacture repair piece complete.

2) nose oleo seals busted on landing, AOG, SOS, ATL who will be here about lunch time.

3) pressurisation defect and re-seat to do.

While Oscar Golf was having a time-expired engine change completed, John Mason was delayed with Foxtrot Yankee at Basle on the night of Friday 23rd. with a mag. drop that led to a night stop for the crew and 85 passengers. The weather continued to be murky with Yankee Kilo late to that airport on Saturday morning due to being fogbound. The aircraft came back from the last Basle that day with a heavy vibration and fluctuating boost and revs on number 2 engine.

Early on Sunday 25th. the Venice and Genoa tours were combined by November Oscar before the final week started, with the accent swinging towards freighting. Fog still wrapped Manston in its clammy vapour on the morning of Monday 26th., delaying the take offs of two DC4s to Basle and November Papa to Lyneham. November Oscar flew a Dusseldorf-Basle passenger flight on Monday and over the night of 27th./28th. flew freight Manston-Manchester-Hanover-Manston; an engine had to be feathered due to a severe oil leak on the way to Hanover. Later that Wednesday, back in passenger trim, the DC6 was diverted into Geneva on the evening Basle. November Papa spent most of the week going to Aden and back, Foxtrot Yankee carried out cargo work Manston-Heathrow-Copenhagen-Milan-Heathrow-Manston, while Oscar Golf took freight to Madrid. On Friday 30th Yankee Kilo carried a full load of passengers from Southend to Munich, routing back via Basle early the next day.

Manchester and Heathrow would figure prominently in the programme for the rest of the year as Air Ferry had contracted to operate some of the B.E.A. and Lufthansa international scheduled freight services from those two destinations. The aircraft would operate on detachment at these airports, sometimes for two to three weeks, occasionally calling into Manston while passing if that was considered necessary.

October The month started with a mixture of passenger and freight work as the inclusive tours ran down and there were a few late seasonal charters, the second half of the month was all freight work.

November Oscar had positioned to Lyneham on the last day of September and on 1st October flew out via Istanbul-Sharjah-Gan-Cocos and Perth to Adelaide, returning the same route to Manston on 10th with a total time of 88 hours 40 minutes. A co-captain or senior first officer was usually carried on these long trips, on this occasion the crew included David Laker and Patrick Hope. The aircraft carried her last passengers of the year with a Jersey charter on Friday 14th., night stopped there and came back via Perpignan for the last visit to that airport in 1966. Then, on Sunday 16th., there was a return to Jersey to collect the 84 passengers, no doubt a DC4 charter at the time of booking. The following Tuesday it was back to Lyneham for a flight to Aden, routed out through Athens and Cairo, and back via Cairo and Rome on the 22nd. The aircraft did not fly again that month.

November Papa flew the last two Venice tours, the second not leaving until nine o'clock on Sunday 2nd., the aircraft returning Venice-Gatwick-Gatwick, where she went U/S and came back to Manston. After a Perpignan, a Cologne-Genoa and another Cologne, the DC6 changed over to cargo trim. On Monday 10th. the aircraft flew freight Manchester-Berlin, positioned to Milan, and went from there to join Oscar Golf at Heathrow from where she operated services to Copenhagen and Milan before returning to Manston on the 14th. Over the 17th./19th. the DC6 flew Manston-Milan-Heathrow-Milan-Heathrow-Manston. A Manston-Heathrow-

1966 OIL LIFT AND A NEW LIVERY

AIRCRAFT .... D.C.6. G. APNO

Date (1)	Daily Number of Flight Hrs (2)	Time Since New Hours	Mins.	Time Since Renewal of Certificate of Airworthiness Hours	Mins.	Landings	Particulars of all maintenance work, overhauls, repairs, modifications and mandatory inspections to the aircraft or its equipment. Particulars of any defects occurring in the aircraft or its equipment and of the rectification of such defects including a reference to the relevant entries in the Technical Log. Certificate that in carrying out the overhaul, repair, etc., all mandatory requirements applicable thereto have been complied with. (5)
Brought Forward		19947	08	7549	20	5866	
10.66	6.50	19953	58	7556	10	1	The current Check I period has been extended by 10 hrs to 410 hours. Authority: Chief Inspector's Concession No.
	5.15	19959	13	7561	25	1	
	5.15	19964	28	7566	40	—	Check I carried out at Manston to Approved Maintenance Schedule. Check II carried out at Manston to Ap...
	15.05	19979	33	7661	45	2	Ref: MANST/DC6/4 No.3 ARB App. Ref: 45DC 6/2. Ref: MANST/DC6/14 ARB App. Ref: 40/3/1
	8.15	19987	48	7600	—	1	Inspection Records Ref: No.3/1 Filed at Manston. Inspection Records Ref: 40/3/1 Fil...
	7.50	19995	38	7567	50	—	Signed: K. Barker Authority: A1/2677/69. Signed: [signature] Authority
	8.20	20004	08	7576	20	2	AIR FERRY LTD. Date: 13.10.66. AIR FERRY LTD. Date: 13...
							Tech Log Sheets 1517 to 1652
							3. CHECK I & C. of A. RENEWAL
							Certified that this aircraft is approved for renewal of its Certificate of Airworthiness.
							H.D. [signature] Air Registration Board 13th October 1966
Carried Forward	2000 4	05	—	—	—	5875	

109

TWILIGHT OF THE PISTONS

Munich-Manston followed on the 24th., there was an Ostend for training and a local flight before the aircraft positioned off to Hurn on the last day of the month.

The contribution made by Foxtrot Yankee that month was fairly brief. The DC4 operated three of the dwindling Basle tours, on the first of these she went U/S at Basle when the captain's gyro instruments stuck on take off. After a freight flight Manston-Manchester-Budapest-Manston on 3rd./4th., she went into the hangar on check for the remainder of the year.

November Papa at Heathrow, October 1966
(Air Britain - J.J. Halley)

Going back to the beginning of the month, the weekend of 1/2 October really saw the end of the tour work. Oscar Golf operated the last Barcelona and carried what would be her last passengers, back from Basle, on Monday 3rd. The series of freight services out of London Heathrow, with an aircraft on detachment there, began on 4 October when Oscar Golf flew to Heathrow via Milan. The aircraft carried out virtually daily flights to Le Bourget and also went to Milan, Copenhagen, Brussels and Amsterdam. There was a brief stop at Manston en route to Heathrow on the 10th., and the aircraft returned to Manston on the afternoon of Saturday 15th.

Between 19/22 October, Oscar Golf made a many-legged flight, Manston-Southend-Amsterdam-Malmo-Southend-Brussels-Orly-Lisbon-Orly-Brussels-Southend-Amsterdam-Malmo-Manston, and made the short journey to Southend and back the following day. On Thursday 27 October, while Yankee Kilo was on the last leg of her Heathrow schedule, Oscar Golf positioned to Heathrow to continue the Le Bourget service and made a brief return to Manston on Saturday afternoon, the 29th., before resuming freight work with a Heathrow-Frankfurt-Dusseldorf-Heathrow run at 0200 the next day. Oscar Golf had gone U/S at Heathrow with the nose leg flat, and the visit to Manston was for the seals to be renewed; back at Heathrow on Sunday the air pressure on the nose oleo was reported low again.

Oscar Golf with small tail marking, at Heathrow   (Eddie Fuller collection)

After the weekend tour work, Yankee Kilo went back to Munich on Sunday 2nd. to return the previous Friday's passengers to Southend. In the early morning the next day, while empty outwards to Perpignan, she had to return to Manston from some distance away recording a time of 3 hours 52 minutes. The flight was not repeated and was undoubedly sub-chartered; that night Yankee Kilo flew the last Basle of the season. The Maintenance Book was not as clear as usual in the first days of October, but Yankee Kilo had one delay at this time due to Tech. log snags, and a lightning strike to the port aileron trailing edge member.

The aircraft then did some training and combined a Maastricht charter with a Perpignan tour. Yankee Kilo flew the last DC4 Perpignan on Sunday 9th., and later that day was diverted to Brussels to collect the returning passengers, who should have been uplifted at Maastricht. Very early on Monday 10th. Yankee Kilo, piloted by Captains Vines and Honeyman, with Mike Waddingham as F/O, left for Lyneham, late for two reasons, a Britannia was stuck in the mud on the taxiway, whether at Lyneham or Manston is not known, and also due to a captain wanting cups of tea; a fact which drew a wrathful comment from the engineer waiting to go home.

1966 OIL LIFT AND A NEW LIVERY

From Lyneham the aircraft went to Aden and had to make a technical return there on leaving, coming back from Cairo to Manston on the 14th. On Saturday 15th., three hours after Oscar Golf had returned from Heathrow, Yankee Kilo positioned there to provide continuity on the Le Bourget and Milan schedules, and to make one flight to Jersey, before returning to Manston from Copenhagen on Friday 28th. In all there were 42 flights into Heathrow during October.

November   The flying hours achieved that November easily eclipsed all others and were nearly 50% up on the three previous years put together. The bulk of the activity came from the contracts for the scheduled freight service flown from Manchester and Heathrow, plus the M.O.D. long range work.

The Heathrow services continued and were operated by Oscar Golf from the 1st to the 22nd. November, although the nose oleo pressure problem continued. The aircraft flew the service on the 1st., but Dave Jennings went off to Heathrow as further servicing was required. November Oscar meanwhile, left Manston to replace Oscar Golf at 0005 on Wednesday 2nd., after a delay when she returned from the runway with the captain's inverter U/S. The DC6 flew three services, two to Frankfurt and one to Stockholm, and came back on the 5th. Oscar Golf had returned to Manston on the 2nd. for the defects to be cleared and the next day went to Ostend, before returning to Heathrow, from where the routes covered on the detachment were mainly Frankfurt and Copenhagen, but journeys were also made to Milan and Malmo.

On the occasions it was necessary for some of the engineers to work at Heathrow, they were not supposed to use the B.E.A. canteen as it was considered these facilities were for their staff only and in a nationalised airline the canteen was technically subsidised by the government. The same principle also applied to the B.E.A. canteen at Gatwick.

After spending most of November on detachment at Heathrow, at 2025 on Tuesday 22nd. Oscar Golf positioned from there to Manchester to operate two Frankfurt schedules and two Frankfurt-Dusseldorfs, one crew being Stan Hunnable and Mike Waddingham. She then returned to Manston on Sunday 27th., went to Ostend on a training sortie next day, and at 0900 on the 29th. started another freight flight, this time via Brussels, Orly and Lisbon. In all the aircraft only spent some seventy hours of the month at Manston.

Yankee Kilo started the Manchester contract and during the month had four detachments up at Manchester. The first departure from Manston, on the night of Tuesday 1st., was delayed due to the crew being late and then with a low fuel warning switch defect on an engine. The scheduled service operated Manchester-Frankfurt-Dusseldorf-Manchester at approximately 0100 hours, although this varied quite a lot, on four mornings each week from Wednesday to Saturday. Between the three Air Ferry aircraft that operated the route in November, this service was flown on each of the scheduled days, except that of Wednesday 16th. Yankee Kilo's first detachment ended with a different route, early in the evening of Saturday 5th., the aircraft flying Manchester-Prague-Manston.

Yankee Kilo went back to Manchester on Thursday 10th., taking over from November Papa and flew two services, although the one on Saturday did not go on to Dusseldorf, and with a return to Manston later that day. There were two local flights before a return to Manchester on Thursday 17th., for three services, and back to Manston on Saturday. Then there was a change over to passenger trim to enable the only passengers to be carried in November, and the last for 1966. The charter was for Luton-Rome on the night of the 23rd. where Yankee Kilo stopped for four nights and returned the group from the Eternal City to Luton on Sunday 27 November. After a long Manston-Ostend training sortie on Tuesday 29th., it was back to Manchester once more.

DC6 on the Cocos Islands, late 1966   (Patrick Hope)

111

TWILIGHT OF THE PISTONS

On the first of the month, November Papa left Hurn and travelled via Istanbul out to Riyadh, returning via Athens on the 4th. The connection between Bournemouth Airport and a Saudi Arabian city is almost certainly due to the presence of a B.A.C. factory at Hurn, and the supply of defence equipment to the Royal Saudi Air Force, who used British aircraft such as the Lightning, together with military support equipment. After this, on Tuesday 8th., November Papa went to Manchester from where she flew the Frankfurt-Dusseldorf service for two days and operated Manchester-Stockholm-Manston on the 11th. Three days later, the DC6 positioned to Stanstead for an engineering check which would last for the rest of the year.

November Oscar covered some of the Heathrow services as mentioned. Between 7th and 19th of the month the DC6 flew the second Adelaide, out via Lyneham-Istanbul-Sharjah-Masirah-Gan-Cocos and Perth, and routing back the same way, but missing out Masirah. The flight added a welcome 94 hours to the year total. On the 23 November the aircraft flew the second Riyadh delivery, following virtually the same route as her sister aircraft had used, but stopping at Kuwait on the way out.

December With two aircraft on check, the remaining three were kept well occupied in the last month of the year. December was again dominated by the Manchester and Heathrow work, the former running all month, and the latter up to Christmas Eve; all three aircraft in use operated both services.

November Oscar was the first to position to Heathrow on Friday 2nd., the Houchin at Manston was U/S and the aircraft was started by the trolley acc.:'But only just.' The DC6 remained at Heathrow for some reason until Tuesday 6th., when she flew to Southend and returned to Manston from there on Friday. After a local flight on Sunday the DC6 went back to Heathrow on Tuesday 13th. to operate the Copenhagen-Stockholm route on Wednesday, and positioned LAP-Hurn next day for another Kuwait-Riyadh, coming back this time via Nicosia to Manston.

November Oscar operated the four Manchester schedules from 21 December and came back to Manston on Christmas Eve, this flight being Hugh Tubman's last for Air Ferry, so that, with the exception of November Papa which was still at Stanstead, all the aircraft were in Thanet for Christmas. There was no flying until 28 December when November Oscar took freight from Manchester to Warsaw and finished the year with a training sortie to Ostend.

Oscar Golf returned from Lisbon on 1 December and did not fly again until she positioned to Heathrow on the 6th. The schedule on December 7th. must have been cancelled as Oscar Golf flew Heathrow-Heathrow with a note 'LBG weather,' indicating that Le Bourget was closed. Flights were made to Le Bourget, Amsterdam, Copenhagen and Stockholm and the DC4 returned Heathrow-Manston on the 13th. Next day it was back to Heathrow for five daily services, with a return to base on the 20th. On the 28th. the aircraft positioned to Manchester to operate the final three Frankfurt-Dusseldorf schedules of the year and returned to Manston from the last.

Yankee Kilo had operated the Thursday 1st.and Friday 2nd. schedules from Manchester and called into Manston on the Saturday evening, continuing on to Dusseldorf 1 hour 50 minutes later. At midday on Sunday the aircraft flew the Frankfurt-Manchester leg. Yankee Kilo operated four more schedules, from Wednesday 7th, and returned to Manston on Sunday 11th. On Tuesday it was off to Manchester once more; the third service that week stopped at Frankfurt on Friday 16th. for virtually twenty four hours before

Bill Wood and Paul Horsting   (Anna Turner nee Oates)

1966 OIL LIFT AND A NEW LIVERY

returning to Manchester, and the last cycle returned to Manston from Dusseldorf on Sunday 18th.

There was a need one day for a radio engineer to fly on the DC4 operating the Frankfurt service and Phil Townsend was chosen. He boarded the aircraft at Manston and flew the service to Frankfurt and Dusseldorf before the DC4 headed back to Manchester. In the winter darkness the weather was extremely poor and Phil, in the jump seat, had to endure a protracted and very dicey approach into Manchester.

Christmas Dance, Don Brooker, Anna Oates and Harry Chang (Anna Turner nee Oates)

Christmas Dance, Mrs. Everingham, Liz, Peter Everingham, Anna Oates and Harry Chang (Anna Turner nee Oates)

Morton's DC3 G-AMHJ
4 March 1966

TWILIGHT OF THE PISTONS

From the 20th./24th. Yankee Kilo was based at Heathrow again, flying to Amsterdam, Turin, Copenhagen and Stockholm from where she returned to Manston on 24 December; the aircraft did not fly again in 1966.

STATISTICS

In some ways 1966 saw Air Ferry at its zenith and four records were set. More hours, 1,432, were flown in July 1966 than in any other month of Air Ferry's history and the year total of 8,630 hours was never exceeded. The DC4s carried more passengers and flew more hours than in any other year.

As a comparison, the year totals to date were:

Year	Hours flown	Passengers	Flights made	Airports visited
1963	3,095	70,598	940	41
1964	6,516	153,057	2,520	77
1965	6,239	108,956	2,009	99
1966	8,630	154,309	1,934	91

An article published in the '*Aeroplane*' in 1967 provided some interesting statistics about the two Manston airlines. Although Air Ferry's figures for hours and passengers are slightly understated, the item provides an excellent snapshot of Invicta's phenomenal growth, and also its dependency on short-haul operations.

		Air Ferry		Invicta	
		1965	1966	1965	1966
Stage flights	(thousands)	3.4	2.9	1.9	5.2
Revenue hours	(thousands)	6.0	8.1	2.5	7.6
Passengers	(thousands)	107	153	120	310
Cargo	(thousand tons)	1.5	2.3	0.2	0.4

MANSTON

The year provided a fascinating stream of visiting aircraft with, for the military types, Varsities and Canberras in profusion. The Canberras came from many front line units including No's 3,13,14,16,17,31,85,and 98 Squadrons, in addition to No. 231 Operational Conversion Unit.

In January the military version of the Viking passed through. This was a Valetta from R.A.F. Germany named 'Loreley' It was used for the transfer of senior personnel and the gleaming transport reputedly had a thin fuselage skin from zealous polishing.

The Pyrene Runway Foamer had a busy year with at least three R.A.F. machines making involuntary diversions into Manston. In February a Dominie landed wheels up, while on 16 March Canberra XM244 touched down on the nose and starboard main wheels. After some repairs XM244 flew out again on 22 April. There was a further incident on 3 May when another Canberra made a landing with a suspect nosewheel, which fortunately proved to be in order.

There were Dutch Neptunes and Trackers, a Noratlas of the Italian Air Force and, in June, more Dutch visitors. An F27 brought Queen Juliana of the Netherlands to review the 1st. Battalion Royal Sussex Regiment at Canterbury, the F27 being accompanied by a Cessna 172 of the Netherlands Television Service.

Argonaut G-ALHY of British Midland, 1 April, 1966

Nine Luftwaffe Noratlases descended on Manston on 1 September, and early October saw the Gnat Trainers of the Red Arrows using the airfield for several days. A Royal Canadian Air Force Yukon visited later that month and three Vulcans flew in early in December

Civil aircraft provided similar variety, including company aircraft such as '*Flight's*' Baron, a Heron used by Shell and the Twin Comanche of Wright Rain Irrigation. Guiness Brewers Aztec called in and a Laker Queen Air.

1966 OIL LIFT AND A NEW LIVERY

A late March airline visitor was a DC3 of British Westpoint, teetering on the edge of liquidation; the aircraft passed through again a week later with the airline name painted over.

Two additional DC4s arrived for Invicta, G-ASZT and G-APID, and April visitors were G-ALHY and G-ALHG, Argonauts of British Midland Airways. A short while later, G-APID suffered a nosewheel failure on 20 June while taxiing out for a revenue flight, the surprising spectacle of a DC4 gently sinking onto it's nose,

Balair DC6 HB-IBU, 23 June, 1966

while in motion, a clear memory to those who happened to see it. This event naturally caused programming problems for Invicta and Lloyd International DC4 G-ARWK was called in for sub-charter work.

The star visitor of the year was an elegently proportioned Super Constellation of the American Flyers' Airline, while two Balair DC6s also appeared during the summer. Other airline representation included an Irelfly DC3, a Channel Viscount, Autair Ambassadors, a British Eagle BAC1-11 and a B.U.A. Viscount in the new livery of sandstone and blue.

R.A.F.

There was a formal end to the confrontation in Borneo, enabling the R.A.F. to withdraw forces from this part of the Far East. A significant presence still remained in the Gulf area of course, to protect British oil interests and to meet our treaty obligations to Kuwait.

Transport Command had two new types introduced in the year, the VC10 and the Andover, the military version of the Avro 748 that was already in airline service.

CIVIL

The '*Flight*' survey in April showed that other airlines were also changing to, or extending into, new equipment; the fleets of Autair and Channel Airways now including HS748s. Cambrian was using more Viscounts and British Midland now counted some Heralds in their fleet.

Britannias now featured prominently in the airline lists. B.K.S. had four, Britannia Airways had eight and B.U.A. five. Caledonian had re-equipped from three DC7s to six of the type. Laker, Lloyd and Transglobe had two Britannias each, while the British Eagle fleet now comprised seventeen Britannias and six Viscounts. Transmeridian switched from two DC4s to two DC7s and Dan-Air now operated a DC7 and introduced two Comets to make the transition onto pure jets. Invicta was listed as operating five DC4s and three Vikings.

Laker Airways had been unveiled in February and carried out the first revenue flight in July. Treffield Aviation was another newcomer to the independent scene from February onwards. As mentioned earlier, British Westpoint went into liquidation before the season was really underway, and another operator, A.C.E. Freighters with four Constellations, ceased operations in September.

AIR HOLDINGS

'*Flight*' also recorded the current status of the Air Holdings operating components, the main ones being B.U.A. with five Britannias, four Viscounts, three VC10s and ten BAC1-11s; B.U.A.F. with eight Carvairs and twenty one Bristol Freighters and B.U.(C.I.)A with six Heralds, ten DC3s and four Viscounts.

The Air Holdings '*Group News*' in February reported that the group carried 1,860,000 passengers in 1965. Air Ferry received several credits in connection with the DC6s, the June edition mentioned that Air Ferry would carry over 35,000 passengers to Basle, the centre of many Cosmos coach tours to Italy, Austria and Yugoslavia.

In May, B.U.A. aircraft were represented at the Biggin Hill Air Fair and the VC10 and BAC1-11 attracted attention with a fashion show to interest the crowds. In July a new livery for application throughout most of the group, in sandstone and a turquoise toned blue, was unveiled.

The August '*News*' gave early details of the 1967 Leroy Tours programme with most now being operated by B.U.A. There were many new features, two coach tours of Russia starting from Ostend, holidays based at Vienna, inexpensive holidays to Greece using B.U.A. Britannias, with others to Sicily and the Bay of Cadiz. 'Low cost-high value' holidays featuring flights to Basle with onward journeys by Leroy coaches would be operated by Gatwick BAC1-11s for the first time. The next month '*Group News*' was renamed '*Wingspan*.'

The headline of the November issue was concerned with the Government's travel currency restrictions, which came into force at the beginning of the month. The view was that this would have only a limited effect on overall holiday business. This issue also included an article entitled 'Air Ferry Prosper' with photographs and some details of Ken Sheppardson, Ron Illsley, Don Brooker, Mike Austin, Charles Carroll and Dick Sanders. At this time Air Ferry employed some two hundred people.

In December, Air Holdings acquired Lyons Tours and the Chairman's Christmas message was a combination of satisfaction at progress made, tempered with caution at the never ending need to control costs.

SAFETY
There was a severe accident to one of the independents on 1 September 1966 when a Britannia of Britannia Airways hit ground 1.5 miles short of the threshold while on approach to Ljubljana in Yugoslavia. There were 22 survivors from the disaster which resulted in 95 fatalities.

1966 was a bad year for the larger carriers with Air India, Lufthansa, All Nippon, Indian, Aeroflot, Canadian Pacific, Ansett-ANA, and an Egyptian airline all experiencing severe accidents. An aircraft of B.O.A.C. suffered a particularly unpleasant accident on 5 March when one of their Boeing 707s crashed near Mount Fuji in Japan.

OTHER EVENTS
The United Kingdom again started the year with some severe weather and, by March, was once more in the grip of a political campaign. The General Election resulted in a substantial Labour victory with a majority of ninety seven.

Another aviation personality was lost to the nation in March when Sir Sidney Camm, creator of the famous Hurricane, died. A strike of the Merchant Seamen occurred in May, the dispute lasting for seven weeks and causing considerable disruption to the import and export trades.

Economic problems caused the Government to impose a 'freeze' in July of wages, prices and dividends and to impose cuts in travel allowances. Any concern over this situation was dispelled later in the month in a wave of jubilation when England triumphed over Germany in the World Cup.

Technological events were to the fore in September, a month in which the new Severn Bridge was opened and the nuclear submarine '*Resolution*' was launched. The following month the nation joined in sorrow with a Welsh village called Aberfan after an old coal tip slid down a hillside, the sludge entombing those in its path. The local school took the brunt of the black slurry, the number of children involved making the tragedy especially poignant.

There were two great personal achievements to capture the headlines and evoke the spirit of explorers from an earlier age. Sheila Scott circumnavigated the world by a long route in her Comanche 260 named 'Myth Too', an incredible flight of some 32,000 miles in a single engined aircraft. A pre-war aviator, now turned yachtsman, Francis Chichester, had left Plymouth in August; he arrived in Sydney Australia, 107 days later having completed the longest non-stop solo voyage ever known.

On the world scene the recurring cycle of natural hazards was supplemented by a severe drought and famine in Africa.

The Soviet Union continued to demonstrate technical prowess by achieving the first soft landing of a probe, Luna 9, onto the moon, and political hardness by consigning two novelists to a labour camp for maligning the state by publishing work outside Russia. The U.S.A. response in the space race was to make a perfect landing

1966 OIL LIFT AND A NEW LIVERY

on the moon with Surveyor 1, which sent photographs back to earth.

President DeGaulle sent a shockwave through N.A.T.O. by suddenly announcing in March that France would leave the alliance, a threat carried out three months later leading to the withdrawal of U.S.A.F. units based in France to the U.K. and Spain. One unit, the 66th Tactical Reconaissance Wing, finding a new home at Upper Heyford in Oxfordshire.

The Rhodesian problem continued to exercise the United Nations, in April the Security Council authorised the use of force by the U.K. to prevent any ships from discharging oil intended for Rhodesia. In December, at a time when U Thant agreed to a second term as secretary general, a resolution was adopted imposing sanctions to prevent products, including oil, reaching Rhodesia.

In fiftieth anniversary commemorations some of the herculean struggles of the First World War were recalled, the battle of Jutland in May and later on the fearsome struggles at Verdun and the Battle of the Somme. A postscript to a later conflict occurred in September when two prominent Nazi leaders were released after serving their full sentences as war criminals.

The U.S. put an extraordinary reconnaissance aircraft into service, a fact unknown at the time, as the SR77 Blackbird was shrouded in secrecy. The anti-war movement had now gained momentum with many demonstrations by those who saw Vietnam as an attempt by a technological state to impose its will on a peasant society. Lyndon Johnson was beginning to isolate himself from the protests, reluctant to be the first American president in history to lose a war.

Riots were occurring in the U.S. for the fourth year running and people began to dread the long hot summers. Away in Vietnam there were violent Buddhist anti-Government demonstrations, while in the North Ho Chi Minh reiterated his determination to continue the war for twenty years. The U.S. despatched more troops, bringing the total deployed in Vietnam to 285,000, followed within months by the announcement from China that that country had successfully fired a nuclear equipped guided missile.

Two well known personalities were lost to the U.S. by the deaths of Admiral Nimitz, the architect of the U.S. Navy's victorious wartime Pacific campaigns and of Walt Disney whose cartoons and films had caused so much laughter and delight throughout the world.

Mrs. Wood, Liz, Bill Wood, Harry Chang, Ken Sheppardson, Pauline Pilcher
(Anna Turner nee Oates)

AIR FERRY LIMITED

Tariff

SPIRITS	Double Tot or Miniature Bottle	Quarter Bottle	Half Bottle
Brandy	2s 6d	6s 3d	12s 6d
Whisky	2s 6d	6s 3d	12s 6d
Gin	2s 6d	5s 0d	10s 0d

MINERALS	Per Bottle
Tonic	6d
Bitter Lemon	6d
Ginger Ale	6d
Ginger Beer	6d
Bottled Soda	6d

CIGARETTES	Packet of 20	Carton of 200
Rothmans King Size Filter	2s 0d	£1
Peter Stuyvesant	2s 0d	£1
Players	2s 0d	£1
Senior Service	2s 0d	£1
Piccadilly	2s 0d	£1

PLEASE REFER TO CUSTOMS NOTICE ON BACK PAGE BEFORE MAKING YOUR PURCHASES

CHAPTER 7
1967 A DOUBLE BLOW

THE AIRCRAFT

Douglas DC4   G-APYK   G-ASFY   G-ASOG   G-ARWI

Douglas DC6   G-APNO   G-APNP

The DC6s had been a great success in 1966 and it was intended to operate the same five aircraft fleet in 1967. With the Commercial department already turning their attention to the following year, at about this time consideration was given to re-equipment plans for 1968. Two possible types reviewed were the Sud-Aviation Caravelle and the Comet; with possible acquisition from Aerolineas Argentinias, who operated both types, and Mexicana whose fleet included the British airliner.

Following the high numbers of hours flown, and passengers and freight carried in 1966, the year started on an optimistic note with the continuing contract on the international scheduled freight service operated from Manchester.

THE CREWS

On the aircrew side there was now a very experienced main group of aircrew who remained throughout 1967. Captains who flew all year were Wood, Laker, Nicol, Ashpitel, Hunnable, Ross, Vines, Sissons, Cropp, Kellard and Ahmad. Tony Ahmad was promoted from Senior First Officer to Captain on 1 January together with Vic Surrage, although the latter left towards the end of November. There were two leavers, both in January, Captain Honeyman and Hugh Tubman, who left to carry on flying DC6s out in the Lebanon. The same month brought three joiners; Captain Adcock came from Invicta on the 9th, Captain Roberts the following day and Captain Pullinger on the 16th. Ron Pullinger came to Air Ferry from B.U.A. where his most recent type was the Britannia. Captain Brown left in March and Harry Chang during May.

Captain Ron Pullinger

Keith Sissons took three months off during the winter to fly an Aztec out to Nigeria for Bristow Helicopters on charter to Mobil Oil. Due to the problems in Nigeria, transportation was a problem and communications had broken down. One job that Keith carried out with the Aztec was to fly along the railway network to find out the location of the Mobil railway tankers.

The First Officers all year were Johnson, Jackson, Hope, Horsting, Champneys, Phillp, Waddingham, Watson and Gilson. There were four joiners in January, F/Os Mackie, El Fata from the Lebanon, Bainbridge and Waller.

The cabin crew establishment increased for what was expected to be the highest number of passengers carried to date. They included A/H Barber, Lyn Batney, Bennett, Steward Len Billett, A/H Britton, Lorna Brownridge, Cameron, Sue Chadwick, Mary Coates, Carol Dale, Ann Duffy, Catherine Dunn, Carol Fox, Gray, Greenway, Griffin, Holden, Jenny Holtan, V. Huckle, Liz Johnson, Kavanagh, Hazel King, Leonard, Una Lockeyear, Patricia MacCann, Manning, Molli, Margaret Norton, Anna Oates, Prybil, Hilary Reeks, Sue Smith, Jackie Southee, Maggie Studt, Linda Townsend and Pat Travers.

THE YEAR

The top ten airports visited in 1967 reverted to an all-European list, after the oil lift of the previous year. They were:

Basle	547
Milan	229
Perpignan	150
Manchester	99
Ostend	81
Frankfurt	62
Luxembourg	60
Dusseldorf	49
Luton	43
Palma	30

January The first movement of the year was recorded by Yankee Kilo, which departed for Gatwick and then to Tripoli, on Monday 2 January. Oscar Golf positioned up to Manchester on Tuesday night and, early on Wednesday, as Yankee Kilo was returning direct from Tripoli, Oscar Golf carried out the first Frankfurt-Dusseldorf of 1967. The aircraft continued the early morning schedule on Thursday, Friday and Saturday and returned to Manston later that day. Also that week, Yankee Kilo took freight from Manston to Strasbourg and made a long training sortie which included a landing at Ostend. The only DC6 movement was one with freight by November Oscar, Manston-Frankfurt-Brindisi-Cairo-Manston.

Yankee Kilo positioned to Manchester on Tuesday 10th. from where she departed at 0040 on Wednesday, crewed by Stan Hunnable and Mike Waddingham, to Frankfurt and Dusseldorf before returning, unusually, to Manston. The aircraft then flew up to Liverpool and returned to Manston two days later; while Yankee Kilo was at Liverpool, November Oscar positioned up to Manchester to take over the schedule for the Thursday, Friday and Saturday morning flights after which she too returned to Manston.

Yankee Kilo went to Ostend on the 16th. for training, and the next day November Papa flew a Stanstead-Stanstead before returning from her check back to Manston. Soon after 2215 on Tuesday 17th., Oscar Golf lifted off from Manston en-route for Manchester for another weeks freight flights. The Wednesday schedule did not depart until 0130, but the Thursday and Friday flights left at 0020 and 0033 respectively.

On Saturday 21 January, Oscar Golf left Manchester at 0109, crewed by Captain Adcock and First Officer Gutteridge. At 0414 the aircraft crashed while on approach to Frankfurt, one and three quarter miles from the runway; Oscar Golf was a total wreck and both crew members were killed. The accident was reported on the B.B.C. radio news at 1 o'clock that day and was the first indication to many people of the accident:

Cathy Dunn (Maura Hunnable)

1967 A DOUBLE BLOW

'A DC4 freight aircraft crashed early this morning near Frankfurt Airport with the loss of the two crew. The aircraft was operated by Air Ferry Ltd from Manston in Kent.'

Two days previously, November Oscar had flown to Lyneham for the third Adelaide flight, routed via Istanbul-Masirah-Gan-Cocos and Perth. The crew, including Andy Nicol, Dave Laker, Jeep, and Viv Kellard as navigator, were on Cocos when they heard the news of Oscar Golf. The flight returned, through Perth-Cocos-Gan-Sharjah-Ankara and Lyneham, to Manston on 29 January with another 93 hours recorded. This flight closely matched the first in that the aircraft left the Cocos Islands with some 70 hours elapsed from Lyneham, while the second Adelaide was 36 hours later at this point, delayed due to headwinds over the ocean.

Yankee Kilo went back to Manchester on Tuesday 24th. and flew the weeks four schedules to Germany before returning to Manston on Saturday 28th. There were two variations, the aircraft called into Manston from Dusseldorf after the Wednesday flight for a short stay before going on to Manchester, and the Saturday schedule changed the usual route by calling into Dusseldorf and then proceeding to Frankfurt. November Papa made her first revenue flight after her check, to Riyadh via Hurn-Istanbul-and Kuwait, returning Kuwait-Athens-Manston on 30th. On the last day of the month, after another local-Ostend flight, Yankee Kilo positioned to Manchester once more. So January ended with 291 hours flown, all the revenue flights being for freight, and with an aircraft lost. For the first time since 1963 Air Ferry was now operating four aircraft.

Jeep Jackson in the 'office' (Jeep Jackson)

February For some reason Yankee Kilo returned to Manston at 0235, having stopped only two and a half hours at Manchester. It is likely that she had uplifted cargo and that this was transferred at Manston to November Oscar, as this aircraft continued the schedule at 1220 to Frankfurt and Dusseldorf, then flew back to Manchester to operate the remainder of the weeks service. On Saturday 4th., instead of returning to Thanet, the DC6 positioned Manchester-Southend where it went on check.

Yankee Kilo returned to Manchester the next Tuesday although, unusually, she did not operate on Wednesday. The aircraft followed the usual route on Thursday and Friday and over Saturday and Sunday the aircraft flew Manchester-Manston-Frankfurt-Dusseldorf-Manchester-Manston. After an Ostend on Tuesday 14th., Yankee Kilo again operated the four schedules and came back to Manston on Saturday afternoon. Following another Ostend on Tuesday 21st., it was Yankee Kilo's turn to go on check - at Manston.

After a short Manston-Manston on Wednesday 8th. due to a snag on number 3 engine, Adrian Ross and Jeep in November Papa positioned to Gatwick for a Gatwick-Zurich-Manchester freight flight and returned to Manston the next day. That weekend November Papa carried the first passengers of 1967 with an Amsterdam-Oslo on Saturday morning and returned the group on Sunday night, the aircraft coming back to Manston, empty, on Monday evening. Between the 16th. and 20th. the DC6 operated another Kuwait-Riyadh freight run from Hurn, which was followed on the 23rd. by a lengthy training sortie to Ostend. Over the last weekend the aircraft carried more passengers, this time Le Bourget-Gatwick early on Saturday 25th., and took them back the next night.

TWILIGHT OF THE PISTONS

After a lengthy spell on the ground, from the previous 4 October, Foxtrot Yankee made a local flight on 18 February. The engineers had changed the tail marking during this time and the 'AF' on the fin and rudder was now much larger. On Tuesday 21 February, Foxtrot Yankee took over the Manchester run, operated the weeks four schedules, and came back to Manston at midday on the Saturday. She left again for Manchester on the last day of the month.

PASSENGER TICKET AND BAGGAGE CHECK
Issued by
AIR FERRY
LIMITED
MANSTON AIRPORT KENT

YOUR ATTENTION IS DRAWN TO THE IMPORTANT NOTICES
AND CONDITIONS OF CONTRACT PRINTED ON INSIDE COVERS

A publicity sheet produced for 1967 was aimed at Travel Agents and Inclusive Tour operators. The sheet explained that the IT charters were a series of flights booked by an IT Company who arrange a complete holiday for an all inclusive price. Air Ferry in 1967 operated these for Clarksons, Cosmos, Lyons, Leroys, Vista and Sunair Holidays to Spain, Switzerland, Italy, Luxembourg, Norway and Tangiers.

The sheet also gave some details for Affinity or Closed Group charters, which were flights carrying closed groups of members of associations or clubs which exist for purposes other than travel. It also explained that the flights could be performed with no restriction on the individual fares. Sports and Supporters clubs, factory and social clubs and other common interest groups would fall into this category as also would parties going to a special event, although tariff exemption would not necessarily be granted for these.

At this time Air Ferry had at least two sets of brothers on the staff, George and Gerry Cavell in the hangar, while Roy Doherty was in the hangar with Al in the Bonded Store. Al's abiding passion was Country & Western music, and in his spare time he performed on stage at various venues in Kent, where his way of singing in the Jim Reeves style was very popular.

March Air Ferry had been strong on the Finance side as both Tim Leigh and Mike Austin were qualified accountants. It was now considered that there should be a position of Leroy Group Chief Accountant, and Mike was given this post; necessitating a move to Tunbridge Wells and the exceptionally speedy acquisition of a driving licence as the motor bike was not thought quite appropriate for this elevated status. Mike's place at Manston was taken by Les Rickards. Rick had worked at Aquila Airways, the last operator of flying boats on scheduled and IT services in the U.K. He later spent some eight years in Lagos with Nigeria Airways; joining virtually at the beginning of this company following the closure of the West Africa Airways Corporation. While with Nigeria Airways, Rick spent some time as a Revenue Accountant, Chief Cashier and finally as Chief Accountant.

Foxtrot Yankee had a very busy month, flying every scheduled freight service from Manchester except one. The DC4 departed Manchester at 0055 on Wednesday 1 March for Frankfurt, where for some reason she was delayed for over twenty four hours, only returning to Manchester at 11 o'clock on Thursday morning. In the meantime, November Papa positioned up to Manchester on Wednesday and operated the Thursday morning schedule to Frankfurt and Dusseldorf. Foxtrot Yankee then flew the remaining two services and came back to Manston on Saturday 4th. Training sorties were flown on Sunday and Monday, then four services to Germany from Manchester and back to Manston on Saturday 11th. The exact replica of this was flown the following week, including the training, and with a return on the 18th.

1967 A DOUBLE BLOW

That evening Foxtrot Yankee took freight Manston-Frankfurt-Brindisi-Cairo-Brindisi-Frankfurt-Manston, getting back on Tuesday, and going off later that day to Manchester for the scheduled service, flown only three times that week with a return to Manston on Friday 24th. The DC4 took freight to Benghazi over the weekend and went back to Manchester on Tuesday 28th., again flying three services, but this time the last of the series, and reappeared at Manston on Friday 31st. at the end of what had proved to be an eventful contract.

On 23rd. March Yankee Kilo had an air test after her check, this DC4 also now bearing the enlarged 'AF' tail markings. Later that day she carried the first tour passengers of the year to Rotterdam and before the end of March flew another Rotterdam and two Basles, all with passengers, and an Ostend training sortie.

For the DC6s, November Oscar had a quiet month, returning from her check at Southend on the 11th. and now looked extremely smart with a large 'AF' on the tail in place of the somewhat undersized union jack which had previously adorned her. In the remainder of March the aircraft operated two freight charters, a Manston-Manchester-Prague-Manston and one to Bremen from Manston, plus two lengthy Ostend training flights.

As previously mentioned, November Papa was called to assist at Manchester on the Thursday 2nd. scheduled service, the aircraft remaining there until the next day, from where she flew to Hanover before returning to Manston. After this came a leisurely trip to Athens, taking passengers out very early on Monday 13th., and returning with them late on Saturday night. The next flight looks unusual in the records without more facts to provide an explanation; the aircraft flew Manston-Frankfurt-Milan-Perpignan-Valencia-Malaga-Tenerife-Frankfurt-Manston between 22/27 March, apparently carrying 53 passengers on the Milan leg, although this could have been an instance of the crew being economical with the paper work! At the end of the month November Papa was at Istanbul, en-route to Saudi Arabia.

The most unusual visit of the year at Manston, in terms of what happened as a consequence, occurred on 31 March when Cessna 172 G-AVDC flew in. As it was leaving, the light aircraft taxied past November Oscar while the DC6 was running up it's four powerful engines, and the hapless Cessna was promptly blown upside down, to the surprise and consternation of its pilot. Over the weekend of 19/21 May the fork lift was loaned to Northern Air Services to lift the Cessna onto a lorry.

Foxtrot Yankee and Yankee Kilo, Invicta's new hangar at right   (Roy Doherty)

April   There were two passenger flights on 1 April, both to Berlin, by Yankee Kilo and November Oscar which left within twenty five minutes minutes of one another. Yankee Kilo did some training and flew passengers to Basle, Bremen and Rotterdam. Between 10th. and 25th. April the aircraft made a series of flights in and out of Luton, which were cleverly arranged to fit in with tours through Manston, to minimise the effect of empty positioning legs. The first two, for example, Manston-Luton-Basle-Manston and Manston-Luton-Bremen-Manston both carried passengers on two of the three legs and this pattern was repeated to these destinations and to Luxembourg. The Bremen flight mentioned above had an unintentional extra landing as it

TWILIGHT OF THE PISTONS

was diverted into Ostend on Wednesday 12th. through bad weather at Manston. There was also a Luxembourg-Gatwick from which a Bordeaux-Dublin charter was flown, the passengers being returned after a Luxembourg-Luton flight two days later. Over the last part of the month Yankee Kilo did more Ostend training sorties and tours to Rotterdam.

Yankee Kilo, 27 April, 1967

When it was time for the annual budget speech, Ken Sheppardson anxious for any news that might affect the finances, asked Peggy Marshall from Accounts to sit in his car and make notes as the speech was broadcast on the radio.

Foxtrot Yankee did not fly until 10th. April when she positioned to Cardiff and spent the next two weeks based at Rhoose Airport, flying passenger charters to Beauvais and Rotterdam, the last one returning via Gatwick to Manston on 25 April. After this the aircraft went to Rotterdam, the most frequently used airport that month, to Le Bourget and took over the Luton work for the last few days.

November Oscar carried out some training in the first week, going to Ostend and making ten landings on Monday 3rd. On Sunday 9th. a new inclusive tour destination, Bergen, appeared in the programme and November Oscar took the first one with 101 passengers at 1045. The tour lasted six days and provided wonderful excursions through a still snow-covered Norway. After a Manchester-Budapest freight flight the second Bergen routed home through Gatwick on Thursday 13th. undoubtedly because of continuing murky weather at Manston, night-stopped and came back on Friday. There were nine Bergens in April, six operated by November Oscar, which also went to Tangier with the first IT to the Moroccan resort. After that the aircraft operated two freight charters, a Manston-Bristol-Amsterdam-Cagliari-Dusseldorf-Manston and an M.O.D. flight Manston-Lyneham-Akrotiri-Manston. November Oscar's last trip of the month was a passenger charter to Rome.

Reverting back to the beginning of the month, on 1 April November Papa continued on from Istanbul to Riyadh and Dubai, returning through Istanbul and Frankfurt. After a local flight on 5 April there were two journeys to Aden from Lyneham, unusually without coming back to Thanet in between them, and with a Lyneham-Lyneham of 30 minutes before the second departure. After a Bergen on the 19th., the aircraft changed back to freight configuration and, after a slight delay due to a door warning defect, flew Manston-Lyneham-Malta-Manston. On return a dent in the prop. spinner had to be dressed out, and left for final plannishing by J Mills at a later date. The aircraft then resumed passenger work for the remainder of the month to Rotterdam, Bergen, now with a large AF on the tail, and to Le Bourget and Tangier.

Lorna Brownridge and Jenny Holtan shared Maggie Studt's flat for a time. Life was exciting for young air hostesses and, as they found Maggie's drive for efficiency extended to too many cleaning duties, they found somewhere else to live.

May   This month was a spring miscellany of passenger work, using Luton and combined with the emergence of 1967s inclusive tours from Manston to some new destinations, and also some freight flights.

Since the loss of Oscar Golf, Ken Sheppardson had been looking for a suitable DC4 available for lease to fill the gap and, on Tuesday 2 May, direct from Cairo, G-ARWI flew into Manston. Previously used by Air Ferry on occasion for sub-charters, the Lloyd International aircraft now went into the hangar to be prepared for her new work; the labourers being kept on all the following Saturday to carry on the job of rubbing down the letters on the aircraft. Back in 1944, Whisky India had joined the U.S.A.A.F. the week after Oscar Golf. Post-war she flew with American Airlines, Alaska Airlines and finally came to Lloyd in the U.K. in 1962.

Some crew changes had occurred since January, Captains Brown and Chang had left, and Captain Davies came in March, staying until the end of August; at one time he flew for Nigeria Airways. Bill Isaacs came back in April, F/O Nay joined the same month and First Officer Fisher started on 15 May; new to the area he found accomodation above the small cafe opposite the church in Minster. Don Nay and Dick Fisher were friends from the same training course at Oxford. On leaving the air force, Dick had bought a tobacconists shop in Bournemouth which he ran until, one day at the local airport, he met one of his ex-service colleagues descending the steps from an airliner, and resolved to take up flying again. The arrival of Whisky India heralded a small group of Lloyd aircrew also coming to Manston for a time, these were Captains Steel and Morriss with First Officers Dykes, Miles and Sigurdson; Bill Steel arriving for what would be his third season with Air Ferry.

1967 A DOUBLE BLOW

The passenger work through Luton connected to Bremen, Luxembourg and Basle continued throughout the month and was shared by all three DC4s once Whisky India was in service. Yankee Kilo was on a Check 1 during the first week and, on 4 May, Dave Jennings completed his part of this work prior to transferring to his new duties as a Flight Engineer the following week.

On Sunday 7th., Foxtrot Yankee was delayed leaving for Bremen when number 1 engine failed to start, blowing the mags. out, and later on the aircraft arrived at Luton with the number 2 feathered, this believed to be due to CSU failure. In the first two weeks, between the Luton flights, Yankee Kilo went to Ostend on training, flew the first tour to Perpignan at 1705 on Saturday 6 May, and on Sunday 14th. called into Calais on the way back from Basle.

On 13 May Foxtrot Yankee took the first Saturday Madrid tour and on the return to Manston on Sunday this aircraft also stopped at Calais. Lorna Brownridge was on this flight and recalled the aircraft having cabin heater problems. It is not known if the use of Calais was technical, to collect some passengers or due to weather. On Monday, however, both DC4s returned to Calais, Foxtrot Yankee's number 1 initially proving difficult to start and blew the mags. out again. The Sunday night Perpignan was definitely a diversion, as Foxtrot Yankee went into Toulouse due to weather.

With high overheads, Ken Sheppardson had to run a tight ship as regards the finances, and the need for economy was occasionally considered somewhat mean. Passengers on the longer flights were provided with packed meals but this concession did not extend to the crews. Some of the pilots had an agreement with the stewardesses who provided them with something to eat, quite a few of the hostesses being excellent cooks.

Lorna Brownridge (Lorna Monje nee Brownridge)

On one flight captained by Keith Sissons, it could have been 1966 or 1967, Cathy Dunn brought a very appetising tray of mushroom soup up to the cockpit, but unfortunately tripped as she entered. On the cockpit floor of the DC4 there was a trap concealing the fuel dump shute control and Cathy spent the next hour cleaning soup from this.

In the third week Whisky India made her first revenue flight, to Basle flown by Stan Davis, and Yankee Kilo took the Saturday Milan tour on the 20th. November Oscar, having had auto pilot defects in the week, had worse to come when she was towed with the torque link connected and rendered U/S. The aircraft was defuelled, the aerials disconnected, and the DC6 was brought into the hangar to be jacked up for work on the nose leg. After checks for retraction, free fall, correct steering, damage to the torque link and for correct wheel spin, the aircraft was considered serviceable. This drama, being on Saturday, led to several aircraft changes from those programmed. Yankee Kilo went twice to Basle on Sunday, the first a change of programme with Whisky India and the second, flown by Ron Pullinger and Mike Waddingham, held up by a traffic delay.

TWILIGHT OF THE PISTONS

Yankee Kilo was called upon to go to Milan again for the flight due out on Monday 22nd., although this finally departed at 0150 on Tuesday. November Papa had been duly refuelled, departed on time, but returned from the runway with instrument defects. Although Harry Burgess was called in, the defects could not be cleared, and Yankee Kilo substituted. Foxtrot Yankee was having radio trouble about this time, Phil Townsend leaving information for Ron Blake next morning, and Whisky India substituted for her. The activity quickened in the last ten days, with all three DC4s going into Luton and also flying tours from Manston, especially to Basle, the most used airport, with Foxtrot Yankee going there on twelve occasions within four days and Yankee Kilo eight times in three. Foxtrot Yankee had a change of role with a Manston-Tunis-Manston freight flight on the 23rd./24th., the first and only occasion this airport was used by Air Ferry.

During the week Yankee Kilo suffered a lightning strike, this time on the starboard aileron, and temporary repairs were carried out while Whisky India substituted to allow time for this to be done. There were only two delays on the night of Friday 26th., when Yankee Kilo's departure for Perpignan was held up due to a door warning defect and November Oscar, already delayed through Foxtrot Yankee being late, had an instrument defect and stood on the end of the runway for twenty minutes. The weather caused some problems on the last Saturday night and Sunday morning; it was Whisky India's turn to have a lightning strike, and on return from Perpignan she had to have a compass swing because of this. Yankee Kilo had a leak in the cabin roof in the vicinity of the cabin heater in the heavy rain. Whisky India finished the month in Nuremburg, having brought a full load of passengers from Glasgow at 0210 on Wednesday 31st., and returned these nocturnal travellers from Nuremburg at 0035 the next morning.

Another M.O.D. freight flight to Kuwait and Riyadh was operated by November Oscar from Hurn at the beginning of the month, coming back through Cairo. The DC6 then switched to IT work, including Bergen, Tangier and the first of the Milans. This flight was late leaving due to the runway being closed while foam was cleared away following an earlier emergency. Between 15/17 May, November Oscar reverted to freighting by flying out of Heathrow, to Copenhagen and twice to Milan. The latter visits were to the second of Milan's airports, Linate, whereas the tour flying used Milan Malpensa. Included in the tour work for the rest of the month was the first Venice, coupled with a Milan, the first Tuesday night Madrid, and five consecutive Milans over the last few days.

> *Steve Pigg, ever one to be on the airfield however early, recalls an early morning flight by an unnamed captain about to start the engines on one of the DC6s. Eddie Edgar, hands thrust deep into the pockets of his white coat, growled across to Steve: 'You watch the mess he makes of this,' as the big engine coughed and spluttered in wreaths of smoke.*

November Papa had a similar month to her sister aircraft, although she went to Rome on 6 May, one of only three passenger charters there that year. The DC6 went from Hurn to Riyadh in the second week, coming back through Khamis Mushayt and Jeddah, returning direct from there to Manston in 12 hours 35 minutes. The aircraft flew a Manston-Oslo-Bergen-Manston, the departure for Oslo being delayed due to weather at Bergen, and arrived back with two lifejackets missing, presumed stolen. Both DC6s flew Basle-Manchester tours. The Milan tours built up rapidly with, from Saturday 20 May, daily flights to this destination, a continuity only broken on 11 July for a sub-charter.

June The season was planned to be at the maximum aircraft utilisation, at a fairly evenly distributed level, through the months of June until September in terms of hours to be flown and passengers carried. Some problems were encountered in the first days of the month, November Papa returned from the runway on the night of the 1st. with no VOR, but no defects were found, and the malfunction was put down to freak weather conditions.

The Perpignan on the night of 1/2 June was flown by Keith Sissons and Bill Isaacs in Yankee Kilo. During Friday 2nd. the engineers were unable to clear all of Yankee Kilos' defects and Foxtrot Yankee was switched over on the programme for Basle. With Whisky India on a Luxembourg-Luton, this probably accounted for there being no 2200 Friday Perpignan, although Yankee Kilo went to Basle at 1900.

Early on Saturday 3rd., three consecutive aircraft arrived back with defects, both DC6s and Foxtrot Yankee from Basle. This was the first of five Basles running at the beginning of that days programme. Yankee Kilo flew the second at 0135, the aircraft being listed as having some radio defects. November Oscar took the next

1967 A DOUBLE BLOW

and when Whisky India had a technical delay on the fourth, when number 1 was difficult to start, it was still only 0910. The fifth Basle was by Yankee Kilo, somewhat late after all the pressures, but the aircraft arrived back with nil defects.

One of the Ground Hostesses, Patricia Dobson, had flown back with her family on this tour and, immediately changing into her uniform, she went on duty in Traffic and assisted with the ticketing of the passengers for the 1700 Perpignan while Yankee Kilo was readied for this flight. After the routine work was completed, Patricia played with some of the children on the tour before the flight departed from the tarmac, in good time and with no technical delay.

Yankee Kilo headed out over Dover, as she had done so many times before, but over France the familiar journey changed to one of terrible proportions. At 2104 the aircraft crashed some thirty five miles from its destination after striking a spur of the Pyrenees, with all on board being killed. The DC4 had been carrying 83 passengers and 5 crew; Captain Pullinger, Bill Isaacs, Richard Fisher with Hostesses Catherine Dunn and Patricia MacCann; now all were gone.

The passengers had included an infant, two entire families from the East Riding of Yorkshire, some children and six young men aged eighteen to twenty from South London, who had decided to make their first air trip together. A five-month old baby was orphaned when her young parents died. One young woman had a premonition of disaster and left the coach taking passengers from Victoria to Manston. Her mother, going to see her other daughter, a Lyons courier waiting to meet the flight, continued with her journey and was one of those killed.

The accident was picked up as front page news in the Sunday papers and, back at Manston, Peter Everingham on duty in Traffic tried to ensure there were no papers on sale in the terminal. He achieved this although, of course, many arriving passengers on the coaches had already purchased their papers on the way. A BAC 1-11 departed Manston for Perpignan at 0500, although it is not known if this was to collect the passengers who were due to return on Yankee Kilo, or was the 0230 programmed departure.

Everyone at Manston was very shocked, one of the Invicta DC4s had preceded Yankee Kilo to Perpignan and the two groups of passengers boarded their aircraft at the same time. One of the Invicta ground hostesses had exchanged some banter with the young men at the end of the Air Ferry queue and could not get their faces out of her mind.

Lorna Brownridge had been on many of the Perpignan flights and was originally down as part of the crew for Saturday's 1700 departure. She had gone and asked Len Billet, who prepared the rosters, if she could have the first June weekend off. Len had agreed to at least put Lorna on standby, and substituted Cathy Dunn in her place. Lorna, naturally, was the subject of terribly conflicting emotions, of relief that she had not been on the aircraft and a feeling of guilt for some time that the roster had been changed at her request.

The weekend programme meanwhile continued. November Oscar was delayed at Palma on Sunday morning due to distributor problems, not getting back until 0130 on Monday when this unit was changed; the aircraft having to be moved into the hangar for the work due to the weather conditions. Eddie Edgar appended a final note to another wet night: 'P.S., can I now finish what remains of my holiday?'

Some of the passengers' families came to Manston in the days following the accident, traumatic visits for them and for the staff who met them, especially for Ken Sheppardson as the General Manager. Other visitors were from the Air Accident Investigation team from the Civil Aviation Authority, a presence that would last some time.

The unseasonal weather also gave Whisky India a pounding. She arrived back at 2230 one night and a brief check around the aircraft at hail stone damage revealed too much work for the night shift to rectify. The aircraft was made the standby with a survey being required in daylight to assess all the damage. Some days later, on arrival back from Basle with high oil consumption on one engine and an oil leak on another, there was a technical discussion on Whisky India's fuel system. This was a recurring theme as she came back from a Bremen-Luton on the 16th. with the MIDAS U/S and another fuel system query.

The two remaining DC4s were worked very hard for the rest of June and indeed for the remainder of the season. Foxtrot Yankee and Whisky India flew 680 hours between them in June and the two DC6s flew 555 hours. The activity concentrated on the three main tour destinations, of the 252 flights in the month, 193 went to Basle, Milan and Perpignan.

TWILIGHT OF THE PISTONS

With just two DC4s again, there were problems in maintaining the schedules without any unplanned unserviceability and there were many sub-charters in 1967. There were at least seven to Perpignan in June and probably more. Transavia of Holland's DC6, PH-TRB, flew in to provide sub-charter back up on Saturday 10th., and operated through until Monday night. The tractor driver made himself unpopular that Sunday as he took home the keys to the tractor fuel tank and the GPU.

PH-TRB was back at Manston at 0030 on Saturday 17th. and had a troubled weekend. Between flights she had some snags worked on by the engineers, including a retraction test on the nose leg micro switch, and she arrived back from Perpignan on Sunday with number 3 feathered, although she was serviceable and left for Basle three and a half hours later. The daily programmes for this weekend, carefully kept by Steve Pigg down the years, show the flights rostered for this aircraft were operated by Captain Merriam with a crew of four and an Air Ferry hostess.

Foxtrot Yankee in the hangar

Barcelona now appeared on the DC4 IT programme, at 2200 on Sundays, with Whisky India making the first departure, somewhat late, at 0055 on Monday 19th. Whisky India was delayed due to engine starting problems then, on arrival back from her second Basle flight, a cracked cylinder required a change. The next two Basles were covered by Foxtrot Yankee substituting for her and November Oscar substituting for Foxtrot Yankee. By Tuesday, Whisky India was back at Luton, with that nights Perpignan sub-chartered and another sub-charter being required on Thursday 22nd.

Transavia helped out again over the weekend 24th./25th., with both PH-TRB and PH-TRA operating this time. On Sunday there was an unusual event when Whisky India's number 4 starter switch was inadvertently operated causing the propeller to turn. The cabin roof of the bowser standing underneath suffered a cut, but the prop was undamaged and an alignment check was satisfactory. That day PH-TRA returned from a flight needing a heavy weather check and positioned back to Rotterdam on Monday while, that night, an Invicta DC4 operated LK121, the 1900 tour to Basle. Also on Monday night, both DC6s suffered delays before leaving. November Papa's was due to an incorrect fuel load having been put aboard, needing a defuelling exercise before going to Milan, while November Oscar on a Palma had a query by Captain Laker on her number 4 engine hours although, after a Milan next day, it was the number 2 engine that was changed - and number 3 had a half-life check.

On Tuesday night, the 27th., while Whisky India was on the way to Basle, Foxtrot Yankee had to make a technical return from an hour out, due to number 3 engine running rough, and Whisky India finally took the Perpignan flight four and a half hours late at 0230; the second Basle for Tuesday night being sub-charterd. Foxtrot Yankee had an air test on Wednesday, but the result was not satisfactory, and number 3 was changed.

Whisky India was delayed going to Basle early on Thursday 29th, the number 3 engine and propeller were time expired and the Ministry contact, Mr. Humphries, had to be telephoned with a request for an emergency extension at 0230 in the morning. Eddie noted that: 'Mr. Humpries will be up here today to sort it out!' That night, and Friday 30th., were two more Perpignan sub-charters, as Whisky India was excluded from the programme, and Foxtrot Yankee was operating the nights Basles. For this weekend, and for most of the remainder of the season, the assistance came from the DC6 of the French company Transunion, with F-BOEV rostered for the Friday night flight.

For 1967 the DC4 Perpignan programme was a 2200 departure each weekday night, at 1715 on Saturdays, and two Sunday departures, at 0230 and 1130. The DC6s made a fortnightly day flight on Saturdays, the tour on Saturday 24th. prompted Bill Wood to request a storage for fire masks and hats as these items were being lodged in spaces round the radio station. June, being a peak month, featured some Saturday/Sunday 2200 flights, most of which seem to have been taken by the chartered aircraft. The flights using Luton continued through most of the month with Whisky India carrying out a Bremen-Luton to fly into that airport for the last time on Monday 26th. In addition to these, and the main tours, the two remaining DC4s also went to Luxembourg on six occasions.

1967 A DOUBLE BLOW

The DC6s went mainly to Milan with usually 12 flights per week and over 50 flights in June. There were night flights each day and with two on Wednesdays, Thursdays and Sundays, and afternoon flights on Saturdays and Sundays. November Papa went to Milan on Thursday 8th., the captain reporting that number 2 engine had only 1 hour 25 minutes to being time expired. The engine was changed next day, with an air test in the evening, before she took the Friday Milan; this flight had 110 passengers and needed some additional life jackets to be put on board by the engineers.

The other DC6 ITs were mostly at night, with departures to Tangier at midnight each third Tuesday and Saturday; to Madrid each third Tuesday and Saturday at 2200, and to Venice each third Monday and Friday at 2200. The Palma tours were more frequent and left every third Monday and Friday at 2200, while the Sunday flight departed at 1030, operating every second week in June and weekly from July onwards. A series of passenger charters by the DC6s between Manchester and Basle started in mid May and lasted until October. Although only six or seven a month, they caused some difficulties when the programme came under strain with some sub-charters occasionally being required on the IT flights from Manston.

On top of this busy programme, some Scandinavian airports were also visited; Oslo by November Oscar, and Helsinki and Copenhagen by November Papa; this aircraft also flew an Edinburgh-Rome passenger charter at the end of June.

Two aircrew joined on Monday 5 June; with all the attention sharply focussed on the tragedy of the previous Saturday night the new Second Officers, Alan Breedon and Simon Searle, must have wondered what they had let themselves in for. Alan soon took to the local scene by living in a caravan situated not far from the end of the runway.

July   June had passed in a dogged determination to keep the programme running, in spite of the ill fortune that had struck so hard and so unexpectedly. A feeling of being under seige had intruded into what had been an almost normal season after the arrival of Whisky India. The media and the specialist press had covered the two accidents and now the Ministry checking procedures intensified, with check captains riding on some operational flights as well as training sorties. These had been quite frequent since January and intensified during the ensuing five months. Ostend was used almost exclusively for training, of the 81 flights there in 1967 only four were for programmed passenger tours and two more were weather diversions. The remaining sorties, seventeen in July alone, accounted for 241 flying hours, and these figures exclude Manston-Manston local flights.

Tony Ahmad returned from one IT flight on which a check captain had ridden in the jump seat, laughing that the 'thumbs up' gestures he and his first officer used to confirm communications between them were understood, had almost resulted in their thumbs going up one another's nostrils. The training for the new aircrew was completely destroyed; as one recalled: 'The Ministry tore into everything.'

This was another hectic month with the flights to Basle, Milan and Perpignan accounting for four fifths of the activity. The first Saturday, Whisky India arrived at Manston with a part of the wing leading edge skin torn away, and Transunion's F-BOEV went to Perpignan in her place. November Oscar had been delayed going to Milan, as the captain had arrived late, and came back with a defective cylinder due to a damaged piston, the cylinder was changed. To add to the night's difficulties, Foxtrot Yankee came back from her Perpignan with a dead magneto on number 3 engine.

The Tangier that day was sub-chartered and November Papa flew the early Sunday Perpignan four and a half hours late. The flights scheduled for the Transunion DC6 to operate included two Perpignans and a Basle, while an Invicta DC4 was again on the programme for Monday's 1900 Basle. Whisky India on the following Basle was delayed there with a fuel pump defect, traced to a booster coil, that was rectified by Balair with a sharp tap from a blunt instrument! Following the Wednesday night Perpignan, Whisky India went on a Check 1 and had the wing leading edge and also nose wheel beam repairs carried out, and did not fly until Saturday afternoon, resulting in sub-charters for the Thursday and Friday night tours.

The weekend of 7/9 July passed fairly uneventfully, with F-BOEV again in support, although November Papa was delayed on a Basle due to having a wheel and brake pad changed. Another Basle that week was held up for an unusual reason, while a foreign body dropped into the control pedestal of a DC4 was extracted.

The weekends of course were extremely busy and any build up of delays naturally affected the later Sunday departures. For the weekend of 14th./16th., both Transavia and Transunion flew in to provide support, the

TWILIGHT OF THE PISTONS

French DC6 being F-BNUZ, which flew a Basle and a Milan. Whisky India came back from Basle with many defects, leading to Foxtrot Yankee taking the next one in substitution, and resulting in the 2200 to Barcelona on Sunday 16th. finally leaving on that aircraft, over six hours late, on Monday morning. Although the Monday night Perpignan departed close to time, Whisky India was then diverted into Toulouse.

In contrast to the earlier years when the Vikings tended to keep to schedule and the DC4 programmes creaked under the strain, now it was the DC6 schedules that came under most pressure. The rest of the Tangier tours and those to Palma, Madrid and Venice went well, while the Manchester-Basles continued. In addition, November Oscar went to Helsinki twice and to Copenhagen, while November Papa took a charter Glasgow-Tarbes on Monday 17th. and returned the group a week later. Interestingly, as so often happened, 103 passengers were on the outward leg and only 101 returned; one often wondered what stories lay behind the number changes. November Oscar flew an extra Milan on Friday 14th., going on to Edinburgh and then back to Manston.

Foxtrot Yankee taxies in   (Steve Pigg)

Whereas the main Milan tours had run well to schedule in the traumatic month of June, with only four of those having significant delays, July was just the reverse. There were about seven flights with delays and at least ten were sub-chartered, with a big break affecting Tuesday 18th. until Thursday 20th., with four consecutive flights missed. On Tuesday, November Oscar flew a Manston-Manston, returning with the number 2 engine feathered and a cylinder exhaust rocker arm fractured, she was replaced by November Papa on the Basle-Manchester. On Wednesday, after a Basle, some distributor studs sheared on this aircraft and the propeller and other components were removed for engineers to come over from Sabena in Belgium to assist with the repair. A Britannia of Britannia Airways, G-ANBE, came in that day to provide support. On Thursday, November Oscar had to have an engine change, with the Britannia being recorded as being over an hour late arriving on the sub-charter that she was flying.

Transunion's DC6 was back for the weekend of 21st./23rd., while both the DC4s and DC6s had some technical difficulties. Foxtrot Yankee needed jump leads changed at Basle, while Whisky India came back from the runway with a dead magneto. November Oscar was late off the chocks to Milan due to an electrical fault and then had to return from the runway to collect some fortunate passengers who had arrived late, and very nearly had their holiday spoilt.

On Tuesday 25th., Whisky India again returned from the runway, this time with an RPM defect and Captain Kellard made a duplicate inspection before leaving for Basle, although an adjustment was still required on arrival back. On her next flight, another Basle early on Wednesday, the aircraft was delayed due to poor weather at the Swiss airport. Later that day November Oscar was in the wars when some propeller blades were damaged by stones during a ground run and the DC6s were changed over, while the blades were cleaned up in the hangar. November Papa, as substitution, was then held up because the petrol bowser was unserviceable and one was borrowed from Invicta.

For the last weekend, F-BNUZ came back to Manston once more and November Papa had problems. She came back from Palma with an undercarriage snag and on Saturday numerous retraction tests were carried out before the aircraft was cleared on an air test during the afternoon. Transunion's DC6 then had the sheer bolt in the tow bar break, resulting in the mainplane striking some steps, but fortunately without any material damage. By this time November Papa, which had operated a Basle-Manchester-Basle, came back with more undercarriage snags as the nose leg seals were leaking again, but this was rectified before Sunday mornings Palma.

August   Two B.U.A. pilots, Captains Underhill and Roocroft, joined Air Ferry on 1 August and resumed their association with the DC6s they had operated previously.

1967 A DOUBLE BLOW

This was the height of the summer in terms of hours flown, although the profiles of the four months from June to September were remarkably similar in terms of hours, numbers of flights, and the fact that four fifths of these were to Basle, Milan and Perpignan. The DC4 utilisation also reached its peak in August. Prior to the 1967 season, the highest number of hours flown by two aircraft in a month was in July 1966 by Foxtrot Yankee and Yankee Kilo with 676 hours which, with Oscar Golf's contribution added, gave a total of 992. The hours flown by Foxtrot Yankee and Whisky India from June to September in 1967 were 680, 749, 829 and 724 respectively; an amazing number considering the reason this became necessary.

Whisky India started the month with a tour to Dinard, only visited on five occasions by Air Ferry. The Milans on the night of Thursday 3rd. were not trouble free, November Oscar went unserviceable there, an engine reverse defect classified 'AOG,' while the departure from Manston of her sister aircraft was held up, firstly when the Flight Engineer found a cracked exhaust segment, and then while a spare for November Oscar, a feathering pump, was made ready.

On Friday, Whisky India had to make a technical return after leaving for Basle due to an electrical fault and was replaced by Foxtrot Yankee, but she was back on the line for the nights Perpignan, albeit an hour or so late. At the weekend, Transunion's F-BOEV came in again, the Saturday nights Milan left at five minutes past midnight, via Basle, while the DC4s had a torrid time due to defects and poor weather. Whisky India was delayed for a wheel change and a change of fuel load, while Foxtrot Yankee was held up prior to going to Perpignan with an electrical fire warning defect on start up. At Perpignan she returned there and the writer's records have the note:'To collect passengers,' so it is probable that one of the coaches returning from Spain had been delayed and the aircraft went back to collect some of the tour that had arrived late. The aircraft arrived back at 0015 with a heavy oil leak on number 1 engine that was traced to a cracked cylinder rocker cap, but the engineers had her away for the Sunday Barcelona, although somewhat late again, at 0120 on Monday morning.

On Monday 7th. August, November Oscar had a propeller change while November Papa had a cylinder change following an oil leak. Next day November Papa returned to the tarmac with a mag. drop, unusual on the DC6s, before crew training at Ostend. That night the aircraft came back after take-off for Milan with a feathered number 3 engine and Charles Carroll decided to sub-charter the flight to B.U.A. On Wednesday 9th., Foxtrot Yankee went to Ostend on crew training, with four headsets installed for the Ministry Inspectors on board.

For the weekend 11th./13th., F-BOEV flew in again and was positioned on the pad ready when, on start up, all the starter motors failed and an electrician had to be sent for. The Air Ferry DC6s somehow had to be changed over, as both had delays due to positioning the aircraft and changes of fuel load; November Oscar leaving for Milan at 0005 on Sunday, with her sister aircraft departing to Tangier twenty minutes later. Transunion's Echo Victor then had more snags, with a fuel priming solenoid defect, before going to Basle.

Trans-Union's DC6 F-BOEV 5 August, 1967

Invicta also had their incidents of course; on 11 August a DC4 returning from a pilgrimage to Lourdes was reported in the paper to have burst a tyre after a forced landing. The aircraft had to land at Manston because of hydraulic trouble although, as the passengers came from Cardiff, that was presumably the destination.

TWILIGHT OF THE PISTONS

The next week brought problems for Whisky India with, on different flights, a delay as 'AOG' for a windscreen wiper motor, a return from the runway with a dead mag., followed by another return due to a feathering switch; on Tuesday 15th. she had an engine change. Also that day, Foxtrot Yankee returned off the runway with a dead cut mag. and the jump lead and mag. board unserviceable, leading to a two hour delay before departing to Basle.

The Palma on Friday 18th. was held up when November Oscar returned from 1 hour 20 minutes out with the aircraft flown back in high blower, with a suspected faulty low blower clutch. The flight had to be sub-chartered, while the DC6 went into the hangar for an engine change. The staff experienced their own difficulties, one of the engineers being called home due to a domestic problem. With the weekend round again, Transunion's Echo Victor was back and the programme ran well.

There was some stormy weather during the latter part of the month. During the Wednesday morning of the 23rd., Foxtrot Yankee came back from a Basle having suffered a lightning strike. Poor weather affected the rest of that day and for days after that. On Thursday 24th., both DC6s went to Milan on time and returned to Manston the following morning, albeit late, but Foxtrot Yankee coming back from Perpignan three hours later had to put into Southend. Bad weather over Switzerland also caused two delays the coincidence of which would have been hard to predict. Whisky India on the 0140 to Basle on Monday 21st. was diverted to Zurich and the same aircraft, leaving at 0130 on Monday 28th., was subjected to a similar diversion.

Poor weather continued through the weekend 25th./27th., with Transunion's Echo Victor helping again. November Oscar's Saturday Madrid was held up due to an unserviceable inverter found during the preflight check and, on return, was diverted into Gatwick. The DC6s continued under pressure; before November Oscar's Palma on the 28th., an engineer started a scare in operations about short engine hours available and: 'Then panic broke out with Mr. Humphries phoned by Operations.' November Papa needed an air test next day, a late one at 2325, and left for Milan an hour later.

Whisky India had one last delay, the aircraft had arrived back from Basle with snags, but the captain agreed to take the aircraft, which finally left for the 31 August Perpignan at 0355 on 1 September. With autumn approaching, the Luxembourg ITs began to build up with six being flown by the DC4s in the last half of the month.

November Papa   (Eddie Fuller collection)

The less frequent DC6 tours and the Manchester-Basles kept close to schedule, considering the hectic pace of the year although, as mentioned, the main exception was the Milan tours, which again took most of the strain with just over twenty five percent. being late or sub-chartered. November Papa went to Oslo the on 9 August, making a practice ILS approach at Stanstead on the way back, and made the last visit to Helsinki on the 25th. As mentioned previously, there were numerous check flights to Ostend in the month and all four aircraft participated in this. The Ministry checking continued; one pilot had terrible trouble with an instrument rating renewal, and problems were found with the check procedures of another which invalidated the training he had carried out.

September   September was remarkable in two ways, the weather during the month caused the most diversions that Air Ferry encountered, and the sighting of the flying saucer. During the morning of the 1st., November Oscar needed some work at Basle which was carried out by Balair. Foxtrot Yankee had a defect on number 4 engine with an RPM drop and timing defects on both mags., her Perpignan being taken by Transunion's Echo Victor. Apart from a slight delay between Perpignans, when Whisky India had new brake pads fitted,

1967 A DOUBLE BLOW

the weekend ran well until Sunday night's Milan. November Papa returned to the tarmac with a radar snag, but finally left at 0225, the captain agreeing to do this with the wing heater unserviceable.

The weather problems were severe on the night of Monday 4th., and the following morning November Oscar returning from Venice went to Stanstead, Foxtrot Yankee coming back from Perpignan put into Southend, flying the next Basle from there and then returning to Manston. Whisky India en-route from Basle ended up at Lydd, from where she flew to Luxembourg, returning this time to Southend, from where she flew a Basle before coming back to Manston.

On Friday night, the 8th., Foxtrot Yankee arrived back from Basle with number 1 engine feathered, due to reduction gear damage, and the motor was changed during the night. F-BOEV came in for her regular visit and was unserviceable early on Sunday morning with sparking plug trouble, and again in the afternoon with an ignition fault.

Foxtrot Yankee on finals, 12 September, 1967

There were similar difficulties with fog and poor visibility from Wednesday 13th. through to the end of the weekend. Whisky India went to Zurich instead of Basle, to Frankfurt instead of Luxembourg, and on Saturday night returned from Perpignan via Ostend, due to limits at Manston. November Papa coming back from Madrid the same night landed at Gatwick and flew the next Basle tour from there. F-BOEV was in support again that weekend, needing some plugs changed on Saturday that she must have had on board, as they were listed as: 'Transunion's.'

The Milan on Saturday was extremely late as November Oscar, off chocks at 2310, returned to the tarmac for a banging noise in the hold to be investigated. The cabin heater was checked and found to be backfiring severely and, when this was sorted out, the fog that caused the other aircraft to divert away from Manston had clamped down; the DC6 finally left at 1010 on Sunday 17th. By the end of Sunday the delays had not all been resolved, both Perpignans were many hours late and this had rippled through to delay the nights Barcelona. In spite of all this, and still with only two DC4s, it was amazing what was achieved and not many of the Perpignan tours had to be sub-chartered.

The weather at Basle continued to be poor on Monday, delaying two flights there, while on another, Foxtrot Yankee was held up at Basle with a dead cut mag. which was rectified by Balair changing the jump lead. On inspection back at Manston the engineers changed it again owing to the poor condition.

Whisky India left Manston at 1245 on Tuesday 19th. and again diverted into Frankfurt, where the aircraft stayed for twenty four hours before coming back empty. The pilots were unable to start the number 2 engine and Eddie Edgar was called in to go to Frankfurt, while Ron Illsley was appraised of the situation at 0250. A Milan tour was delayed once more on Wednesday 20th., when November Papa had a snag on one engine and then it was noted a propeller on another had only two hours left, a concession being obtained for another five hours to complete the flight. The next nights Perpignan was held up so that an 'AOG' de-icer pump, obtained from Southend, could be fitted to Foxtrot Yankee.

For sub-charter work the next weekend it was Invicta's DC4s that were programmed to operate Basles on Saturday and Sunday, 23rd/24th September. By the 25th. of the month the poor weather had moved to Italy, and November Oscar went to Rimini as the alternate to Venice.

On Wednesday 27th. a midday Luxembourg did go to that airport, but this time Whisky India stayed there for virtually twenty four hours and again returned empty. Keith Sissons and F/O El Fata brought Whisky India back on a three engine ferry; this time it was a cylinder problem, and when the aircraft was brought into the hangar at Manston they found metal in the filter so the engine, number 4, had to be changed.

TWILIGHT OF THE PISTONS

DAILY PROGRAMME FOR SATURDAY SEPTEMBER, 23RD 1967

ALL TIMES G.M.T.

ROVE	A/C	STD - STA	SECTOR	LOAD	FLT NOs	A/CREW	C/CREW
1	FY	0000 - 0030	BSL - MSE	61	LK 144	MORRISS SIGURDSSON	MANNING SOUTHEE
2	FY	0120 - 0340 0430 - 0650	MSE - BSL BSL - MSE	POSN FOR 82	LK 102 LK 102	SISSONS MILES	MILLI OATES
3	INVICTA D.C.4	0130 - 0350 0440 - 0700	MSE - BSL BSL - MSE	POSN FOR 84	LK 146 LK 146		
4	HP	0000 - 0520	MIL - MSE	93oINF	LK 232	VINES HORSTING DUNLOP	FOX GRIFFIN TOWNSEND
5	MI	0000 - 0540	PGF - MSE	74	LK 214	ROBERTS BAINBRIDGE	HOLDEN PRIBYL
6	HO	0000 - 0545	BSL - MSE	89	LK 254	LAKER JOHNSTON TILLEY	HOLTAM LOCKEYEAR REEKS
7	MI	0830 - 1050 1150 - 1410	MSE - BSL BSL - MSE	POSN FOR 83	LK 104 LK 104	EAMES WATSON	BARBER CAMERON
8	HP	0850 - 1050 1150 - 1350	MSE - BSL BSL - MSE	27o2COMPS 83o2COMPS	LK 153 LK 154	UNDERHILL CHAMPNEYS JENNINGS	BILLETT DALE HORTON
9	FY	0930 - 1150 1250 - 1510	MSE - BSL BSL - MSE	POSN FOR 83	LK 105 LK 106	CROPP RAY BREEDON (S/V)	BRITTON DUFFY
10	HO	1230 - 1350 1615 - 1735	MSE - LUX LUX - MSE	84 84	LK 331 LK 332	ROSS SIMPSON SHERWOOD	OATNEY KAVANAGH SMITH
11	HP	1430 - 1720 1830 - 2120	MSE - MIL MIL - MSE	17 54	LK 233 LK 234	NICOL HOPE BLANDFORD	BENNETT DALE GREENWAY
12	MI	1510 - 1730 1830 - 2050	MSE - BSL BSL - MSE	52 77	LK 107 LK 108	STEEL WADDINGHAM	BARBER CAMERON
13	FY	1730 - 2050 2200 - 0120	MSE - PGF PGF - MSE	69 75	LK 215 LK 216	HUNNABLE GILSON	STUDY SOUTHEE
14	MI	2210 - 0030 0130 - 0350	MSE - I BSL - MSE	42 83	LK 109 LK 110	ROBERTS BAINBRIDGE	KING LEONARD
15	HO	2230 - 0120 0230 - 0520	MSE - MIL MIL - MSE	POSN FOR 81	LK 220 LK 220	VINES PHILLP TOGHILL	BROWNRIDGE GRAY TRAVERS
16	HP	2340 - 0425 0525 - 1010	MSE - TMG TMG - MSE	98 102	LK 249 LK 250	WOOD HORSTING DUNLOP	COATES CHADWICK JOHNSON

1967 A DOUBLE BLOW

AIR FERRY LIMITED

DAILY PROGRAMME FOR SUNDAY SEPTEMBER 24TH 1967

ALL TIMES G.M.T.

MOVE	A/C	STD - STA	SECTOR	LOAD	FLT NO:	A/CREW	C/CREW
1	FY	0000 - 0120	PGF - MSE	75	LK 216	HUNNABLE / GILSON	STUDT / SOUTHEE
2	FY	0230 - 0558 / 0650 - 1020	MSE - PGF / PGF - MSE	82 / 81	LK 217 / LK 218	ASHPITEL / FATA	HOLDEN / PRIBYL
3	VI	0000 - 0350	BSL - MSE	83	LK 110	ROBERTS / BAINBRIDGE	KING / LEONARD
4	VI	0440 - 0700 / 0800 - 1020	MSE - BSL / BSL - MSE	POSN FOR / 82	LK 112 / LK 112	EAMES / NAY	HOLTAM / LOCKEYEAR
5	NO	0000 - 0520	MIL - MSE	81	LK 220	VINES / PHILLP / TOGHILL	BROWNRIDGE / GRAY / TRAVERS
6	INVICTA D.C.4	0820 - 1040 / 1140 - 1400	MSE - BSL / BSL - MSE	POSN FOR / 73	LK 148 / LK 148		
7	NO	0840 - 1035 / 1135 - 1330	MSE - BSL / BSL - MSE	POSN FOR / 104	LK 402 / LK 402	UNDERHILL / JOHNSTON / JENNINGS	BRITTON / KAVANAGH / MOLLI
8	NP	0000 - 1010	TNG - MSE	102	LK 250	WOOD / HORSTING / DUNLOP	COATES / CHADWICK / JOHNSON
9	NP	1110 - 1440 / 1540 - 1910	MSE - PMI / PMI - MSE	POSN FOR / 104+INF	LK 416 / LK 416	ROSS / SIMPSON / TILLEY	BATNEY / MANNING / NORTON
10	FY	1120 - 1340 / 1440 - 1700	MSE - BSL / BSL - MSE	POSN FOR / 84	LK 114 / LK 114	MORRISS / SIGURDSSON	BILLETT / REEKS
11	VI	1230 - 1470 / 1615 - 1755	MSE - LUX / LUX - MSE	82 / 83	LK 331 / LK 332	STEEL / MILES	CAMERON / DALE
12	NO	1430 - 1720 / 1830 - 2120	MSE - MIL / MIL - MSE	16+2COMPS / 74	LK 295 / LK 236	NICOL / HOPE / BLANDFORD	BRITTON / KAVANAGH / SMITH
13	FY	1900 - 2120 / 2210 - 0030	MSE - BSL / BSL - MSE	81 / 84	LK 115 / LK 116	HUNNABLE / GILSON	DUFFY / SOUTHEE
14	NP	2150 - 0040 / 0140 - 0430	MSE - MIL / MIL - MSE	POSN FOR / 103	LK 244 / LK 244	ROOCROFT / CHAMPREYS / SHERWOOD	GREENWAY / LEONARD / OATES
15	VI	2200 - 0200 / 0300 - 0700	MSE - BCN / BCN - MSE	48 / 80	LK 427 / LK 428	CROPP / WADDINGHAM	STUDT / BARBER
16	NO	2230 - 0120 / 0230 - 0520	MSE - MIL / MIL - MSE	POSN FOR / 48+2COMPS	LK 222 / LK 222	VINES / PHILLP / TOGHILL	FOX / GRIFFIN / TOWNSEND

These programmes are from Steve Pigg's collection

TWILIGHT OF THE PISTONS

The freight season was coming round again and November Oscar carried out a Manchester-Hanover charter. On the 29th her sister aircraft was at Manchester for a Basle tour, going on from there to collect passengers from Milan.

Both the DC4s and November Papa again carried out training and checks at Ostend in September, but it was November Oscar which made the front page.

> *The Air Holdings newspaper 'Wingspan' for October had a front page article entitled: 'Saucer Sighted' which read: 'When Captain Fred Underhill picked up his Air Ferry flight report sheet at Palma airport on 10 September he did not realise that when he landed back at Manston it would contain notes on a 'flying saucer' seen over the Pyrenees!*
>
> *But as dusk approached, the crew of DC6 'November Oscar' witnessed the incredible. Says Fred: 'It appeared first as a blur on the horizon travelling across our bows at a terrific speed, about seventy miles away. We could see it was metallic and going so fast it had a haze around it. Shape-wise it looked like an upturned ice-cream cone.*
>
> *By now I was quite convinced I must be imagining things. But my first officer, Patrick Hope and engineer Brian Dunlop, who by now had seen the thing, confirmed my thoughts. Just to check, though, I buzzed through to steward Len Billett and asked him to look out left. He was flabbergasted too. In fact Len could see it from the cabin for longer than we could.*
>
> *All in all we on the flight deck saw the saucer for about two and a half minutes I suppose. After crossing us it swung down, below and behind us now travelling much slower about our speed - 300 mph.'*
>
> *Back at Manston the incident was reported to R.A.F. air traffic control. A top level investigator will be talking first hand to Captain Underhill.'*

There was some talk of the sighting being a U.S. spacecraft, and that N.A.S.A. had been to Manston, but the manned Gemini series of space flights had ended in late 1966, so the mystery remains.

Reg Eames left at this time, and the final note in the engineers' book for September was an important administrative item, to ensure the aircraft had the correct document aboard to allow them to uplift fuel abroad on credit: 'Please ensure the fuel carnet is changed in November Papa.'

October   The inclusive tours virtually ended in October. Both DC4s flew the remaining Basles, with Foxtrot Yankee having to make a return from the runway with a mag. drop on Sunday 1st., while Whisky India took the last tour there on Saturday 7th.

Adrian Ross, Ken Sheppardson and Pauline Pilcher (Anna Turner nee Oates)

1967 A DOUBLE BLOW

Both DC4s also went to Luxembourg, the most used airport in the month with eighteen flights. On Wednesday 4th. Whisky India's number 3 engine failed on take-off from Luxembourg with a full load of passengers, the crew being Keith Sissons, George Gilson and Simon Searle as P3, but they continued on back to Manston. Keith was left reflecting that it was a good thing number 3 had not failed a week earlier, when he brought the DC4 out of that airport on the three engine ferry, or he would been down to two motors on the same side at a very critical point. Poor weather affected these tours and Foxtrot Yankee was diverted to Frankfurt en-route for Luxembourg on the 6th.

> *On one of the Luxembourgs, the crew reported back an engine fault on a DC4, and Tony O'Reilly put the names of the engine bay fitters into a hat to decide who should go out to make the repairs. This fell to Roger Pearce and Barry Bull who, when they arrived and checked the aircraft, found that no work was needed and were able to join the tour which, on that occasion, visited Frankfurt. (Roger Pearce)*

> *One of the freight flights loaded at Manston consisted of a cargo of bullion, the weight being so great that only one layer was able to be spread along the length of the cabin floor. (Peggy Marshall)*

They changed an engine on Foxtrot Yankee on Friday 13th., and when they manoeuvred the DC4 out of the hangar, the tractor driver parked the aircraft on pan 17, the hangar corner one; damaging the starboard wing tip and aileron trailing edge in the process. Repairs were made and the next flight took passengers to Ostend on Sunday.

On Saturday, Whisky India took passengers to Ostend at 0930 and must have been scheduled to make another flight later on as the engineering notes read: 'No 1330 take off, bad weather.' This must have cleared, as at 1725 Whisky India took the final Perpignan, incredibly the last occasion that an Air Ferry DC4 would make this journey. On the 20th., Whisky India took 81 passengers to Munich, and went unserviceable there with an ignition defect, so Foxtrot Yankee flew over to Munich on Sunday night to collect the passengers. Whisky India finally left for Manston at 1255 on Monday.

On the 24th., Foxtrot Yankee returned to Manston from nearly an hour out to Luxembourg due to poor weather there, and the aircraft finally left an hour and a half later to Brussels as the alternate.

Foxtrot Yankee had an engine change on the last Saturday, while on Sunday 29th. Whisky India with 84 passengers aborted a flight to Luxembourg with number 4 feathered due to low oil pressure and high oil temperature. As Foxtrot Yankee was by then already on the way to Luxembourg, it fell to November Oscar as substitution to make the final Luxembourg tour of the season. This change was unexpected, with the DC6 in freight trim, but the engineers commenced reseating at 1230 and by 1515 she was on the way to Luxembourg.

November Oscar operated four times in passenger trim and three in freight configuration during October. After a Basle and a Basle-Manchester, she returned to Manchester for a freight flight to Le Bourget and followed this with two cargo journeys from the Lightning fighter base at R.A.F. Binbrook in Lincolnshire to Luqa airfield in Malta. The aircraft was delayed leaving on the second one due to poor weather at Binbrook and returned through Milan, with 23 passengers, presumably service personnel from Malta, although they could also have been some of the last tour passengers from Milan. The reason for going into Milan was that the number 2 main booster pump was unserviceable and required changing there. Back at Manston, Mr. Reilly and the spares needed were prepared for the flight out to Milan on November Papa, which called there en-route with the Venice tour late on Friday 6th.

After a Pisa tour, the last Palma, and some training, a Milan-Heathrow freight flight followed for November Oscar. A Tangier tour came next and then a Middle East flight from 16th. to the 25th. with cargo from Hurn, the crew comprised Bill Wood, Jeep Jackson, the flight engineer and a navigator. At Istanbul they had to return with the number 1 engine feathered in the climb, due to an exhaust leak. Back on the ground, they sat waiting for assistance, but none came as there was a religious festival in progress. Bill said: 'We might as well clean the engine,' a job that Jeep remembers for the amount of skin taken off his hands by the petrol and also for the surfeit of Turkish cigarettes smoked.

After five days they continued to Kuwait and on to Jeddah, where they encountered more difficulties. Their destination, Khamis Mushayt, was a military base up in the mountains and the DC6 was required to lose some weight before delivering their cargo of spares for the Royal Saudi Air Force. There was a dispute with the Saudi customs; one set of officials declared they would not be permitted to take-off with the freight, while another said, equally emphatically, they could not go without it. To complicate matters, a search of the hold revealed a considerable quantity of '*Playboy*' magazines, presumably put aboard to entertain the military in the mountains.

Always phlegmatic and calm, Bill Wood finally said: 'If you can't resolve this, we must see the top man.' 'You mean the King?' they asked. 'Yes,' replied Bill. The King did hold routine audiences and, after duly appearing and explaining the position, they were allowed to proceed. At Khamis Mushayt, a base with no customs presence, other items of a celluloid and liquid nature were taken from the hold, and the crew joined their hosts for a film show in the only large room with white walls that could be used as a screen. It was almost an anticlimax to return via Cairo to Manston.

November Papa flew the last of the Basle-Manchester tours, also went to Malta from Binbrook, and then took the final Venice tour with the variation mentioned above. Another Binbrook-Malta followed and, like her sister aircraft, although twenty four hours later, returned via Milan with passengers recorded, 29 this time. After an engine change and a Check B, the appearance of major R.A.F. stations on the programme continued, with a freight flight from Waddington to Malta, this flight was delayed leaving as no refuelling crew was available. The DC6 came back from Malta with the number 3 engine feathered.

There was then a charter from R.A.F. Brize Norton to Akrotiri, captained by Andy Nicol, this flight returning through Milan Linate and Heathrow to Manston. From the 18th. to the 21st. November Papa flew a Manston-Tripoli-Kano-Lagos-Malta-Manston freight journey. Andy Nicol took over this charter from Tripoli; the Tripoli-Kano leg had to be at night so that astro navigation could be used, and they had a B.U.A. navigator with them. Part of the cargo, four rams, was dropped off at Kano before the aircraft proceeded on to Lagos. Keith Sissons was also in this crew as he had experience of Nigeria.

The DC6 closed the month with a longer flight, which routed Manston-Manston-Stanstead-Nicosia-Dhahran-Nicosia-Stanstead-Liverpool-Athens-Jeddah-Nairobi-Athens-Manston. This charter started badly on Saturday 21st., as the aircraft returned to the tarmac with unserviceable cowl gill motors that were changed. The aircraft was also checked generally, after a normal landing, but with 41,000 kg. overweight! After all this there was no flying on the last day of the month.

November There was no flying on the first day of November either, but on the following one the DC4s took the final two passenger charters over to Ostend. Whisky India spent the rest of the month freighting with a Hamburg, a Heathrow-Zurich-Basle-Heathrow and a journey up to Manchester, where she stayed for two nightstops and then came back, the aircraft was listed by the engineers as delayed due to fog at Manchester.

Foxtrot Yankee went with freight to Hamburg on successive days and over the 18th./19th. carried out two Heathrow-Viennas and returned to Manston from the last one, having gone unserviceable with a cracked cylinder in Vienna and required an engine change back at Manston. This was a long duty flight and the crew was Captain Cropp, Keith Sissons as co-captain and Don Nay.

On Tuesday 21st. the aircraft went to Rotterdam, just 46 passengers recorded, and then positioned empty back there, after a delay leaving due to poor weather, where it night stopped. On Wednesday she returned to Manston and that evening flew back once more to Rotterdam for another night stop, before returning to Thanet early on Thursday.

Over the 10th./11th., Foxtrot Yankee had been positioned on pan 17 for some defects to be cleared and the aircraft to be cleaned externally, after this it was moved onto pan 16 into wind. This was followed by an air test and during the next two days the aircraft was positioned to pan 6 for use in the heater investigation, still going on with regard to Yankee Kilo's accident. After this the original heater in the nose, that had earlier been removed, was replaced.

On the 3rd., Bill Wood and Mike Waddingham gave November Oscar and air test. Meanwhile the climate in Africa was still attractive, with the last two Tangiers on Sunday 5th. by November Oscar and on the 15th. by her sister aircraft, although neither was trouble free. November Oscar had a prop. change and 500 hour check followed by an air test, before going to Tangier. She arrived back from this flight with a supercharger unserviceable. November Oscar changed to freight trim and flew a Manston-Brussels-Orly-Lisbon and returned the same route. Her next revenue flight was Ministry work, leaving Manston on the 17th. for Lyneham-Athens-Tehran-Karachi-Columbo-Changi, and coming back via Karachi and Beirut on 25 November. Next day it was off to Lyneham once more, although late leaving from there as the engineers had a call out at 0130 regarding a feathering pump defect. The stores were called in and Messrs. Cavell, Robson and O'Reilly travelled to Lyneham with Eddie O'Callaghan at 0625. After repairs, the DC6 followed the same route to arrive at Changi in Singapore on the last day of the month.

November Papa was due for a C of A air test on the 1st. that was postponed, it was postponed again next day due to weather, and for a third time the following day when the message came through that a Beirut freight flight was booked and the DC6 was needed for it. The aircraft carried out the cargo flight, Manston-Heathrow-Rome-Beirut-Manston, and finally had its C of A test flight on Thursday 9th. The aircraft then went into the hangar to rectify some defects and they found a tooth off the number 4 engine gear wheel in the sump. After another air test the aircraft was readied for the last Tangier, as mentioned, although there was a delay when she came off chocks and returned with an engine snag.

The next day, Thursday 16th., the DC6 took passengers to Turin, had three night stops and returned them on Sunday. Then the aircraft was converted to freight trim and a drift sight fitted for the last flight of the month, to Saudi Arabia from Hurn, calling at the capital Riyadh, Khamis Mushayt and Jeddah. All four aircraft made local flights, or ones over to Ostend during the month.

The last appointment of the year occurred on 22 November and was a significant one. Additional equipment had been arranged for the 1968 season and two 800 series Viscounts were to be leased from Channel Airways at Southend. Captain Lockwood, who was previously a Comet and Viscount captain with Middle East Airlines, joined Air Ferry as Operations Manager. Don Brooker was still recovering from his serious illness at this time, and Peter Lockwood took over from Captain Madelaine of B.A.F. who had been covering the position.

Now with more Viscount expertise available there were some intensive sessions for 1968 costings, involving Charles Carroll, Rick and Peter Lockwood, in Ken Sheppardson's office. With profit margins very tight in the industry, some care had to be taken with prices being worked out to pence per seat. One discussion concerned flights to a new destination, Gerona, and someone said: 'The Viscounts will take longer taxiing,' whereupon Shep growled: 'You'll just have to bloody taxi faster.'

December

'I had joined the company as a DC4 copilot, straight from basic flying school, along with Simon Searle the Monday morning after the Perpignan accident. When the C.A.A. descended on the company our further training was completely wiped out and we spent several months working in the movement control doing load sheets and similar work, generally making ourselves useful for the operating crews. Slowly we eventually managed to get some flying time in and I was finally line-checked in December.' (Alan Breedon)

December was very much a freight month for three of the aircraft. Foxtrot Yankee went to Kuwait via Brindisi and Beirut, returning through Brindisi and Zurich to Manston, before positioning to Heathrow for flights to Oslo and Milan. She then made two Ministry flights from Lyneham to Bahrein via Benghazi. For the second the aircraft had a DC6 type galley fitted, and returned through Brindisi, Milan and Heathrow to Manston on the morning of Christmas Eve. The DC4 then went on check at Manston, an overhaul that would last a month.

Whisky India spent the month flying mainly from Heathrow to various European destinations, including Vienna, Linz, Zurich, Dusseldorf, Milan and Copenhagen, returning to Manston between flights. The aircraft had to turn back after leaving Manston for Heathrow on the 10th. with a wing de-icer motor defect. On the 13th., Whisky India flew Manston-Goteborg-Gatwick where she went unserviceable with a radio defect, next day positioning to Heathrow where she went U/S again, and came back to Manston on Saturday 16th. for the snags to be cleared. The DC4 then returned via Amsterdam to Heathrow. The Heathrow flights were a B.E.A. cargo division charter, Alan Breedon spent a week on these before a spell of little work for the DC4s over the Christmas period followed.

A/C	arr	Dep.	WED 13·12-67
WI	0600		s/plug change commenced at 0600. completed 07:30. #2 feather pump u/s — #1 eng oil pressure gauge u/s. — A/c cleared
	13:05	12:30	Depart Copenhagen.
F-1	07:50		Position in hangar — check I commenced — 08:10
WI			U/S at Gatwick Radio.

THURSDAY 14/12/67

| F4 | 1805 | | RUN UP CHECK I at 0830 SNAGS CLEARED BY 15-30. |

Friday Dec 15th 1967

WI			U.S at London Heathrow
NO.	16·15	0330	With defect cleared by 2150. Loading started at 2215 Loading completed at 0230 Delay due to de-fuel.
WI	0130	0430	Returned from L.H.R. CLEARED of SNAGS AT 0300 Hrs DEPARTED TO AMSTERDAM AND COPN DUE TO RETURN AT 23:50 SAT.
	0440	0530	N°3 ENGINE SNAG. Heathrow Rela... u/s

WINGSPAN

Vol. 3 No. 15 — Air Holdings Group Monthly Newspaper — DECEMBER 1967

Sir Myles urges:
FIGHT FOR PROFIT

Bristow outlines policies

Gatwick Becomes Nerve Centre

'EVERYBODY who values his job and the future of this great company will have to put his back into it to see that our productivity is increased, that costs are reduced and sales go up.' These are the tough words used by Sir Myles Wyatt, chairman of BUA at Gatwick on 8 December to over 120 managers and captains at a meeting held to 'introduce' BUA's newly-appointed managing director Mr Alan Bristow.

The Chairman also referred to the airline's 'quite sizeable losses' but stressed that Mr Bristow was 'very well fitted in every way' to carry out the task ahead.

Tribute

He paid tribute to Mr Max Stuart-Shaw, the new vice-chairman, who, he said, 'has had two years of hard and productive work in getting many things done behind the scenes, and is now taking on the very important and difficult task of planning the future of this airline'.

In a forceful speech Mr Bristow set out to explain his 'philosophies' and to give a broad picture of intentions. After just 3½ days in the seat he was able to announce several new measures. These include the appointment of 'specialists and professionals' to the board of BUA, an ideas awards scheme, the general BUA operational pattern and the planned concentration of all facilities and staff in the Gatwick area.

Mr Bristow also addressed a general staff meeting in Gatwick hangar one on 13 December and has already held a series of management 'teach-ins'. The new MD has set himself a critical time-scale for application of his ideas.

At the first Gatwick gathering Mr Bristow said his policy in one sentence 'is to lead BUA and to make a profit'. He described the basic elements of any commercial enterprise as falling into five main categories—people, ideas, management, methods and money.

'If you have the people with the ideas and capable management it is not difficult to find methods and markets in which to make money, to use money to make more money.'

'I am determined to weld BUA into a homogeneous, proud, go-getting and ultimately profitable airline,' he proclaimed. But he could not do this by himself; it could only be achieved by a first-class team. 'I am going to form a management team,' he said, 'and this team will be known as BRISTOW'S COMMANDOS.'

The forecast loss for 1967 was £532,000, for next year £1.1 million 'and at the rate we are going the '69 loss would be £1.4 million'. The present economic crisis and everlasting upward trends in costs coupled with these losses would seem to make the Commandos' task near impossible. 'That is what Commandos are for—to achieve the near impossible . . . and I do not like being associated with failure,' he emphasised.

Team

The team would consist of four new directors of BUA—commercial, operations, technical and financial directors. The appointments would be announced on 1 January. 'The going will be tough and the demands I will make on the skill and stamina and loyalty of the team will be of Commando calibre,' said Mr Bristow.

Every facet of the company's organisation and activity would be explored and analysed by the

Continued on page six, col. five

Group Prospers, BUA flags

MOUNTING losses by the Group UK airlines were a depressing feature of generally satisfactory financial results announced by Air Holdings last month. The Group trading profit for 1966 was £507,343, compared with £52,116 in the previous year.

Sir Myles Wyatt said that the UK airlines made a combined loss of £328,674 in 1966 and that 1967 figures would undoubtedly be still worse, perhaps in the region of £500,000. The prospects for next year were by no means encouraging.

The board of Air Holdings is 'very seriously concerned, not only with the present position of the long-term prospects for independent operators'. But the board welcomes the formation of the Edwards Committee and its inquiry into the industry.

The directors' report states that strenuous efforts are being made both to reduce costs and to obtain increased revenue. 'I am confident that the steps which are being taken will reverse this trend,' says Sir Myles.

Other companies in the Group achieved satisfactory results in 1966 and are expected to sustain their success in 1967 and subsequent years.

Gatwick Manor
for large or small parties

'One of the top eleven restaurants outside London'
EGON RONAY FOOD GUIDE

Near Crawley, Sussex
Telephone: Crawley 24381

Stuart-Shaw shapes forward planning

THE top management re-shuffle in BUA was announced by the Chairman, Sir Myles Wyatt, on 5 December. The appointments had been finalised that day.

In his staff message Sir Myles said: 'With effect from today Mr Max Stuart-Shaw, CBE, MInstT, becomes vice-chairman of BUA. Mr Alan Bristow, OBE, FRAeS, Croix de Guerre, becomes managing director of BUA and joins the board of BUA(CI).

As vice-chairman Mr Stuart-Shaw, who of course remains on the boards of BUA and BUA(CI), will have special responsibilities for forward planning and for duties in relation to the presentation to the ATLB of the long-range route application and for the preparation of evidence for the Edwards Committee. Mr Stuart-Shaw will also deal with such matters as airline bi-lateral traffic rights and inter-airline pooling negotiations.

Mr Bristow has been on the board of BUA since its formation in 1960. In his new appointment as managing director he will be responsible for the overall direction of BUA and will take a close interest in the affairs of BUA(CI).

During the last war Mr Bristow, who is 44, served with the Merchant Navy, later becoming a pilot in the Fleet Air Arm. In 1946 he left to join Westland Helicopters as chief helicopter test pilot. In 1947 he became managing pilot of a French com-

Continued on p. seven, col. four

£½m. deal for ATL

IN a deal worth about £½m, Aviation Traders are to manufacture freight doors for five BEA Vanguards, which are to be converted into cargo aircraft. ATL will install the doors in at least two of the aircraft and the first will arrive at Southend next October. The second follows in February, 1969.

Each door measures 136 in by 76 in and is generally similar to that fitted by ATL to some BUA Britannias. The 'new' cargo planes will supplement BEA's all-cargo Argosies on European and domestic routes.

Initial interest came from the State airline in July, 1966, when Aviation Traders were asked to tender for the contract. It is also likely that the Group firm will design and install a complete above-floor cargo system for the BEA Vanguard fleet and some additional Hylo orders are possible.

ANNE KING gets an unexpected bonus from Bob Monkhouse after winning the Miss Wingspan title at the Group Ball in London last month. Anne, who reached the finals as Miss VAT, wins a silver trophy and an Horizon holiday for two. Nineteen girls from Group companies and bases throughout the UK competed in the beauty contest organised by *Wingspan*. More Ball photographs on page four.

New MD at Redhill

MR GEORGE RUSSELL FRY, DFC, has been appointed managing director of Bristow Helicopters, following Mr Alan Bristow's new appointment. Mr Bristow becomes chairman of the Group helicopter firm.

Early action is planned to strengthen the helicopter firm management team now that Bristow has left Redhill. This be done by re-arranging some the present team. New appointments will be made on the side and in the field of management.

More about Bristow's managing director in 'People' page two.

Page 5: XMAS SPECIAL

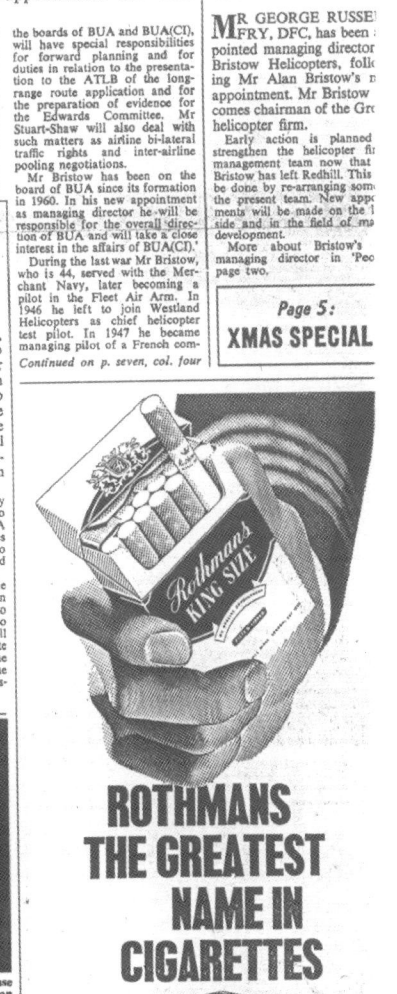

ROTHMANS
THE GREATEST
NAME IN
CIGARETTES

TWILIGHT OF THE PISTONS

On the 18th. there was a Geneva before the aircraft went back to London for a Heathrow-Copenhagen-Heathrow over the 20th./21st., going U/S again at Heathrow. The aircraft positioned on the 21st. from Heathrow to Gatwick where Les Dray and Len Mees met the aircraft to clear the defects. The last of her itinerant journeys started that day and the aircraft proceeded Gatwick-Basle-Rotterdam-Las Palmas, the return journey direct to Manston taking 9 hours 10 minutes, arriving back on Christmas Eve two hours after Foxtrot Yankee.

In Accounts: Peggy Marshall, Maggie, Ann Cowley and the writer (Peggy Marshall)

Air Ferry's new DC4 had an atrocious fuel system which, on the long flights, evoked fears of sudden stopping of the engines and which was probably due in whole or in part to the provision at some time of an extra belly tank. DC4s normally had four main fuel cocks, usually manually operated; Whisky India had more cocks and they were electrical. I wrote a three page overview of the system as an operating guide. (Keith Sissons)

November Oscar returned from Changi through Karachi, a leg of 12 hours 05 minutes, and Tehran, on December 4th. There was a training flight to Ostend on the 6th., and then flights from Heathrow to Milan and Stockholm followed. After this the DC6 made three journeys to Saudi Arabia. The first was delayed leaving Manston, en route for Hurn, as it was necessary to de-ice the tailplanes, while the second was Manston-Istanbul-Dhahran, with a return the same route.

The third flight was another from Hurn where it proceeded Istanbul-Dhahran-Riyadh, and should have returned back through Istanbul, where Andy Nicol was due to collect more funds. Istanbul was iced up and the DC6 was diverted into Ankara where the weather was also very poor. Pan Am de-iced November Oscar, while Andy scraped together the remainder of his travellers cheques and paid the balance with a personal cheque, a quick visit being made to his bank manager with an explanation on return to Thanet.

There was just time to fit in a Basle-Cagliari-Basle with passengers before Christmas. After a Check B, November Oscar went to Liverpool, after initially turning back with a rough number 3 engine, which ran well after the front and rear sparking plugs were changed. The aircraft then took freight between the 28th./30th. from Liverpool-Benghazi-Khartoum-Nairobi and came back through Benghazi to Manston. On the last day of the year the aircraft was at Benghazi once more, this time en-route to Lusaka.

The last freight work for November Papa was a Brussels-Orly-Lisbon and return before the aircraft, crews and engineers embarked on quite an expedition - to Afghanistan! When B.U.A. operated the DC6s, an agreement was in place with Ariana Afghan Airlines that, when the DC6s operated by the latter were on a major check, the B.U.A. aircraft would carry out Ariana's scheduled passenger service between Kabul and Gatwick. One of these checks became due in December and, as the undertaking had transferred to Air Ferry, November Papa was called upon to do this work.

On 9 December the DC6 positioned to Gatwick and on Sunday 10th. flew out on the first service via Frankfurt-Beirut-Kandahar to Kabul. After a local flight on 13th., November Papa went to Amritsar on 15th., returned to Kabul and then started for Gatwick via Kandahar-Tehran-Beirut and Frankfurt, arriving back on Saturday 16th. About this time Eddy Roocroft positioned along the route to Beirut and succumbed to appendicitis, where he was treated at the American Hospital there. Andy Nicol then went out to take his place and was based in the Lebanon for most of the remainder of the service.

The aircraft completed another service between Sunday 17 December and Saturday 23rd., returning via Munich to Gatwick on this occasion. The DC6 was met at Gatwick by a servicing party from Manston and the same night left once more for Frankfurt. This schedule included an Amritsar-Delhi leg and, as the year ended, the aircraft was nearly back to Frankfurt to end the third service.

1967 A DOUBLE BLOW

One recollection regarding the culinary efforts of the crews was that they used to heat up tins of beans on the cabin heaters at Kabul. (Jeep Jackson)

When the Ariana charter to Afghanistan started, I was one of the four engineers who accompanied November Papa to that foreign, barren land. We were based in Kabul, living in a comfortable Russian built hotel, but with a monotonous diet. Due to the long-haul nature of the aircraft schedule we didn't see the aircraft too often. If the visibility was bad in Kabul, which it was at times as the airfield height was some 5,000 feet above sea level, there was a diversion to Kandahar many hundreds of miles to the south. We engineers wore out a pack of cards in just three weeks. (Paul Noller)

Frank Tilley: the Kabul Charters (Andy Nicol)

Eddie Edgar: the Kabul Charters (Rose Edgar)

So 1967 ended, it had been quite a year.

STATISTICS

The year provided the passenger total record for the airline with 179,786 passengers carried. The flying hours, at 8543, were just 87 less than the record achieved the previous year. Two individual aircraft records were also achieved. The most flying hours in one month was achieved by Foxtrot Yankee, with 415, and the record for the most passengers ever carried in one month was taken by Whisky India, with 12104; both of these were in August. The year was also the one in which the DC6s flew the most passengers and the most hours. There were, in all, 1,838 visits to 111 airfields and airports

TWILIGHT OF THE PISTONS

MANSTON

The best publicity article produced about Manston was one by the '*Aeroplane*' in its issue of June 14th., attention from the aviation press that would have pleased everyone had the timing not been so unfortunate. Air Ferry was still very shocked at the loss of Yankee Kilo, and an enormous effort was being put in to keep the programme running with just four aircraft.

It was still a good article and gave a review of the two Manston airlines. The first part reviewed Hugh Kennard's civil career and the Manston background leading up to the takeover. The rest of the article is worthy of reproduction almost in full:

'Then the fun really started. Hugh Kennard immediately contacted the other tour operators which were then committed to fly with Air Ferry in 1965. He managed to persuade most of them to transfer their business to the new company which he then proceeded to form. After what were probably the most heated hearings in the history of the Air Transport Licensing Board, tour operators were allowed to choose whether they would stay with Air Ferry or switch to Kennard. As it was, about half of the business originally booked for Air Ferry transferred to the new company, which was appropriately enough named Invicta Airways (after the legendary White Horse of Kent, famed for its obstinate unconquerability).

Hardly surprisingly, rumours flew around at this time that Air Holdings planned to close down Air Ferry. Staff started to move from Air Ferry to Invicta, some out of loyalty to Kennard, others out of natural fear of landing up without a job. However, the position soon began to stabilize with the early appointment of Captain Kenneth Sheppardson as general manager. Capt. Sheppardson had just successfully completed the task of starting up Sierra Leone Airways on behalf of Air Holdings.

He wasted no time in making it clear that Air Ferry was still very much in business. But at this time a more subtle development was also at work to ensure the survival of Air Ferry. On its

Air Ferry Vikings in new livery.
From top,
Victor Foxtrot, Oscar Whisky and Charlie Hotel

takeover of Leroy Tours, Air Holdings appointed Douglas Whybrow as managing director. Mr. Whybrow had long been interested in the organisation of air transport - he had previously been instrumental, with Freddie Laker, in building up Air Charter and Channel Air Bridge - and he now saw Air Ferry as an opportunity to prove that a large enterprise could still offer really low-cost air transport if it was properly organised. With Whybrow determined to demonstrate to Air Holdings that Air Ferry was a viable

1967 A DOUBLE BLOW

proposition, the position of the company was again securely established.

Needless to say, relations between the two airlines were severely strained in 1965. Invicta had to operate from temporary premises while building a new hangar and terminal. Some staff still felt a little uncertain where their loyalties should lie. But fortunately it was a good year for business and total traffic through Manston rose by 50% with rather more than half going to Invicta. The situation was further resolved by an even more successful year in 1966 when each of the two carriers managed to double their business. As it became clear that there was enough traffic to support both Air Ferry and Invicta, the inevitable mistrust gradually began to subside.

As far as Invicta's 1966 operations were concerned, the growth was affected for a while during the peak summer months by abnormal engine unserviceability following sub-contracted overhauls. However, immediate remedial action was taken by the transfer of engine overhaul work to other more satisfactory contractors and the reorganization of the company's engineering department.

With an efficient organization Kennard is now planning 1967 as a period of consolidation with only a slight growth in traffic, while plans are being laid for the future introduction of more modern aircraft.

Mr. Kennard - known generally to his 200 plus staff as Mr. K - is very much the boss of the family business. But growth has recently brought more delegation. In strong contrast, Capt. Sheppardson down the road runs Air Ferry in a relaxed, democratic way. Whereas Invicta is typified by dogged determination to succeed, in Air Ferry one is conscious of quiet confidence. This comes partly from the comforting thought of Air Holdings standing there in the background. To some extent it reflects the proven success of the management: last year they achieved a 'very satisfactory' return on capital. Another key factor is the very obvious team spirit which exists among its executives.

Ken Sheppardson rather modestly looks upon himself not as the big chief but as the co-ordinator and prefers to disturb his men as little as possible. The organization is very simple with Sheppardson reporting in effect to Whybrow (on matters of policy only) and five managers reporting to Sheppardson (Captain D Brooker, operations; R Illsley, engineering; Michael Austin, accounts; Dick Sanders, sales; and Charles Carroll, commercial). The staff numbers just under 200. Like Invicta, Air Ferry is also now going through a period of consolidation before moving into the turbine era, the most likely next move being the acquisition of Viscounts.

Another noticeable difference between the two airlines is that Air Ferry concentrates more on longer-haul contracts. For example, the Air Ferry average passenger haul of 350 miles in 1966 compares with only 250 miles for Invicta (the very low Invicta figure is largely explained by the emphasis it puts on short cross-Channel services). Air Ferry also goes for a small number of large contractors (examples: Clarksons, Cosmos, Lyons). And whereas Invicta has only recently started going for freight, with Air Ferry this is already big business. (Whereas Invicta has roughly twice the passenger business of Air Ferry, its rival carries five time as much cargo, mostly on contract).

As much as anything it is this diverging character which is now healing the wounds inflicted in 1964 and 1965. And nobody is happier to see this reconciliation than those who have made their working home at Manston.'

Following the two crashes, there were some feelings of irony that Air Ferry, with a good organisation and structure, should have been so unfortunate. There had been stories of dramas at Invicta in that first year of scrabbling for existance, and one captain had left under a cloud following a dispute about aircraft serviceability. Without going out of context too much in time, this dispute went to court in 1969, when the pilot sued Invicta for damages, and the airline counter-claimed against him for lost business.

The year provided the usual crop of planned and unplanned visitors to Manston. U.K. airline movements included Britannias belonging to Caledonian, British Eagle, B.U.A., Britannia, Transglobe and Laker. The British Eagle visit fell into the involuntary category, as G-ANCG 'Trojan' was barely airborne en route for Woomera in Australia when undercarriage trouble became apparent and the aircraft was diverted to Manston. There it made a successful wheels-up landing on the prepared foam strip and the passengers evacuated the airliner with some alacrity.

TWILIGHT OF THE PISTONS

There were visits by elegant Ambassadors of Autair and Dan-Air and by Viscounts of Channel, B.U.(C.I.)A and B.E.A. One of the Channel aircraft, G-AVHE, would return later on lease to Air Ferry. Other types represented were Hs748s of Skyways Coach-Air and Channel, and a B.U.A. BAC1-11. Also from the U.K. register was a Morton Heron and Doves of Cardinal Airways and Scottish Aviation.

There were some exotic birds amongst the foreign visitors; a Norwegian Convair 240, an Electra of The American Flyers Airline, and a German DC7 from Sudflug.

Invicta recorded two movements away from Manston, with DC4s G-APID leaving on 28 February and G-ASZT on 29 September, both with the airline name erased.

The military birds of passage were equally colourful that year. The faithful Varsities appeared frequently and there were other trainers such as the Beagle Basset and HS Dominie. Avro Anson communications aircraft visited the station, a type first seen at Manston over thirty years earlier. In March, five Royal Navy Hunters from Brawdy passed through and in June five Jet Provosts from the College of Air Warfare based at Manby in Lincolnshire. In between those visits a Whirlwind of the Queen's Flight brought the Prime Minister, Mr. Wilson, for a visit to Margate. Other interesting visits came from a Hastings of the A.&A.E.E. at Boscombe Down and on 6 November AB910, a Spitfire of the Battle of Britain flight.

Whirlwind of 22 Squadron, 9 September, 1967

Vulcan XH483, 4 August, 1967

Javelin XH764 'C' of 29 Squadron

Operational aircraft seen in 1967 included Wessexes from No.'s 18 and 72 Squadrons, and Hastings from No. 24, 36 and 70 Squadrons. One Hastings brought in a spare wheel, a very large item, for another, TG581, which had landed earlier in the day. There were also Argosies, Andovers and, a familiar sight and sound of those days, the Army Beavers, which took off with a rasping noise that echoed right across the airfield and the surrounding countryside.

There was a highlight on 14 May, especially for fans of the type, when five Javelin F(AW)9s of No. 29 Squadron flew in from Nicosia, where they were being replaced by Lightnings. The squadron landed during a storm and one of their number, XH764 'C' made such a heavy landing that its career ended at that point. The Station Commander had an affection for the big Gloster all weather fighter, and in August XH764 appeared on display with the Manston Spitfire. Other visitors of note were a Royal Navy Sea Vixen, and on 9 November three Vulcans and a VC10. Five days later another unplanned movement occurred when a Victor

146

of 543 Squadron from Wyton had to make an emergency landing in the dark.

There were several foreign military visitors to remember, the Canadian T33 which appeared regularly, usually just before a weekend, and the 12 May when the U.S.A.F. came in numbers. There were three types of helicopter, a Sabreliner communications aircraft and an F100 fighter with a very blackened rear fuselage that departed some days later after an engine change. Another memorable influx was by the French display team, the 'Patouille de France,' which gave some celebrated displays over several years with their Fouga Magisters. Ten of these beautiful trainers, with their distinctive butterfly tails, carried out a stream landing at Manston, backed up on this visit by two Noratlas transports.

Manston itself had a change of 'ownership' during the year as, in August, the station changed from No.1 Group Bomber Command to No. 19 Group Coastal Command, although still remaining a Master Diversion Airfield.

R.A.F.

The re-equipment of the transport squadrons continued with the introduction of the Lockheed Hercules. Already well proven by the U.S.A.F., the Hercules became one of aviations success stories and continues in service at the time of writing. R.A.F. Transport Command was replaced in August by Air Support Command, a move towards an eventual two-command structure within the service.

CIVIL

After a reasonably buoyant period, 1967 was a hard year for the travel industry with issues such as the U.K. sterling crisis and the six day war in the Middle East doing little to add confidence.

Fleet changes recorded in the '*Flight*' survey tended to reflect the cautious mood as, with one or two notable exceptions, such as the Channel Viscount acquisition from the U.S., additions and disposals tended to be in small numbers. The trend of additional equipment was mainly for turboprops with their additional speed and smoothness, and clearly indicated the way that airlines would need to go.

Autair, still expanding, added a DC4 and three Heralds while B.K.S. added two Viscounts, but disposed of a Hs748. Britannia, having lost one of their fleet at Ljubljana, were down to seven Britannias while Caledonian and Transmeridian made no changes to their 1966 line up.

Cambrian added three Viscounts, while Channel acquired nine of the type but had phased out their DC3s. There were some pure jet additions, Dan-Air with another Comet, Laker a BAC1-11 and British Eagle with five BAC1-11s, although they recorded two Britannias less than 1966.

Lloyd International reduced in size by leasing Air Ferry a DC4 and disposing of their DC6, while British Midland added three Viscounts, disposed of three DC3s and phased out their Heralds. Invicta were listed with five DC4s and five Vikings, correctly reflecting that Victor Delta, acquired from Air Ferry, would not fly with them. Skyways Coach-Air, down at Lympne, added two Hs748s while the newcomer, Treffield Aviation acquired three Viscounts.

AIR HOLDINGS

The '*Flight*' survey listed B.U.A.F. with nine Carvairs and fourteen Bristol Freighters, quite a change in four years from three Carvairs and twenty five Freighters. B.U.(C.I.)A added two Heralds to their fleet and a Viscount, while disposing of eight DC3s. B.U.A. itself still flew three VC10s, ten BAC1-11s and four Britannias, one down from 1966, and no Viscounts were listed; as they were in 1966 and 1968 it could be that an error was made, or the three aircraft were leased out to another operator for 1967. The Britannia sold went to new airline, Donaldson Line Air Services.

The January edition of '*Wingspan*' gave a review of 1966 operating statistics. Group aircraft had carried a total of 2,240,659 passengers, a 16% increase of the final figure for 1965 of 1,928,447. Freight, at 106,357 tons was 17% above the previous year total of 91,780 tons. The car ferry operation had, in fact, temporarily reversed the downward trend although there were still many problems for B.U.A.F. in their attempts to maintain a viable business, and the 'Deep Penetration' routes, started so optimistically with the Carvairs in 1964, were closed during the year.

Wingspan had several references to Air Ferry in the year although, in view of the accidents, not all of them were welcome. The February edition included a resumee of the facts known regarding Oscar Golf and the June/July issue reported that Yankee Kilo's flight recorder had been played back, the first time that the particular system, SADAS, had actually been used.

The April editorial explained the facts regarding the end of an era for long range trooping flights. The contract held by B.U.A. for the carriage of servicemen and their families to the Middle East would terminate at the end of the year, as would the British Eagle contract to the Far East, with R.A.F. VC10s now able to do the work. An article on Lyons Tours, at this time among the top half dozen tour companies in the U.K., in this issue confirmed that the large majority of their holidays starting from London used chartered aircraft of group associate Air Ferry, or of Invicta Airways.

The midsummer issue reported the restructuring of B.U.A.F. into British Air Ferries in an attempt to turn this business into a more separate organisation, the company would be based at Southend, and with a board headed up by Lewis Leroy as Chairman.

In September, '*Wingspan*' reported that Air Ferry were seeking a new Operations Manager as Don Brooker was in hospital. Captain Len Madelaine, deputy chief pilot of the group was currently in charge of this area. This issue also reported that Air Ferry would operate some of their shorter range charters in 1968 from Lydd, the reason given was that Manston was becoming overcrowded and that Lydd offered ample capacity. This switch meant a welcome boost for Ferryfield, which lost its long range B.U.A.F. flights earlier in the year.

A profitable line for Air Ferry was the sale of Swiss watches on their flights, at £4.17.6 each. Charles Carroll reported that over two thousand had been sold already in the year.

The October edition noted that Dick Sanders, Air Ferry's Sales Manager, was leaving the group after ten years, and in November, '*Sylvia*' reported that the Assistant Commercial Manager at Air Ferry, Peter Covell, married Marianne Tunbridge, who for seven years was a Leroy courier.

Wingspan in December gave what is so obvious with the benefit of hindsight, a coded signal of breakers ahead for the group. Sir Miles Wyatt and the newly appointed B.U.A. Managing Director, Alan Bristow, said in uncompromising terms that it was vital that costs were reduced and that sales and productivity must increase. An article under the heading: 'Group Prospers, B.U.A. flags' stated that: 'Mounting losses by the Group U.K. airlines were a depressing feature of generally satisfactory financial results announced by Air Holdings last month.' The Group trading profit for 1966 was £507,343 but the U.K. airlines made a combined loss of £328,674 and it was indicated that the 1967 figures would be worse, probably in the region of £500,000. The prospects for 1968 were by no means encouraging. The report also said: 'The board of Air Holdings is 'very seriously concerned, not only with the present position but of the long-term prospects for independent operators.' But the board welcomes the formation of the Edwards Committee and its enquiry into the industry.'

The 'People' section in January revealed that one of the senior Air Holdings men most involved with Air Ferry would be leaving the group at the end of January 1968. This was Douglas Whybrow, who had reluctantly reached the conclusion that he had little confidence in the future of the Air Holdings Group, and relinquished directorships of Lyons, Leroys and Air Ferry and also the chairmanship of Canaries Hotels.

His relationship with Lewis Leroy had also deteriorated as he described much later in his book. 'I had soon found that the business was in decline, the number of clients dropping by an average of 8% a year. This was largely because Leroy's original business, which was well managed, was touring holidays, and there had been a continuing swing to stay-put sunshine vacations. Leroy was too late in the field to have the muscle to get the right beds at the right price and, as happens even now, people found themselves paying higher prices in inferior rooms. Complaints mounted but Leroy shrugged off my concerns; I was not happy. I had told him about the discussions with the Chairman about B.U.A.F. and one day he went to Wyatt and convinced him that he could rescue the air ferries if he was made chairman and would expect me to join the board. The idea was ludicrous and I refused. From then on Leroy sulked, had an '*Engaged*' notice permanently fitted to his office door and communicated with me only by memorandum.' As his original three year contract with the Leroy Group, the largest group tour firm when he joined it, expired in January 1968, Douglas explained his concerns to Sir Miles Wyatt who was understanding and agreed to an amicable severance.

As most of Air Ferry's Leroy work had long ago been siphoned off by B.U.A., these problems in the immediate holding company in Tunbridge Wells were not generally known at Manston.

1967 A DOUBLE BLOW

SAFETY

On 4 June, within twelve hours of Yankee Kilo's accident, disaster struck a British Midland DC4M Argonaut, which crashed in Stockport while approaching Manchester Airport. The aircraft was seen to be losing height over the town with the engines revving; when it was down to 500 feet Manchester control was stating that the airliner should have been at 1,850 feet, with six miles to go to the airport. There were 84 passengers and crew on board of which 72 were killed. The passengers were returning from an eleven day package holiday with Arrowsmith Tours in Majorca. The aircraft struck a disused warehouse before landing on an electricity sub-station and bursting into flames. Fuel feed problems were later found to have cut the power to the engines. The aircraft involved, G-ALHG, had been one of the visitors to Manston in April of the previous year.

Later on a B.E.A. Comet crashed into the Mediterranean, one hundred and seventy miles west of Cyprus. Fears of a repetition of the Comet 1 disasters briefly resurfaced but the accident was later attributed to other causes.

OTHER EVENTS

One of the early news items of the year was the attempt in January on the world water speed record on Coniston Water in the Lake District, which unfortunately ended in disaster and the death of Donald Campbell. The Soviet Premier, Mr. Kosygin, visited Great Britain and paid a visit to Scotland. At the other end of the country, at Filton near Bristol, the British Concorde was taking shape, as was the French version at Toulouse and which would be complete by the end of the year.

An environmental problem on an enormous scale was caused in the spring when a giant oil tanker the '*Torrey Canyon*' came to grief on the southern coastline. Vast quantities of oil were discharged into the sea causing havoc to the marine life and bird population and the wreck was eventually bombed in an attempt to break up the vessel and fire the oil. A maritime event on a happier note occurred in June when Francis Chichester completed his epic round the world voyage and was knighted in recognition of his endeavours.

The government was in the throes of a currency crisis during the summer and a pay freeze was enforced; the problems continued through to November when sterling was devalued for the first time since 1950. August saw the liner '*Queen Mary*' leave New York on her final cruise; although slightly smaller than the '*Queen Elizabeth*' and not quite so fast as the '*United States*,' the '*Queen Mary*' epitomised the age of stately travel in these large ships. In September the new cruise liner the '*Queen Elizabeth 2*' was launched, and Gibraltarians voted to stay British after two hundred and fifty four years. Britain's military commitments in the Far East were by now considered too costly, and at this time a gradual withdrawal began from the bases 'East of Suez.'

In November, France vetoed Britain's attempts to join the E.E.C. and there was a bad train crash at Hither Green on the Hastings to Charing Cross line which resulted in the deaths of 55 people.

In America things were not going well; in January the First Lady wrote in her diary: 'A miasma of trouble hangs over everything,' and the President was having nightmares that offensive action by the U.S.A.F. over North Vietnam could trigger the start of World War Three. After his visit to Britain, Mr. Kosygin made a journey to meet Mr. Johnson in New Jersey to discuss world affairs. The summer brought another round of race riots, especially in Detroit, and these allied to the anti-war protests gave rise to fears about the fate of the nation itself. By November a grim sense of siege hung over the 'White House' and the President called in a group of veterans, called 'The wise men,' who had all previously held high office, to advise him. After an extensive briefing and much consideration, their decision was that the President had no other course of action than to actively pursue the war.

The space race between the U.S. and the Soviet Union had become very expensive for both sides, although work continued on developments that gave such prestige, and the possibility of gaining some military advantage. A Soviet Cosmonaut, Colonel Komarov, became sadly the first person to be killed in space.

In May the headlines were taken up by the marriage of Elvis Presley to Priscilla, just before the Middle East took centre stage. In June the six day war occurred after Egypt moved against the U.N. peacekeeping force, which had been based in the Canal Zone since the fighting in 1956. Israel attacked airfields in Egypt, Jordan, Syria and Iraq and pushed ahead on land at a spectacular pace. By 7 June the Israeli Army was at the Suez Canal and the west bank of the Jordan was occupied. Israel at last had access to the Jordanian sector of Jerusalem and to a place of great religious significance, the Wailing Wall.

Brian Dunlop and Patrick Hope   (Jodi Hope)

CHAPTER 8
1968 PROP JETS AND FINALE

AIRCRAFT

    Douglas DC4   G-ASFY   G-ARWI

    Douglas DC6   G-APNO   G-APNP

    Vickers Viscount   G-AVHE   G-AVNJ

For 1968 Air Ferry would use a fleet of three types, the two DC4s, the two DC6s and two 800 series Viscounts, the latter leased from Channel Airways at Southend.

CREWS

With the coming of the Viscounts, additional crews were needed and from B.U.A. came Captains Dunn, Collyer and Saunders with First Officers Parker and Watt. Captain Adams joined in February and Bill Steel returned for the season. Paul Horsting was promoted to Captain on 15 April and Captain Mayo came in June. Other pilots to join during the season were First Officers Bullock, Tyler and Styles.

There were leavers, too. David Laker and Paul Ashpitel left in February and Viv Kellard in June. Bill Wood also went, on 3 July, to take up the position of Instrument Rating Examiner on the DC7 at Dan-Air.

Occasionally crews would have a brush with Customs and it was not only the civil ones. There was one story that, at another station, an R.A.F. aircrew came under suspicion and a V bomber was virtually taken to pieces in a hunt for illicit items. One night in July, a hostess back from Basle at 02.30 was caught with a duty free watch; feeling suitably petrified she was relieved to be told the matter was only between her and them, provided that was all! The result was a fine and, of course, the confiscation of the prized watch.

The cabin crew line up included two more stewards for this season, Michael Bopst and Lionel Heady. Michael, being German, was able to converse with Maggie Studt, now Chief Air Hostess, in her native tongue, no doubt intriguing to the passengers! The air hostesses were Liz Arden, Lyn Batney, Hazel Baynham, Bennett, Lorna Brownridge, Sue Chadwick, Chanell, Lyn Chilton, Mary Coates, Carol Dale, Maria Eisenhut, Jill Field, Gray, Jackie Hanson, Harvey, Jenny Holtan, Hunt, Liz Johnson, Hazel King, Janet Lamont, Roswitha Mayo, Margaret Norton, Parish, Hilary Reeks, Ann Rippon, Sue Smith, Sandra Sparrowhawk, Maggie Studt, Lyn Thorn, Linda Townsend, Pat Travers, and Woodman.

The flight engineers who flew with Air Ferry, although possibly not all in the 1968 season, included F/E Blandford, Jock Chisholm, Brian Dunlop, Doug Erswell, Des Froud, Dave Jennings, Sherwood, Roy Simmons, Frank Tilley, Les Toghill, Arthur Ward, and 'Timber' Wood, the latter from B.U.A.

THE YEAR

The top ten airports in 1968 were:

	Visits
Basle	295
Perpignan	280
Ostend	175
Manchester	98
Milan	86

Gatwick	74
Zurich	46
Luxembourg	43
Rotterdam	41
Newcastle and Le Bourget	40

January   Foxtrot Yankee, which had last flown on Christmas Eve, spent much of the month on a Check 2, and a working party from Scottish Aviation was at Manston assisting on this overhaul. Just prior to November Oscar's Ndola flight, as mentioned below, the Air Ferry manpower was transferred from Foxtrot Yankee to ensure the Check 1 on the DC6 was completed. Following her check the DC4 made a test flight on 25 January. The next day she left on a freight flight to Freetown on the west coast of Africa, stopping at Casablanca in both directions.

Foxtrot Yankee (John Somerville)

Whisky India was on freight work all month starting on the 3rd. with a Le Bourget; she was due to carry out training the following Monday but, after a delay for a mag. drop, was then unable to take off due to an R.A.F. emergency. Between the 9th./11th. the DC4 flew Manston-Teesside-Goteborg-Milan-Heathrow-Manston, and then went to Bordeaux on the 16th.

On the 17th., Keith Sissons and Mike Waddingham flew Whisky India Manston-Teesside-Goteborg, this time returning direct to Manston. By the time they reached Goteborg, an airport near the coast, darkness had fallen and the weather was very poor. It was intensely cold with a low cloud base and, to make matters worse, rain was falling onto ice on the runway.

A.T.C. had informed Whisky India that, although there were snow banks on the sides of the runway, the surface braking action was 'good'. There was no mention of a stiff cross-wind blowing so that when they touched down and Keith applied the brakes there was no braking action at all. They were pretty helpless as the cross-wind drifted the aircraft towards the snow-banked side of the runway and, as they slowed down, the rudder became progressively less effective. The DC4 gradually weather-cocked, in seeming slow motion, as they proceeded towards the end of this none-too-long piece of ice-covered concrete, getting closer to the snow banks.

They eventually slithered to a stop before things became too serious but they had to have the undercarriage well on one side cleared of all the ice and snow they had scooped up while acting as an involuntary snow plough. Keith's comments to A.T.C., who had caused them to land outside the official slippery runway limits, were unprintable.

1968 PROP JETS AND FINALE

It was so cold the next morning when they left that, after starting up with some difficulty and taxiing out, they had to give up and return to the apron to have a hot-air blower directed onto the flight deck to unfreeze the instruments.

G-APNO at Basle
(Rolf Siegrist via Robert Stitt)

On the 22nd. Whisky India flew a Cardiff-Goteborg which had to return via Lydd, necessitating a night stop at the B.A.F. base. The last trip of January was Manston-Teesside-Oslo-Brussels-Lisbon, and the aircraft night stopped in Portugal on the last night of the month.

November Oscar, in Entebbe at the start of the month, continued on to Lusaka in Zambia and returned the same way as the outward route, via Entebbe and Benghazi to Manston. After this came a flight from Hurn through Saudi Arabia, calling at Dhahran and Khamis Mushayt before going on to Dubai in the Trucial States. Then there was an Ostend training sortie and a Check 1 prior to the long haul from Gatwick through Benghazi and Nairobi to the other oil lift destination of Ndola. On return the DC6 went back into the hangar for an engine and a propeller to be changed. This work, and a problem with an inverter, delayed the next freight flight out from Hurn to Saudi Arabia again, and then proceeding from there to Bahrein and Dubai. There was a five hour training session at Ostend on Friday 26th. before the aircraft left at midday on Saturday for Gatwick to take over the Ariana work. November Oscar departed from Gatwick with 60 passengers, her first of the year, at teatime on Sunday and with only one stop, at Beirut, flew out to Kabul. The aircraft flew to Lahore and Amritsar before returning to Kabul by the end of the January.

On the first day of the year, November Papa had completed the third Ariana Gatwick service, the DC6 being met at Gatwick by a servicing party from Manston and left again the same day to return to Kabul. Back in Afghanistan, the DC6 flew to Delhi and Amritsar, then back to Kabul, before setting out once again for Gatwick, arriving there on Saturday 6th. After a check over by the engineers on the weekly visit the service was repeated, out Sunday 7th, with a return through Munich to London Gatwick on the 14th., then after servicing back out to Afghanistan the same day and return on Sunday 21st.

The most eerie event to occur to Air Ferry staff undoubtedly happened to an engineer out in Kabul and is best described in his own words as they appeared in the '*Monarch*' magazine:

'Once upon a time (there's a beginning for you), an aircraft engineer was standing on the tarmac at Kabul, doing watch duty while one of his company aircraft was being ground run.

It was a long engine run and as a small distraction the engineer almost subconsciously noticed a small ball of paper being blown towards him by the ever present breeze that one finds at a location nearly 6,000 feet above sea level.

Some seven months prior to this time, another aeroplane operated by the company had been prepared for a night flight to Perpignan in southern France, taken on a full load of passengers, and in the small hours of a Sunday morning had eased its way south from its airport in Kent. It never landed in Perpignan, crashing instead into Mt. Canigou in the Pyrenees. All 88 people on board lost their lives. Only the very public crash of a similar aircraft type at Stockport in England, prevented the usual all-engulfing press attention making more of the disaster in France.

Meanwhile, back in Kabul, the engine run was still roaring on, and the little ball of blue paper was blowing nearer to our engineer, who by now was wondering how close to him the breeze would bring it on its journey along the great stretch of tarmac, he was determined not to take a step forward or back to make it 'happen.'

TWILIGHT OF THE PISTONS

A look up at the flight deck showed that the two men were engrossed in the interior of the cockpit and their readings. A glance at the left showed the windblown object to be moving by the starboard wingtip. Another glance to the cockpit, the propeller disc slowing showed the run was complete, silence at last, now where was that piece of paper. Good Lord, just here in front of me. Bend down to pick it up, unscrew it, flatten it out, read it.

IT WAS THE RE-FUELLING CHIT FOR THE FLIGHT FROM MANSTON TO PERPIGNAN, SEVEN MONTHS BEFORE THAT ENDED HIGH IN THOSE MOUNTAINS SO FAR AWAY.

I know this is true, because I was that engineer. (Paul Noller)

Other engineering staff who went out to Kabul were Eddie Edgar, Jock Robson to look after the electrics, and Bob Ratcliffe, airframe. Off duty some of them purchased as souvenirs the long rifles used in Afghanistan but, on arrival back at Gatwick, these were unfortunately confiscated. Bales of Kashmir wool were another product for sale and some of the crews bought a length large enough for a suit to be made from.

When Paul Noller returned from Kabul after Christmas, Phil Townsend went out to replace him as the radio engineer. The DC6 stopped at Beirut on the way out, the Indian passengers making many purchases at the airport, especially small transistor radios.

The DC6 taking Phil out was diverted to Kandahar from Kabul and then to Lahore where, on arrival, one fuel tank was empty, one held six gallons and a third, thirty. There was some enmity between Pakistan Airways and Ariana and the flight number was changed by adding a letter to slightly conceal the nature of the flight stopping at Lahore. They proceeded the short distance to Amritsar, followed by Kandahar where a spare engine was left, and then to Kabul.

The next service left Gatwick on Monday 22nd. and did not make the usual secondary journey from Kabul, although there was a local flight of 30 minutes from there on the 24th. The aircraft returned, stopping at Naples and Frankfurt, to Gatwick on Saturday 27th. By this time, November Oscar was already at Gatwick to make the next scheduled departure on Sunday 28th. Having completed seven of the varied Ariana services, November Papa returned to Manston for a Check 1 and some training at Ostend on Wednesday 31st.

The crews were appalled at the behaviour of the passengers on the Ariana flights; most of which were Indian immigrants to the U.K., who sat on the floor and ate off the seats. On arrival back at Gatwick the aircraft were in a very dirty state, so bad in fact, that Gatwick Airport Services declined to carry out the aircraft cleaning, and the servicing party from Manston was sent to do this. At the end of the charter the aircraft had to be stripped of internal furnishings, the carpets taken up, and the curtains and seat covers were burnt.

From: '*Not Many People Know That,*' an article in K.A.H.R.S:

The Afghanistan service required the plane to depart Gatwick on Sunday afternoon, for Kabul via Frankfurt, then to Amritsar, returning to Gatwick the following Saturday. A small party of engineers had to be stationed at Kabul for the duration of the operation.

Passengers arriving at Kandahar after the long flight from Beirut, disembarked and made hopefully towards the terminal building. The airport stood in incongruous isolation in a surrealistic landscape; from a vast barren red plain there rose gigantic outcrops of rock, while away to the east, the snow covered peaks of the Hindu Kush floated disembodied in the clear blue sky.

The terminal building was a most unusual design, with a ground floor plan in the shape of an annulus, it was made up of what I can only describe as hoop shaped sections, the whole thing loooking like a large scale model of the top half of an Elizabethan ruff, both ends of each section were glazed giving the interior a bright appearance. On entering however, one was confronted by rows of brand new, never been used, counters. All the necessary equipment for producing hot water had obviously never gurgled and hissed to produce a single cup of coffee or tea, shelves in the rows of glass cabinets had never held a slice of Swiss Gateau or a pre-McDonald's hamburger. The bemused passengers wandered aimlessly around in the echoing spaces, but there were no staff to approach and request guidance from, for the history of this building was as strange as it's appearance.

1968 PROP JETS AND FINALE

In the days when Civil Aviation was spreading so confidently, what with the many aerodromes left over from WWII and the arrival of such aircraft as the DC7 and Super Constellation, it was decided that an airport at Kandahar would be perfect as a cross roads of the air, planes arriving from Europe would refuel and proceed to such destinations as India, the Far East and all points to Australasia. Construction went ahead, probably Pan-Am was in the picture somewhere, this airline was behind Ariana, the chief pilot and chief engineer were both seconded to Kabul from Pan-Am. Then, just before the airport was completed, along came the jets and Kandahar Airport was stillborn, jet airliners having different operational disciplines to those of the piston engined variety. And so there it was, a convenient alternative when Kabul was closed due to weather, used mainly by a few DC3s, but as far as one could visualise, there was very little prospect of recovering the original expenditure. (Phil Townsend)

DC6 at Kandahar (Phil Townsend)

On 10 January the first of the Viscounts, G-AVNJ flew in from Southend, piloted by Peter Lockwood. The aircraft was in Channel Airways colour scheme although without the airline name. Next day, similarly painted, Captain Lockwood ferried G-AVHE over from Southend. Both aircraft were to be repainted and made ready for their inclusive tour work in an 83 seat configuration at Manston. On January 26th., November Juliet went to Ostend on training as the only movement for the new type.

TWILIGHT OF THE PISTONS

February In January the only passengers carried had been on the Kabul run and February was similar for most of the month. Foxtrot Yankee however, carried only freight. She made a flight Manston-Basle-Cairo-Rome-Manston, followed by two Goteborgs, and a Heathrow-Copenhagen-Heathrow. On the 19th

Foxtrot Yankee, winter 1967/68   (Peter O'Sullivan)

she flew to Zurich and on to Heathrow where she had a radio defect that resulted in Paul Noller being called in to go to London Airport. The DC4 spent the remainder of February away from base on a contract serving Zurich-Stuttgart-Zurich, some cycles ending at Heathrow and some at Manchester. There was a variation on Saturday 24th., when Vienna was the destination instead of Stuttgart and at the end of the month Foxtrot Yankee was at Heathrow loading for another service.

This month Air Ferry pilots were involved in what was almost certainly the third and last strike in the company's existence. The 1965 and 1968 ones were driven by membership of the Air Holdings group and support of B.U.A. pilots in their grievances about conditions of employment. It is probably fair to say that commitment to strike action on both occasions was in indirect proportion to age and seniority, although some of the younger ones were reluctant to become involved.

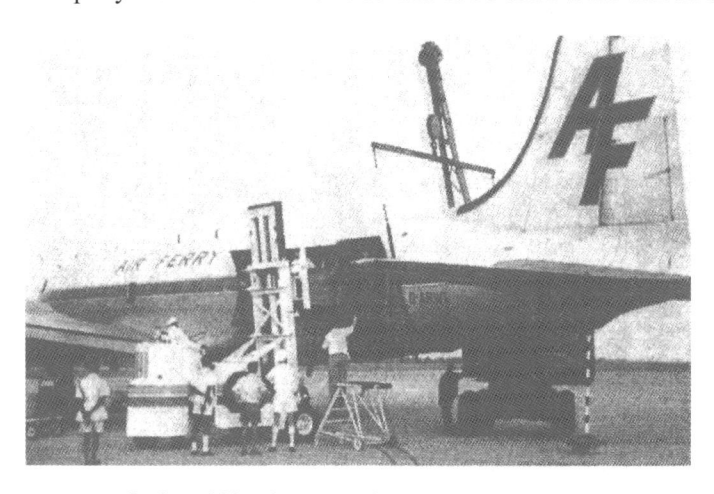

Arthur Ward supervises the unloading in Sierra Leone (*Wingspan*)

The action occurred during the Zurich contract and John Cropp, Bill Steel and Keith Sissons were three who declined to be involved. When they drove to Manston one of the pilots was on picket duty at the service road entrance and, looking very uncomfortable, said: 'I have to do this, I am reminding you that there is a strike on.' Keith gave his colleages a line check so that they could operate in the right hand seat for this charter by Swissair. They were stationed in Zurich, and the original three were later joined by Eddie Adams, Alan Breedon and Simon Searle for the duration of the contract.

One interesting feature of this scheduled freight service was that Foxtrot Yankee operated to a timetable and, as they flew over Rye at night, Keith Sissons used to flash the landing lights, which on the DC4 could be operated in the retracted position, to his wife Shirley down below.

1968 PROP JETS AND FINALE

G-APNO at Manchester (P.A.Tomlin via Robert Stitt)

TWILIGHT OF THE PISTONS

Whisky India, at Lisbon at the end of January, returned through Brussels to Manston. Her next flight was an epic one involving the transportation of a five ton reel of cable from Manston to Freetown for use in a dredger. On the 8th. the flight was cancelled because they were unable to load the heavy and unwieldy cargo on board. As the weight placed in the freight door would have tipped the aircraft on its tail, it was necessary to borrow a strop from Lydd to hold the tail while the front was ballasted. After that the reel was loaded and slid forward in the aircraft. At that point, on Friday 9th., they were unable to start the number 2 engine, with the mag. blown out. The starter was changed, and Frank Strainge called in, who found a booster coil U/S so the flight was cancelled again until Saturday.

Next day, after a ground run, Captain Sissons requested two hundred gallons of extra fuel for which John Verrion was called in. When this was aboard Keith Sissons had to abandon the take off as number 4 was not giving maximum take off RPM, but after the pulley wheel was changed, and another ground run, the aircraft finally departed at 1050. The long haul to Sierra Leone was via Casablanca and Robertsfield, the latter a leg of 11 hours 50 minutes. Whisky India's landing at Robertsfield on Sunday was probably because Freetown, an hour and a half flying time away, had closed. After a fourteen hour break the aircraft took off once more, and arrived at its destination at midday on Monday. There, Flight Engineer Arthur Ward supervised the unloading of the reel that had required special wooden supports to be made by A.T.L. to avoid damaging the floor.

On take-off from Freetown the crew had one more problem when a drive pump on the engine went U/S, but the aircraft arrived back at Manston alright on Wednesday evening, the flight recording 37 hours 5 minutes. Some idea of the load that was carried on this occasion can be made by comparing the Casablanca-Robertsfield leg with Foxtrot Yankee's Casablance-Freetown flight, over a similar distance, on 27 January which took 9 hours 15 minutes.

Whisky India went to Ostend for training on Sunday 18th., and on Saturday 24th. had to make an early start. The DC4 made a positioning flight to Rotterdam to take the first Manston passengers of the year to Goteborg and, after a night stop, returned via Rotterdam late on Sunday evening. A second passenger flight was carried out by November Oscar that weekend to the same schedule, although she collected her passengers from Amsterdam for Goteborg. After another Ostend for training, the second of three in the month, Whisky India took freight to Malmo and then returned to passenger work on Wednesday 28th. with a flight to Marseilles. It is probable that this charter and also possibly the ones to Goteborg were for ships crews

November Oscar completed her Kabul service via Beirut direct to Gatwick on Saturday 3 February, and left on Sunday for the last of the series. This arrived back at Gatwick on Sunday 11th. and the DC6 returned to Manston later in the morning. From the 19th./23rd. it was a return to cargo work with a journey Manston-Brussels-Istanbul-Kuwait-Abu Dhabi-Bahrein-Nicosia-Manston. Next day the aircraft made the passenger flight already described, and completed the month with another freight flight. The aircraft was delayed leaving for this, returning from the runway with a radio defect, and then flew Manston-Frankfurt-Cairo-Zurich-Manston.

November Papa concentrated on freight, she flew Manston-Zurich-Shannon-Manston and then made a long trip from Bordeaux via Benghazi, Khartoum and Nairobi to Tamatave in the Malagasy Republic, and returned through Nairobi, Benghazi and Southend. There was one more trip, from Hurn to the three Saudi Arabian destinations between the 12th./16th., before the aircraft left Manston next day on the flight up to Prestwick for a Check 3.

For the Viscounts, Hotel Echo did not fly at all in February as she was undergoing work in the hangar. The exterior was stripped down for a repaint and the interior virtually gutted for changes to the cabin furnishings and the seating capacity. November Juliet made three training sorties, to Ostend, to the B.A.C./de Havilland base at Hatfield and to Stanstead. By the end of the month the aircraft was in the hangar for paint stripping.

March In March, Foxtrot Yankee continued her itinerant lifestyle, working from Heathrow and Manchester; she had left Manston on 19 February and it was not until 17 March that she returned. The patterns varied, but the first programme of the month flown is an example. The aircraft left Heathrow on Friday 1st. and flew Zurich-Basle-Zurich-Manchester, then Manchester-Zurich-Vienna-Zurich-Heathrow; the next cycle ending back at Manchester and so on, with the airports served by Zurich being Vienna and Stuttgart.

1968 PROP JETS AND FINALE

The Zurich-Basle leg mentioned above was not in fact part of the schedule, but a three engine ferry by Keith Sissons for repairs by Balair and, later on, a return to Zurich was required early on the morning of Saturday 16th. Basle was used again on the 10th. but whether programmed or a diversion is not known.

Two more freight journeys followed, a Gatwick-Le Bourget and a Rome-Cairo-Rome which returned to Manston on Friday 22nd. The next day it was a change to passenger flying with a charter Calais-Cardiff-Calais. There were no flights for nearly a week by Foxtrot Yankee, the aircraft going into the hangar for the replacement of time expired items and for 'white top' cleaning. Then on Friday 29th. she positioned up to Newcastle for another period away from base, making the first of a series of passenger flights from Woolsington Airport to Beauvais on the last two days of the month.

Whisky India only flew between the 8th. and the 25th. of March, beginning and ending this period with training sorties to Ostend, and spent the time in between on freighting. On Monday 11th. there was a Gatwick-Zurich, followed a few days later by a Teesside-Helsinki charter. Then the aircraft left for Aden via Rome and Cairo, returning direct from Cairo in exactly 13 hours and with number 3 engine backfiring in flight. The DC4 then went into the hangar for the defects to be cleared and, after that, they had a job getting her out on Wednesday 20th. due to the high winds. That morning Whisky India took off but returned with the number 3 running rough, but finally departed for Gatwick. The aircraft flew two more Gatwick-Zurich charters, returning from the second to Manston on Thursday evening.

The DC6s similarly concentrated on cargo work. November Oscar had two abortive attempts at training on the 2nd. and 4th., returning from the runway both times, once due to poor weather and then due to a mag. drop. The flight to Ostend was achieved on Tuesday 5th., then November Oscar set off for old territory the next day routing out through Birmingham-Benghazi-Khartoum-Entebbe and Beira, in Mozambique, to Durban in South Africa. The Beira stop was a diversion from Blantyre due to fog. The aircraft returned Entebbe-Benghazi-Manston on the 11th. After a quick flight to Lyons next day, November Oscar positioned back to Birmingham later on the Tuesday for the second of the Durban trips. This one followed the original proposed route of a stop on the way out at Blantyre in Malawi, and at 50 hours 40 minutes took three hours less overall.

After an Ostend on Monday 18th. November Oscar positioned next day up to Scottish Aviation for a check and for some hours both DC6s were at Prestwick before November Papa flew back to Manston at the completion of her overhaul. On her return, the DC6 went into the hangar before her next flight for the renewal of the floor boards and stowing of aircraft spares. Then, between 25th. and 30th. March, November Papa was back to revenue work with more cargo from Hurn to Saudi Arabia, via Istanbul to Dhahran, Khamis Mushayt and Jeddah, with a return through Athens to Manston.

This trip came up during a time when there was not much work for the DC4 and the company was looking for someone to go along as loadmaster. We had one genuine article, but it was felt he needed an assistant and when I volunteered it helped them get away without hiring in from outside. My idea, of course, was to spend as much time as possible on the flightdeck and try to learn as much about the DC6 as I could in the hope that it might somehow allow me to get a promotion onto the type. It didn't happen, needless to say, but I had a grand time nevertheless and thoroughly enjoyed myself. We took some cargo outbound to somewhere in the general direction of Saudi and ended up in Dhahran the night before we were due to fly across the desert to Khamis, which is south of Jeddah on the other side of the country.

As well as myself and the loadmaster freeloading so far, we had been carrying a navigator just for the next sector, one which I now fly regularly with just one other pilot in the cockpit, plus inertial navigation and a flight management system. The reason for our trip to Khamis was to extricate some Airwork personnel who, I believe, had just lost the contract for maintaining the Saudi Air Force equipment there. The flight across the desert was uneventful, our seconded-from-B.U.A. navigator appearing to find all the wadis and oases he was looking for; the only thing of note being the run-down of the engines when we landed at this six thousand feet above sea level airfield. I believe I heard the flight engineer muttering about damn mixture controls.

We taxied onto the apron area, only to see a long line of white men lining the edge, all with suitcases packed and raring to go. Much consternation ensued when we explained we wouldn't be leaving until the following morning because, before we could go off duty, we had to transfer their seats from the cargo holds - where they had been while we carried freight on the main deck - and reposition them onto the rails in the passenger cabin. This would put us out of hours to continue. Wrong! Airwork personnel knew all about aeroplanes, and the seats were in place in about half-an-hour. But we still stayed the night anyway.

The next day we left, flying to Athens via Jeddah, where we had to stop for fuel, due lack of performance out of Khamis I assume. Now the loadmaster and I became stewards, of a sort. We served the meals to them in their seats but for a drink service we arranged several bar boxes and some wooden planks from the cargo floor into a makeshift bar, and they came to us. This worked quite well and there were no complaints. Luxury they weren't looking for, just a ride out of a military camp in the middle of the Saudi desert. They had apparently lived dry for the past eighteen months, apart from a few illicit stills on the camp, but at Athens they all tried to make up for this eighteen month deficiency in one night.

We were all put in the same hotel for the night, not a first class establishment either, and I remember there being very little sleep possible. There were doors banging, drunken songs being sung, the occasional crash of breaking bottles etc. all night long; the further into the night we were the louder the singing and signs of inebriation. Next morning there were, it would seem, several of our passengers missing, but they were eventually dug out from various disreputable bars and shady places and we finally managed to get them the last leg of the journey back to their loved ones. Truly an interesting experience, especially for a non-boozer like myself. (Alan Breedon)

Hotel Echo was the first of the Viscounts to appear in full livery, making her first Air Ferry flight, and first revenue flight, with 66 passengers to Alicante on 8 March. The flight was commanded by Captain Lockwood, and the aircraft returned to Manston on the 10th. After an Ostend for training on the 19th. she positioned to Le Bourget on Thursday 21st., and over the next three days carried out a series of passenger charters from there with two to Geneva and four to Cardiff.

November Juliet positioned to Le Bourget a day later than her colleague, and this was her first flight in full Air Ferry colours. The Viscount was delayed leaving, having to return to the tarmac with an unserviceable compass, then had a further delay awaiting spares from Southend. Peter Lockwood made the first revenue flight from Le Bourget to Cardiff on Saturday 23rd., a second Le Bourget-Cardiff-Le Bourget followed next day and then both Viscounts returned to Manston on Sunday night.

It must have been sometime in late March or early April that the rumour flashed round that Air Ferry was to close at the end of the season. Alan Bristow was widely credited as actually taking the decision; B.U.A. BAC1-11s were under utilised and it was known that Bristow wanted Air Ferry's work, especially Cosmos, to fill them. Alan Jones recalls a helicopter coming into Manston about this time with the B.U.A. managing director aboard.

Ken Sheppardson did not prevaricate, the rumour was true, but meanwhile there was much work to be done and there would be incentives offered to retain staff through to the closure at 30 September. For many people, pride in Air Ferry was enough to keep them as long as possible, but there were commitments to meet and the future to think about. A retention payment, and some redundancy pay, would obviously be welcome. However unpalatable the thought of closure was, at least it was to be an extremely well managed one, in sharp contrast to many others in the airline industry.

There was the feeling, as Hugh Kennard had predicted, that Air Ferry was to be brought down by the bigger politics of Air Holdings. It was particularly frustrating that it was the unprofitabiltiy and falling markets of B.U.A. and B.A.F. that required the commando action that Sir Miles and Alan Bristow were advocating back in December. As before, at the time of the takeover, Air Ferry's trade was reasonably lucrative and easy to take away; very galling when the travel industry was back on growth. Gone now were the plans to re-equip with Comets, although Alan Jones recalls that the manuals for the De Havilland airliner were actually in the

WINGSPAN

Vol. 3 No. 18 — Air Holdings Group Monthly Newspaper — MARCH/APRIL 1968

IT'S OFFICIAL—
BUA leaves Air Holdings

NOW it is confirmed—British United Airways and other transport companies are leaving the Air Holdings Group. This move follows a series of complex negotiations, which were delayed by the death of Sir Myles Wyatt. The whole share capital of BUA, BUA(CI), BU(Manx) Airways, BUA (Services), Morton Air Services and Airwork International (Bristow Helicopters) will be acquired by British & Commonwealth Shipping Co. on behalf of itself and others. These concerns will form a new BUA Group, which also includes Sierra Leone Airways, Uganda Aviation Services and Gambia Airways.

A joint statement says: 'British & Commonwealth and Air Holdings feel that it will be advantageous to separate the air operating companies from the remainder of the Air Holdings Group.'

New company to be formed

British & Commonwealth propose to form a new company (name to be announced later) which will hold all the shares of the companies acquired. Sir Nicholas Cayzer is to be chairman of this new company in which B & C will have a controlling interest. The directors will include Hon Anthony Cayzer, Mr J. A. Thomson, Mr Alan Bristow and Mr G. Russell Fry. Sir Brian Mountain has also expressed his willingness to accept a seat on the Board.

Mr Anthony Cayzer will be chairman of British United Airways with Mr Alan Bristow as deputy chairman and managing director. Mr Thomson will join the Board. Mr Max Stuart-Shaw, Mr R. W. Cantello and Mr J. O. Charlton are leaving the Board. The special directors are Mr Ted Bates, Mr J. R. Sidebotham, Mr Bill Richardson and Mr Jack Bes, while Mr W. B. Caulfield will be appointed an additional special director. The composition of the Boards of the other companies will be announced later.

Chairman for a limited period

Consequent upon the sudden death of Sir Myles Wyatt, Sir Errington Keville—currently a director of Air Holdings—has consented to become chairman of the company for a limited period. Mr R. L. Cumming, presently financial director, is appointed managing director. The Board of Air Holdings will therefore comprise Sir Errington Keville (chairman), Sir Nicholas Cayzer (deputy chairman), Mr Cumming (managing director), Sir Donald Anderson, Sir Brian Mountain, Mr F. A. Bishop. As a result of these changes and by agreement Mr Charlton will resign as chief executive of Air Holdings on 31 May.

The main companies owned by Air Holdings are now as follows: Airwork Services, Aviation Traders, BAF, Air Ferry, Safe Air, Lyons, Whitehall and Leroy.

The new BUA Group employs nearly 5,000 people. Its fleet consists of 45 airliners and 80 helicopters.

SPECIAL MESSAGE FROM SIR NICHOLAS CAYZER

For a long time British United Airways and its associated companies have played a leading role among the independent airlines in this country, and Airwork International (Bristows) has a world-wide reputation for its helicopter operations.

I am anxious that we shall continue to be leaders in these fields.

So far as the airline is concerned we have a very difficult task for we are denied a fair share of the market.

As a Group our only hope of going forward will be to secure that the undertaking is profitable. To achieve this end we shall have to work together as a team; we shall need a real spirit of enterprise; a determination to succeed and the enthusiastic and loyal support of all who work for the Group. Good Luck and Good Business.

A MESSAGE FROM SIR ERRINGTON KEVILLE

In this first message to each of you throughout the companies which now form the Air Hold-
Continued on page ten, col. two

Chairman's sudden death

A MEMORIAL service for the late Sir Myles Wyatt who died on 15 April was held at St Martins-in-the-Fields, London, on 26 April.

The death of Sir Myles, chairman of Air Holdings and many Group companies, was sudden and unexpected. He had been working a normal and full day at Portland House right up until Easter. Sir Myles, who was 64, died at his home, Alresford Hall, near Colchester, Essex.

A personal tribute to Sir Myles by Mr R. Loudon Cumming, a senior colleague for over 30 years, is published on page 10.

The names of Sir Myles Wyatt and the Air Holdings Group are synonymous. From the time that he joined Airwork as general manager in 1934, the late chairman was the major builder and
Continued on page four

Gatwick Manor for large or small parties

'One of the top eleven restaurants outside London'
EGON RONAY FOOD GUIDE

Near Crawley, Sussex
Telephone: Crawley 24301

4/- in the £ OFF
NEW BRITISH TYRES
BRIGHTON TYRE SERVICE LTD.
37 Lewes Road, Brighton
14 Beach Road, Eastbourne
Eastbourne 37961 Brighton 63632

WELCOME FOR 28,000

Helping to attract 28,000 visitors to the Lydd Air Show on Easter Sunday was 'Miss Ferryfield', Maureen Coleman, a 24-year-old BAF air hostess.

The Air Show, which was opened by aviator Shiela Scott, featured a flying display and static exhibition. Stars of the event were the Red Arrows RAF aerobatic team and ATL director Bob Batt who demonstrated his Prentice aircraft.

stores; so near and yet so far.

News of the impending closure was swiftly picked up by the local press, always quick to monitor threats and opportunities to the poor employment prospects in Thanet.

April Foxtrot Yankee operated out of Newcastle throughout April carrying passengers to and from Beauvais and Rotterdam, plus two Ostends. On Sunday 21st. a Rotterdam routed back to Manchester, with a return to Newcastle the next morning, and on Tuesday 23rd. the DC4 flew Newcastle-Rotterdam-Gatwick. Hotel Echo flew Manston-Rotterdam-Gatwick-Manston that day with an electrician and a fitter on board for Gatwick, and carrying spares for Foxtrot Yankee. More work was found to be necessary however, and the

Whisky India (John Somerville)

DC4 positioned Gatwick-Manston during the afternoon for her only appearance at Manston in the month. This diversion was a brief stay of three hours to clear the defects before returning to Newcastle via Rotterdam. On the 29th. Foxtrot Yankee went unserviceable at Rotterdam with the ILS glide receiver U/S, and the Radio Inspector flew out, via Invicta, to clear the defect. On 30th. April the the aircraft positioned Newcastle-Leeds to carry on the Rotterdam tours from there. This series was easily the most sustained period of activity by one aircraft with Foxtrot Yankee, away from base, carrying passengers every day from 30th. March to 5th. May, a total of thirty seven consecutive days.

November Papa, 10 April, 1968

Two crews operated, based in a hotel in Newcastle they shared a hire car so that while one crew was on duty the other one could use the car for running around and to make some sight seeing tours of the area. The crews included Keith Sissons, Mike Waddingham, Jenny Holtan, Hazel King and Hazel Baynham. In one of his out of Air Ferry activities, Keith Sissons had assisted in making an episode of '*Doctor Who*,' in which he had flown a helicopter as part of the action. Annoyingly, this episode was shown during the time they were at Newcastle and Keith never did see it.

Between flying the DC4s and converting to the DC6s Keith had another opportunity for a freelance journey and implored Ken Sheppardson to let him have two weeks leave. This trip involved a seaplane licence,

1968 PROP JETS AND FINALE

flying a Grumman Mallard from Luton on a long journey out to Gabon in Africa and return. It was not until they had flown to numerous places, and collected some very businesslike passengers, that Keith realised the aircraft's owner was reconnoitering a route for the Biafran transport runs. On landing at Paris, by this time alone, Keith unfortunately scuffed a tyre on the Mallard and ended up collecting a new one from England and then taking it out as hand baggage! After this had been fitted he completed the journey back to the U.K. On Keith's return, Shep was not too amused that one of his captains had accumulated 100 hours flying in 10 days, while on leave!

Hotel Echo, 12 March 1968

November Juliet, April 1968

Whisky India did not fly until 10th. April, being in the hangar on a Check 2, with a working party from Scottish Aviation assisting, and then alternated between freight and passenger work. She took freight Liverpool-Brussels on the 10th./11th., followed by passenger flights to Cologne and Rotterdam. A cargo flight to Malta came next and then tour flying once more to Basle, Beauvais and Rotterdam. Between 23/26 April the DC4 went off to Freetown again, routed through Casablanca out and return. Ostend was visited on four occasions, with passengers on the 15th. and the rest for training. After the training flight on the 29th., the engineers started an engine change and checked the cabin and nose heaters in accordance with A.R.B. notice number 41.

It was not until Tuesday 30th. that November Oscar emerged from her check, and then it was just for a short local test flight at Prestwick. As the only DC6 doing revenue flying in April, November Papa was also involved in both passenger and freight work, starting with cargo flights to Beirut via Rome and a Manchester-Le Bourget. Between 13/18 April the aircraft flew passengers Amsterdam-Rome and return, Manston-Stockholm-Cologne-Manston, and a Rotterdam-Rome-Le Bourget-Rome-Rotterdam. Then the seats came out during the morning of Thursday 18th. for a positioning flight to Hurn, delayed starting as the flight engineer was late, for more cargo to Kuwait and the three usual Saudi destinations. After a training sortie to Ostend, from which she returned with a propeller defect, and two Rotterdams with passengers, one via Gatwick; November Papa left on the last day to Frankfurt for another cargo journey.

With the introduction of the jet turbined airliners, at long last the long climbout and circuit over Manston required by the piston engined aircraft joining the airways at Dover was no longer a feature, the Viscount could easily join direct. (Paul Noller)

The Viscount revenue flying was all passenger work, with Hotel Echo starting with a Le Bourget-Gatwick, this flight delayed leaving as there was no hostess, and later going to Stockholm, Basle and Ostend. On Saturday 13th. the aircraft had a technical return from a charter to Rome with 58 passengers, and November Juliet substituted. Hotel Echo did not fly again until an engine change had been made and a visit made by the Dowty representative for number 1 propeller servicing; after this the aircraft had an air test on Saturday 20th.

On the 23rd., Hotel Echo flew the Rotterdam-Gatwick mentioned above, and then put in some lengthy training flights both flying locally and over to Ostend. A 'Manston-Manston' on Friday 26th. was of nearly five hours duration and recorded an impressive twenty three landings! The Viscount completed April with a charter to Hanover.

Early in the month the engineers were working on November Juliet with a weight saving exercise that was in progress for several days. The Viscount only flew between 12th./20th. April, taking passengers to Rome, Ostend, Rotterdam and Gatwick-Le Bourget. On Sunday 14th., the Viscount flew a group of staff and their families across Kent to the Lydd Airshow where she was in some demand for joy rides during the day. The last flight of the month was a Rome-Gatwick charter.

Norman Watson was one of the pilots selected to fly the new type, as was Don Nay, although he had worked through the DC6 technical and passed the examination.for this type

Paddy Roberts and Ann Rippon (Ann Rippon)

Several of the pilots shared a house locally, the main occupants being Norman, George Gilson plus Alan Breedon and an Invicta pilot. It is not known if the caravan was unavailable then, or if a Thanet winter had influenced Alan's change of accomodation.

May   The hours flown in May, 591, were the second lowest for that month in Air Ferry's six year history. There was a telex from Leeds on Wednesday 1st. that Foxtrot Yankee's main cabin lights were U/S, and Joe Russell arranged a seat on an Invicta aircraft for an electrician to go to Rotterdam to meet Foxtrot Yankee.

Geneva: Mike Waddingham directs the traffic for Lorna Brownridge, not known, Hazel King and Sue Chadwick (Hazel Kyd-Grant nee King)

164

1968 PROP JETS AND FINALE

The DC4 continued with the Leeds-Rotterdam work, returning via Ostend to Manston on the 5th. After an Ostend for training, there was a Geneva with freight that was delayed starting when the aircraft returned from the runway with a mag. drop and mag. blown out; the jump leads were changed and the aircraft was away at 0400. After that the aircraft positioned to Gatwick on the afternoon of Friday 10th., and flew Gatwick-Madrid early on Saturday with 13 passengers and presumably some cargo; the aircraft returned direct to Manston late Sunday evening, still with the 13 passengers. After an Amsterdam tour, the Basle inclusive tours built up, and these would be the main work for the DC4s in the last season. Near the end of the month the aircraft made two freight flights, a Manston-Birmingham-Brussels-Gatwick-Manston, and another Geneva, although with an engine change in between. The aircraft completed the month with a Basle IT on the night of Friday 31st.

November Oscar, 2 May, 1968

'I liked the DC4s, they were steady; I wasn't so keen on the Viscounts as the rear swung.' (Ann Rippon)

Whisky India went to Calais and Antwerp with tour charters on the first day, all flown by Paddy Roberts and Mike Waddingham, and over the 2nd./4th. made a cargo trip to Dhahran via Athens. The crew on this flight was Keith Sissons, Paul Horsting as co-captain and Simon Searle. Considering the empty flight back, Paul suggested: 'Why don't we do it in one leg?' They left Dhahran at 0915, and 17 hours 15 minutes later switched off at Manston. Adequate fuel remained on return, had a diversion been necessary, but they had exceeded the duty times slightly, and Keith received a gentle reprimand for this.

On the afternoon of Sunday 5th., the DC4 flew over to Rotterdam and on to Leeds to provide the continuity for Foxtrot Yankee, which had returned to Manston earlier in the day. These flights to Rotterdam and Beauvais carried on until the return from Leeds to Manston on Wednesday 15th. The flight on the 13th. combined two charters, by travelling Leeds-Beauvais-Southampton-Beauvais-Leeds. The DC4 did not fly again until she joined in the IT work to Basle on the 25th. Another Basle, a Basle-Gatwick and an Ostend with just 42 passengers followed, this flight delayed leaving due to bad weather that affected Manston for several days. The aircraft closed the month with a Zurich-Shannon freight journey.

November Oscar came back from Prestwick on 1 May and spent most of the month on charter and tour passenger work. After an Ostend for training there was a Birmingham-Berlin, a Geneva on the 11th., and a Madrid with a night stop. On Friday 17th. November Oscar collected passengers from Brno in Czechoslovakia, the only time Air Ferry went there, and brought them to Birmingham. By this time the first tours were getting underway to Genoa, Manchester-Basle, Valencia, and Tangier. On Monday 27th. the DC6 took passengers Gatwick-Vienna, and next day positioned to Hurn, with Adrian Ross in command, for freight to Dhahran via Frankfurt and Istanbul, with a return to Manston on the last day of the month.

November Papa, at Frankfurt on 1 May, continued to Cairo and returned, via Zurich, to Manston. It was then back to passenger configuration for flights to Berlin and the first Genoa IT, before removing the seats once again for cargo Dusseldorf-Dakar. This was followed by another journey from Hurn to Kuwait and the usual three airports in Saudi Arabia, a stop of nearly four days being made at Riyadh. Another freight journey followed on the 27th., the departure held up due to a technical defect, then the DC6 returned to the tarmac as there was no clearance over France for approximately an hour. The flight finally proceeded Manston-Cagliari-Amsterdam-Gatwick, the last leg on the 28th. being a diversion due to the bad weather at Manston. A re-seating and service crew set off from Manston for Gatwick with Les Dray in charge, and the next day the DC6 took the first passengers to Venice and returned home to Manston. The month ended with a Manston-Basle-Manchester-Basle-Manston that was late getting away from Manston due to fuelling troubles.

TWILIGHT OF THE PISTONS

In addition to the Leeds telex on the 1st., another one came from Calais when Hotel Echo reported low batteries and GPU and was unable to start. By means of another flight on Invicta, Messrs. Green and Brown set off to give assistance, armed with two recharged batteries. Hotel Echo also made several training sorties early in May, and flew charters Manston-Southend-Hanover-Stanstead-Manston and Manston-Glasgow-Southend-Glasgow-Manston. After an eight day gap, a Manston-Manchester-Gerona-Manston followed, and then another gap of a week before flying again, once more to Gerona. Early on 27 May, Whisky India had returned from Basle to Gatwick, presumably due to weather, and as mentioned, November Oscar flew a Vienna from there; during the day Hotel Echo flew from Manston to Gatwick and return, possibly with crews or spares. That night Hotel Echo's Gerona flight diverted into Lydd on the return; with passengers on the outward leg only, the aircraft lived up to the name the engineers sometimes used of 'Home Empty.' On the 29th. the aircraft took the first Barcelona and ended May with a Manston-Basle-Berlin-Basle-Manston charter.

November Juliet made an internal flight, Manston-Manchester-Southend-Manchester-Manston on the 9th., and only flew on training until Saturday 18th., when she took the first of the Gerona tours to Spain. Other flights included a Milan-Zurich, a charter over the 24th./26th. that was late leaving due to a fuel pump being changed, and then flew Manston-Alicante-Manchester-Gerona-Alicante-Manston. A charter to Brussels recorded another delay due to weather. and the month ended with a Gerona that positioned empty to Manchester twenty four hours later, for an early morning departure from that airport.

June The months of June-August saw the second most intensive period of flying by Air Ferry and was only exceeded by July-September 1966, and the three DC4/ two DC6 combination at that time. The two DC4s spent virtually all the month on IT work to Basle and Ostend; there was a Basle tour by DC4 every day of the month with a second flight on Saturdays and Sundays.

With the programme lightly loaded compared to previous seasons the DC4s did not experience too many dramas, although Foxtrot Yankee was held up twice on Sunday 2nd., firstly due to the non availability of departure pans and then because the passengers did not show up on time, a situation repeated for a Le Touquet a few days later. The aircraft had an air test on the 14th., for a filter check on number 1 engine. At 1950 on Saturday 22nd., Foxtrot Yankee came back from Basle with defects including an unserviceable radio which was AOG'd for spares, and the stores had to do a 'tunnel meet' during the night when one of the storemen from Manston met a counterpart from Southend at the Dartford Tunnel; a convenient meeting place in those days.

> *During one flight, on what was considered a very bumpy ride with one of the DC4s, Hazel Baynham found one passenger not showing too much confidence in the journey by staring straight ahead, muttering and with a rosary in her hand.*

Whisky India carried out the DC4 schedule for Sunday, and Foxtrot Yankee's last significant entry in the maintenance handover book for June was on Saturday 29th., when the first officer flooded numbers 3 and 4 and the mags. were blown out on the latter. Whisky India had an air test on the 7th. and was delayed in Basle on the 15th., with a dead cutting mag. which Balair cleared, so the aircraft was expected back: 'Early Sunday, weather permitting.' Flights other than to Ostend and Basle were infrequent, Foxtrot Yankee went to Le Touquet and Maastricht, and Whisky India to Rotterdam. It was now a case of '*sic transit gloria*' for these aircraft, and their hours in 1968 were the lowest flown by the type in the six years.

The DC6 programme was now well into its stride, the tours to Tangier, Palma, Venice and Valencia and about half of the Munichs were evening departures, although on varying days, from Manston between 2100 and 2230. These followed a nine day programme cycle of departures for the aircraft, although a ten day holiday for the voyageurs by the time their home to airport travel was included. In June there were two cycles running for Tangier and Palma having eight and six departures respectively. There was also a Saturday morning tour to Munich at 0830 while the Genoa tours also departed each Saturday morning although some two hours later.

Flights to Milan were much more frequent with an occasional tour operated by the Viscounts. In June the Milans left on Mondays at 2230, Wednesdays at 1100, Saturdays at 1800, Sundays at 1500 and with some additional flights at other times. In addition, there were some Basles, the Friday Basle-Manchesters and occasional extra charters.

1968 PROP JETS AND FINALE

CAYZER, SEEAR & CO. LTD.
INSURANCE BROKERS

Telephone: SISSINGHURST 361
Cables: SEMGRET LONDON
Telex: 95179

HARTRIDGE HOUSE
CRANBROOK
KENT
and at LLOYD'S

DIRECTORS:
SIR NICHOLAS CAYZER, Bt. (CHAIRMAN)
LORD ROTHERWICK (DEPUTY CHAIRMAN)
P. A. DUCK   J. K. SEEAR
R. W. LAST   I. O. SHORT, A.C.I.I.
J. A. THOMSON, C.A.

Your ref.

Our ref.

CERTIFICATE OF INSURANCE   G-APNO   22nd May, 1968

THIS IS TO CERTIFY that as Joint Insurance Brokers with C. T. Bowring & Company (Insurance) Ltd., we have effected Insurance with Companies and Lloyd's Underwriters as follows:-

A/C: BRITISH UNITED AIRWAYS LIMITED &/or Subsidiary &/or Associated &/or Affiliated Companies &/or SAFE AIR LIMITED &/or BRITISH AIR FERRIES LTD., &/or BRITISH UNITED AIRWAYS (C.I.) LTD., &/or MORTON AIR SERVICES LTD., &/or AIR FERRY LTD., &/or Subsidiary &/or Associated Companies - for their respective rights and interests.

Period: 1st June, 1968 to 31st May, 1969 both days inclusive.

IN RESPECT OF ALL AIRCRAFT OWNED &/OR OPERATED BY THE INSURED UNDER THEIR MAIN AIRCRAFT FLEET

COVER: THIRD PARTY LIABILITY, FREIGHT &/OR MAIL LEGAL LIABILITY AND PASSENGER LEGAL LIABILITY

LIMITS: (a)   Third Party Liability

£3,000,000 any one accident, each aircraft

(b)   Freight &/or Mail Legal Liability (as required)

(i)   £1,250,000 any one accident, each aircraft, but
(ii) £2,500,000 any one accident on the ground outside aircraft.

(c)   Passenger Legal Liability

(i)   £3,600,000 any one accident, each aircraft, but
(ii) £4,125,000 any one accident, each aircraft in respect of flights commencing or landing in U.S.A.

Schedule of aircraft at 1st June, 1968 as attached. Additions and deletions automatically covered as per policy terms.

Subject to the terms and conditions of the policies issued or to be issued.

For and on behalf of
CAYZER, SEEAR & CO. LTD.

Director

Branches at: Bristol, Exeter, Guernsey, Maidstone and Plymouth   London Office: Dowgate Hill House, 14 Dowgate Hill, London, E.C.4

Ron Blake still made occasional trips to check on the performance of the radio equipment, one of these was to Goteborg. At any time, but particularly in poor or bad visibility, the correct functioning of the aids was critical. It is considered that Air Ferry nearly suffered a DC6 crash in Switzerland, it could have been 1966, 1967 or 1968 and, on this or another occasion, Captain Ross insisted that all the radio equipment be removed and sent off to be checked and recalibrated by Collins, the manufacturer. No faults were found and the view held was that some interference to the aids occurred at Basle. A railway line passed near to the approach and the suspicion was that interference could occur when a train passed. Balair's operations room were quoted as saying once: 'We know about that, you have to be very careful on ILS.' Fears of these problems would unhappily recur later, to Invicta.

November Oscar, already late for Tangier on the 1st., came back from the runway with sparking plugs failed on three engines. The next day the DC6 took the only non-Viscount tour to Gerona operated by Air Ferry. An extra flight that first week was a Manston-Rome-Cairo-Athens-Manston freight journey, for which the aircraft was given an extra twenty four hours on her Check B. On her return the engineers were unable to position November Oscar in the hangar for two hours owing to Customs clearance problems. The aircraft also took a Barcelona, the few 1968 tours there usually being flown by the Viscounts. Perpignan was another mainly Viscount destination, but the DC6s flew some, with November Oscar making her first visit of 1968 on the night of the 10th/11th.

Anna Oates at right   (Anna Turner nee Oates)

The second Basle on Sunday 9th. was another delay for this aircraft when it was brought into the hangar for a main wheel change and the tyre to be pumped up. Later in the month, November Oscar, already delayed on Tuesday nights Tangier, needed an air test, by Adrian Ross and Mike Waddingham, at 0135 on Wednesday 19th., and finally departed for Morocco at 0300. After going into the hangar on the 24th. for a Check 1 and a clean, the aircraft went to Oslo on the 25th., held up starting for fifty minutes with no crew. Later that day November Oscar combined a Basle with a Basle-Liverpool-Basle charter. The DC6 went back to Oslo early on the morning of Thursday 27th., returning on this occasion via Gatwick, and probably causing the sub-charter of the Valencia due at that time, and which did not operate.

Len Mees at left

1968 PROP JETS AND FINALE

November Papa worked hard, going to Valencia, Munich and Genoa on the first day. After two Milans she operated a Basle-Berlin-Basle, replacing November Juliet on this flight as the Viscount had a recurring compass defect, and also went to Helsinki in the first week. Other events in the month were a return from Palma through Le Touquet in the early hours of Saturday 15th., and the DC6 came back from a Basle next day with defects to the radar and autopilot that resulted in Harry Burgess being called in. She then flew a Manston-Basle-Liverpool-Basle-Manston that night. On the 22nd., November Papa went to Munich and arrived back with a fire warning on the number 1 engine and November Oscar went to Basle in her stead. There was a flight Manston-Edinburgh-Oslo-Manston on the 25th., and another Oslo direct the next day.

November Papa departed for Palma at 2105 on the last day of June with 103 passengers aboard, the aircraft returned after forty minutes with a smell of burning. As the DC6 touched down very heavily loaded, an overweight landing check had to be carried out. The engineers carried out a ground run and checked all the systems including radio, electrical, engines, pressurisation, cabin heater and wing heater, but were unable to reproduce the symptoms. At the request of the captain and operations, an electrician and an airframe fitter went on the flight, and the aircraft finally departed for Palma at 2355.

The Viscounts flew 405 hours between them, the majority from the many flights through Perpignan. For 1968 one of the Viscounts was to be actually based in Perpignan and this led to some complicated programming of routes. Tours to Perpignan were flown as usual from Manston by one Viscount, and some DC6 flights, while the Perpignan based Viscount flew to Manchester, Liverpool and Birmingham from there in addition to the Perpignan-Manston-Perpignans. The aircraft on detachment rotated approximately on a weekly basis and Ken Sheppardson based an engineer over in Perpignan for on site support, with Ted Williams being selected for this task. There were also five tours to Barcelona in the first half of the month and, between 18 May and 4 June, the Viscounts went to Gerona on seventeen occasions.

November Juliet started June flying Manchester-Barcelona-Manchester-Gerona-Birmingham-Gerona-Manston. The Viscount substituted for November Oscar, which was still in freight trim, for Wednesday 5th's. Milan and on the 7th. flew a charter Manston-Gatwick-Mahon-Gatwick-Manston. On return the aircraft had defects, and a generator balance was carried out after a complaint was received from the tower. The Viscount was AOG'd for autopilot spares from Channel Airways and Cyril Nurthen duly left in the mini to collect them from Southend. The Viscount flew three Perpignans on Saturday 8th. then at Sunday lunchtime, after a delay leaving while there was an instrument swap with Hotel Echo, went to France for the first detachment at the French airport. November Juliet was based there for a week and operated to Manchester, Birmingham and Liverpool, before coming back to Manston on Sunday 16th. The next week November Juliet operated out of Manston and went back to Perpignan on Sunday 23rd. for another weeks detachment before returning home again on Sunday 30th.

Hotel Echo also travelled widely. At the start of the month her Gerona on the night of Saturday 1st. left late due to traffic problems over France. Over the 5th./6th. there was a Manston-Luton-Dusseldorf-Luton-Manchester-Barcelona, where the aircraft remained until Saturday 8th., and then flew Barcelona-Manchester-Perpignan-Manston-Perpignan. In the second week there was a Manston-Gatwick-Vienna-Gatwick-Manston, a C of A air test on the 11th., and the usual tours before being Perpignan based between the Sunday 16th. and Sunday 23rd. The aircraft went unserviceable at Perpignan on Wednesday 19th., requiring a brake unit change and spares were sent from Manston by the first available aircraft. The aircraft came off the chocks at Perpignan but returned to the pan and, when it arrived at Manston early next morning, was unserviceable due to the autopilot and a compass. There was a Manston-Gatwick-Vienna-Manston on Monday 24th., and on Friday 28th. a Manston-Le Bourget-Binbrook-Le Bourget-Manston. The Viscount had been delayed on this flight due to poor weather at Paris and a DC6 Basle-Manchester that day was also delayed through weather. Quite a month.

The opening times of the duty free shop at Perpignan were sometimes not helpful to the crews. There was one especially hot day when a Viscount was loaded prior to departure, the aircraft bar stocks were very low and there was no opportunity for an uplift at the shop. The hostesses calculated they only had enough stock to permit one pack of twenty cigarettes per customer, and were nearly lynched on admitting this to their perspiring and irritable passengers, the men by now without their shirts and most of the women down to bras. 'Do you often get flights like this?'

TWILIGHT OF THE PISTONS

Hilary Reeks asked Ann Rippon. When based on detachment at Perpignan the crews often used a town square featuring a nude woman statue as a meeting place, referred to by them as 'starkers square.' (Ann Rippon)

DC4 cockpit, Foxtrot Yankee

July This was another busy and complicated month. The DC4s kept up their tour work, again visiting Basle every day and Ostend frequently, fog in Belgium delaying Sunday 7th's first flight there. The night Basle by Foxtrot Yankee on Tuesday 2nd. was diverted into Le Bourget on the outward route due to poor weather at Basle, and the DC4 had another Basle diversion on the 10th., going into Gatwick on the return because of high crosswinds at Manston. The aircraft had some freight work, going to Bordeaux on the 17th., Whisky India was unserviceable that day, leading to a delay loading, and the weather conditions were still poor. After that Foxtrot Yankee had a Check 1 and an engine change, and then made a cargo flight to Montoire Airport at St. Nazaire on the 19th., the only visit made there by Air Ferry. On the 24th. the aircraft flew Manston-Ostend-Gatwick-Le Bourget-Manston and the following day had a cargo journey Manston-Metz-Basle-Manston; the only previous visits to Metz had been by the two Vikings with freight in January 1966. After that it was a return to Ostends and Basles for the remainder of July.

Whisky India took freight on the 2nd. to Guernsey, the aircraft delayed leaving, although loaded with freight, due to the autopilot and a hydraulic leak. The DC4 went unserviceable at Basle on the 6th. and Balair looked at the mags; although they took the boards off and found water present, all seemed to be in order. On the 11th. the aircraft positioned to Hurn for cargo to the Gulf area, and Air Ferry's last long range cargo haul, flying Hurn-Rome-Nicosia-Beirut-Abu Dhabi-Azaiba-Bahrein-Nicosia-Rome-Manston. The DC4 arrived back on the 17th. with a block time of 43 hours.

On two occasions Whisky India was late going to Basle due to congestion on the apron, and on the 23rd. was delayed over in Ostend when the starter went U/S. There was an Manston-Exeter-Le Bourget-Manston passenger charter on the 29th., and during the afternoon of the next day Whisky India went unserviceable at Ostend again, this time with engine trouble. She had returned after take off with 43 passengers, and Foxtrot Yankee took three engineers and went over to collect them. This flight was definitely a revenue loss as Whisky India had gone out empty, and the half load of passengers that came back on FoxtrotYankee were the only ones carried on the two trips. Over the end of the month Whisky India was on an engine change.

The DC6 activity continued at record level, somehow keeping the tours to Munich, Valencia and Genoa all to time. The Venice and Palma flights had one late each, Tangier two delays and inevitably there were occasional sub-charters. Both aircraft had additional charters from Paris, visited fourteen times by Air Ferry

1968 PROP JETS AND FINALE

Air Ferry — Manston

FLIGHT INFORMATION

Date: 7.7.1968   15.30 Local/~~Greenwich~~ Time

From Captain HORSTING to all passengers on AIR FERRY aircraft G. ARWI

We are flying at 9000 feet at 200 M.P.H.

Our present position is OVER CHATILLON (N. FRANCE)

We shall be passing 40 MILES EAST OF PARIS

at approximately 15.30

We will arrive at BASLE

at approximately 16.30 Local/~~Greenwich~~ Time

The name of your ~~Steward~~/Hostess is MISS GRAY
                                          ✓ HUNT

WHEN YOU HAVE READ THIS PLEASE PASS IT ON TO THE NEXT PASSENGER

AIRCRAFT ARRIVAL AND SURPLUS STORES ACCOUNT

For Official Use Only

Time of arrival	Rotn. No.

Airport: MANSTON
Operator: AIR FERRY LIMITED

Identifying Marks and No. of Aircraft	Flight No.	Arrived from	Date

Description of Goods	Trade Brand	UNITS Description	Number	Identifying Marks and No. of each container
WHISKY		MINS ½		
GIN		MINS ¼		
BRANDY		MINS ¼		
SHERRY		MINS		
CIGARETTES	PLAIN	20s		
	TIPPED	20s		
CIGARS		5s		
TOBACCO		2 oz		
WATCHES				
TRAVEL CLOCKS				
COLOGNE	CARVEN	2 oz		
	DIOR	2 oz		
PERFUME	WORTH	⅓ oz		
	CARVEN	1/6 oz		
	BLUE GRASS	1/5 oz		
AFTER SHAVE	DIOR	2 oz		

Total number of containers

Date .... 196..   Signature ....
                     Commander or authorised person

C.911   Sec. F.2407 (July, 1962)   (Continued Overleaf)

in the month. On the 1st., one DC6 flew Manston-Le Bourget-Dublin-Manston, and the other Manston-Le Bourget-Edinburgh-Manston. November Papa went into the hangar for a Check 1 and after this, on the 3rd., both DC6s flew Manston-Le Bourget-Southampton-Manston, one of the latter causing that nights Venice delay of some eight hours. November Papa also went to Helsinki in the first week and November Oscar's Manchester-Basle early on Friday 5th. was diverted into Zurich.

Also this season there was a time when, for some reason, aircraft were not permitted to enter French air space. This occasionally necessitated long taxi drives to connect up with airports or hotels and after one of these journeys the Air Ferry crew, including Hazel Baynham, found themselves accomodated in the same hotel as a British Eagle crew which, after a few drinks, marked the occasion by throwing a fully uniformed air hostess into the swimming pool.

November Oscar went to Munich on the 6th., delayed starting with technical log defects, and the aircraft was operating with the radar unserviceable; in addition the DC6 came back from this flight with the radio aerial and tail beacon broken. On Monday 8th. July, November Oscar's Munich returned via Gatwick, and the next day the aircraft had an extra flight, Manston-Le Bourget-Gatwick-Manston. The Milan and Perpignan flights that had departed at 0130 that morning had been held up leaving for three hours due to an R.A.F. emergency landing. There was another delay on Wednesday night when the Tangier, operated by November Papa, did not leave until midnight. Paris featured again for November Oscar with a Le Bourget-Exeter on Thursday 11th. when the aircraft had defects and, probably for this reason, there was no Palma that night, this being sub-chartered to a Laker Britannia. With sequential registration letters, it was very easy to confuse the two DC6s, and a potentially bad situation was averted on the afternoon of Sunday 14th. when it was discovered the aircraft bound for Basle and Milan had the wrong baggage loaded and there was a delay while the suitcases were frantically changed over.

The third week saw November Oscar flying a Glasgow-Tarbes on the 15th. and followed this with a Valencia. At midday on Tuesday 16th. November Oscar returned from the runway with engine defects that were cleared but the DC6, flown by Adrian Ross and Patrick Hope, came back after an hours flight with the flying controls stiff to operate. The engineers checked the flying controls from cockpit to the rear, the underfloor panels were removed and the cables checked. The aileron system was also checked and the autopilot and servos were removed. Finally, an air test at 1825 registered everything satisfactory, and the DC6 went to Milan at 2235.

November Oscar flew Manston-Gatwick-Oslo-Manston on Thursday 18th., this flight left an hour late as November Papa went unserviceable on the line and the aircraft were changed over. On return, November Oscar went into the hangar with an autopilot defect and then had an air test on Friday. There were omissions from the flight log of Palma on Thursday night and Milan on Friday due to this unserviceability, and to November Papa being on a Basle-Manchester.

On Monday 22nd. November Oscar flew Tarbes-Glasgow, returning the group from the previous week, piloted by Tony Ahmad and Mike Waddingham. Being a religious tour to Lourdes, the group said their 'Hail Mary's' before take off, the passengers somehow conveniently distributed priest and nun alternately. By the time the aircraft landed the bar stocks of Ann Rippon, Mary Coates and Hostess Eisenhut were exhausted except for some perfume! On the 23rd. November Papa went to Milan in place of her sister aircraft as the latter's tail beacon was unserviceable and, to the fury of the engineers, there was no giraffe and no beacon in stock!

The fourth week went well until the weekend. On Friday 26th. November Oscar was two hours late leaving for a Basle-Manchester due to the clearance of flight defects, and then returned to the tarmac with engine trouble. November Papa came back from Saturday's Munich with fluctuating boost torque on number 4, had an air test during the afternoon, and was over three hours late going to Basle as a result. This DC6's bad weekend continued as she arrived back with a radar defect, and then the aircraft was backed into the steps on return to the pad, which damaged the trailing edge of the port elevator. This was repaired, but the aircraft was delayed five hours: 'Through circumstances too numerous to mention,' per Eddie Edgar, before going to Palma. She then came back from that with the original trouble, boost fluctuation on number 4, still apparent. On Sunday, November Papa went to Basle but came back in the late afternoon with the troublesome number 4 feathered after the boost dropped off in climb, and the engine was then changed.

1968 PROP JETS AND FINALE

G-AVHE
(Eddie Fuller collection)

Saturday nights Tangier had also departed late, and the evening Milan on Sunday the 28th did not operate. There was more Le Bourget work over the last few days, a Manston-Le Bourget-Dublin-Le Bourget-Manston by November Oscar, and a Manston-Edinburgh-Le Bourget-Exeter-Manston and Manston-Southampton-Le Bourget-Southampton-Manston, both by her sister aircraft. On the last day November Oscar was also on an engine change with the crane, needed to assist in this work, arriving late.

The Viscounts concentrated on Perpignan, plus a few Milans. Hotel Echo was on detachment at Perpignan for the first week, returning on Sunday 7th., and November Juliet, with the exception of the 21st./23rd., covered the France based operations for the remainder of the month. Hotel Echo flew Perpignan-Rotterdam-Rome-Athens-Perpignan over the first two days, then went unserviceable at Perpignan, with a Laker BAC 1-11 being sub-chartered to carry out her flight. Ernie Brown and Bob Ratcliffe were called in to go to Perpignan, via Gatwick and Gerona. It seemed that the Viscount, after standing at Athens all night, and having been refuelled

Viscount at Basle (Rene Zurcher)

and reoiled, had flown to Perpignan without any defects, but on arrival there the engines were found to be covered in oil. After this was sorted out, Hotel Echo flew Perpignan-Birmingham-Manston-Perpignan on the night of 3rd./4th. and the engineers came back on November Juliet in the early hours of the 4th. July.

On Monday 8th. Hotel Echo took a charter Manston-Gatwick-Vienna-Gatwick-Manston, making the nights Perpignan late in the process, this tour leaving at 0135 on Tuesday. On Tuesday night Hotel Echo, on the 2130 from Manston to Perpignan, had to land at Toulouse before continuing to its destination, Air Ferry's tenth and last diversion over six seasons to the French airport. There was an internal flight, Gatwick-Newcastle-Gatwick on the 11th. and Hotel Echo came back from Perpignan on the 13th. with a brake unit leaking that was changed. The aircraft went to Stanstead for training or calibration on Wednesday 17th. then took passengers to Ostend. There was a Manston-Gatwick-Hamburg-Manston charter the next day, which was reversed the day after that, and on the 25th. there were two flights to Dusseldorf.

TWILIGHT OF THE PISTONS

1968 PROP JETS AND FINALE

Monday. 26 Aug/68.

	ARR	DEP.	
NO.			Check "B" A/c Cleared 16.00 HRS.
		22.15	No Tech delay.
NJ.	09.45	10.20	
NP.		11.35	Defects Cleared A/c on Line 10.58 HRS.
	19.25		Nil snags.
WI.			Engine Change 11.00 HRS. No 3. (A.T.L. filters) Engine Installed connected + Prop fitted 21.00 HRS.
HE.			No 4 Prop + Intake anti icing Brush pack U/S. carry fwd defect. Fillis Check carried out.
		15.35	A/c on Line 15.00 HRS. 70 mins delay Tech
PY.	18.00		Back from C/training with Nos 3 + 4 Engine defects. A/c Cleared 16.48 HRS.
		21.35	
HE.	19.20		No 4 Prop + Intake Brush pack fitted A/c Cleared 20.00 HRS.
		22.35	No Tech delay.
NP.		00.10	Departed 90 mins. Late due to crew problem.

K Barker.

TWILIGHT OF THE PISTONS

The Perpignan tours from Manston were scheduled at 2130 Monday to Friday, 2230 on Saturday and Sunday and with one or two extra flights on those days. In addition, the DC6s had two tours on a nine day cycle. The Perpignan based Viscount operated to Manchester, Birmingham, Newcastle and Manston, with the changeovers occurring less frequently than in June, although there were switches for the detached Viscount to come to Manston. Hotel Echo had remained at Perpignan on Wednesday 10th. and in a neat switch November Juliet flew, albeit many hours late, the Perpignan-Manston. After a Milan she flew the Manston-Perpignan leg that night, while Hotel Echo returned Perpignan-Manston. There was another switch on the 21st., with November Juliet flying Perpignan-Manston at 0935 and Hotel Echo going out to France at 1335. Considering the pressure on everyone the programme ran well although there were occasional hitches; some unexpected ones causing annoyance such as one Sunday when the David Brown tractor went unserviceable, the other tractor was punctured, and one had to be borrowed from Invicta to move the aircraft.

On the 14th. July November Juliet was AOG at Perpignan for a spare radio unit, which was located at Southend, and when the aircraft arrived at Manston on Sunday afternoon it was changed. The Viscount was back at Manston that night, still with a radio defect for which there was no spare, although she left again for Perpignan at 2350. November Juliet flew the second Manston-Gatwick-Vienna-Gatwick-Manston on 22nd.July. Next day Hotel Echo came in from Perpignan at 2340 with radio and radar defects, the flight delayed through this and poor weather. The captain was reluctant to fly the aircraft, and the passengers went out to Perpignan on November Juliet after a delay of five hours. Three days later, November Juliet had a pitot head defect and this time Pony Moore set off for Perpignan to give assistance. On Monday 29th., although the Perpignan based Viscount operated, the Manston based flight was sub-chartered to a Channel Airways Viscount that was unable to depart on time due to an emergency on the runway, and finally left at 0255.

August The summer seemed to be going at twice the usual rate with September's closure in everyone's mind. The DC4s almost achieved another complete month of daily flights on the Basle programme, with the usual four movements each weekend but on one day only, Thursday 29th., no tour departed to the Swiss airport. Early in the month Foxtrot Yankee flew a Manston-Lille-Gatwick-Manston, and a Manston-Gatwick-Basle-Gatwick-Manston, in addition to the usual tours.

The DC4 was in the hangar for a short time with an undercarriage defect, had a C of A air test on the 7th., and a return to the pan with a faulty jump lead before going to Basle the next day. After a Manston-Gatwick-Le Touquet-Gatwick on the 13th., Foxtrot Yankee flew Gatwick-Wildenwrath-Gatwick-Le Touquet-Gatwick-Manston the following day. There was an echo of summers past on the 30th when, after a Check 1 the previous day and an air test that morning, Foxtrot Yankee departed on a Friday daytime flight to Dusseldorf.

Whisky India was held up on Sunday 4th. as her crew was late arriving back on Foxtrot Yankee from Ostend due to poor weather, a recurring theme in early August. The aircraft, on an afternoon flight to Ostend on Tuesday 6th., was diverted into Southend on the way back due to weather. Both DC4s went to Ostend on the 17th. one of which was to take a Boys Band, the crews for that charter were Paddy Roberts and Don Bullock outwards, with the return by Bill Steel and Alan Tyler. Ann Rippon and Carol Dale completed the journeys with bar sales of £2.19.6d!

Whisky India had two freight flights. The aircraft returned back at the start of the first due to a mag. drop and radio defects, before leaving at 0020 on Saturday 10th, and flew Manston-Heathrow-Copenhagen-Manston, being diverted into Manston from Heathrow on Sunday morning due to weather. The other cargo journey was Manston-Oporto-Liverpool-Manston on the 28th./29th. Apart from Basle and Ostend, the DC4 also carried passengers Dublin-Le Bourget, to Dinard and to Dusseldorf.

On the 26th. the aircraft had an engine change, the A.T.L. fitters helping with this; next day Ernie Brown fell from the steps and sustained a broken ankle, and the day after that Whisky India was back in the hangar for an undercarriage retraction test to clear a defect. On the last day of the month Whisky India went unserviceable with a hydraulic defect and Foxtrot Yankee took the Ostend although, later on, Whisky India, after another delay due to a CSU oil leak and more hydraulic system defects, went to Basle.

For the DC6s it was another action packed month, one in which November Papa took the record for DC6 hours in a month and November Oscar the record number of passengers, beating her sister aircraft by three! In total, too, more passengers were carried in August 1968 than in any other month in Air Ferry's history.

1968 PROP JETS AND FINALE

Tours to Genoa, Palma and Valencia all operated close to schedule as did the departures from Manston for those to Venice, Tangier and Munich, although on these three routes there were some weather difficulties at the destinations. In addition to these, the Basle-Manchester tours continued and the frequent Milans, twenty three in August.

In the first week, November Oscar flew Manston-Dinard-Le Bourget-Edinburgh-Manston, the only time a DC6 went to Dinard, and on Monday 5th. the aircaft went to Dusseldorf. Oslo was visited by November Oscar on the 13th. and after the nights Milan the DC6 was taken into the hangar as the port undercarriage leg was leaking; the Check 2 in progress on Hotel Echo was stopped and the aircraft moved out to make room for the DC6. The dangers in the hangar environment were underlined with Ted Friend getting some cleaning fluid in his eyes and needing some attenion. That night November Oscar departed for Tangier on time, but bad weather over the Mediterranean caused a stop at Gibralter on the way out. Both DC6s had some exhaust trouble found by the flight engineers, one had some loose bolts and the other a blowing exhaust.

November Oscar flew to Luxembourg on Monday 19th., the departure held up for a time due to late passengers, and then returned to the pan with the number 3 gill motor unserviceable. Fog caused long delays on the 21st., affecting November Juliet with one of six hours from Perpignan, both DC6s were also six hours late, while Whisky India topped those with a nine hour hold up on a Basle tour. On Monday 26th. adverse weather hit another tour, causing a diversion by November Oscar into Rimini on the way to Venice.

On the 1st. of the month, November Papa on a Manchester-Basle diverted to Gatwick on the way back to Manston, Patrick Hope was one of the crew. The aircraft came back from Tangier early on the 3rd. with radio defects, which delayed her Genoa due to the top rotating beacon being unserviceable and the giraffe was also U/S! On Sunday the aircraft's Munich had a weather diversion into Frankfurt, before continuing to its destination. The aircraft was the busier of the DC6s in the week commencing the 5th., flying Tuesday night's Perpignan and making an extra charter Manston-Exeter-Le Bourget-Manston.

The weather was unseasonable on the 9th. with November Papa being taken into the hangar for flight defects to be cleared due to the conditions outside. The rotating beacon defect recurred on the 11th. delaying the departure to Valencia. November Papa also flew two Manston-Gatwick-Oslo-Manstons, a Helsinki and in the last week flew charters to Le Bourget from Dublin, Southampton and Edinburgh. In the early hours of Saturday 31st., November Papa flew into Turin, the only visit in 1968 and possibly an alternate to Milan as, although a Friday departure was not one of the usual services at that time, there were some in September.

Perpignan continued to dominate the Viscount's activity and just a few flights were made to other destinations. The Perpignan based Viscount operated one flight most days, with usually two flights from Friday through to Sunday, to Manchester and Birmingham, although Hotel Echo went on two occasions to Newcastle and November Juliet flew to Teeside. November Juliet was Perpignan based at the beginning, middle and end of the month, with Hotel Echo taking over from Sunday 4th. to Sunday 11th. and from Sunday 18th. to the 25th. The Manston based Viscount operated to time virtually all month, the main exceptions being the DC6 substitution on the 6th., and one on the 8th. that left at 0030 the next morning.

> *One fine bright morning a Viscount taxied smoothly from the Manston runway, went past the junction leading down to the hangar and the flight line and stopped on a pan too narrow to permit turning unaided; the crew were somewhat embarassed as they had been watching the rabbits gambolling on the grass and missed the turn off. (Ann Rippon)*

On Monday 5th., November Juliet flew Manston-Gatwick-Vienna-Gatwick, operating the Manston Monday night's Perpignan from there at 0045 on Tuesday, and then flew back to Manston for a Check 2 to be carried out - and missing that nights Perpignan, as mentioned. November Juliet resumed for the Perpignan on Wednesday 7th., coming back, for some reason, via Heathrow to Manston the next morning.

Perhaps November Juliet's most celebrated charter was an internal one on Saturday 10th., Manston-Brawdy-Gatwick-Manston. Brawdy was an R.A.F. station and one of the nearest operational airfields to the Milford Haven oil terminals where the Queen was opening a new installation. The charter was to ferry a group of Gulf Oil executives to Gatwick.

TWILIGHT OF THE PISTONS

The proper starter for the Viscount engines was not available and the R.A.F. rigged up a bank of batteries to provide adequate power to turn the Darts for starting. When Captain Saunders pressed the button there was a flash, immediate disintegration of the temporary starting gear, acid all over the place, and great embarrassment on the part of the R.A.F.! (Michael Bopst)

Accounts, from left: Malcolm, Peter Hand, the writer, Maggie, Ann Cowley, Peggy Marshall, Rick Rickards, Carol Strainge, Brenda and John Williams (Peggy Marshall)

The Perpignan based continuity was changed on 13th. when November Juliet flew Perpignan-Ostend-Ostend-Manston and then operated three nights Perpignans from Manston. She went back on detachment there on Friday 16th., delayed leaving with brake trouble, and Ken Barker had to be called in. There was another Perpignan tour delay later in the month, when the aircraft was delayed because too much fuel was loaded at Manston and the Viscount had to be defuelled. Other work by this aircraft included Ostend, Milan, another Manston-Gatwick-Vienna-Gatwick-Manston and a Luxembourg.

Hotel Echo came back from Perpignan on the 3rd. with nose wheel shimmy, this had been the first of three departures there that day, the last being delayed leaving when an oil pressure light would not go out on number 1 on start up, and the pressure switch was changed. Late on the 10th. the Viscount came in from Perpignan with the door seal pressure zero and a nosewheel due to be changed, the aircraft went back to Perpignan and returned from her detachment there at 0720 next morning, when the defects were cleared.

Hotel Echo had her lower forward aerial mast damaged by the 'baggage department' on the 27th., and on the 30th. there were still traffic problems as her Perpignan was held up as the aircraft came back on the pan, unable to get airways clearance, this problem being repeated Saturday morning on the next Perpignan. Flights made other than the Perpignan work were to Dusseldorf, Luxembourg, Milan and an Ostend for training

September September arrived, still a busy month with a thousand hours to fly, although the tours were now winding down. The DC4s again flew mostly to Basle and Ostend. Whisky India went to Luxembourg, and a 2035 departure on Monday 9th. to Zurich was almost certainly a diversion of the nights Basle. On the 20th. September, Whisky India, after a delay when she returned from the runway with high oil pressure and oil temperature, flew Manston-Le Bourget-Basle-Manston. Her last visit to Ostend, flown by Captain Steel on Saturday 28th., started off with a delay while a broken aerial was replaced and was marked by engine trouble at Ostend. November Papa flew over with Eddie Edgar and Frank Strainge to collect the waiting passengers and clear the defect, and Whisky India was back on the line for the nights Basle. The next day the aircraft went to Basle again, but for the last time on her final revenue flight, once again with Bill Steel in command.

Foxtrot Yankee visited Calais four times on Saturday 7th., going unserviceable there on the last flight with a burst tyre. The engineers went over to Ostend on the 0830 Sunday service with a jack, wheel and some tools, Whisky India flying Manston-Ostend-Calais-Manston to deliver them. Foxtrot Yankee also flew Manston-Amsterdam-Gatwick-Manston on the 9th. and went back to Gatwick next day for a charter to Cognac, Air Ferry's only visit there, returning to Gatwick after a night stop. The crew was Stan Hunnable, Alan Breedon, Ann Rippon, Liz Johnson and Maria Eisenhut. While three hostesses on a DC4 was one more than usually carried, they were kept busy providing hospitality to the passengers, including in-flight champagne, on an unusual charter, as Alan's recollections show.

Several things made this trip memorable, not the least of which being that Ann managed to wangle herself on it as well. At this time not only were we considered to be a pair, but she had

1968 PROP JETS AND FINALE

by then also wangled herself into the Chief Hostie's good books sufficiently to be able to ask for and get little favours - like going as extra crew on a jolly. Our passengers were quite dismayed when they rolled up at Manston, and found they would be flying on a DC4 - steam-driven bag of nuts and bolts seemed to be their impression.

Again the flight down there was uneventful (shouldn't they all be?), and once they were all off the aeroplane the crew were met by a representative of Courvoisier who advised us that we were all to eat at a particular restaurant in Cognac and charge the bill to them, that we were invited to the banquet they were throwing that night for the Whitbread people, and also to the tour of the distillery the following day. And that included the extra person whom they had not been advised about. So a great thirty-six hours was had by all, chauffeur driven limousines to and from the various functions, a freebie blow-out, an insight into how good Cognac is made - including the compulsory stop to try the finished product (somewhat lost on a person like me, I'm afraid), and a freebie bottle of the stuff to take back with you. After that we left them to their own devices, because tomorrow was the return flight and a little rule concerning throttle to bottle came into effect.

We had a last lunch at the aforementioned restaurant, where I discovered a delightful dish called omelette au fine herb. *The little crunchy bits in it were delicious, and I took to them like a duck to water, not ever, would you believe, having tasted garlic before this time. Shortly after the meal was over I was advised of what I had done in no uncertain terms by the rest of the crew, and had to spend the remainder of the day facing outwards. When we left Cognac on the return trip we managed to get clearance to fly down the local river at one thousand feet all the way to the coast line, ostensibly to let our passengers get a birds eye view of the region in which their latest product was grown, but mainly of course for the hell of it ourselves.*

Once we had left the coast we climbed to normal cruising level and settled down to routine flight. By now our passengers had got used to the idea of flying in a DC4, and were beginning to like the idea because it didn't travel as fast as the modern jets and, therefore, the journey took longer - which translated into more drinking time at the company's expense. Once again I believe a makeshift bar was arranged down the back, and people were encouraged to go for their own drinks. Sometime during the cruise someone got the usual idea of passing the time by requesting a visit to the flightdeck, and this quickly caught on.

In no time flat we had a string of people coming up front to see what we were doing, and then continuing back down the full length of the cabin for their next drink, forming a continuous chain of mildly inebriated party goers pushing past each other in the aisle. But moreso through the narrow passage to the flight deck. I can still remember looking over my shoulder at one stage to see the latest entrant in his sodden shirtsleeves, perspiration rolling down his face and everywhere else it could flow from. 'Didn't think it was that hot,' I quipped, only to be advised that it was like a blast furnace down the back - not that he was complaining, you understand. There followed some light banter, until there was suddenly a dawning of realisation in the skipper's eyes. He asked the next person in the line not to come through the door, and then stared hard at the wall of the narrow entry passage, on which was located the control for the cabin heating. Sure enough, it was on full hot, having been pushed into that position by one of the visitors coming in as he squirmed his way past one of them going out. That discovered, normal service was quickly resumed, and a load of extremely happy Whitbread reps. were delivered back by early evening. And that was the end of another great outing with Air Ferry - except for one extra little thing in my case on return to Manston.

Apparently we had run out of co-pilots, and the evening Basle flight was sitting on the next stand full of passengers just waiting for me to climb aboard and assist the captain in starting the engines. The only thing being the skipper was Bill Steel, whom I affectionately remember as being the only pilot I've met in my entire career who was as nice as pie outside the cockpit but became a grumpy old sod when having to operate an aeroplane. And I had not yet recovered

TWILIGHT OF THE PISTONS

Sunday 1st Sept 1968.

EY.	08.40	No tech delay.
	10.15	Arrived "S"
NP	09.25	Departed, returned from runway 09.50 spark plug defect No.3 eng. Defect cleared 10.10.
~~WI~~	10.15	
WI.	10.50	No tech delay.
	12.40	Arrived "S"
NJ.	12.45	Arrived with defects.
WI	13.45	No tech delay.
	19.15	Arrived with defects.
ME	14.05	No tech delay.
NP.	14.45	Arrived.
	15.50	
NO	16.35	No tech delay. 15 mins late.
	22.05	Arrived.
EY.	21.40	No tech delay.
NO	22.05	Arrived with defects.
	23.40	No tech delay.
NP	20.30	Arrived with defects.
	22.10	No tech delay.
NJ.	23.25	No tech delay

1968 PROP JETS AND FINALE

from the effects of the lunchtime meal in Cognac. That was a quiet trip, believe me, with me trying to spend the whole time with my mouth shut peering out of my side window, and Bill doing his best to counteract my aroma with the one he was generating from his pipe! (Alan Breedon)

Foxtrot Yankee also went to Luxembourg, flew a Manston-Basle-Manchester-Manston that was delayed due to the late arrival of the captain, and then came back from the runway with a dead cut mag. The next flight, on Sunday 15th. to Ostend, was also delayed, this time for two and a half hours due to weather. The aircraft also visited Le Bourget and Maastricht. On Thursday 26 September, at 2010 in the evening, Foxtrot Yankee departed on her last trip to Basle and two days later she set off, with Captain Horsting in command, on her last revenue flight, to Amsterdam. After a night stop, Paul Horsting landed Foxtrot Yankee back at Manston just before 1940 on the evening of Sunday 28th. Whisky India also arrived back from her last flight that day as mentioned, and so ended six seasons of DC4 operations.

The DC6s still had much to do. In September the tours to Venice, Munich and Palma flew to time, and each of these came to an end during the month; the Basle-Manchesters also finished. The Valencia and Genoa tours operated on schedule although there was one more of each of these to come.

November Oscar's Basle-Manchester on Thursday 5th. went on to Zurich, undoubtedly a diversion. The DC6 came back from Milan early on Sunday 8th. with the nosewheel torque links needing to be changed because of severe nosewheel shimmy. The defect was cleared by 0440 and the aircraft left for Tangier at 0700, quite a feat, although some eight and a half hours late. A message came back later, informing operations that the DC6 was stuck there with a leaking seal on the hydraulic pressure regulator, and the aircraft came back to Manston, empty, during Monday afternoon.

Very early on Wednesday 11th., November Oscar again left for Tangier, this time four hours late, having taxied back from the runway with an ignition defect, and did not return to Manston until almost exactly twenty four hours later, although on this occasion bringing back the passengers. There were still some Basle-Manchester flights, and on the 26th. the aircraft went to Berlin with 84 passengers before going on to Basle. On Saturday 28 September November Oscar made her last revenue flight, to Basle, and was flown by Captain Ross.

November Papa returned from the runway on Saturday 1st. with a sparking plug defect before going to Basle. It fell to this aircraft to make the final flights to Venice, Munich, Palma, Milan and Tangier, and a busy month of tour flying came to an end on the last day with a Berlin charter, presumably returning the group taken out four days previously.

There were 60 flights to Perpignan in September, all but four by the Viscounts, and November Juliet flew the most hours of the six aircraft in the month, the only time this happened. Hotel Echo was based at Perpignan at the beginning of the month and on Thursday 6th. the aircraft flew half a Perpignan tour on return from the detachment there, the Viscount arriving at Manston with many defects and was AOG'd. November Oscar, on the Milan tour, was recalled from the runway to carry Hotel Echo's passengers, and the DC6 then combined two tours by flying Manston-Perpignan-Milan-Manston. November Juliet was refuelled to return to Perpignan in place of Hotel Echo, positioning there empty at 0350 on Saturday 7th, and remained until Sunday 15th. On the 9th. Hotel Echo's flight was delayed awaiting spares for November Juliet in Perpignan while, after the flight on the 12th./13th., Hotel Echo had an engine defect that required two combustion chambers to be removed for the turbine to be inspected and the fuel controls reset.

Hotel Echo went back to France from the 15th. to the 22nd. On the 21st. it was November Juliet that was delayed, awaiting spares for Hotel Echo at Perpignan, making the latter's return to Manston six hours late. Back at Perpignan, and until Friday of that week, November Juliet operated the last Perpignan-Manchester-Perpignan, the last Perpignan-Birmingham-Perpignan and also carried out a flight on the 27th, Perpignan-Manchester-Gatwick-Valencia-Perpignan. Hotel Echo also operated several Luxembourg tours and went to Rheims on the 11th.

During the month November Juliet flew a Manston-Gatwick-Vienna-Gatwick-Manston charter, with a Manston-Vienna-Gatwick-Manston two weeks later, a Gatwick-Amsterdam, and went to Milan and Luxembourg. The Viscount arrived back from the Milan on the 4th. with a severe oil leak that required the engine removal for rectification.

The last of the Big Pistons: from left Keith Sissons, Margaret Norton, Brian Dunlop, Pat Travers, Patrick Hope and Hazel Baynham   (Hazel Brooks nee Baynham)

The last of the Big Pistons, Jodi with the crew   (Jodi Hope)

There was a mass exodus of the aircrew on 30 September as most of the pilots, the flight engineers and cabin staff left. For the staff which remained there was the task of clearing up, and the disposal of all the equipment and fittings that had been needed to run the company.

Not all the impressions of that last summer remain in the U.K., one of the respondents to the 'Flight' letter of 1994 was from Rene Zurcher in Switzerland who recalled Air Ferry's close affinity with Basle and enclosed some photgraphs taken at the time.

October   There was still some revenue to be earned in October. The first six days saw November Papa making flights to Ostend, Luxembourg and twice to Basle. The aircraft then flew the last Valencia and, on Saturday 5 October, made her last revenue flight, commanded by Keith Sissons, to Genoa. '*Flight*' was on hand to record this last passenger flight by a DC6 in the U.K. and printed an article under the heading of '*The Last Of The Big Pistons.*'

November Juliet started the month by positioning empty Manchester-Gatwick to operate two Gatwick-Cologne-Gatwick charters, followed by Gatwick-Perpignan-Manston. On Friday 4th. the aircraft flew Manston-Castle Donington-Munich, returning on Saturday to Manston via Perpignan, Air Ferry's last visit to this airport of mixed fortunes. In the first few days, Hotel Echo flew three Luxembourgs and Air Ferry's very last Ostend on Friday 5th. The aircraft next day returned the passengers back Munich-Castle Donington,

1968 PROP JETS AND FINALE

the flight being delayed due to waiting for the passengers, while November Juliet, on a Luxembourg that day, was also late by taking on extra fuel due to the weather.

There was no flying on the following Monday and next day Hotel Echo had technical trouble and off-loaded the 83 passengers who, after a short delay, went to Luxembourg in November Juliet. This Viscount then arrived back at Manston with the number 4 engine feathered to record the last serious technical fault of the season.

Wednesday 9 October saw the first of the aircraft departures when Captain Nicol flew November Oscar to Lydd. The next day it was the turn of November Papa, also flown to Lydd by Andy Nicol and accompanied on this flight by Jeep. Each delivery took most of a day to carry out and Andy was paid £20 each for them. An hour and a half later, Whisky India left for Southend, flown by Captain Adams. 'Air Ferry' had been deleted and the aircraft left with an all white fuselage. In this respect Whisky India was the exception as the other five aircraft all left in their full colours.

The DC6 was the lovliest transport aeroplane I ever flew. (Keith Sissons)

Foxtrot Yankee, the final departure

Viscount (Steve Pigg)

The passengers have gone!

The Admin Block

183

TWILIGHT OF THE PISTONS

For a few days the Viscounts continued with the Luxembourgs, Hotel Echo had an air test on Saturday 12th. and November Juliet made the last visit to Basle returning, after a night stop, on Sunday evening.

The most emotive departure was on Wednesday 16th. when Foxtrot Yankee started up, her motors wreathed in smoke as they had been hundreds of time before, and Captain Adams moved her onto the apron and turned off up the taxiway to the runway. After take-off she circled round to the right and flew back low over the Air Ferry buildings before climbing away for the short flight to Lydd. An era had ended.

Now there were just a few Luxembourg flights to the end, and one of these, on Tuesday 22nd., was probably diverted to Brussels. On Sunday 27th. the last two revenue flights took place, Hotel Echo flown by Captain Lockwood and November Juliet by Captain Cropp. This departure was recorded, sadly but appropriately, by Ken Barker as: 'The last of a great many.' The Maintenance Handover Book too was redundant - for twenty eight years! The Viscounts were both returned to Southend by Captain Adams, Hotel Echo on 31 October and November Juliet at 1100 on Wednesday 6 November, bringing down the curtain on the last Act of Air Ferry.

The Tower on 30 October, 1968

The only time that the Accounts harmony group ever sang was over the tannoy during the clearing up, when a visit was made to the now deserted Traffic office to check for any items which needed saving. (Peggy Marshall)

With the demise of Air Ferry trade in the 'Jolly Farmer' in Manston village undoubtedly declined. If someone from Air Ferry, or Invicta, was unavailable but known to be in the hostelry the answer was: 'Sorry he is not in operations, he must be in 'forward operations.' The 'Jolly' was a helpful tavern, in response to a telephone enquiry of: 'Are you open?' the retort was usually: 'If you are coming, we are open'.

STATISTICS

The sixth and final season saw the second highest passenger total for a year and the third highest number of hours flown. There were 1,866 flights to a record number of 124 airports for one year.

The flying in August, so near the end, resulted in the highest number of passengers ever carried in one month by Air Ferry, 41,655. Also in August the DC6s recorded the highest number of passenger and flying hours in any one month, and the Viscounts carried their highest number of passengers.

MANSTON

Two early movements into Manston were by two 700 series Viscounts, once operated by British Eagle, on delivery to Invicta; these were G-AOCC and G-AOCB; the former bearing the name 'Sylt' during the summer. The civil visitors included an Irish registered DC4 and an involuntary appearance on 9 May when a Skyways Coach-Air HS748 made an emergency landing and the nosewheel collapsed, a radio report gave this as the eleventh foam landing at Manston. Another, probably unwelcome, visitor that day, although for a different reason, was a Hiller UH12 of Bristow Helicopters; Alan Bristow being now associated as the prime mover in the closure of Air Ferry. Yet another arrival that day was a Lancashire Prospector, a rare animal on the aviation scene.

In June one of Transmeridian's 'Seven Seas' came in as did two British Eagle Britannias and a CL44 from Transglobe. The first three of these movements were to uplift arms for Nigeria, the aircraft loaded well away from any possible public, or press, interest. On 27 June a Beagle 206 brought in a prospective buyer of the DC6s for a discussion, and probably a viewing as well, as both aircraft were on the airfield.

1968 PROP JETS AND FINALE

Messerschmitt under a threatening sky, 10 May, 1968

109s at Manston (Alan Jones)

The Red Arrows, Russian Roulette, Summer 1968

Other aircraft seen that summer were B.A.F. Carvairs, and a rare Avro 19. There was also a Martinair DC9, showing how the Dutch Airline had progressed from their DC4 equipment of the early sixties when they operated as Martins Air Charter. Two Dan-Air Comets visited and also Channel's new Trident. In the twilight of their operating lives, Ambassadors were seen quite often at Manston in 1968, one being Dan-Air's G-AMAG which ended up making a wheels up landing on 30 September, and G-ALZZ which spent the season in Skyways Coach-Air livery, but reappeared on 9 September once again wearing its Autair colours.

The military visits were also punctuated with emergency landings, a Victor starting these incidents on 8 January by touching down with the nosewheel up or only partially extended. There were movements through the station by Britannias and Hercules of Support Command, HS125s, and, on two occasions in September, visits by five Jet Provosts, one being the 'Macaws' display team of the College of Air Warfare. Two Yugoslav Air Force jets came through on 12 September en-route to the Farnborough Air Show, a Soko Jastreb and a Soko Galeb; they returned on 23rd of the month. September also saw visits by a CL44 of the R.C.A.F. and the huge R.A.F. transport, the Short Belfast.

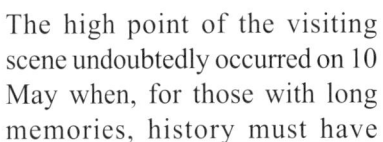

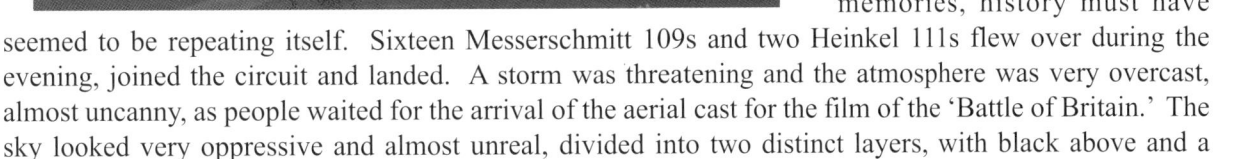

The high point of the visiting scene undoubtedly occurred on 10 May when, for those with long memories, history must have seemed to be repeating itself. Sixteen Messerschmitt 109s and two Heinkel 111s flew over during the evening, joined the circuit and landed. A storm was threatening and the atmosphere was very overcast, almost uncanny, as people waited for the arrival of the aerial cast for the film of the 'Battle of Britain.' The sky looked very oppressive and almost unreal, divided into two distinct layers, with black above and a narrow band of pale blue pressed down underneath.

The Messerschmitts and Heinkels were joined on 15 May by a photographic aircraft, a wartime North American Mitchell. Used for air-to-air filming, this bomber was painted with a dayglo rear fuselage and tail, half red and half green wings, with black stripes marked with orange on the port side of the fuselage and light green on the starboard; the nose was silver.

The making of a film commemorating the 'Battle of Britain' had long been mooted, with fierce feelings generated both for and against. Many felt that, however much could be put in in the way of resources, it would not be possible to do justice to the subject; on the other hand, if it could be done properly, what an achievement this would be. Over a long period of time the project went through many difficult and almost impossible twists and turns, the eventual making of the film produced by Harry Salzman and directed by Guy

Hamilton was worthy of a book of its own, and received one, written by Leonard Moseley. In the end, most of the doubters conceded that the film was beautifully done and with an excellent musical accompaniment; the German scenes in the Pas de Calais were especially effective.

The aircraft which flew into Manston that May evening were not the genuine articles, but licence built variants produced by CASA in Spain for the Spanish Air Force, and both types were powered by British Merlin engines.

R.A.F.
During 1968 the role of the Victors in the Strategic Deterrent scaled down and these versatile aircraft switched over to the tanker and reconnaissance roles. A new type for the R.A.F. inventory was now well on the way, with the first flight of the production model of the Hawker Siddeley Harrier having taken place at the end of 1967. The vertical take off fighter was shown off in a preview at Dunsfold and production was building up there for entry into service in 1969.

Two famous names disappeared from the R.A.F. organisational structure in 1968 with the merger, on the R.A.F.'s 50th birthday, of Bomber and Fighter Commands into a new Strike Command.

CIVIL
The '*Flight*' survey broke with tradition that year and came out on 24 October. It correctly reported that Air Ferry operated two Viscounts - for three more days! Elsewhere the picture was generally one of quiet confidence and movement onto more turbine equipment. The faithful Ambassadors and Vikings were gone from Autair who had now acquired three BAC1-11s; BKS, now British Air Services, had added five Viscounts, while Britannia had added the first of many of the type that would come onto the register in future years, two Boeing 737s.

British Midland had disposed of the last Argonauts and increased their Viscount fleet from three to seven. Caledonian had two less Britannias but now operated three Boeing 707s, while Channel had two Tridents and a BAC1-11; Dan-Air were up to four Comets. At this stage Invicta were shown with four DC4s and two Viscounts. For their freight work Transglobe had reduced the Britannias and equipped with four CL44s, the swing-tail Britannia development by Canadair. Transmeridian, meanwhile, had gone from two to five DC7s. A new operator from April was Monarch at Luton, who operated three Britannias while Treffield was not listed, having closed down at the end of 1967.

AIR HOLDINGS
B.U.A. had basically the same fleet, three Britannias, three VC10s, ten BAC1-11s and three Viscounts, while B.U.(C.I.)A. were operating seven Heralds, four DC3s and four Herons. Reflecting the decline in business with cross-channel traffic now down to 5% of the market, from the 27% at its peak, B.A.F. had five Carvairs and five Bristol Freighters.

The March/April edition of '*Wingspan*' unveiled to staff at the numerous group locations that B.U.A. and other transport companies were to leave Air Holdings. The whole share capital of B.U.A., B.U.A. (C.I.), B.U. (Manx) Airways, B.U.A. (Services), Morton Air Services and Airwork International (Bristow Helicopters) would be acquired by the British & Commonwealth Shipping Co on behalf of itself and others. These concerns would form a new B.U.A. group which also included Sierra Leone Airways, Uganda Aviation services and Gambia Airways.

A new B.U.A. group holding company would be formed, of which British & Commonwealth would have a controlling interest. Mr. Anthony Cayzer would be chairman of B.U.A. with Alan Bristow as deputy chairman and managing director.

The now much smaller Air Holdings group, in its new form, would have Airwork Services, Aviation Traders, B.A.F., Air Ferry, Safe Air, Lyons, Whitehall and Leroys as the main companies.

'*Wingspans*' other front page lead was about the sudden death of Sir Miles Wyatt on 15 April at the age of 64. This unexpected loss delayed the complex negotiations regarding the change in group structure and, for an interim period, Sir Errington Keville had taken over as chairman of Air Holdings.

1968 PROP JETS AND FINALE

SAFETY

A British Eagle Viscount sadly marred the safety record on 9 August when a major fault in the main busbar resulted in the loss of all electric power, and the aircraft crashed onto the Munich to Nuremberg autobahn.

OTHER EVENTS

In the U.K. that year London Bridge was dismantled for sale to the U.S., the first open Wimbledon tournament occurred, and the inaugural flight of the cross-channel SRN4 Hovercraft took place from Dover to Boulogne. In September the Victoria Line was opened, the first complete underground line to be built in London for sixty years. The Rhodesian issue had still not been resolved and there were talks in Gibralter between Britain and Southern Rhodesia. Another issue to evoke strong views at this time, especially by the Conservative politician Enoch Powell, was that of Asian immigrants from Kenya to Britain.

In December Tom Jones was awarded a golden disc for 'Delila,' and the *Queen Elizabeth 2* made her maiden voyage on the Clyde from John Brown's shipyard to Greenock. Earlier in the year, in April at Hockenheim, Britain lost one of the supreme artists of the motor racing world when Jim Clark was killed.

Dark shadows were cast over the international scene in August by the Soviet invasion of Czechoslovakia. The Eastern Bloc satellite had been moving towards a more open society and the swift action by the U.S.S.R. brought an end to the 'Prague Spring,' a daring game of political chess which had been watched by the free world with interest mixed with apprehension for Alexander Dubcek and his colleagues. In Britain, Parliament was recalled to debate the issue, while in America an emergency meeting of the U.N. Security Council was convened to consider the ever present fear that one move might be the cover for another one elsewhere.

Earlier on, in a year of continued space exploration, came the news from the U.S.S.R. that the worlds first cosmonaut, Yuri Gagarin, had been killed in an air crash. Towards the end of 1968 the American space project made two impressive flights, an eleven day mission by Apollo VII, followed in December by the emotive flight of Apollo VIII, when the first men to break free from the gravitational pull of the earth set off towards the moon. The spacecraft orbited the moon during Christmas and returned safely to earth on 27 December.

Those had been the high spots of the year for America, otherwise much of 1968 passed in doom and gloom. Two prominent political figures were assassinated, Martin Luther King the civil rights leader in Memphis and Bobbie Kennedy, the brother of the late president, in Los Angeles while he was running for the presidential nomination of the Democratic Party. He had attracted much support from the anti-war and civil rights movements, both continuing to dominate the United States.

During the year the Vietnam war was in a critical stage. There were now over 500,000 Americans in Vietnam and the commander wanted more. The Tet offensive by the communists in April was a decisive turning point. The U.S. forces had achieved a very considerable tactical victory and yet somehow, in the sprawling confusion, the media took delight in portraying it as a strategic defeat for America. With student protests not only in the U.S., but France and Britain as well, some thought the West would slide into anarchy. President Johnson called another meeting of 'The wise men' after Tet and found that their views had altered; they had all changed round and now sought to distance America from the struggle.

TWILIGHT OF THE PISTONS

Captain Reg Eames who flew for the 1964, 1966 and 1967 seasons.

DC6   (John Somerville)

CHAPTER 9
OSCAR GOLF AND YANKEE KILO

OSCAR GOLF

'*Flight*' in the issue of 9 February 1967 devoted some space to the accident, starting with a leader entitled '*The Safety Gap*. This item began:

'A DC4 crashed on the approach to Frankfurt three weeks ago. It was a far-away cargo flight and it attracted little notice. The crew of two died; if it had been a passenger service fifty people could have been killed. Another British airliner had been fatally at the wrong height or place. There have been ten such British accidents in the past ten years, killing 370 passengers and crew.

This is an appalling record. After the tragedy at Ljubljana it was soon established that the probable cause was a wrong altimeter setting - another case of confusion between QNH and QFE. It would be wrong to jump to firm conclusions, and in any case the matter is officially in foreign hands (as are 70 per cent of British accidents). But a formula can always be found for quickly promulgating lessons that might save lives. It is possible - we put it no higher yet - that a strong QNH/QFE campaign after Ljubljana might have averted a further tragedy.'

The leader ended:

'The British airline safety record is not good by comparison with those of other countries, notably Australia and the U.S.A. Government departments are not responsible for accidents, but they are responsible for the accident record. If they are not, who is?'

A further article gave much more information:

'Less than two weeks after the accident to Air Ferry's DC4, G-ASOG, which hit trees 1 3/4 miles from the threshold of runway 25R at Frankfurt at 0414hr GMT on January 21, the Board of Trade has issued a statement of known facts about the accident. The aircraft was on an all-cargo flight from Manchester. The crew of two were killed.

The BoT statement gives details of the weather at the time: cloud ceiling was 2,000ft with patches at 300-400ft in the approach sector; ground visibility was about 2,500 metres; slant visibility was five miles; wind calm. The QFE was 1005mb and the QNH, 1018mb; airfield elevation is 368ft. Both the runway and approach lighting were on.

The accident is being investigated by the Federal German authorities, assisted by BoT inspectors, and the wreckage, including remains of the radio installation and flight instrumentation, is being examined in detail. The statement ends by saying : 'Preliminary examination indicated that two of the altimeters (one on the captain's panel and one on the co-pilot's panel) were set to QNH (1018mb) and a third altimeter to the standard setting (1013mb). There are no indications that the aircraft was on fire before impact and it appears that the aircraft was in the approach configuration when it struck the ground.'

Normal procedure would be for one pilot to have his altimeter set to QFE so that on landing his altimeter would read zero; the other pilot would have QNH set on his altimeter so that on touch-down his altimeter would show the airport elevation. If both altimeters were set to the higher setting and the pilot in control was under the impression that his altimeter was set to QFE the

TWILIGHT OF THE PISTONS

aircraft would be lower than it should have been by the same height as the airfield elevation above sea level. On a 3 degree glideslope, assuming flat terrain surrounding the airport, this would mean that at airfields 300, 600, 900 and 1,200 ft above sea level, aircraft with mis-set altimeters (i.e. QNH instead of QFE) could be expected to hit the ground one, two, three and four miles from the threshold respectively. Uneven terrain would produce wide scatter of these points.

That the pilot of the DC4 was under a misconception about his height information is pure supposition at this stage. For the final analysis the report of the Federal German investigators must be awaited.'

The '*Aeroplane*' issue of the same week also included cover of the accident as did '*Wingspan*' in the February edition.

The actual report, issued by the Federal Office of Civil Aeronautics, Federal Republic of Germany and dated 5 February 1968, was a thorough and detailed review of every aspect of the Frankfurt crash.

The aircraft taxied to take-off at Manchester at about 0047 hours but returned to the ramp because of a fault in the door warning device. Take-off finally took place at 0119 hours and Oscar Golf's proposed flight route was via Congleton beacon, airways Amber 1, Amber 2, Blue 3, Dover beacon and airway Green 1 to Frankfurt.

After passing the Frankfurt VOR and taking a heading of 090 degrees, the aircraft was instructed by Frankfurt approach control to turn 180 degrees towards the ILS localiser, and about five minutes before the accident it was cleared for an ILS approach to runway 25R. About three minutes before the accident the aircraft was on its final approach at a distance of about 8NM from the airport.

At about 0413 hours, i.e. about two minutes after the last radio transmission to the control tower, when about 2,700 metres from the threshold of runway 25R and approximately 100 metres left of the ILS-centreline and approaching at a flat approach angle and on a heading of about 260 degrees, the aircraft first struck an oak tree with the starboard wing 35 feet above ground, and after snapping off several more trees it continued on a track of about 280 degrees, finally hitting the ground. The aircraft was destroyed by the impact and the ensuing fire.

The report gave details of the technical status of the aircraft and listed the total airframe flying time on the day of the accident as 35,525 hours 50 minutes.

Before take-off from Manchester the aircraft was refuelled with 1,670 USG of fuel and thus in addition to the necessary fuel for the route Manchester-Frankfurt and the route to the alternate airport Dusseldorf, had a reserve of approximately 560 USG, giving an endurance of approximately six hours. The estimated take-off weight was 30,903 kg; the estimated landing weight 29,006 kg. The approved maximum take-off weight was 33,470 kg., and the approved maximum landing weight was 29,100 kg. The centre of gravity for take-off and landing was approximately 20 percent. standard mean chord. The approved centre of gravity range was between 16 and 32 percent. standard mean chord. The freight transported weighed 7,067 kg. and consisted mainly of machines, machine parts, bales of material and chemicals.

The Pratt & Whitney engines were all within the approved running time of 1,520 hours; number one had only been installed at Manston on 16 January with 25 hours running since that time and the other engines had run 1,077, 507 and 746 hours respectively since their last overhaul. The propellers similarly complied with airworthiness directives; the approved running time was 1,600 hours and although number two had run 1,632 hours approval had been given for an extension to 1,680 hours.

Weather information came next and, according to the evidence of a pilot who followed G-ASOG after an interval of approximately three minutes, there was a slant visibility of approximately 5 NM and cloud layers with base 300 to 400 feet and tops 600 to 800 feet in the approach sector, so that the approach lights were intermittently visible over the accident site at ILS glide path height but not the runway lights.

The review of ground aids to navigation covered the serviceability of the ILS system. Two special flight calibrations carried out after the accident showed that the course line and approach angle indicated by the localiser and the glide path lay within the required tolerances. This was confirmed by a pilot who followed

OSCAR GOLF AND YANKEE KILO

G-ASOG about three minutes later and by three other pilots who landed approximately 40 minutes before and one to two hours after the accident. There was reference to the fact that there had been some fluctuations in the glide path indications up to five days before and three days after the accident. Precision approach radar was not in operation although this fact had been promulgated in a NOTAM.

Radio communications were good and recorded transmissions showed that the flight was carried out in accordance with the directions of the air traffic control units.

As happens in all such cases, the examination of the wreckage was meticulous. The first point of impact of the aircraft was about 160 metres from the main wreckage and about 12 metres above the ground on an oak tree, part of the starboard wing tip was found in the immediate vicinity of this oak. Both wings were torn into many fragments, some of which were burnt, by contact with numerous trees. It was concluded from the traces of fire on the ground and the fragments of the wings, that the aircraft must have caught fire immediately after the tearing away of the integral tanks, about 20 metres after the first contact with a tree.

A section on the airframe reported that, because of the high degree of primary and secondary destruction by impact and fire, it was not possible to determine whether there was a structural failure. However, from the state of the fragments not destroyed and the fact that the accident occurred in conditions which did not present any peak loadings, it was concluded that a failure during flight of any main components could be excluded with a high degree of confidence.

The section on the powerplants pointed to similar conclusions. No indication of failure during flight which could have led to the accident were found in the four power units, which were badly damaged by the impact. The distortion of the propeller blades, the fact that the propellers were torn off all four engines, the fact that the fifth tooth of the toothed segment of all the propellers was damaged, and examination of the shim fractures led to the conclusion that all four engines were running effectively at the time of impact and that the propeller blades were at an angle of 28-30 degrees.

From the ascertained blade pitch angles and the few significant indications of the engine instruments, it was concluded that the output of the engines on impact was probably more than 600BHP. According to the determined carburettor air temperature gauge readings and a ram air flap found closed it could be concluded that warm carburettor air was probably being used.

Details of the aircraft systems also pointed to these all being serviceable on Oscar Golf. The aircraft had sufficient lashing and securing equipment for the cargo, which had been employed.

The fire extinguishing system was probably not operated.

The elevator, rudder and aileron trimming was probably in a neutral setting. The landing flaps were extended symetrically to about 30 degrees. No fault or deficiency could be found in the remaining components of the control system.

All three undercarriage units were in the lowered and locked position.

The aircraft had all the radio and navigational equipment necessary for the planned route. All equipment included in the equipment list for the aircraft was present.

The crystal for the channel of the ILS installation for runway 25R at Frankfurt was present in the UHF glide path receiver. This unit was probably in good working order until the time of impact.

The rotary transformer of the marker receiver was running on impact as were both turn and slip indicators, both directional giro units and the gyro horizon indicator. The DC/AC supply was intact and all vacuum operated instruments were running until the impact; the remote compass was in order and the landing lights were retracted.

The analysis section of the report covered the competency of the crew, the technical status of the aircraft, and all other circumstances surrounding Flight BE/LH 2200 and could not point to any factor to which the accident could have been due. The conclusion was that the accident was probably attributable to the fact that the crew did not set the altimeters in the final approach according to the instructions in the operations manual.

This error was aggravated by the fact that the final approach check list did not coincide with the altimeter setting procedure.

An alteration to the check list of the operations manual as an immediate measure was undertaken on 23 February 1967.

How fortunate most of us are that our mistakes at work are usually capable of corrective action. The clinical analysis of a sequence of actions is of course vitally necessary in the interest of flight safety but a report of this description graphically illustrates the terrible consequences which follow from an error or omission.

To be almost to the runway at dead of night over Germany and to see trees looming up must have been the most awful thing; it is likely that Peter Gutteridge was the first to notice the trees appearing to the right of the aircraft and that he grasped the control column but was unable to prevent the accident. The 3 and 4 switches on his side were in the off position showing he had done all he could in those last seconds.

A very poignant cameo occurred a few days after the crash and concerned a young lady on the staff who was friendly with Peter and who had been taking a few days off. She had heard of the accident but was not aware of the severity and telephoned in to Air Ferry for some details. When the operator said: 'They are being brought back tomorrow' Peter's friend still did not realise the full significance and made some remark such as: 'Oh, good,' giving the operator the difficult task of telling her what had happened.

* * * *

YANKEE KILO

The newspapers on Monday 5 June had two serious accidents to report with the British Midland Argonaut crash following on Sunday morning and devoted much space to them.

The Daily Telegraph had front page articles, photographs, a leader article, a casualty list and several other stories about the Perpignan crash. The leader, entitled '*Disaster in the Air*,' included the following paragraph:

> '*Aircraft disasters have their own peculiar horror because, so often, those who are killed or maimed are cut off at moments which ought to be happy. Another element peculiar to such accidents is the very high probability of complete loss of life; in all present-generation aircraft with high cruising speeds, the sheer violence of the impact and fire risks immediately after it leave only a small chance of getting out alive. All these factors tend to produce, in the public mind, disquiet about present trends in civil aviation. As aircraft become, for economic reasons, ever larger, must it inevitably follow that the toll taken by the air must rise? Need these eggs (all precious to someone) necessarily be put in one basket?*'

It was reported, quite incorrectly, that the crew called the control tower at Perpigan to say they could see the runway and that a visual approach and landing would be made. There was speculation that the lights seen were of the town of Pannes (Prades was probably intended here) and that Yankee Kilo had omitted to change course on leaving Toulouse and was still in the Barcelona air corridor.

Villagers in the little town of Vernet-les-Baines heard the aircraft pass overhead 'extremely low'. It continued up the valley with the landing lights on. It was thought that the pilot saw a mountain ahead of him and attempted to retrace his course. In making the turn, the right wing of the aircraft brushed a hilltop. Fragments of the wing and the two engines were embedded in the trees at the top of the hill. The fuselage carried on into a ravine.

The local Thanet papers also reported the details at the weekend. Captain Pullinger had lived locally with his wife and family and a couple from Broadstairs, Frederick and Kathleen Jones, had also been aboard Yankee Kilo. Mr. Jones had worked at Pfizers and his wife for Vyes, a leading food store chain in Kent.

Later in June *The Daily Telegraph Magazine* included an article entitled: '*The Black Mountain*' which noted that there had been nine accidents in the vicinity of Perpignan since 1951. The article, by Andrew Duncan, began:

OSCAR GOLF AND YANKEE KILO

'The forlorn remnants of this summer's first air crash in which 83 holiday makers and 5 crew died still litter the slopes of Mount Canigou in the Pyrenees. A stream struggles through the centre of the wreck, lazily carrying with it the occasional crushed carton of duty-free cigarettes. Lumps of fuselage are lodged in the scorched trees, and momentoes of individual disasters lie untouched nearby: children's water wings, a pair of new white high heels, unopened packets of cine film, combs, bathing costumes, a crumpled bucket and spade...

It is an unpleasant and unforgettable sight. But for people in nearby villages it is not unusual. This year's crash - on June 3 - was the third on or very near Mount Canigou since October 1961. A total of 162 people, mostly Britons heading for holidays on the Costa Brava, have died. All three crashes were at night and involved charter planes about to land at Perpignan, in southern France, which has an unmatched record of catastrophe. Nine planes have crashed in the past 16 years in the mountains on three sides of the airport - known somewhat dramatically as 'the graveyard of airliners'. Canigou, the highest point, lies 40 miles west.

On summer weekends 8,000 people land at Perpignan and take a two hour coach trip to Spanish resorts. They pay from 30 guineas for 15 days, all inclusive, to fly by DC4, the type of plane that crashed in June. A jet flight could be £10 more, but not necessarily any safer, as all planes undergo rigorous safety checks by the Air Registration Board.

Perpignan airport itself is not considered dangerous and has a Category A classification which means the procedures are straightforward. London, New York and Hong Kong, for instance, are Category C.

Why, then, have 219 people been killed in the vicinity?

'There are always 1,001 reasons, but no one really knows when the crew are killed,' said Burns Andrew, British Eagle station manager for two years. 'The approaches are difficult, but not dangerous. I've seen plenty of worse ones - Naples or Berlin Templehof where you descend between two blocks of flats.'

Investigations have usually produced one of three answers: navigational error, bad weather, or interference from the radio stations at Madrid, Andorra or Pals. But in the villages surrounding Mount Canigou there are those who think the coincidences are too awesome to be explained in any of these ways. Moreover, the last crash took place in perfect weather.

'I don't know what to think anymore,' says Pablo Casals' neice, Henriette Touron, who runs a cinema in Prades, a few miles from the most recent accident. 'I used to believe there was something in the mountains that affected navigation in bad weather. That was because our car radio never worked during a storm. But now...who knows? The only certain thing is that when one hears an aeroplane one thinks, 'Oh no, not another accident.'

Superstition is not a common characteristic of the Catalans. 'We are very objective, like the Chinese,' says Louis Monestier, mayor of Prades. 'We don't believe in miracles or mysteries.' And yet, in the case of Mount Canigou, 9,137 feet, some people have begun to wonder.

By night, during the frequent thunderstorms, Canigou provides a spectacle that would effervesce even the most blase psychedelic. Sheet lightning illuminates vast areas of gaunt cliff. Rust-coloured rocks jut out on all sides of you. Thunder echoes down the valleys. And then everything is eerie and still and you hope the next lightning won't be too close. A fox rushes frightened through the trees. Then more lightning just ahead. It is a virtuoso performance.

'People speak of the magic of Canigou' says Anna Maria White, 71 year old widow who has lived at Vernet-les-Baines since 1924. 'There must be something strange here because no one can understand why the crashes happen. I think there is an easy explanation somewhere. They say that signals coming from Perpignan are not clear because of mineral deposits left over from iron mines.

TWILIGHT OF THE PISTONS

The terrible thing is that before all three crashes we have heard the planes circling overhead, looking for a way out. You despair because you know in a few minutes they are going to crash, and you are in bed, and can do nothing. It's terrible, worse than a nightmare, and it feels as if danger is all around. Before the last crash the pilot seemed to speak to me, 'Where can I go?' I said to myself, 'Don't be so silly, they'll be alright'. Then there was an awful boomf.'

At Py, half a mile from the last crash, some of the 146 inhabitants agree with their mayor, Rene Pedeil: 'There's iron in the mountains, but it has nothing to do with the crashes. It's simply that the Pyrenees are a barrier. I saw the plane come over and thought it would hit the village. Then it turned, the wing tip hit a ledge, and it plunged on to the mountain and caught fire. It was like the atomic explosions you see on telly.'

The '*Flight*' leader on 8 June also started with a review of the accident toll;

'Two major British air disasters in 12 hours is tragic enough. What makes them even more grievous is that they bring to 22 the number of serious British independent-airline accidents in the last 10 years. The record is appalling. Since 1957 11 British independent airliners - the majority of them on charter flights carrying inclusive-tour passengers - have flown into high ground with the loss of 409 passengers and 49 crew. The Air Ferry tragedy was the ninth to occur in the Perpignan region since 1951, and was the fourth involving British holidaymakers.'

An article inside gave greater information, including the comparison that between 1955 and 1967 BOAC and BEA had suffered 11 fatal accidents, on scheduled and non-scheduled routes, while the independents had been involved in 26. Mention was made that it was inevitable that the standard of safety achievable on charter operations, because of their greater irregularity and less frequently visited destinations, could not be as high as that on scheduled flights. Another article, entitled '*Black Weekend*', gave the known brief details regarding the Perpignan and Stockport accidents.

'*The Aeroplane*' on 14 June focussed on the regulatory aspects in a leader titled 'Authority = Safety'. The article began:

'Against some absolute datum, there can be no doubt that 20-year-old aircraft are less safe than modern, well developed equipment. Otherwise what have we been achieving in the way of technical progress?

Measured against the same absolute datum, some airfields are more dangerous than others. However, we do not need to operate aircraft to absolute standards. In practice we make allowance for the relative unreliability of the piston engine, and introduce special procedures and higher minima at doubtful airfields.

The struggle to maintain this uniformity of standards, and the effort to provide the continual improvement of the overall level is, at the official level, the responsibility in the U.K. of the Board of trade and Air Registration Board.

It is the BoT's intention to conduct an internal re-examination into the methods and manner in which these bodies are fulfilling their functions.

The coincidence of two major air disasters to U.K. charter operators within the space of a few hours is bound to arouse public concern, and the official announcement will give impetus to the self-analysis that had, in any case, already been embarked on in the Civil Aviation Department. By tragic chance, the U.K. has had a recent lesson to ponder - the 1965 Vanguard accident.

It is to be hoped that panic measures similar to those which resulted from that crash (such as the blanket increase - and introduction of an arbitary standard - in weather minima) will not be repeated this time. They contribute little towards safety.

The 'Letters' page of that issue of '*Aeroplane*' included a plea from '*Pilot's Wife, Leics.*' about the dangers of night duty. This read:

'No doubt there will be a thorough investigation by the U.K. Board of Trade into the recent air disasters, and after a suitable delay the causes will be found to be unknown, or due to an error in judgement, navigation or aircraft maintenance. It is also quite likely that some minor and irrelevant mistakes by traffic clerks and operations assistants will come to light. However, as the enquiry will be carried out by the same body which governs the hours an operator may require his crews to work, I am most concerned that one of the major contributory factors may not even be mentioned.

I refer to the fact that both accidents occurred on long night flights, with duty times probably well over 12 hours, and I suspect in one case with a doubtful rest period beforehand including either dead heading to the place of departure, or a rest period in a hotel during the day followed by some 14 hours on duty. While this is no doubt legal, I for one will not rest until night duties are further restricted to a period of 10, or at the most, 11 hours duty time. I want my husband, his colleagues and his passengers to stay alive.'

The final report, issued by the French Ministry of Transport was released in Paris on 25 April 1968. This commenced with some statistical information about the accident, at about 2106 hours, the location being the Commune of Py at the place known as 'Cicereus' (Pyrenees Orientales) 50km SW of Perpignan Airport. It went on to give details of the notification of the accident and the constitution of the committee of enquiry.

Ingenieur en Chef Guillevic, the duty investigating officer, was notified by 2200 hours and left Paris by the earliest air service, joining the local investigating officers in the early afternoon. He made his first examination of the wreckage at the scene of the accident, together with the British accredited representatives from the U.K. Accidents Investigation Branch and representatives from Air Ferry.

Details were given of the crew and the aircraft, total flying time listed as 42,662 hours 46 minutes, and a note about previous incidents said that examination of the airframe records had not revealed the occurrence of any incident of interest for the enquiry.

Similarly the technical records of the power plants and propellers did not reveal any evidence which would throw light on the accident.

The meteorological conditions did not indicate any difficulties from that source, although there were thunderstorms over northern Spain there was no record anywhere of any localised thunderstorm activity. Similarly, all radar observations in southern France, including Marignane and Montpellier, gave an 'echo nil' report which seemed to exclude the existence of large air masses.

Various witnesses confirmed that the weather conditions were good:

- *The Py climatological observer reported: 'sky entirely clear'*

- *The Prades police reported 'sky clear'*

- *Monsieur Henri Saly, vine grower at Trevillach, stated: 'The sky was starlit and clear. At the surface there was no wind.'*

- *Finally, M Paul Gahagnon, who was at Py, stated in his evidence: 'The night was very fine, dark but starlit.'*

In the area of the accident sunset was at about 1945 hours; there was no moon at the time of the impact.

Air Ferry's normal procedure was for the crew to report to the Company's Operations (Flight Despatch) one hour before departure. The crew then obtained the weather forecasts for the flight and completed the company's flight plan. The resultant fuel estimates were transmitted to the Operations which prepared and completed the load sheet. This procedure was followed on 3 June.

The flight plan, prepared by Brian Koering, was filed at Manston and sent in the normal manner to London Southern ATCC, Paris ACC, Marseille ACC, Perpignan Aerodrome, Lydd and to Compagnie de Navigation Mixte, the Air Ferry agent at Perpignan.

TWILIGHT OF THE PISTONS

Yankee Kilo received taxying clearance at 1714 from Manston Tower and take off clearance 17 minutes later. At 1741 the aircraft called London Airways, reported at Dover and was held until flight level 60 was reached before proceeding to Lydd. Yankee Kilo passed over Beachy Head at flight level 70 at 1813 and was handed over to Paris Control. The French coast was reached at 1824 and Chartres at 1851. From there the flight progressed to Chateaudun at 1900. At this stage Invicta's G-ASPM, also going to Perpignan, was flying some ten miles ahead of Yankee Kilo and slightly higher and Yankee Kilo reported at Nevers at 1928 that it was climbing to flight level 90.

The aircraft was passed from Paris to Marseille Control before reporting at Clermont Ferrand at 2003 and at Mende at 2025. From this point some areas of doubt seemed to exist in the transmissions; Yankee Kilo stating that it would be abeam Montelimar at 2044. Marseille Control immediately asked for confirmation that this should be Montpellier, Montelimar being practically on the same parallel as Mende. Yankee Kilo corrected itself but shortly afterwards gave the estimated time of arrival at Perpignan as 2110 whereas Marseille Control considered 2100 more appropriate. Control asked for confirmation and the aircraft replied 2210, then corrected itself and confirmed 2110. Marseille Control persisted by repeating 2110 and Yankee Kilo answered 'affirmative.'

At 2043 the aircraft reported to Marseilles Control that it was abeam *Montelimar* at flight level 90 and gave 2052 as the estimated time of arrival at Papa 3 (an entry point into Perpignan TMA). This estimated time was appropriate but made the estimated time of arrival at Perpignan even more difficult to accept. Marseille Control, whose controller had himself corrected Montelimar to Montpellier, asked the aircraft to maintain flight level 90 and call again at Papa 3. This point was reached at 2050 and Marseille Control's last contact was to clear a descent to flight level 70 and asked Yankee Kilo to call Perpignan Approach.

At 2052, two minutes after having been requested to do so, the aircraft called Perpignan Approach and still gave 2110 as the estimated time of arrival although both Marseille and Perpignan Controllers considered this to be an error. The aircraft was given the QFE, QNH and the surface temperature and requested to call again at flight level 70. At 2055 the aircraft reported at level 70 and Approach asked it to call again at level 50.

At 2100 the aircraft reported that it was approaching flight level 50. Perpignan Approach acknowledged receipt and asked it if it had the aerodrome in sight. From the transmissions Perpignan Approach thought that Yankee Kilo had the airfield in sight, telling the aircraft to report downwind for runway 33. When the controller checked again the reply came: 'Yankee Kilo negative, we will be with you in about five minutes.'

There was then a repeat of the controller thinking that the field was in sight as he again told the aircraft to report downwind for the runway; when a few seconds later Yankee Kilo asked for QDMs, Perpignan Approach was surprised and asked it to repeat its request and then asked for a transmission which was never made. There was no reply to any subsequent calls. Just before the accident the quality of communications was sometimes poor which, with the additional absence of any correct standard phraseology, led to misinterpretation by the controller. Captain Ashpitel assisted by listening to the tapes and endeavouring to clarify the transmissions made by the aircraft.

There was a comment in the report that the Perpignan Controller did not check the aircraft's bearing during the communication at 2055 when Yankee Kilo would have been on a magnetic bearing noticeably further to the north than was expected.

Invicta's DC4 Papa Mike, flying just ahead of Yankee Kilo, did not report any particular difficulty with any of the navigational aids.

Yankee Kilo was carrying a SADAS flight recorder which was recovered and the five parameters in use, time, magnetic heading, altitude, indicated air speed and vertical acceleration ('g') were analysed as also was the film taken, at one frame per 10 seconds, from the French radar. The track showed a deviation to the south west at which had commenced shortly before Mende and by Papa 3 was some 15 km west. The flight path at 2059 was headed clearly for Prades with the aircraft less than 30km west of Perpignan Airport, descending to about 5,700 feet and making good a track of about 225 degrees. Yankee Kilo flew over Prades at about 2102 hours and then, some three minutes before the impact, when it was about 4,400 feet, went into a wide left-hand turn for two minutes, then into a fast right-hand turn of about 90 degrees, immediately followed by a fresh steep left-hand turn during which normal acceleration peaks of as much as 2g were recorded and a clear variation in altitude in both senses. The impact was positioned at shortly after 2106 hours on a northerly track at an altitude of about 3,800 feet.

It was after the pilot switched on his landing lights, by this time the crew were beginning to be anxious, that he saw the mountain and endeavoured to turn back on a reciprocal heading by making a tight left-hand turn with a bank of about 60 degrees. It was during this turn at the recorded speed of 290 km/hr when the aircraft, still steeply banked and going onto the northerly heading, struck a rock spur with the port wing outboard of No. 1 engine.

On the impact, in an area named 'Sauteilles' the entire port wing broke away from the fuselage at the wing root and disintegrated over a sparsely wooded plateau with a slight slope in approximately the direction of the aircraft's heading at the time of impact. The wing wreckage was scattered over about 300m. The heavier parts, engines 1 and 2 and the port undercarriage unit, were arrested by trees at the end of the plateau at the point where the slope became steeper. After losing it's port wing, the aircraft followed a ballistic trajectory across the 'Ravin de Bareu' without striking any trees and then crashed into a rock wall at an angle of about 60 degrees to the horizontal, 450m north of the first point of impact and 220m lower down. This was at Cicereus on the right bank of the Mountain torrent 'Le Bareu'.

The wreckage was searched for clues but it was the pathology tests which revealed that there had been an unusual level of carbon monoxide present in the cockpit. On 7 September 1967 during a fresh search of the wreckage the Janitrol cockpit and passenger cabin heaters were found and also a light alloy duct which provided warm air for the pilot's foot warmer.

Malfunctioning of the heating system was not unknown in the DC4 but had usually given warning of this by fumes; as part of the minute examination of all the features, part of a duct of the same type was removed for comparison from a DC4 maintained by Air France.

The enquiry concluded that the immediate cause of the accident was that expert examination of the Janitrol cockpit heater had established with certainty the fact that burnt gasses passed into the cockpit and were therefore the source of intoxication to the crew.

The estimated time of arrival given by the aircraft of 10 minutes later than would be expected was probably due to an allowance for the landing procedure. Perpignan aerodrome, which was particularly well lit, should have been in sight on the left hand side of the aircraft but allowing for the mistake in the estimated time of arrival it is probable the crew looked for the aerodrome too late when the aircraft was no longer in a favourable position. From the communications from Yankee Kilo it was clear that the crew never thought it had identified the airport.

The aircraft indicated at 2104 it's height of 4,000 and was therefore below the minimum altitude fixed on the flight plan when, by estimating 'we will be with you in about five minutes,' it still did not have the aerodrome in sight.

The final opinion of the commission was that the accident occurred following a collision with the mountainside which resulted directly from a series of errors on the part of the crew; failure to use all means of radio navigation available in the aircraft, error in dead reckoning, descent starting from a point which had been inadequately identified, failure to observe the safe altitudes fixed on the company's flight plan and, perhaps, mistakes in identification by visual reference to the ground. This irrational conduct of the flight can be explained by the phenomena due to intoxication by carbon monoxide coming from a defective heating system.

Finally, it was stressed that the misunderstandings which occurred between the aircraft and the Perpignan controller, as a result of language difficulties and in particular the non-existence of any standard phraseology, and also the failure to check the aircraft's magnetic bearing by means of the D/F equipment during the communication at 2055 hours, may have constituted additional aggravating circumstances.

* * * *

Accidents by their very nature are terrible things and it is not the intention to speculate or to cast aspersions on the official reports which are rather like an accounting balance sheet, a strict attempt to provide a true and fair view at a point in time but which can be similarly susceptible to errors, omissions or different professional opinions of the facts available. Air Ferry's accidents still evoke some strong feelings among those who were involved and it is only natural that the engineers especially, whose working lives are devoted to total technical integrity, should be sensitive to any verdict which includes some reference to mechanical causes. Aircrew are equally acutely aware of the propensity of human nature, in instances where no definite cause can be established, to attribute the mishap to the pilot.

There is a story of a Viking accident, some years before Air Ferry, where the cause of the crash was attributed to failure to maintain flight following an engine failure. This conclusion was undoubtedly correct although the report was silent on the fact that the aircraft had been overloaded on take-off, and the company concerned was known to follow this practice on occasion.

In Oscar Golf's case a view was held by some that the captain collapsed onto the controls at a critical point during the approach. Although completely within limits, Oscar Golf was heavily loaded and the feeling was that Peter Gutteridge, being slightly built, may not have had the strength, even if he had had the time, to correct such a terrible emergency. If there was any truth in that theory, and it had not occurred, the fact that the altimeter was mis-set may have been noticed and not resulted in an accident at all. Another theory, still held by some, is that the aircraft was lined up for the approach on the brightly lit autobahn.

Ron Illsley flew over to Frankfurt as part of the investigation. He went through much of the wreckage and later told his colleagues that, prior to the crash, the airframe had been in a marvellous condition with no sign of corrosion.

Being such a traumatic event, the Perpignan crash evoked several theories, some typical press speculation. One at the time considered the accuracy of the radio equipment and some senior men, including Bill Wood, Len Madelaine and Ron Blake gathered in Ken Sheppardson's office to consider this. The trace from the flight recorder clearly indicated a succession of accurate pir points over the beacons, almost to the end, and Len made the comment: 'It wasn't the radio.' Later on, as part of the routine, the Accident Investigation Board went through all the tec. logs. Another idea, still referred to, concerns the possibility that the ADF was incorrectly tuned into the Barcelona beacon without being noticed.

Some of the senior engineers are still quite vehement that it is not correct to apportion all the blame onto the heaters; these were known to give trouble on DC4s and the engineers' testing practices included regular checks on them prior to flight. If there was any hint of trouble the area was blanked off which, in turn, led to some bitter complaints from the pilots at being cold. The medical evidence and the fact that any weakness was considered to have been undetectable to the human eye may seem to go against this theory but aviation engineers have their own deep feelings, rather like the complete affinity of seamen for the intricacies of their element.

Many tests were carried out on the heaters, including one at Manston where the engineers actually bored holes in the casing, the heater was refitted into the DC4, and a ground run carried out without registering any significant measurement on the equipment used.

Douglas Whybrow was present for some sessions of the enquiry before he left and it was mentioned that the crew travelled to Manston together and were caught in a traffic jam for half an hour, hardly moving, there was no wind and it was suggested that they could have picked up some of the carbon monoxide during that time. Hardly evidence but another factor to consider. Douglas had many years previously undergone a near catastrophic incident from vehicle fumes escaping into his car while on a long and arduous drive in Germany and this comment would undoubtedly have had particular significance to him after such an experience.

We will never know for sure and anyone who has driven a car, let alone been the pilot of an aircraft, will have known the feeling on occasion of: 'There but for the grace of God, go I.'

* * * *

OSCAR GOLF AND YANKEE KILO

On 17 December 1996 the writer sent a letter to the Mayor of Py asking for any information he might be able to give. By the 28th a reply was received which included leaflets about this beautiful Nature Reserve area and a photograph marked to show how frighteningly close Yankee Kilo came to obliterating part of this tiny village.

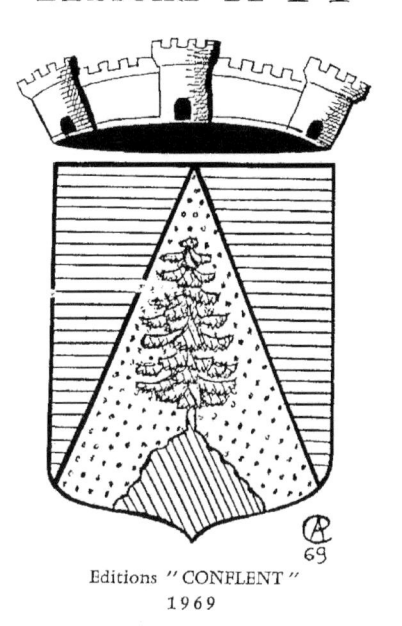

DOCTEUR BAILBÉ
JEAN VIALLET

Histoire de PY

Editions "CONFLENT"
1969

LA CATASTROPHE DU DC-4

Le 3 juin 1967, vers 23 heures, la population de Py entendit soudain le vrombissement énorme d'un appareil géant volant à basse altitude. Soudain, une terrible explosion se produisit.

Le Maire, M. Pideil, sa secrétaire de mairie, Mlle Calvet et toute la population se précipitèrent dans les rues du village éclairées déjà par les lueurs sinistres de l'incendie de l'avion.

L'infortuné DC-4 avait heurté la crête de la montagne au lieu-dit « Sauteilles » et s'était désintégré dans le ravin de Cirerens où coule le ruisseau du même nom.

Quatre-vingt-huit personnes étaient à bord et sous l'effet de l'explosion en vol les pauvres corps furent dispersés dans le vide et s'éparpillèrent, déchiquetés, sur tout le flanc du ravin ! La carcasse de l'avion acheva de brûler au fond du ravin et les corps qui restaient encore furent carbonisés !

Immédiatement, M. Pideil alerta les autorités, et les secours ne tardèrent point. Hélas ! il ne restait plus qu'à recueillir les pauvres restes (tâche bien pénible) et à les grouper pour les ramener en Angleterre d'où ils venaient tous.

L'avion appartenait à la Cie Air-Ferry-Limited.

Selon le rapport d'enquête du Ministère Français des Transports, publié en décembre 1968 par le Board of Trade Britannique, l'équipage se trouvait intoxiqué par des émanations d'oxyde de carbone dégagées par un système défectueux de chauffage ; dans les minutes qui précédèrent l'accident, les réflexes du pilote furent amoindris, son jugement faussé. Lorsque la montagne surgit devant lui, le pilote essaya de l'éviter (dit toujours le rapport mais trop tard, et... l'aile gauche heurta l'éperon rocheux !...

TWILIGHT OF THE PISTONS

Accueil et Découverte en Conflent
66360 PY - 68 05 53 65 Pyrénées-Orientales

A Sauteilles
B Ravin de Bareu
C Cicereus

CHAPTER 10
POSTSCRIPT

OTHER EVENTS

The Labour Government continued until 1970 when the Conservatives under Mr. Heath took over. North Sea Oil was booming, Britain joined the E.E.C. and a long period of industrial unrest and militancy began. A short, sharp, Middle East war occurred in October of 1973 when Syria and Egypt attacked Israel. By the end of that month many of the oil producing states sent shivers through the western world by vastly increasing the price of oil, while at the same time cutting production. At home, action by the miners and electricity power workers led to the government declaring a state of emergency; a three day week for industry followed with many firms resorting to work by candle light in that cheerless winter.

Two general elections to clear the air in 1974 resulted in Labour having no overall majority in the first and of Harold Wilson having just three in the second. Margaret Thatcher became the first woman to lead a political party in Britain as the country limped into the second half of the seventies, with another currency crisis and inflation peaking at over 24%. The Conservatives took power in 1979, the same year that White Rhodesians finally decided to end their thirteen year struggle to hold on to power, and voted to approve a constitution that would lead to an African dominated government. Zimbabwe was founded the following year.

The change of government did not lessen Britain's internal problems and the winter of 1979 was one of discontent, marked by strikes and disruption to normal life. High inflation was seen again in 1981; by then Britain had lost some 15% of it's manufacturing base and there was more social disorder. The economy went through depression and recession for some eight years.

In 1982 the Falklands Islands were recovered by a task force after being invaded by Argentina, one factor in the landslide election result the following year which was the second of three consecutive wins by Mrs. Thatcher.

Britain experienced some extremes of weather during these years with a hurricane in 1987 and a very severe storm just over two years later.

The years since Air Ferry closed have seen enormous changes, technical and economic. The motorway network has been greatly expanded, the Channel Tunnel constructed and the Dartford Bridge built. Town centres have first been ripped apart to allow the construction of fashionable shopping precincts, and then fought a losing battle to keep many businesses viable when much trade has transferred to out-of-town shopping centres built on green field sites. Now there are video recorders, personal computers, compact discs and a whole range of electronic wizardry.

Social changes have been even more dramatic; although standards of living have risen, the years of high unemployment and welfare dependency have led to many stresses and strains. Animal rights have recently assumed a high priority as many practices condoned for years are re-evaluated. Who in 1968 was familiar with the sight of their parents in trainers and track suits, let alone their grandparents!

Soviet weaponry continued to improve throughout the unstable 70s, and the U.S.S.R. believed it could threaten the free world almost with impunity. The introduction of a new IRBM in the mid 1970s upset almost overnight the strategic balance, and by 1979 the deployment of SS20s rendered the situation dangerously unstable.

The U.S.S.R. was also suffering significant problems while trying to fund high expenditure on space exploration and military hardware from a centrally directed economy. The Soviets became embroiled in a war in Afghanistan where the native Mujahideen were an intractable enemy, to the point where the conflict was perceived as the U.S.S.R.'s Vietnam. Pulling out of Afghanistan was a visible sign of the debilitating effect of such an involvement, even for a superpower, and gradually the iron grip over the satellite countries relaxed. This particularly affected Poland, Czechoslovakia and East Germany, ending with the breaching of the Berlin Wall in 1989. Finally, at midnight on 2 October 1990, Germany was reunited, and a gathering of world leaders met in Strasbourg in November 1990 to formally celebrate the end of the cold war. Eventually the changes in the Soviet Union led to the virtual rejection of communism and the break up of the U.S.S.R. in August 1991; an unimagineable scenario during the years of confrontation.

The ending of the Cold War brought dangers of its own, including instability in the former U.S.S.R. and its theatres of influence. From the time of the revolution in Iran there had been a gradual growth in religious fundamentalism, often coupled with strong anti-western feelings which sometimes boiled over into subversion and international terrorism. These convulsions surfaced in the long civil war in the Lebanon, the dreadful ten year Iran-Iraq War and the Gulf War; when Kuwait was invaded by Iraq in August 1990, Britain, along with her allies, fought the Gulf War some months later to liberate this small state. Individual acts of terrorism, such as the bombing of the Pan-American Boeing 747 at Lockerbie, highlighted the dangers of factions and splinter groups.

The Americans finally reached the moon on 21 July 1969 when Apollo XI made a safe landing in the Sea of Tranquility. There were to be five more moon landings, interspersed with Soviet space flights, which were working to perfect a link up with a space station. Soyuz 11 underlined the dangers of space exploration in June 1971 when the crew of three died on re-entry to the earth's atmosphere.

In America, Lyndon Johnson died on 22 January 1973 and five days later, with the signing of the Peace Treaty in Paris, the Vietnam war at last ended for the U.S. Another two years would pass before the North Vietnamese finally took control of the South and many more will elapse before historians ultimately decide, as written in *'Many Reasons Why,'* whether the war was one of the fundamental conflicts in history or if the Americans invested Vietnam with an importance it need never have acquired. Persistent rumours circulated down the years of missing U.S. servicemen still imprisoned in Asia and, as recently as 1992, Senate hearings heard testimony that POWs were indeed left behind; it is a chilling thought that a Phantom or B52 crewman, shot down while Air Ferry operated, was still in Asia nearly thirty years later.

SAFETY
Total safety in travel will always be an unattainable objective, design faults, maintenance omissions, human error and bad weather to name but a few potential hazards will never be eradicated. Public transport is still susceptible to disasters, in 1987 Townsend Thorenson lost their ferry 'Herald of Free Enterprise' with many casualties, while British Rail has suffered fatal crashes into the mid 1990s.

Accidents such as those feared in the 1967 edition of *'Flight'* have occurred, although fortunately safety has improved through the years. As predicted of course, if an incident occurs to a wide bodied jet, many people are involved. The losses of a Turkish Airlines DC10 in 1974, a DC10 at Chicago in 1979 after an engine separation, and of a Japanese Boeing 747 in August 1985 being examples of this; the last accident alone causing the loss of 517 people. In March 1977 the worst accident to date occurred, when two Boeing 747s collided on the runway at Tenerife.

Some of the disasters that have happened have been through the perversity of human nature rather than operating accidents, such as the sky-jackings which caused a blot on the aviation scene. Other incidents included the shooting down of the Korean Airlines Boeing 747 over Sakhalin Island in 1983, and the bombing of aircraft such as an Air India 747 over the Atlantic.

For the independents, Dan-Air suffered a bad accident in July 1970 when a Comet, en route from Manchester to Gerona and carrying 107 Clarkson passengers and 7 crew, flew into a mountain near to the end of its journey, with the loss of all on board.

There have been accidents in the U.K. which led to loss of life and caused the safety experts to seek to head off similar risks of danger in the future. A B.E.A. Trident crashed at Staines in 1972 after take-off from Heathrow, and British Airtours suffered a take-off accident to a Boeing 737 at Manchester in August 1985. A British Midland crash in January 1989 occurred when an aircraft making an emergency landing at East Midlands airport came down onto the M1 Motorway.

POSTSCRIPT

CIVIL

Only a month after Air Ferry's closure, British Eagle collapsed. As with so many of the independents there had been a long struggle to remain viable. Air Holdings had considered acquiring Eagle at one time but were concerned at the financial position, then there had been the link up with Cunard for a while. The closure prompted an emotional response from the newspapers; such was the affection in which the company was held that many of the staff were prepared to allow their pension fund to be used in a forlorn attempt to allow British Eagle to continue.

Transglobe also closed by the end of 1968 and in the years that followed many famous names disappeared, one of the first being British United Airways which was purchased by Caledonian in November 1970. Channel went into receivership in February 1972 while Skyways International, which succeeded Skyways Coach-Air, was absorbed by Dan-Air two months later.

During the early 1970s there was a great race for volume in the inclusive tour market, that led to some large losses being incurred by the major players such as Horizon, Thomson and Clarksons. Autair, which changed its name in 1970 to Court Line, had expanded considerably with Clarksons as a main customer. The '*Flight*' survey of October 1970 recorded eight BAC1-11s on strength, with two more on order. Following a trend initiated by Braniff in the U.S., the 1-11s were painted in multi-coloured livery with each aircraft a different pastel shade; 'Halcyon Sun' was yellow overall, while other aircraft were green and mauve.

The interdependency of the two firms was such that Court Line obtained control of Clarksons in 1973 to protect their market. As mentioned, the oil producing countries tripled the price of oil in late 1973 and this, together with the strains of the fearful competition for market share, took their toll. In early 1974 the three day week caused the vital cash flow of deposits to dip sharply and Horizon Holidays collapsed; Clarksons undertook to carry their passengers and to pay an element for goodwill. This caused a long dispute with British Caledonian which fought for compensation for its loss of Horizon business; Laker had responded promply and picked up a share of this work. Finally, on 16 August 1974, Court Line suddenly went under in circumstances evoking memories of the Overseas collapse many years earlier. Some businesses build up such an aura of success and invincibility that they seem almost to defy the laws of gravity and the fall, when it comes, is all the more spectacular.

Through 1980-81 the recession deepened and affected carriers world wide; it was estimated that at this time the equivalent of fifty five Jumbo Jets were flying the Atlantic route with empty seats.

By 1981 the names of B.K.S., Cambrian, Transmeridian and Lloyd had all gone. After a strenuous fight against the large trans-atlantic carriers, Laker Airways went into liquidation in January 1982, followed by Invicta International Air Cargo in October of that year.

During 1987 Caledonian was absorbed by British Airways although the name still adorned the aircraft; scheduled services were scrapped and the once proud independent was operated as British Airways holiday airline. Dan-Air, one of the old and proud flag carriers, operated through to November 1992 when it, too, closed; the forty year history brought to an end when ownership transferred to British Airways.

Of the airlines operating when Air Ferry ceased only three now remain; Britannia and Monarch at Luton and British Midland at Castle Donington. Reflecting the enormous changes that have taken place, in 1995 Britannia had over 3,000 staff and a fleet of Boeing 757s and 767s. Monarch flies a mixed fleet of Boeing 737s, 757s and Airbus 300s and 320s.

Balair still flies, although the company was merged with another in 1978 to become Balair-CTA. As reported in '*Flight*' in March 1995, the Swissair board was considering transferring Balair operations to Crossair, another of Swissair's partly owned subsidiaries.

Over at Schipol, Martinair, the company which operated a DC4 as Martin's Air Charter, is an international operator with a fleet which includes Boeing 747s and an A310, with large types on order.

Financial pressures have not only affected the U.K. carriers down the years, the mighty Pan American, after years as the sick man of the industry, was forced out of business on the 4 December 1991.

TWILIGHT OF THE PISTONS

Changes have also taken place at the civil airfields. Wymeswold is long closed and the airfield returned to agriculture although the great runways, and much of the crumbling perimeter track, remains. There are many buildings left, some used for industrial purposes, while others, including the tower, slowly rot away. The elegant T2 hangars where the DC4s were once overhauled are still there, one in active use as a Go-Kart centre.

Ramsgate Airport has disappeared beneath a housing estate and Lydd, although still on the active list, is dreadfully quiet nowadays. The old airfields are never forgotten though, articles on Ramsgate have recently appeared in '*Air Britain*' and the *R.A.F. Manston History Club Magazine*, the latter by Roy Doherty, in which he wrote of the 1957 season when the concession for pleasure flying was held by Island Air Services.

Nicosia Airport, visited so often by Air Ferry transports, was a victim of the partition of Cyprus and has remained unused for many years, while Beirut International was another airport to suffer through a war situation over a long period.

So familiar are we now with the wide-bodied jets that it seems amazing that the first one to visit Britain, a Pan-Am 747, landed at Heathrow on 23 January 1970.

Another flight, even more remarkable in many ways, was by Dick Rutan and Jeana Yeager in December 1986 when they piloted their Voyager around the world. The flight, without refuelling, was airborne for a fraction over nine days.

R.A.F.
The R.A.F. has changed considerably since since 1968. The Red Arrows still delight the crowds having celebrated their 25th. anniversary in 1989, although the Gnat Trainers were replaced by Hawks from the 1980 season. The 'V' Force has gone and the only bombers that remain are for museum duty or on fire dumps. Vulcans came off the operational list in March 1984 while the Victors of No. 55 Squadron continued in the tanker role at Marham until as late as October 1993.

The mighty Phantom has been and gone through the R.A.F. inventory in these intervening years since Air Ferry closed, how quickly they have passed.

In 1996 the Tornado was the main operational type, equipping fourteen squadrons, the O.C.U. and two detached flights. Other front line types include the Harrier and the venerable Jaguar.

During this time many famous military airfields have become surplus to requirements and have closed their gates for the last time.

MANSTON
If Air Ferry now seems a great distance ago, the days when the powerful Hawker Typhoons flew from Manston are even more remote. The pilot mentioned in the excerpt on No. 609 Squadron in Chapter 1, Jean de Selys, was killed in August of that year when the tail separated from his Typhoon as he came into land. He was buried in Minster cemetery, virtually the closest point of the village to the airfield, and still lies there today; an unusual feature as the mortal remains of many Belgian pilots were exhumed and returned home after the war.

Air Ferry had barely closed when Invicta underwent a transformation. Hugh Kennard had merged the company with British Midland Airways, which led to consternation at the loss of jobs at Manston resulting from the reduction in local activity. This venture did not last very long as, by June 1969, Hugh broke off the association and acquired the Manston assets to form a new company, called Invicta Air Cargo Ltd. All-freight work was pursued until 1971 when two Vanguards were acquired and the name changed again, to Invicta International Airlines Ltd.

On 10 April 1973, one of Invicta's Vanguards carried out a day shopping trip from Bristol to Basle. The charter was for a West Country womens' club, mainly from four Somerset villages, and ended in tragedy when the airliner overshot the runway at Basle in driving snow and crashed into a mountain. The accident killed 105 out of the 144 passengers and crew. Hugh Kennard went out to Basle although, as he said not long before he died: 'There wasn't much I could do.'

POSTSCRIPT

The Vanguards were later used for cargo work, as also were Boeing 707s; and Hugh Kennard finally sold out his shareholding in 1981, the company going into liquidation the following year.

The airfield itself looks much the same nearly thirty years on from Air Ferry. Now there is a fine Spitfire and Hurricane Memorial Building to house TB752, which has been at Manston since September 1955 and the Hurricane which was acquired later. The first occasion that the writer saw the Spitfire was on a Combined Cadet Force visit to the station in July 1956; sleek Sabres whined round the perimeter track to the runway and red baseball caps were everywhere. In those days TB752 was silver overall, the cadets were permitted to climb inside, and there were birds nests in the cannons.

No. 617 V.G.S., which moved to Manston in 1970, is still there although No. 1 A.E.F. left the airfield in 1996. Helicopter cover for Air Sea Rescue has had a chequered history due to perceived needs for economy and to service changes. The Whirlwinds of No. 22 Squadron left in March 1969, against a background of much local protest and there was a gap of just over two years before a civilian unit, Bristow Helicopters, came to Thanet. In October 1974 the rescue work was transferred back to the R.A.F. and this time the Wessexes, mainly of 22 Squadron, remained until late 1993 when they were withdrawn once more and based at Wattisham in Suffolk.

The Air Ministry Fire School continues to provide essential training, burning aircraft at the end of their active lives, occasionally including a redundant geriatric jet transport from the civilian side.

In 1977 some test bombs used in the Dams trials were found at Reculver, and Manston was involved in two successful cross-channel flights; in 1979 of the man-powered Gossamer Albatross and in 1982 of the Solar Challenger. Between those dates, in 1980, the runway foamer, which was now quite old, was withdrawn from service.

From 1984-1985 some rebuilding was carried out on the station and the runway was resurfaced.

Most of the Air Ferry accomodation has gone, the terminal, the administration building and the huts. The hangar is still there, although in a very dilapidated condition, Invicta used it for storage for many years. Manston is now listed as Kent International Airport and there is a modern terminal block where the old administration building once stood.

The Invicta engineering facilities are used by Jet Support who provide maintenance and overhaul facilities, specialising in the older big jets. Adjacent to this area are the modern buildings of TG Aviation which provide a range of training and aircraft hire services..

The station's illustrious past is kept alive by a thriving History Club which use as their Headquarters an unpretentious wooden hut which must have been passed by hundreds of thousands of people, with barely a glance, as they drove past along the western entry roads. This building is of great historic significance as it was the aircrew briefing hut in WWII and, in its time, has been visited by dignatories such as Mr. Churchill and General de Gaulle.

Elsewhere in Thanet, transport undertakings have been started and ended. The Pegwell Hoverport provided employment for some ex-Air Ferry staff, including the air hostesses. Peter O'Sullivan, who worked there, recalls an ex-Air Ferry stewardess who regaled him with stories of holding umbrellas over flight crew in unpressurised cockpits and wiping coffee stains off cabin roofs on bumpy flights. The hovercraft operations were eventually transferred to Dover while, much later, a shipping company, The Sally Line, was established at Ramsgate.

Air Ferry has not been forgotten down the years although coverage has naturally turned to aviation interest magazines rather than the business press. These included a section in the greatly prized *British Independent Airlines since 1946* and, more recently, photographs in *Golden Age* and *Vintage Glory*.

STATISTICS
In all, Air Ferry aircraft flew 40,314 hours over the six years of operations and carried 834,931 passengers and much freight. Sixteen different aircraft were used covering four main types.

TWILIGHT OF THE PISTONS

Foxtrot Yankee easily took the records for hours flown, at 9,228 and passengers carried of 190,524. It is an impressive statistic that two DC4s, Foxtrot Yankee and Yankee Kilo, together flew 37.8% of Air Ferry's total hours and 37.5% of all passengers carried.

AIRCRAFT

Air Ferry's Bristol freighter G-AMLL went to Canada where she was used by North Coast Air Services and was finally withdrawn from use; one source indicated that this was caused involuntarily by sinking through the ice on a lake, but this had not been substantiated.

The end of Bravo Xray has been chronicled earlier, of the four Vikings sold to Invicta only Victor Delta did not fly with that airline. Oscar Whisky is listed as being withdrawn from use in 1967 and Victor Foxtrot in 1969, it is likely that these two, probably plus Charlie Hotel and Victor Delta, were all broken up at Manston in 1969. The writer recalls some talk of an air hostess being offered one to use as a caravan for some £150, a tantalising prospect from this distance but at the time any preservation aspirations of those tempted were usually defeated by factors such as cost, logistics and small gardens.

Foxtrot Yankee was acquired before the end of the year by the Aviation Development Corporation in Malta. On 21 December 1968 Stan Hunnable and Jeep Jackson gave her an air test at Lydd, now with the U.S. registration of N3454. In October 1969 she passed to International Aviation Development and was operated by LAVCO, finally being broken up at Hal Far in Malta during 1979.

Whisky India returned to Lloyd International and was overhauled by Aviation Traders before being sold in December 1968 to Air Fret, who passed the DC4 on the same month to the Federal Nigerian Government.

About November of 1968 Ken Sheppardson contacted me to see if I was yet gainfully employed and, when he received a reply in the negative, he asked me if I would like to help Paddy Roberts deliver G-ARWI to Lagos where it had been sold to the Nigerian Air Force. Needless to say I jumped at the chance, partly because of the lolly but also because I had worked in a bank in Nigeria for four years before taking up flying and wanted to go back and posture in front of some of my mates so that they could see I had made it as a proper pilot.

We had to pick up the aircraft at Southend and, after one false start when Paddy's compass was found to be frozen, we taxied out; took it down to Tripoli the first day and on to Lagos the next. Tripoli to Lagos was to be VFR over the Sahara, no navigator this time. We plotted our track line, somewhat to the west of what we had actually had to file for in order to get clearance out of Tripoli, because Paddy was not happy with the dearth of radio aids in the south of Libya and wanted to get closer to some which might be operating in the south of Algeria. Once he considered we were out of radar range we drifted over to our chosen course, staying inside Libya for which we had overflight clearance, but quite some way from the designated airway. Our track line was annotated with times for passing various ground features which we reckoned should be visible to us, and plodded on using every radio aid we could find for cross checks and the like.

The wind at our altitude had been forecast to be ten knots from the west at the start and ten knots from the east at the finish of the desert crossing so, taking the practical viewpoint, we ignored it. All our landmarks came up as expected and on time and the navigation turned out to be no problem. Even with all Paddy's planning we spent about four hours out of reach of any ground aid, including VHF stations, by the end of which time he was just about sitting on the edge of his seat counting every blade passing of the propellers. I, of course, being young and inexperienced could not envisage any breakdowns and the subsequent horrors which might follow and was quite happily plotting my way through this fascinating sightseeing trip, and offering to finish off Paddy's packed lunch if he was finished with it.

When we finally picked up the Kano NDB we required less than a ten degree heading change to track into it and arrived at Lagos as the sun was going down. Lagos by this time had been involved in a civil war for about four years and was nothing like the friendly place where I had spent so many happy hours. Military all over the place, roadchecks everywhere and not many friendly faces to be seen. (Alan Breedon)

POSTSCRIPT

After being withdrawn from use the aircraft was kept in storage for some years and eventually broken up in 1977.

The Viscounts went back to Channel Airways as mentioned and were later broken up at Southend.

DC6 at Cotonou, Phil Townsend on the wing   (Phil Townsend)

Balair carried out the flying required by the International Red Cross and, at the time of the Air Ferry closure, were engaged on the Biafran Air Lift in Africa. The trouble in this small country, seven years on from the British departure from her previous colony of Nigeria, had been caused when the Ibo tribe attempted to secede Biafra from Nigeria, and caused the civil war that raged from 1967-1970. Balair operated two of their own DC6s there, but one was due for a major overhaul, a Check 4 that would last for three months, and the other had reached the end of its service life and was due to be scrapped.

LEASE/PURCHASE-AGREEMENT

It is this day mutually agreed between the

      Air Ferry Limited
      Portland House,
      Stag Place,

      L o n d o n S.W.1

      (hereinafter called "the owner")
      of the first part

and

      BALAIR LTD.
      P.O. Box 173

      4002 B a s l e / Switzerland

      (hereinafter called "the tenant")
      of the second part

that:

Article 1

a) The owner shall let to the tenant and the tenant shall take on hire two Douglas DC-6A/B aircraft with the registrations G-APNO / serial number 45531 and G-APNT / serial number 45532, (hereinafter called "the aircraft") more particularly described in schedule A hereto.

b) Air Ferry Limited hereby certifies that it is the legal owner of the aircraft and such aircraft is not subject to any lien, encumbrance, mortgage or charge of any kind.

Article 2

The owner will put at the disposal of the tenant the aircraft (tanks empty) at 10th January 1969 at *SOUTHEND Airport / UK*.

POSTSCRIPT

With Air Ferry's DC6s available, Balair purchased these and, as part of the agreement, asked if Air Ferry could supply a small band of engineers on a three month contract to go out to Africa to maintain the fleet. This would give the Balair staff a rest as they had been providing engineering cover on a three months on and three months off basis, quite an onerous duty for a relatively small firm. (Phil Townsend)

The Air Ferry closure, coming at the end of a season in an area of high unemployment, meant that those who worked on the aircraft had no real alternative than to seek employment elsewhere and probably going into lodgings for a while if they were successful.

I was one of a small band who, finding themselves with no work, flew out of Southend to Basle. It was January when we arrived in Africa and the change to a very hot climate was something of a shock, alleviated somewhat when one of our recent workmates who had accepted a position at Luton wrote describing how he had spent the night in his car trapped in a snowdrift on the Thanet Way on his journey home for the weekend. (Phil Townsend)

The aircraft had operated from the island of Fernando Po but, following some trouble there, a new base was established at Cotonou, the main port of Dahomey. To avoid the danger from gunfire of a daylight landing in Biafra the aircraft operated in darkness and sought to achieve three trips a night. The aircraft were then available for maintenance by the engineers during the day although some care was needed by mid morning when the aircraft became too hot to touch. These flights could be extremely dangerous and the civil crews showed great bravery, not only by doing the work but sometimes by bringing back very damaged aircraft. (Phil Townsend)

In Balair's hands, November Oscar and November Papa became HB-IBS and HB-IBT respectively and, if they had to be involved in a conflict, at least it was for humanitarian purposes. The DC6s were both flown from Lydd to Wymeswold for work prior to going to Africa by Adrian Ross and Jeep, November Oscar on 30 December 1968 and November Papa the next day. The DC6s later flew to Southend, November Oscar on 9 January 1969 by Tony Ahmad and Jeep, to be readied for departure and to pick up the engineers. On the airlift, the aircraft bore the name 'INTERNATIONAL RED CROSS' along the cabin roof in red, and with a bold red cross on the tail. November Oscar flew from Southend to Basle on 11 January 1969 to join Balair.

The Biafran war caused November Papa's career to be cut short, as she crashed on the approach to Uli airstrip on the night of 6/7 May 1969, the four occupants being killed. There were not any ex-Air Ferry crew on board as far as can be ascertained, although it is likely the captain was named Nicol. Some years previously Andy Nicol was aware of another captain, named Alan Nicol, when his insurers needed some clarification and it is possible that this man was the unfortunate pilot.

After the airlift, November Oscar, as HB-IBS of course, was operated by Balair on much more Red Cross work and later in their own livery for some years. The next owner was Conair Aviation Ltd. in Canada where she acquired the registration of C-GIBS. Conair has operated a mixed fleet of aircraft for many years on fire control duties, a far cry from inclusive tours to Genoa. November Oscar arrived at Conair's Abbotsford base

C-GIBS (G-APNO)
in 1995
(Robert M Stitt)

in September 1982 and has been part of the fire control fleet ever since. Her fleet number is 451 of which '51' appears on the tail. She is equipped with a 12-compartment, 2,500 imperial gallon retardent delivery system. There are nine DC6s on strength and these are based at airports in British Columbia, Alberta and the Northwest

TWILIGHT OF THE PISTONS

Territories during the summer months, each with a Piper Aerostar birddog. Each aircraft flies between 60 and 150 hours per year, depending on the severity of the fire season.

Robert M Stitt, Conair's Marketing Manager, has written articles about November Oscar and the rest of the fleet which are maintained in a superb condition. Some of November Oscar's former operators at Balair still have a lot of affection for her as she was the last piston engined airliner operating scheduled passenger services in Europe, and there are many who hope that she may return to Switzerland after she is finally retired.

Included in the items Robert provided for this history was a copy of the lease by Air Ferry to Balair of HB-IBS and HB-IBT. This was initially for three months and the figures quoted are for each aircraft. The rental was at $22,000 for 200 hours per month with additional hours at $80. The insurance cover was £150,000 in respect of total loss, which of course unfortunately happened in respect of HB-IBT, and there was also an option to purchase at $250,000. This was exercised for November Oscar, the DC6 holding her price so well that the price charged by Balair to Conair, over thirteen years later, was only $10,000 less.

STAFF
Hugh Kennard is dead. After he sold out his Invicta shares he turned again to his other abiding interest, the renovation of old cars. He set up a company in Canterbury and traded there until the business moved to Chilham in March 1995.

He collapsed from a heart attack, onto one of his cars, on 2 June 1995 and died the following day. The funeral was held at Linton, near Maidstone, where the Kennard family once farmed and above which Hugh had flown in 1940. In a moving ceremony Jeremy read the lesson while Julian read extracts from '*The Eagle Squadrons.*' Brian McAvoy gave the address and told of Hugh Kennard's kindness to many people; he ended with the immortal words: 'Never in the field of human conflict was so much owed by so many to so few.'

Audry went to America after she left Invicta and continues to lead a busy working life by running her own travel business in London.

Of those who ran the catering in the early years, Jeremy Kennard now lives in London while Gwen Jackson (Laycock), is retired in Thanet.

The man who, with Hugh and Audry, started it all is also gone. Lewis Leroy retired and later lost his wife. Some time after this he died in tragic circumstances, a sad epithet to a lifetime of opening horizons for so many.

Unfortunately it has not been possible to obtain any news of Ken Sheppardson in recent years. *The Flight World Airline Directory* in March 1984 listed him as the General Manager of Management Aviation at Bourn. This company operated a fleet of helicopters on a wide range of duties, including support for the

Ken Barker,
Airframe/
Engine
Inspector
(Joan Barker)

POSTSCRIPT

offshore oil and gas industries, but by 1987 had joined up with British International Helicopters based at Dyce.

The last few years have seen the passing of some of the senior, and therefore older staff, such as Ron Illsley, Jim Jones and Ken Barker from the engineers; Ken sadly died only days before the reunion in March 1996.

After Air Ferry, Eddie Edgar went out to Nigeria for eighteen months, and then worked for B.U.A. at Gatwick as a flight engineer, during which time he was seconded to Pan American for eight months in Kabul. After B.U.A., he joined Dan-Air and became a lecturer in aerodynamics at Odiham but sadly, a few years later and only fifty three, he contacted bronchitis which affected his heart and he died in Odiham Hospital. Eddie is one of those who will always be remembered for his hard work and dedication, a great loss.

As is to be expected with the passage of time, many of the old staff are scattered; while some remained in Thanet others have relocated for work or family reasons. Space does not allow a biopic of everyone but some details can be given. Many well known names are included in those who still reside in Thanet, some now retired; Robbie Thomson who went to Skyways for a while, Frank Strainge, Phil Townsend, Dave Ellis, Roger Pearce to name but a few. Roger also worked for Skyways and later for Shorts at West Malling.

Ron Blake joined Invicta for a short time and then went out on the Biafran Air Lift with Frank Strainge, Eddie Edgar and Phil Townsend. After that he was with B.U.A. at Gatwick, in charge of the avionics workshop, and considered one of the best jobs in the industry. Living away from home is not for everyone, and Ron returned to Manston with Invicta, working on the Vanguards. He has his own business, Airborne Radio Services in Thanet. Frank Strainge also returned to Manston and rejoined Hugh Kennard when the firm was Invicta International.

Paul Noller and John Williams work with Monarch at Luton. Ernest Brown is also in Luton, he was with Invicta until 1982 and then became a supervisor with Britannia until he retired some three years ago.

Cyril Nurthen and Les Mees went up to Wymeswold while the DC6s were being readied for their Red Cross duties, the atmosphere in the hangar highly pungent, with the big aircraft being sprayed while other work was going on.

After a while with Skyways Coach-Air and Hoverlloyd, Cyril spent four years in New Zealand looking after the DC3s of Field Air, a top dressing company who carried out this hazardous agricultural work at very low level. He then returned to Manston as an Inspector in the engine bay for Invicta, acclimatising to the somewhat longer overhaul life for Proteus engines of 10,000 hours! Cyril remained with Invicta to 1982 and now runs hotels in Thanet.

John Cornwell is far away in Ross-Shire, but not too far to spot the brief item about Air Ferry on teletext. After the closure John moved over to the R.A.F. side where he worked for the M.O.D. until 1990. Of the Doherty brothers, Roy still lives in Ramsgate while sadly, and just as his career was becoming established and recordings being marketed, Al succumbed to a heart attack in 1981. As mentioned, Roy is an active member of the Manston History Club.

Les Dray is in the West Country, still working on aircraft, and Len Mees, although retired, has seen his son follow him into engineering, appropriately working for A.E.M which still operates, although now on the Haine Road Estate.

Of those who manned the stores, Reg Hampton is still in Thanet, as are Gerry Cavell and brother George. Alan Jones, who once painted the U.S.A.F. Sabres and Albatrosses in the loop hangar, and always a modeller of note, has turned his hand to aviation art and produced some stunning paintings. Ted and Sally Maycock have now been mine hosts at 'The Bull' at Otford for some 20 years.

From Traffic, Joe and Sheila Russell have both passed away, Sheila at a relatively young age and not much over fifty. Ingrid Osborne is a senior manager in the N.H.S. and a magistrate, while Richard Grist does much to help young people. Patricia Dobson emigrated to Australia, where she achieved her ambition to be an air hostess, and flew for fifteen years with Trans-Australia Airlines.

Alan Wood from tarmac, who followed Hugh to Invicta and flew as a steward with them, died in 1994 and there is a commemorative tree on the airfield in his memory.

TWILIGHT OF THE PISTONS

Mike Willetts who was in Operations for most of Air Ferry's time, went to America; an avid gardener, Traffic were on notice not to telephone unnecessarily on a Sunday afternoon and so interrupt *'Gardeners' Question Time.'* Brian Koering went to Caledonian; to Laker Airways, which he rated a good company; and to Air Europe where he became Operations Manager.

Mike Harradine has continued a successful career in aviation, he worked for many years with Hugh Kennard in various ways and, among his responsibilities, currently runs a company in Ostend. Herfurth is now Belgavia, and one of the largest aviation enterprises in Belgium. Some of the staff there intended to come to the reunion via the jet foil but due to a low load it was cancelled that night, although the operators blamed the weather!

Rick Rickards spent eleven years with T.W.A. at Heathrow and, in 1990, achieved a long held ambition by gaining his PPL.

Douglas Whybrow is now retired and lives in Dorset. As is fitting after a long and well known history, B.U.A.F.s' reunions take place annually, alternating between Lydd and Gatwick. Like many of the old airlines there is a fierce *'esprit de corps'* and Douglas' book *'Air Ferry,'* published in 1995, gives a very interesting story of the vehicle ferry operations. The title was not intended to place special emphasis on the old names issue; he had hoped to use the excellent title of: *'When Cars Could Fly,'* but the publishers insisted on a name higher up the alphabetical index!

> *While it can always be said that distance lends enchantment, many people had similar feelings at the time; Ann Bay (nee Cowley) recalled in 1995: 'They were great days, just like one big family.'*

CREWS

As mentioned in the narrative, the compilation of this history has attracted attention from people who did not even work for the company. Howard Meredith worked for B.U.A. from 1961 until the takeover by Caledonian, and flew to Verona on November Oscar in 1966, he remembers being on duty the night that news came through of Yankee Kilo's crash.

One impression, in retrospect in later years, was how kind and approachable the crews were, not a feature necessarily exhibited by professionals in other walks of life. This is not only a personal view but one repeated by people who have written in during the course of this work. Chas. Finn-Kelcey, a Britannia Boeing 767 captain, wrote recalling the buoyant aviation industry that used to flourish on the Kent airfields. In his 'teens surreptitious jump-seat rides were arranged on day trips and he remembers the kind people who spurred his ambitions to be a pilot, such as Peter Wannop, Vic Surrage and Ronald Pullinger.

Many of the stalwarts of Air Ferry days have gone, incredibly including Tony Ahmad who was a senior Boeing 747 captain for Hong Kong Airways and sadly succumbed to cancer within the last couple of years. Tony flew for Tradewinds and at one time was with International Air Services at Gatwick, who operated DC8s and CL44s, as also was Bob McNay.

Hugh Tubman flew DC6s in the Lebanon for four years and spent another year operating DC3s from Lympne. He later joined Invicta as Operations Manager and sadly died in 1980 at the early age of 61.

Bill Wood continued with Dan-Air until he retired. From the DC7BF Bill converted onto the jets and flew Comets and the Boeing 727., he retired in Horley and died in April 1996. At Dan-Air Bill was joined by Jeep Jackson, Patrick Hope, Simon Searle and Les Toghill. Simon is currently with British Airways, European, at Gatwick. Paul Ashpitel flew Avro 748s for Skyways Coach-Air and later joined Dan-Air when it took over Skyways. Peter Souster retired to Cyprus.

John Page left Air Ferry to fly with Aer Lingus as a co-pilot on Viscounts and Boeing 707s. Later on he spent fourteen years with Laker Airways where he qualified as a C.A.A. Instrument Rating Examiner and Type Rating Examiner on the BAC 1-11, Boeing 707 and DC10/30 aircraft. He was responsible for the Berlin base and became Chief Training Captain. He was appointed Director of Flight Operations for Novair International Airways and Head of Flight Operations for Cyprus Airways. Now back once more in his native Eastbourne, he is currently Training Manager/Chief Pilot for Hughes Flight Training.

POSTSCRIPT

Time to sort out duty times

SIR—May I comment on the letter from Capt Kahn (*Flight*, April 30)? I have been retired from aviation for some six years, having notched up some very considerable hours as pilot, radio operator, and ex-wireless operator/air gunner. I had many years in command, finishing up with five years flying Boeing 707s.

There is little likelihood that Capt Kahn will ever be responsible for any "tragic accident or loss of life". Like all the other tired and weary aircrew before him, he will alert himself at the critical times to ensure that the job is done with safety. The companies know this, and act accordingly. Indeed, Capt Khan will play his part as a responsible man and, like symbiotic lichen, will keep the system working.

No, the price will be paid not by the passengers or even by the company, but by Capt Kahn himself. He will damage his own health and endanger his life expectancy by co-operating with a system of rest and duty periods which will take their toll of him and his colleagues. There is no need for this to be so. The problem of how you keep an airline viable is one with which we all have to live. As far as I can see no-one has found a solution to the fatigue problems involved.

It is my profound belief that the solution is being sought in the wrong place. By the very nature of the exercise it will always be difficult to create a system of rostering which will answer the problem. But there must be, and is, a solution. It should be found in just the same way as an aircrew is created, by training. The training of operations staff should include the study of aircrew management, and aircrew themselves should understand that they should have an appreciation of what is happening.

All of us tended to return to base with an air of cheeriness which was usually interpreted as, "We enjoyed that, and are raring to go again", even when we were whacked and perhaps shattered. What is needed is for there to be an understanding that aircrew get tired over a period of unnatural working hours.

The boss or head of operations going down the route will enjoy his "trip", and will not be in the same position as the crew. He will often tend to wonder why the crew get tired so easily. He has not been at this particular stint for the last few months. After a period of difficult rostering the crew will get tired in such a way that even light work will not restore the situation. And a roster that ops. may think is easy may add to, and not relieve, the level of strain.

What is important is that it should be recognised by *all* that crew should not be trusted to say say how they feel about fatigue. All rostering should be done on the basis of minimising difficulties of unusual patterns of working which are synonymous with flying.

When it is possible to give more rest time down route it should *always* be done, on principle. When it is possible to choose between "normal operating times" and obvious non-body times, then the best rostering should be used to ensure the most restful option. If a crew can be left in bed during night-time (when they are already there), then the opportunity should always be taken, even if it is only for an extra half-hour. At this end of the rest period the crew are probably asleep, so an extra half hour here is an extra half hour of real rest ... sleep.

When we have to move the aircraft to night-stop position for example, and are stranded on the other side of the airport without steps, then the three hours it takes to get off the airport should not come out of rest.

There should never be a situation where the crew are got out of of bed to fly the aircraft back to base at one or two o'clock in the morning, when the aircraft is not needed. Aircrew (captains) should never be wakened from sleep to be told something which could wait until call time. Where possible, someone should watch over the crew call, so that if a flight is delayed the crew can be left asleep. The 24hr stopover should be seen as particularly difficult for rest patterns.

Many more situations could be added. However, let it be remembered that crews are, in the main, willing horses, and should be protected on the grounds of common sense as well as common humanity. Capt Kahn should then be able to look forward to a more deservedly relaxed work pattern, so that upon retirement he might enjoy the few remaining years with feelings of pride in achievement and respect for his employers and the professional operations staff who made it all possible.

This week I had a telephone call to say that an old friend at Tradewinds had died, and I have just read an obituary of another old friend, John Michie. Before the last of us shuffle off and leave things unchanged, let me tell you that my memories of Skyways and John are of a year when I did 1,160hr as a radio operator on Yorks while training, at my own expense to become a pilot. At another time I had my leave cancelled five times because the company could not give me one month away all in one go to get up to date and sit my ATPL. My leave, you note, not time off.

Under that regime I spent 11 years regarding five hours sleep as "sufficient"; I spent several years out of the pension scheme because Skyways of London did not have, in my days, a scheme for Radio Officers. And to this day I draw a paid-up £90 a year which does not change. I ended my flying with Tradewinds at Gatwick, and for the last four years of my working life was kept out of their pension scheme because I was too old to be in it.

Having started by putting my age on to get into the RAF as a wireless operator/air gunner, I went on to age 59 to get together enough to live on (my total pension from all sources after 42 years of aviation comes to £3,300). Having spent my savings at age 35 to become a pilot, I had hoped to fly on to age 60 or more, to at least retire as if I had been aircrew, but sadly my health broke down. With a blood pressure of 240 over 140 and a bladder infection I could not shake off, I gave up trying to persuade the Rylands, Jones's, Michies, and Du Canns to try to put things right, and retired to try to re-establish an otherwise robust health and claim a few years for myself.

It was always my belief that the company's success was my success, but sadly the latter part did not always get over to the employers. Can I commend to younger pilots the book *Fate is the Hunter* by Ernest K. Gann? Everything in that book happened to me, and I think it should be required reading for all who might wish to understand modern aviation and the breadth of the achievement. Let us hope that we might eventually get the human side right as well as the technical, and then the achievement will truly be complete.

STANLEY K. HUNNABLE
72 Stone Road
Broadstairs
Kent XT10 1EB

WHAT'S ON

May 16 FlightSafety International, three-day international procedures course, Savannah, Georgia, USA; tel: (718) 565-4120.

May 16-17 ICC/Ifapa/Interavia international symposium on airline computer reservation systems, "Competition, Concentration, and Customer Satisfaction", Intercontinental Hotel, Geneva. Contact: Geoffrey Lipman, Ifapa, PO Box 462, 1215 Geneva 15, Switzerland; tel: (41-22)-98-52-55.

May 17-19 University of Sheffield/Brüel and Kjaer, 3-day course, "Sound Intensity: Theory and Practice". Contact: Short Course Office, Department of Mechanical Engineering, The University, Mappin Street, Sheffield S1 3JD; tel: 0742 758555 (ext. 5151/5169).

May 18 The Royal Institute of Navigation, "The Integration of Flight Control and Navigation Systems", Dr J. F. Meredith, 16.30, Royal Entomological Society, 41 Queens Gate, London SW7 5HU. Contact: The Director, The Royal Institute of Navigation, 1 Kensington Gore, London SW7 2AT; tel: 01-589 5021.

May 18-20 Flight-test conference, San Diego, California, USA. Contact Robert Tuttle; tel: (505) 848-5608.

May 19 RAeS Halton Branch, annual general meeting and "Dambusters", Jim Shortland, 7.30 p.m., RAeS Clubroom, Building 26, Henderson Parade Square, RAF Halton. Tel: 01-499 3515 (ext. 253).

May 19 RAeS, 28th Lanchester Memorial Lecture, "Experimental Real-gas Hypersonics", Prof. H. Hornung, 7.00 p.m., 4 Hamilton Place, London W1V 0BQ; tel: 01-499 3515 (ext. 253).

May 19 RAeS Man-powered Flight Group, annual general meeting, 4 Hamilton Place, London W1V 0BQ; tel: 01-499 3515 (ext. 253).

May 19-24 International Federation of Airline Pilots' Association's annual conference.

May 20-21 IMechE, two-day seminar, "Propulsion in the 21st Century: update scenario for the 21st century aero engine design", 9.00 a.m., Manor Hotel, Meriden, Warwickshire. Contact: Aerospace Industries Division, Institution of Mechanical Engineers, 1 Birdcage Walk, Westminster, London SW1H 9JJ; tel: 01-222 7899.

In a discussion recently John made a comment echoed by other pilots about Captain Wood; 'I liked flying with Bill.'

John Kenton-Page

Jeep Jackson went on to become a senior captain with Dan-Air until the closure and flew 5,000 hours on Comets, 6,000 hours on Boeing 727s and later flew the Airbus A300 and the Boeing 737-200. Twenty five years on from his memorable trip into Khamis Mushayt, he returned there at the controls of a V.I.P. Boeing 727. He now works for the C.A.A., flying a desk for much of the time, although he does get to use the Bae Hs 725 in the course of his work. He remembers the DC4 as a nice aeroplane, but hard work!

While Jeep carried on with Comets and obtained his command, Patrick Hope flew on the Boeing 707 and achieved his captaincy not long after Jeep. Patrick sadly died some fifteen years ago in an aircraft accident at Shoreham.

Keith Sissons went back to Nigeria when Air Ferry closed and flew DC4s for Pan African Airlines, a U.S. operated passenger and cargo company, rather like Air Ferry. Keith happened to meet Alan Bristow at that time and was asked what he was doing. He said: 'Pan African,' and Bristow asked: 'Why don't you settle down and get a steady job?' Keith replied: 'I would if you'd stop closing down airlines.'

Keith also spent some time ferrying Islanders to Australia and then worked some more for Air Holdings. They had obtained the sales agency for Tri-Stars and one of the companies who acquired them was Trans Canada who insisted their Vanguards be taken in part exchange. These aircraft were leased to various firms; Keith flew the Vanguards in the Lebanon and Sweden and was out in Indonesia for a time, operating them with Ken Sheppardson.

Later on, Keith flew Vanguards on both passenger and cargo work for Invicta, CL44s with Transmeridian and the great Belfast for Heavylift at Stanstead, although he is best known to aviation enthusiasts for his display flying of the B17 'Sally B' over some twenty years. He has had various colleagues in the cockpit, including Mike Waddingham. Sometimes 'Sally B' stars at other events, particularly the reunion visits that are still made to the derelict wartime U.S.A.A.F. airfields, or when remembrance ceremonies are held at the impressive American Cemetry at Madingly. It is a spine tingling experience to stand on one of those old bases and to see the Fortress ease into the circuit and turn for a low pass over what is left of the main runway; the veterans, of course, are visibly moved.

Adrian Ross went on to be a training captain on BAC 1-11s, he retired to Majorca and sadly died in January 1996, just before the reunion could take place, and which Paul Horsting had hoped he might attend. Paul is still flying, as a senior captain on Boeing 747s with Cathay Pacific Airways, for which company he is the Manager of International Operations.

Stan Hunnable had been happy at Air Ferry as Maura recalls, being nearby he could sometimes sail his boat, as he was later still able to do when he moved to Tradewinds, for whom he flew the CL44. He later trained out in Dallas on the Boeing 707. He retired in 1982 and died in 1993, at sixty nine. Always concerned with aircrew health, and the injurious effects of extended duty times, Stan wrote a long letter to *Flight* on the

POSTSCRIPT

subject in 1988 that drew some interest and sympathetic response.

Andy Nicol is retired and lives in Birchington. By December 1968 he was back on DC6s, this time out in Saudi Arabia. He gave up flying in 1974 and remembers the DC6 with affection as being the quietest and nicest aircraft to fly. He recalls Foxtrot Yankee as the best of the DC4s, and the fastest, although with a lower fuel capacity; while Yankee Kilo's best features were the brakes, a disc type not used on the other DC4s he flew.

Viv Kellard flew Vanguards with Air Bridge Carriers and on his final charter fell seriously ill in a hotel in the Gambia with what turned out to be cerebral malaria. Don Nay was in the crew and they frantically tried to organise a jet to fly Viv out for attention, but he died while they were doing this.

Vic Surrage flew the BASCO DC6s from Aden, and was with Invicta; at some time he flew Air Atlantique's DC6. While flying a Nigerian registered DC4 he had to belly land the aircraft at Manston. Vic was known to be very ill in recent years. Frank Hargreaves, Frank Simpson, Paddy Roberts, Stan Davis and Flight Engineer Jock Chisholm, who was in Biafra, are all now dead. Another captain no longer with us is Eddie Adams who went on to fly Laker DC10s.

British Air Ferries saw several ex-Air Ferry pilots. Eddie Roocroft and Phil Phillp were both on Heralds until retirement, and Peter Lockwood and Harry Chang were also there until the early 1990s. Following the closure, Phil Phillp went to BASCO at Aden and then participated in the Biafran Relief Work. The unit he joined was called Joint Church Air, which operated black finished DC6s bearing a two fishes insignia on the fin. He recalls being bombed while on the ground by a DC4, which was accomplished by the simple method of rolling bombs down the fuselage and out of the door; and reflects that this operation could have been by an ex-colleague now working on the government side. He also flew Martinair's DC6, where he gained his captaincy, and later flew for Channel, Balair, East African Airways and finally B.A.F. with whom he flew until retirement about four years ago. Phil's stint at Balair reunited him with relief work, and with November Oscar, as he flew her on the Red Cross missions to India, Bangladesh and Afghanistan.

Norman Watson went to Hunting Surveys flying their Dove and DC3 overseas and then joined British Midland, where he spent two years on Viscounts before converting to the BAC 1-11. After two British Midland pilots and two industrialists set up Alidair, with ex-British Midland and Channel Viscounts, Norman joined them for four years as Training Captain. He then moved to Monarch where he has been for sixteen years and is currently a Training Captain on Boeing 757s.

George Gilson and his wife Irene set up an airline of their own, Chieftan Airways, in early 1987 with two HS 748s at Glasgow. George is currently Operations Director for Hunting Cargo.

Don Nay spent a year flying an air taxi and instructing at his local flying club after Air Ferry closed. Then he joined Invicta and soon gained a command on their DC4s, later converting to the Vanguards. Time on Viscounts with Alidair and Cyprus Airways followed and then nine years with Air Bridge flying the Merchantman, as the cargo version of the Vanguard was named. He spent the last six years or so before he

Reunion
7 March, 1996
from left to right:
Frank Strainge,
Charlie Bailie,
Peter Ling and
Robbie Thomson

had to retire operating Viscounts for B.A.F. Don is still flying, although now a Golden Arrow, while his daughter, with whom he flew briefly at B.A.F., and who gained her A.L.T.P. licence there, is now on Boeing 747s with British Airways.

After delivering Whisky India to Lagos, Alan Breedon managed to get another job a couple of months later, as a Boeing 727 P3 for two years with British West Indian Airways in the Caribbean. That was followed by a year with Channel Airways as a BAC 1-11 co-pilot until they failed, then with Court Line until they too failed. At that time he vowed no more charter outfits and joined Royal Brunai Airlines on day one, along with sixteen others, as a Boeing 737 copilot. Since then he has progressed through command, flight safety officer, line training, base training and authorised examiner; the airline now operating the B757/767 combination. He also had eight years in the office as Flight Standards Superintendent and later as fleet manager on the B757, until he felt he had had enough of that, and returned to a mainly flying and simulator instructing lifestyle. Twenty years on, he is the last of the original sixteen in Brunai.

Don Nay

Don Bullock founded a company called Euroworld for ferrying and broking; he was very involved in the preservation movement. He died in a tragic accident at the Biggin Hill Battle of Britain airshow on Sunday 21 September 1980 when the Invader he was flying crashed. The accident was widely reported and drew the usual media speculation. The discussion continued into March of the following year in 'Flight' when a doctor, whose specialist subject was tropical diseases, made some statements about aircrew fitness that prompted letters from some annoyed readers and one from Keith Sissons in defence of his friend. Keith flew the Fortress at the show immediately after the crash and clearly recalls how very bright the day was, and how frequently he needed to call to his co-pilot for the airspeed as the instruments were difficult to see.

The Mayos retired to Barbados, Bob Vines and Dave Mackie went to Rhodesia and Guy Clapshaw settled in New Zealand. John Cropp now lives in Sussex, while Reg Eames retired to Surrey.

Mrs. Pullinger continued to work with Hugh Kennard for many years, becoming a director of A.E.&M., and also Company secretary, until she retired some ten years ago. Ron and Eileen's daughter Christine came to the reunion; she was Hugh Kennard's secretary and later a hostess on the hovercraft and with B.O.A.C.; their son John is a Lieutenant Colonel in the Army, serving with the U.N. in Angola.

After a long interval of the writer trying to contact former aircrew, without much success, Mike Waddingham compensated for this by recently writing a cameo of his aviation experiences:

'My Air Ferry log book starts on June 15th 1966, training at Ostend with Paul Ashpitel. This was my first 'air line' job, having got my instrument rating a month earlier. I was sad at the thought of leaving behind my life as a solo pilot; jets in the R.A.F. and Cessna's bush flying in Kenya.

On the other hand a new life as part of a team and part of what seemed a large organisation had all the lure of the unknown. I did not expect to really enjoy large multi-engined aircraft, after all you could hardly do a snap roll in a DC4 with passengers could you ?

But there were other pleasures to be found. The sheer size and weight of the aircraft, the skill in handling four engines, the distance travelled, the countries visited, the night stopovers, the girls! It was an entirely new experience and the start of a love affair with aviation and a few others as well!

The DC4 turned out to be a pleasure to fly, and carried 84 passengers in lumbering comfort. They were served lunch boxes and coffee and biscuits, and they were explorers! These were the early days of package holidays and the British were just beginning to explore Europe. Not many people flew then, and they had stories to bring home, together with straw hats, donkeys and bottles of duty free. They told their experiences to their neighbours and the beginning of the 'inclusive tour' trade was established.

POSTSCRIPT

Air Ferry flew them off at the exotic speed of 180 knots to far away places like Basle and Perpignan. In fact those were almost the only two destinations for the first two summer seasons. There are 106 trips to Basle in my log book. If ever Operations wanted one of us for a flight on our day off they would phone and ask if you could do a flight to Miami. If you said 'yes' they would say: ".....Well would you mind going to Basle, someone has gone sick!"

The passengers for the Costa Brava landed at Perpignan. The French were unwilling to provide Air Traffic services to overflying aircraft without some sort of share in the pot. There were no navigation fees at that time, so they decided they would only grant over-flight clearance if the aircraft were to make a landing in French territory. This way they would pick up landing fees, but the passengers had to continue by coach.

Other destinations were therefore a welcome relief. When my first summer season ended in September '66, we started doing freight for B.E.A. out of Heathrow. I recall the first such flight with Reg Eames to Copenhagen. We went out on the town to celebrate. After many beers we returned to the hotel only to find it so full we had to share a room. In the morning I awoke to find Reg conspicuous by his absence. I looked outside and found him camped in the corridor! He had not been able to sleep for my snoring!

The following year, 1967 I thought I should find some decent bachelor accommodation. It needed to be somewhere dramatic and consistent with my new horizons. I stumbled upon Kingsgate Castle. It was a somewhat modern castle built of flint on the edge of the cliffs. It was being converted to about thirty flats when the property company went bust. However two of the flats were finished and the agents wanted £6 a week for each. I took one and Norman Waller took the other.

I was ecstatic. The castle had a mock portcullis, a central courtyard, and a balcony set on the cliff edge. Morever there was a sandy beach on each side, a pub on the next cliff, and a golf course over the road. For a bachelor this was heaven. My former London flatmates re-discovered me and brought all their girl friends down to visit. "We are going to Kingsgate Castle for the weekend," was the best pulling line in Fulham!

I had a job earning £2,700 a year, a brilliant pad, an envious choice of girlfriends, and the Beetles were in full swing. The sixties were living up to their obituary. About this time I met Hazel; I think over a spag bog at Joy Greenway's. She was about 20, came from Faversham, and was convinced that life was not a dress rehearsal! It may have been my charm, or more likely that of the castle that persuaded her to move in.

That summer went by in a whirl. We flew by day and more often than not by night, unwound at the Jolly Farmer, slept on the beach and partied at the castle. One day I came home to find nearly 100 chocolate bars on the mantelpiece. Hazel and the other girls had got hungry on the turn around so they opened the lunch boxes in the back two rows and ate all the chock bars. Hazel realised that these passengers would see the people in front had Sports Bars but they had not, so she brought them all home! I came home to see this lot and thought: 'She must be pregnant!'

The next winter found us doing freight and going to all the cold places again. I remember landing at Goteborg with Keith Sissons and sliding sideways down the ice and snow covered runway. The brakes and steering were totally ineffective and we were slowly turning round. I recall thinking that if we could make it right round we could open up the engines and become the first DC4 with reverse thrust!

Keith and I night stopped at a hotel in town. We were amused to watch two local girls at dinner. As soon as their food arrived two chaps asked them to dance. This happened every course. Keith remarked that it was daft because their food was getting cold. I said: 'They didn't come out for dinner!'

In the spring of '68 I was one of the crews that took a DC4 up to Newcastle for a whole month of day trips to Paris and Rotterdam. Hazel and Jenny Holtan were the hosties. We flew every other day with a day off in between. As they were early starts and late returns we were given hotel rooms for the day while the passengers explored the bulb fields or whatever.

We had spending money too; half a crown an hour away from base! However we found ways of improving our lot. First we hired a car and continued to charge taxi fares to the airport. This gave us wheels for our days off, and we spent every other day exploring the best pubs in the area, or visiting the Lake District.

Soon it became obvious that the cost of four hotel rooms held further potential for mismanagement. So on our day trips we continued to draw funds for four rooms but we all stayed in one! The hotel staff in both Beauvais and Rotterdam were very courteous; they had obviously heard about this sort of thing, but I suspect they were secretly delighted to be able to report they had witnessed it first hand!

The extra cash meant we could dine well in the evenings, and for that month at least our salaries went untouched. However May '68 saw us back at Manston with the package holiday season starting again. We were back to destinations like Basle and Palma. Hazel was into her second season and had passenger management down to a fine art. A rather pretentious lady asked her for "Coffee without cream please." Hazel said: "..Sorry we don't serve cream on this airline; would you like it without milk?"

The DC4 was fairly reliable, but it did have a few weak points. For example it had high tension distribution to it's spark plugs, and this was very susceptible to moisture. Frequently we had engine problems with ignition, but we carried a spares box and a few tools. The passengers would be sat on top of the terminal drinking beer and watching as we spent a couple of hours changed spark leads in our uniforms.

This sort of incident gave us quite a long day when added to the three and a half hours each way. Twelve hours was common, but duty hours were almost unheard of and we were expected to do or die along with the passengers.

Sadly, one crew did die when their DC4 crashed near Perpignan and one of the hostesses on that aircraft, Cathy Dunn, was a good friend. Amazingly I was rostered for this flight, but was taken off to start a DC6 course on Monday. My good fortune was entirely overshadowed by the loss of my good friends. I suppose it was all part of life's rich adventure, and we sunk a few beers for our compatriots and got on with the job.

The Jolly Farmer *pub became the centre of our social life. Bert and Enid almost ran the pub for the benefit of the airline. They also had a remarkably clear premonition of the governments intention to abolish 'closing time'. The airline life was so rich in experience, we had numerous stories to tell and exaggerate in the pub. Many of the girls had come down from places like Manchester. They were in search of adventure and romance, and determined to find it. A small sign on the wall of the pub said "Good girls go to Heaven, bad girls go everywhere!"*

The DC6 seemed several generations advanced from the DC4. The Pratt and Whitney R2800 engines were very advanced and the addition of a Flight Engineer was a distinct advantage. There were so many systems and different ways of doing things. I once counted all the cockpit indicators, warning lights, circuit breakers, controls etc., and it came to over 1,000.

The fuel tanks were divided into two separate systems so that two different kinds of fuel could be carried; a high octane for take-off and an economical fuel for cruise. The radial engines each had 18 cylinders, and each cylinder had 2 spark plugs; a dual ignition system. The distribution was at low tension so there was a spark coil for each plug. To supervise all 144 plugs required a spark analyser; a sort of TV screen where you could select an individual plug and look at the discharge profile.

This told the Flight Engineer if an engine was losing oil or misbehaving in any way. The engines

POSTSCRIPT

were also supercharged (turbocharged) to increase the amount of air fuel mix inserted into the cylinders. This was handy in two situations; mainly for high altitude where the air is thin, but also for take-off where extra push will increase the 'maximum take-off weight' and hence the payload.

While atmospheric pressure on your hall barometer is 30 inches of mercury, (you do have a hall barometer don't you!), the blowers could lift the air pressure to 73 inches for take-off. At this pressure the fuel air mix could detonate so a fine water spray was pumped into the engine; called water injection. The water then required an additive of Methnol to stop it freezing in cold weather. However the power produced was such that if an engine failed on take-off the swing could be catastrophic, so 'auto-feather' was added to feather the pops in the event of failure.

Reunion 1996
from left: Anna Turner (nee Oates), Hazel's sister, Mike Waddingham,
Hazel Kyd-Grant (nee King), and Celia McAvoy

But there again a misbehaviour of the auto feather system (two or more getting the desire to do it together) would also be fatal, so there were interlocks to prevent that. It seemed that every level of sophistication added required two or three extra systems to provide additional safety. Hence the need for a Flight Engineer to monitor all these systems.

Of course the DC6 was also pressurised and could fly much higher, and also it had weather radar. It would be a relief not to have to relive the experience of flying low over the Alps at about 10,000 feet and hitting the centre of a thunderstorm. On one occasion, in a DC4, the hail stones were the size of eggs and were hitting the wind screen at 200mph. The noise in the cockpit was deafening and the glass seemed sure to break. If it did, both pilots would have been battered to death in seconds. We discussed the merits of one of us leaving the cockpit so that the surviving pilot could save the plane if disaster should occur. Fortunately the hailstones abated just as we were about to toss a coin. On landing the engine cowlings were so dented that you would think a giant had been let loose with a sledge hammer!

TWILIGHT OF THE PISTONS

Not only could the DC6 fly higher, but it could fly faster; 240 knots as against 180. This either took us further afield, or got us back to the pub quicker. (If you wanted a happy life you would fit the emotion to the circumstances!) On the other hand if you missed the pub, there was an alternative. Down in Ramsgate was Nero's Night club. If you landed too late for the pub this was a chance for a beer and a dance up till about 2 am.

That summer I somehow managed to pass my Airline Transport Pilots Licence by doing a postal course, but only because three examiners gave me the benefit of the doubt and awarded me the exact pass mark. If they had conferred they might have realised my mind was on other things.

This exam would have entitled me to become a Captain, but before then the world took another turn. The major share-holding in Air Ferry was held by British United Airlines. They were an amalgamation of several smaller airlines such as Silver City. Typically for the time, when they combined, few if any of the managerial staff were sacked. They became top heavy with middle management who expanded themselves into new departments which then took on even more staff. It became a 'jobs for the boys' outfit, and before long they were against the wall.

…. Bristow was in charge, and when he realised his predicament he started cutting jobs, benefits and salaries. There was a strike, and as a subsidiary, Air Ferry was drawn in. We were out on strike for several weeks. We felt strange, it was against our instincts. We had no argument with Air Ferry, it was part of our family. On the other hand we had no wish to let down our colleagues at Gatwick.

In any case it was to no avail. B.U.A. was seriously overmanned and cuts of pay or conditions would not cure the problem; the airline was nearly bankrupt. Bristow looked at the balance sheet; the losses and the assets, and there seemed to be a possible solution. There was Air Ferry, with good holiday contracts, a healthy cash flow and few debts. B.U.A. decided to disband Air Ferry, sell the aircraft, after all the future was in jets, and take the package holidays to Gatwick.

So in September 1968 it was all over. Our enthusiastic band of air and ground crew found itself disbanded. The pilots faced the fact that jets were coming in fast and that they were qualified on aeroplanes which were well past their sell-by date. We set off in different directions. DC6's were still valued abroad and continued to be so in the developing countries. A group of us went to Aden.

Colonel Mad Mitch had not long finished skirmishing with the locals; the Brits had pulled out of Aden leaving the state of Southern Yemen in a total shambles. There was an airline of sorts, the residue of Aden Airways with a few DC6's; it was called BASCO: Brothers Air Services Company.

We had little choice, it was the brothers Baharoon or on the buses. This is not the story of BASCO but there is an Alistair Cook ending to my tale. Hazel came to join me in Aden. We lived in the hotel at Steamer Point, and thoroughly enjoyed making the best of one of God's forgotten outposts. There were chaps from Chartered Bank, Whinney Murray Acountants, Embassy staff; in fact a microcosm of British Society. This combined with the Americans, their Marines, a smattering of French and Italians actually made life quite exciting. Operation full program was the expression of the time.

Sadly the Arabs revoked Hazel's visa and she left for Nairobi initially and then to Beirut where she joined M.E.A. It was a long time before we were to meet again. I left soon after and went to Holland for my last tour on the DC6 with Martinair. My good friend Phil Phillp came too and we took charge of Amsterdam.

A year later saw me back in England doing a Boeing 707 course with British Caledonian, but four years further still and I came up against B.U.A. again. B.U.A. never quite got over the problem of having too many middle managers, and slipped deeper and deeper into debt. The government of the day would not see them going into bankruptcy so they persuaded Adam Thompson of B.C.A.L. to take them over. Adam Thompson should have let them go to the wall and taken over the holiday business and as many managers as he needed. Unfortunately he took

POSTSCRIPT

over the lot, and as we all know B.C.A.L. finally ended up in the hands of British Airways.

For my part, the B.U.A. take over proved too much. They were twice the size of Caledonian, and B.A.L.P.A., the pilots union, convinced B.C.A.L. to split our pilot seniority list and place two B.U.A. pilots between each of us. I was just coming up for my command on the 707, but was put back 8 years overnight. Moreover I was told when I got a command it would be on the BAC1-11. That meant Alicante instead of New York. I decided this was the time to quit.

Thereafter I gradually eased my way out of airline flying into architecture. Of course I still love aeroplanes and take every opportunity to fly myself around on business. I now live in the Cotswolds and have a share in a Cessna Reims Rocket.

And so it was that on March the 7th 1996 I found myself flying back to Manston for the Air Ferry reunion. As I taxied in to the ramp with the sun setting behind me, I was immersed in the memories and emotions of all the events and all the years gone by. And as I pulled up on the tarmac, there standing infront of me, just as beautiful as ever was Hazel. (Mike Waddingham)

Maureen Pople, having been involved with Hugh and Audry for a long time, had some difficulty, remembering back, in separating Silver City from Air Ferry and Invicta, as did Ingrid Osborne and Ronnie Cox, although the latter could in most cases recall the type of hat she was wearing at the time! After about a year at Invicta, Pop flew with Bahamas Airways on VC10s for four years and has lived in Australia ever since. She loves Queensland and the Australian climate, living near the sea with a garden bedecked with coconut trees. She still dreams of flying, usually night flights to Palma for some reason! Pop sent the writer a tape with her reminiscences and her voice is just the same. In addition to the ghastly meals they served she recalled: 'Gee, we worked hard and we played hard. We were all frightfully loyal to the company and pulled together, it was an awful lot of fun.'

Gillian Appleby, Anna Turner (Oates), Hazel Kyd-Grant (King) and Lorna Monje (Brownridge) still live in Kent, Lorna working for Eurostar. Sandra King (Sparrowhawk) lives in Thanet, while Ann Rippon went to the Ballearic Islands. During her time as a hostess with British Midland Ann flew with the hostess who had survived the Argonaut crash in Stockport. Hazel Brooks (Baynham) has lived in Dorset for many years.

Michael Bopst enjoyed a full career, flying on an impressive number of airliners. He worked for Channel, when they operated DC4 G-ARYY, with Lufthansa for many years and for Dan-Air with whom he made an emergency landing in a Comet on foam at Manston. His colleague, Lionel Heady, was flying as loadmaster on the Redcoat Britannia which crashed on take-off in icy weather at Boston in 1980, sadly with the loss of all those aboard apart from the flight engineer.

A reunion, Air Ferry's first, but hopefully not the last, was held in Manston Village on the night of 7 March 1996. Several regretful apologies were received from those unable to be present for health or logistical reasons, but over 80 people turned up, some from quite a distance, and many revisited former stamping grounds not seen since the closure. Both Audry and Jeremy Kennard attended and a pleasant evening, that unfortunately passed all too quickly, was enjoyed by all.

* * * *

Perhaps the last word on Air Ferry should go to Bill Wood, given over the telephone shortly before he died: 'It was a good company, some of the others have said to me it was the best time of their flying lives.'

TWILIGHT OF THE PISTONS

DC4 loading at Manston

DC6 loading at Manston

APPENDICES

Glossary	224
Aircrew - Captains	225
Aircrew - Co-Pilots	226
Aircrew - Flight Engineers	227
Aircrew - Cabin Crew	228
Ground Staff	229
The Aircraft - DC4s	231
The Aircraft - DC6s	232
The Aircraft - Vikings	233
The Aircraft - Viscounts	235
The Aircraft - Bristol Freighters	236
Passengers and flying hours by aircraft by month - 1963	237
Passengers and flying hours by aircraft by month - 1964	238
Passengers and flying hours by aircraft by month - 1965	239
Passengers and flying hours by aircraft by month - 1966	240
Passengers and flying hours by aircraft by month - 1967	241
Passengers and flying hours by aircraft by month - 1968	242
Passengers by aircraft by year 1963 - 1968	243
Flying hours by aircraft by year 1963 - 1968	244
Record months each year - passengers and flying hours by aircraft 1963 -1968	245
Total flying hours by aircraft	246
Aircraft overhauls 1963 - 1968	247
Flights outside Europe 1963 - 1964	248
Flights outside Europe 1965	249
Flights outside Europe 1966	250
Flights outside Europe 1967	251
Flights outside Europe 1968	253
The number of visits to the top ten airports by year 1963 - 1968	254
The number of airport visits by year 1963 - 1968	255
Bibliography	261

TWILIGHT OF THE PISTONS

GLOSSARY

A. & A.E.E.	Aeroplane and Armament Experimental Establishment
ADF	Automatic Direction Finder (Radio Compass)
A.E.F.	Air Experience Flight
AOG	Aircraft on Ground
A.R.B.	Air Registration Board
A.S.I.	Airspeed Indicator
A.T.C.C.	Air Traffic Control Centre
A.T.L.B.	Air Transport Licensing Board
B.A.C.	British Aircraft Corporation
B.A.F.	British Air Farries
B.E.A.	British European Airways
B.O.A.C.	British Overseas Airways Corporation
B.U.A.	British United Airways
B.U.A.F.	British United Air Ferries
B.U.(C.I.)A.	British United (Channel Island) Airways
C.A.A.	Civil Aviation Authority
C of A	Certificate of Airworthiness
C.F.I.	Chief Flying Instructor
CSU	Constant Speed Unit
DFC	Distinguished Flying Cross
E.E.C.	European Economic Community
FIDO	Fog Investigation and Dispersal Operation
F/O	First Officer
GPU	Ground Power Unit
ILS	Instrument Landing System
IRBM	Intermediate Range Ballistic Missile
IT	Inclusive Tour
LAP	London (Heathrow) Airport
MIDAS	Flight Safety Recorder
M.O.D.	Ministry of Defence
N.A.S.A.	National Aeronautics and Space Administration
N.A.T.O.	North Atlantic Treaty Organisation
N.H.S.	National Health Service
NM	Nautical Miles
NOTAMS	Notices to Airmen (Airfield Information Service)
O.C.U.	Operational Conversion Unit
P1(S)	Pilot One under supervision
PPL	Private Pilots Licence
POW	Prisoner of War
QC	Queen's Counsel
R.A.F.	Royal Air Force
RPM	Revolutions Per Minute
SADAS	Flight Safety Recorder
T.W.A.	Trans World Airlines
U.K.	United Kingdom
U.N.	United Nations
U.S.A.A.F.	United States Army Air Force
U.S.A.F.	United States Air Force
USG	U.S. Gallons
U.S.S.R.	Union of Soviet Socialist Republics
U/S	Unserviceable
V1	Vergeltungswaffe 1 - German Flying Bomb
VFR	Visual Flight Rules
V.G.S.	Volunteer Gliding School
VHF	Very High Frequency
WWI	World War One
WWII	World War Two

APPENDICES

AIR FERRY LTD
AIRCREW CAPTAINS

	1962	1963	1964	1965	1966	1967	1968	
Wood W.H.B.	1 Oct	——————	30 Sep	8 Feb	———————		3 Jul	
Souster P.J.		1 Feb —— 9 Dec						then Ops. Man.
Tubman H.		1 Feb	————————	———————	——— 22 Jan			
Brooker D.		1 Feb	————————	——— Jun?				then Ops. Man.
Mc Nay R.		15 Feb	————— 7 Mar					
Stimpson		19/2-May						dates uncertain
Gibson J.		1 Mar	————————	——— 31 Jul				
Salmon B.		May —— Jul						
Hargreaves F.		23/6 -30/11						
Laker D.			10 Feb	———————————	————————	15 Feb		see also F/O
Nicol A.			16 Mar	———————————	———— 5 Oct			
Ashpitel P.			1 Apl	———————————	———— 25 Feb			
Wigley R.			1/4-30/11					
Steel W. (AF & Lloyd)			1/5-30/9			18/5-Oct	1/5-31/10	see also F/O
Mason J.			15 May	——— 15 Dec				
Eames R.	)		Jun-Oct		1 Mar — 24 Mar			
	)				1/6-30/9			
Gwyther C.				3 Mar—31 Jan				
Hunnable S.				15 Mar	——————— 30 Sep			
Honeyman R.				25 Jul	———— 1 Jan			
Chang H.					12 Jan —17 May			see also F/O
Ross A.					1 Mar	——— 30 Sep		
Brown P.					12 Mar — 5 Mar			
Vines R.					25 Apl	——— 30 Sep		
Lloyd F.					4/5-24/6			
Sissons K.					20 Jul	——— 30 Sep		see also F/O
Cropp J.					14 Aug	——— 31 Oct		see also F/O
Lockhart W.					17/8-Oct			
Kellard V.					26 Sep	——— 30 Jun		see also F/O
Surrage W.						1/1-26/11		see also F/O
Ahmad A.						1 Jan —30 Sep		see also F/O
Adcock F.						9/1-21/1		
Roberts A.						10 Jan —30 Sep		
Pullinger R.						16/1-3/6		
Davis S.						6/3-31/8		
Morriss (Lloyd)						18/5-Oct		
Underhill (B.U.A.)						1/8-Oct		
Roocroft E. (B.U.A.)	)					1/8-Oct		
	)					10 Dec — 30 Sep		
Lockwood P.						22 Nov — 31 Oct		
Dunn J. (B.U.A.)							1/1-Sep	
Collyer J. (B.U.A.)							15/1-Sep	
Saunders E. (B.U.A.)							17/1-Sep	
Adams E.							5/2-31/10	
Horsting P.							15/4-30/9	see also F/O
Mayo P.							10/6-30/9	

TWILIGHT OF THE PISTONS

AIR FERRY LTD
AIRCREW CO - PILOTS

	1963	1964	1965	1966	1967	1968	
Steel W.	1/1-15/4						see also Capt.
Winyard K.		1 Feb ——— 7 Apl					
Kellard V.		15 Feb ——— 31 Jan					see also Capt.
Hendley D.	15/2-14/8						
Laker D.		15 Feb ——— 10 Feb					see also Capt.
Hazell J.		1 Mar ——— 31 Dec					
Thomas P.		1 Mar ——— 6 Jul					
Page J.		13 May ——— 14 Nov					
Ahmad A.	29/5-31/10	1 Feb ————————————— 1 Jan					see also Capt.
Isaacs W.	1/8-14/10	Mar-31/10		12/4-11/10	Apl-3/6		
Clapshaw G.		26/1-31/5	16/6-17/7				
Armstrong N		1 Mar ——— 14 Sep					
Johnston P.		9 Mar ————————————— 30 Sep					
Jackson J.		16 Mar ————————————— 30 Sep					
Surrage W.		1 Apl ————————————— 1 Jan					see also Capt.
Gutteridge P.		14 Apl ————————————— 21 Jan					
Davey I.		May					
Green M.		May					
Hope P.		11 May ————————————— 30 Sep					
Eshelby J.		1/6-15/8					
Horsting P.		19 Aug ————————————— 15 Apl					see also Capt.
Sheppardson K.J.		1 Nov ——— Sep?					General Man.
Simpson F.			5 Apl ——— 30 Sep	6/2-30/9			
Chang H.			12 Jul ——— 12 Jan				see also Capt.
Cropp J.				1/3-14/8			see also Capt.
Champneys A.				1 Mar ——— 30 Sep			
Phillp P.				14 Mar ——— 30 Sep			
Waddingham M.				10 Apl ——— 30 Sep			
Sissons K.				12/4-20/7			see also Capt.
Green D.				May			
Gatty N.				12/5-30/11			
Watson N.				17 Jun ——— 31 Oct			
Gilson G.				5 Aug ——— 30 Sep			
Hrycak P.				12/8-19/9			
Mackie D.					1 Jan — 5 Oct		
El Fata W.					15 Jan — 7 Feb		
Bainbridge J.					16 Jan — 30 Sep		
Waller N.					23/1-26/7		
Nay D.					10 Apl — 30 Sep		
Fisher R.					15/5-3/6		
Dykes (Lloyd)					18/5-Jul		
Miles (Lloyd)					18/5-Oct		
Sigurdson (Lloyd)					18/5-Oct		
Breedon A.					5 Jun— 30 Sep		
Searle S.					5 Jun — 30 Sep		
Parker R. (B.U.A.)					15/1-Sep		
Watt I. (B.U.A.)					Feb-Sep		
Bullock D.					1/5-19/9		
Tyler A.					1/6-7/10		
Styles R.					1/7-31/10		
Norwood P.							

APPENDICES

AIR FERRY LTD
AIRCREW FLIGHT ENGINEERS

Blandford Mark
Chisholm Jock
Dunlop Brian
Erswell Doug
Froud Des
Jennings Dave
Sherwood
Simmons Roy
Tilley Frank
Toghill Les
Ward Arthur
Wood Timber (B.U.A.)

AIR FERRY LTD
AIRCREW CABIN STAFF

AIRCREW AIR HOSTESSES

1963
Bell Jill
Bentham Jill
Hathaway Margo
Leete Judy
Mills Jane
Pople Maureen
Starr-Gosling Gillian
Tapp Liz

1964
Firkin Jill
Heffernan Terry
Mills Jane
Pople Maureen
Studt Maggie

1965
Appleby Gillian
Bowery
Britton Heather
Brown
Desmond
Krebstarkies
Lemm
Masters
Mills Jane
Molli
Morgan
Rendall
Rolls
Setchel
Studt Maggie
Willcox Pat
Woods

1966
Appleby Gillian
Barnett
Bird
Byrne
Dunn Catherine
Ereckson
Firkin Jill

1966 continued
Hoffman
Huckle V
Johnson Liz
Manning
Molli
Norton Margaret
Oates Anna
Parsons Odile
Rees
Setchel
Willcox Pat

1967
Barber
Batney Lyn
Bennett
Britton
Brownridge Lorna
Cameron
Chadwick Sue
Coates Mary
Dale Carol
Duffy Ann
Dunn Catherine
Fox Carol
Gray
Greenway
Griffin
Holden
Holtan Jenny
Huckle V
Johnson Liz
Kavanagh
King Hazel
Leonard
Lockeyear Una
MacCann Patricia
Manning
Molli
Norton Margaret
Oates Anna
Pribyl
Reeks Hilary
Smith Sue

1967 continued
Southee Jackie
Studt Maggie
Townsend Linda
Travers Pat

1968
Arden Liz
Batney Lyn
Baynham Hazel
Bennett
Brownridge Lorna
Chadwick Sue
Chanell
Chilton Lyn
Coates Mary
Dale Carol
Eisenhut Maria
Field Jill
Gray
Hanson Jackie
Harvey
Holtan Jenny
Hunt
Johnson Liz
King Hazel
Lamont Janet
Mayo Roswitha
Norton Margaret
Parish
Reeks Hilary
Rippon Ann
Smith Sue
Sparrowhawk Sandra
Studt Maggie
Thorn Lyn
Townsend Linda
Travers Pat
Woodman

AIRCREW STEWARDS
Billett Len   1967
Bopst Michael 1968
Heady Lionel 1968
Wood Alan   1963-64

APPENDICES

AIR FERRY LTD.
THE GROUND STAFF

ENGINEERING

Attwood George
Ayres Bill

Baigent Don
Bailey Charlie
Baker Barbara (Babs)
Barker Ken
Barnes John
Barrett Ivor
Baxter Chris
Blake Ron
Bradley Rowland
Brooks Mary
Brown Ernest
Bulot Cliff
Bull Barry
Burgess Harry

Cavell George
Cavell Gerry
Cawte Colin
Cornwell John

Darch John
Doherty Roy
Dray Les
Dunmill William

Edgar Eddie
Ellis Cliff
Ellis Dave
Evans Arthur

Finnis Brenda
Foat Dick
Francis Derek

Graveney
Green

Hampton Reg
Hopkins Clive

Illsley Ron

Knight Kathleen
Knight Les

Jack R (Bob)

ENGINEERING continued

Jennings Dave
Jones Alan
Jones Jim

Kirkham Peter

Lane B
Ling Peter

Malone Pete
Mason John
Maycock Sally
Maycock Ted
McCreery Sheila
McKinnon Neil 'Mac'
Mees Len
Mills J
Moore Pony

Noller Paul
Nurthen Cyril
O'Callaghan Eddie
O'Reilly Tony (Spike)

Payne Frederick
Pearce Roger
Philbrick Graham

Ratcliffe Bob
Redshaw Charles
Reilly
Richardson Nora
Robson Jock

Simpson W (Bill)
Solly Russell
Spires Gordon
Strainge Frank

Thomson Robbie
Thompson Gerry
Townsend Phil
Tudor Tommy
Twyman Doug

Verrion John

Walker Sid
White Chalky
Wickens
Wilde B
Williams Ted

AIR FERRY LTD.
THE GROUND STAFF

FLIGHT CATERING /CATERING
Cashman Ron
Kennard Jeremy
Laycock Gwen

TRAFFIC
Cagney C
Cooper Sue (Primrose)
Cox 'Ronnie'
Dalton Phill
Everingham Peter
Hope Jody
Osborne Ingrid
Picket Carol
Robert L
Russell Joe
Thompson Lilian

BONDED STORE
Doherty Al
Fern Ian
Illsley Geoffrey

COMMERCIAL / SALES
Carroll Charles
Clark Sylvia
Covell Peter
Harradine Mike
Nias Jenny
Sanders Dick
Wannop Peter

SECRETARIAL
Horspool Maureen
Illsley Carollyn
McIvor Monica

TARMAC
Burns J
Fletcher Ken
Friend Ted
Wood Alan

OPERATIONS
Brown Mike?
Hull Peter
Koering Brian
Morris Peter
Pilcher Pauline
Willetts Mike

ACCOUNTS
Austin Mike
Brenda
Collison Maureen
Cowley Ann
Edwards Peter
Finnis Malcolm
Flemming Valerie
Fusco Carol
Haggerty Olly
Hand Peter
Hennessey Mr
Jerome Paul
Leigh Tim
Maggie
Malcolm
Marshall Peggy
Pinder Mr
Rickards Les R
Strainge Carol
Vanderbyl Peter
Walker Mr
Williams John

APPENDICES
THE AIRCRAFT - DC4s

G-APYK   type C54A-1DC
	10279	Constructor's Number
15.1.44	42-72174	Delivered to U.S.A.A.F.
45	N56006	Hart F Farwell
46		Pennsylvania Central Airlines
21.4.48		Capital Airlines named 'Capitaliner Milwaukee' and 'Capitaliner Baltimore'
55		General Airways, used in Hungarian airlift
13.3.60	G-APYK	Starways
23.7.61		wheels up landing Elizabethville Congo
3.5.62		accident Liverpool
2.63		Air Ferry
3.6.67		crashed Py, Mount Canigou, Pyrenees

G-ASFY   type C54A-10DC
	10335	Constructor's Number
27.6.44	42-72230	Delivered to U.S.A.A.F.
17.6.46		Conversion to DC4 standard number 23 at El Segundo
9.3.47	NC88922	Pan American World Airways named 'Clipper Radiant'
	N88922	later 'Clipper Nurnberg' and 'Clipper Dusseldorf'
17.6.60	HB-ILC	Balair
3.63	G-ASFY	Air Ferry
25.11.68	N3454	International Aviation Development
2.9.69		LAVCO
79		withdrawn from use and broken up at Hal Far Malta

G-ASOG   type C54A-15DC
	10359	Constructor's Number
31.7.44	42-72254	Delivered to U.S.A.A.F.
46	NC75415	Trans Carribean Airways
48	N75415	Leased by Eastern Airlines
14.9.51		accident landing at Miami
24.4.52		Returned to Trans Carribean Airways
53		Leased to Near East Air Transport
		Returned to Trans Carribean Airways
54		Seaboard & Western Airlines named 'Geneva Airtrader'
56		Los Angeles Air Service
57		Meteor Air Transport
58		General Airways
58		Atlas Airways
59		American International Airways
21.12.60	HB-ILB	Balair
63	N9760F	Mary Herzog Stucki / Richard D Ferguson
28.1.64	G-ASOG	Air Ferry
21.1.67		crashed Frankfurt

G-ARWI   type C54B-5-DO
	18349	Constructor's Number
7.8.44	43-17149	Delivered to U.S.A.A.F.
46	NC90450	American Airlines
51	N90450	Alaska Airlines
16.3.62	G-ARWI	Leased by Lloyd International purchased 10.1.64
2.5.67		Leased Air Ferry
10.68		Returned to Lloyd International
12.68		Air Fret
12.68	NAF311	Nigerian Air Force
74		withdrawn from use and stored Lagos
77		broken up

THE AIRCRAFT - DC6s

G-APNO   type DC6A

	45531	Constructor's Number (Number 689 of 704 DC6s)
2.8.58	G-APNO	first flight
10.8.58		delivered to Hunting-Clan Air Transport London Heathrow
3.60		became British United Airways following Hunting/Airwork merger
		flying hours 4682.1
		Africargo schedules and IT work
		flying hours 18246.7
14.2.66		Air Ferry training
29.4.66		Air Ferry delivery
9.10.68		ferried to Lydd on Air Ferry closure
30.12.68		ferried to Wymeswold
9.1.69		ferried to Southend
11.1.69	HB-IBS	delivery to Balair at Basle
		International Red Cross Biafra
14.6.69		return to Basle for tour work with many interruptions
1970		relief work in Biafra, Turkey, Romania and Jordan
1972		relief work in Bangladesh
1973		relief work in Middle East
4.75-6.75		French Croix Rouge Internationale work in Vietnam
		HB-IBS was the first foreign aircraft to gain landing rights to Hanoi
24.6.75		return to Basle
9.75		Portugese Comite Internacional de Cruz Vermelha work in Angola
76		relief work in Beirut, Mauritania and Cyprus
13.2.77		50 year commemorative flight to the Cape of Good Hope
8.7.82		last Balair flight
17.9.82	C-GIBS	delivery to Conair at Abbotsford British Columbia
		flying hours 39358.1
1996		flying hours 41204.5

G-APNP   type DC6A

	45532	Constructor's Number (Number 690 of 704 DC6s)
8.58	G-APNP	delivered to Hunting-Clan Air Transport
3.60		became British United Airways following Hunting/Airwork merger
		Africargo schedules and IT work
3.2.66		Air Ferry training
15.6.66		Air Ferry delivery
10.10.68		ferried to Lydd on Air Ferry closure
31.12.68		ferried to Wymeswold
10.1.69		ferried to Southend
12.1.69	HB-IBT	delivery to Balair at Basle
		International Red Cross Biafra
6/7.5.69		crashed on approach to Uli airstrip Biafra

APPENDICES

THE AIRCRAFT - VIKINGS

G-AHOW type V.498-1A

	124	Constructor's Number
11.10.46	G-AHOW	British European Airways named 'Vanessa'
		Crewsair
		Eagle Aviation Ltd.
	XD636	military serial for Trooping (Eagle)
	G-AHOW	Eagle Aviation Ltd.
	ZS-DKI	Trek Airways Ltd.
2.4.55		emergency landing Messina Airport, Transvaal
	ZS-DKI	Trek Airways Ltd.
	G-AHOW	African Air Safaris
		Air Safaris Ltd.
2.63		Eros Airline (UK) Ltd.
4.4.64		Air Ferry Ltd.
28.10.66		Invicta Airways
		withdrawn from use 9.67 at Manston, broken up approx 69

G-AOCH type V.621-02

	150	Constructor's Number
47	VL231	Royal Air Force Empire Test Pilots' School
	A 82-1	Leased to Royal Australian Air Force
	VL231	Returned to Royal Air Force
6.55	G-AOCH	Field Aircraft Services Ltd.
7.56		Dragon Airways
13.2.57	D-AMOR	Luftransport Union G.m.b.h. (L.T.U.)
	D-BABY	Luftransport Union G.m.b.h. (L.T.U.)
19.10.61		damaged on landing Rhein Main, Frankfurt
14.8.63	G-AOCH	Air Ferry Ltd.
23.3.66		Invicta Airways
		withdrawn from use Manston, broken up approx 69

G-AIVD type V.610-1B

	217	Constructor's Number
16.5.47	G-AIVD	British European Airways named 'Veteran'
52		later named 'Lord Duncan'
		First Air Trading Co. Ltd.
3.56	D-ADAM	L.T.U.
6.57	D-ADAM	Leased to Balair
	HB-AAR	Balair
		Leased to United Nations
2.61		Returned to Balair
18.2.63	G-AIVD	Air Couriers Ltd.
2.63		Air Ferry Ltd.
		C of A expired 3.4.65
23.3.66		Invicta Airways - did not fly with them, later broken up approx 69

233

THE AIRCRAFT - VIKINGS

G-AIVF   type   V.610-1B

	219	Constructor's Number
30.5.47	G-AIVF	British European Airways named 'Vibrant'
52		later named 'Sir James Somerville'
		First Air Trading Co. Ltd.
4.56	D-AGIL	Deutsche Flugdienst G.m.b.h.
1.4.58	D-BARI	Deutsche Flugdienst G.m.b.h.
5.58	HB-AAN	Balair
		Leased to United Nations
		Returned to Balair
18.2.63	G-AIVF	Air Couriers Ltd.
18.2.63		Air Ferry Ltd. as type V.610-3B
23.3.66		Invicta Airways
		withdrawn from use Manston 1969, broken up approx 69

G-AJBX   type   V.610-1B

	249	Constructor's Number
27.1.48	G-AJBX	British European Airways named 'Vital'
52		later named 'Sir Edward Hughes'
53		Eagle Aviation Ltd.
7.54		Eagle Aircraft Services
1.56	D-AFIX	Karl Herfurtner
11.57		Trans Avia Flugdienst G.m.b.h.
12.57	D-BABA	Trans Avia Flugdienst G.m.b.h.
5.58		Werner Nolte t/a Trans Avia
9.1.60	G-AJBX	Continental Air Services Ltd.
60		L.T.U.
60		Maitland Drewery Aviation
		Air Safaris Ltd.
		Eros Airline (UK) Ltd.
4.4.64		Air Ferry Ltd.
		C of A expired 9.5.65, broken up Manston 29/30.10.65

APPENDICES

THE AIRCRAFT - VISCOUNTS

G-AVHE   type 812
	363	Constructor's Number
13.10.58		First Flight
5.11.58	N251V	Delivered to Continental Air Lines U.S.A.
13.2.67	G-AVHE	Delivered to Channel Airways
11.1.68		Delivered on lease to Air Ferry
31.10.68		Returned to Channel Airways
30.5.70		Withdrawn from use Southend
6.72		Broken up Southend

G-AVNJ   type 812
	361	Constructor's Number
10.9.58		First Flight
2.10.58	N249V	Delivered to Continental Air Lines U.S.A.
25.5.67	G-AVNJ	Delivered to Channel Airways
10.1.68		Delivered on lease to Air Ferry
6.11.68		Returned to Channel Airways
23.10.69		Withdrawn from use Southend
6.72		Broken up Southend

THE AIRCRAFT - BRISTOL FREIGHTERS

G-AMLL   type 31E

	13074	Constructor's Number
23.8.51	G-AMLL	Registered to Bristol Aeroplane Company
5.12.52	EI-AFS	Delivered to Aer Lingus
1.1.57	G-AMLL	Purchased by B.E.A. and leased to Jersey Airlines
9.8.59		Delivered to Dan-Air
23.4.63		Acquired by Handley Page part exchange two Ambassadors Aircraft remained at Lasham
11.3.64		Delivered on lease to Air Ferry
11.3.65		Returned to Handley Page
5.66	CF-UME	Delivered to North Coast Air Services
11.5.66		Withdrawn from use and stored

G-ANVR   type 32

	13251	Constructor's Number
23.10.54		Registered to Bristol Aeroplane Company
16.3.55		First Flight
25.3.55		Leased to Air Charter Ltd
24.12.57		Channel Air Bridge
1.1.63		B.U.A.F.
14.1.65		Delivered on lease to Air Ferry
26.3.65		Returned to B.U.A.F.
1.10.67		B.A.F.
16.3.71		Delivered to Midland Air Cargo
12.5.71		Stored at Coventry, did not fly with MAC
9.1.73		Withdrawn from use Bagington
3.74		Broken up

G-AMLP   type 31E

	13078	Constructor's Number
23.8.51		Registered to Bristol Aeroplane Company
21.2.53		Leased to Air Charter Ltd
4.11.53		Purchased by Air Charter Ltd
3.58		Converted to Mk 32
25.2.59		Channel Air Bridge
1.1.63		B.U.A.F.
8.4.65		Delivered on lease to Air Ferry
29.5.65		Returned to B.U.A.F.
1.10.67		B.A.F.
12.11.70		Delivered to Midland Air Cargo
12.5.71	CF-QWJ	Purchased by Lambair
3.77		Crashed Rankin Inlet Canada

APPENDICES

AIR FERRY LTD

PASSENGERS AND FLYING HOURS BY AIRCRAFT BY MONTH FOR 1963

1963	Total pax	Total hrs	Total min	VIKING G-AIVD pax	VIKING G-AIVD hrs	VIKING G-AIVD min	VIKING G-AIVF pax	VIKING G-AIVF hrs	VIKING G-AIVF min	VIKING G-AOCH pax	VIKING G-AOCH hrs	VIKING G-AOCH min	DC4 G-APYK pax	DC4 G-APYK hrs	DC4 G-APYK min	DC4 G-ASFY pax	DC4 G-ASFY hrs	DC4 G-ASFY min
Jan																		
Feb	0	6	33	0	3	25	0	3	08				0	0	00	0	0	00
Mar	71	40	56	0	0	00	0	0	00				71	37	20	0	3	36
Apl	3481	212	21	782	47	20	590	26	25				1587	111	55	522	26	41
May	5783	301	54	506	26	15	890	38	40				2004	110	34	2383	126	25
Jun	13440	515	53	2316	83	35	2304	107	20				3520	142	59	5300	181	59
Jul	13921	509	39	2698	91	43	2082	88	06				4411	177	33	4730	152	17
Aug	15980	585	21	2962	99	28	3513	103	35	0	1	30	5409	216	12	4096	164	36
Sep	12413	526	22	2162	86	45	2091	104	58				2998	140	04	5162	194	35
Oct	3962	252	58	615	56	40	130	12	40	0	0	40	1416	94	33	1801	88	25
Nov	492	41	23	255	18	03	100	13	24				137	9	13	0	0	43
Dec	1055	101	35	484	40	20	210	40	26				74	9	45	287	11	04
	70598	3094	55	12780	553	34	11910	538	42	0	2	10	21627	1050	08	24281	950	21

AIR FERRY LTD
PASSENGERS AND FLYING HOURS BY AIRCRAFT BY MONTH FOR 1964

1964	Total pax	hrs	min	VIKING G-AIVD pax	hrs	min	VIKING G-AIVF pax	hrs	min	VIKING G-AOCH pax	hrs	min	VIKING G-AHOW pax	hrs	min	VIKING G-AJBX pax	hrs	min
Jan	460	99	43	282	37	14	2	17	51	0	0	00						
Feb	934	66	48	144	7	22	75	12	33	0	0	00						
Mar	4663	266	04	428	24	05	491	28	15	564	20	25						
Apl	7471	386	32	1235	63	50	236	13	51	1211	61	00	0	2	35	523	64	52
May	17531	875	25	1820	81	56	1961	103	12	2474	95	02	1103	79	59	928	74	48
Jun	25358	973	42	1927	105	13	3590	116	07	2694	100	08	1164	77	39	1500	98	01
Jul	30753	1071	43	2492	84	04	3627	104	15	3677	108	05	1678	113	24	1353	79	22
Aug	34638	1231	59	3172	133	04	3524	115	27	4306	127	42	2099	127	00	1674	84	31
Sep	23893	975	02	1970	74	51	2397	81	51	3343	94	49	1483	86	15	1238	76	26
Oct	5740	370	02	500	22	47	690	38	14	453	25	40	155	11	48	167	20	15
Nov	480	62	51	0	0	00	251	11	55	68	3	47	0	0	00	0	0	00
Dec	1136	136	38	250	7	39	351	17	20	206	25	10	0	0	00	0	0	00
	153057	6516	29	14220	642	05	17195	660	51	18996	661	48	7682	498	40	7383	498	15

1964	DC4 G-APYK pax	hrs	min	DC4 G-ASFY pax	hrs	min	DC4 G-ASOG pax	hrs	min	BRISTOL G-AMLL pax	hrs	min
Jan	0	0	00	176	42	13	0	2	25	0	0	00
Feb	0	0	00	715	45	40	0	1	13	0	0	00
Mar	1550	100	52	832	48	50	796	25	00	2	18	37
Apl	1334	34	13	1051	66	19	1881	47	17	0	32	35
May	3061	101	31	2937	123	44	3242	150	49	5	64	24
Jun	4590	149	37	5553	158	56	4340	144	29	0	23	32
Jul	5322	184	24	6724	189	15	5880	193	54	0	15	00
Aug	6552	190	27	8240	215	33	5066	197	50	5	40	25
Sep	4510	152	28	4757	155	53	4191	177	11	4	75	18
Oct	1492	80	30	1314	82	28	958	37	51	11	50	29
Nov	160	9	45	0	5	30	0	0	00	1	31	54
Dec	75	14	16	82	27	37	163	6	17	9	38	19
	28646	1018	03	32381	1161	58	26517	984	16	37	390	33

238

APPENDICES

AIR FERRY LTD
PASSENGERS AND FLYING HOURS BY AIRCRAFT BY MONTH FOR 1965

1965	Total pax	hrs	min	VIKING G-AIVD pax	hrs	min	VIKING G-AIVF pax	hrs	min	VIKING G-AOCH pax	hrs	min	VIKING G-AHOW pax	hrs	min
Jan	841	104	39	74	2	30	82	1	20	120	7	16	0	0	00
Feb	1156	151	16	0	0	00	0	0	40	219	17	05	79	4	40
Mar	2380	370	58				196	14	07	0	0	00	139	14	05
Apl	11138	345	44				881	42	10	1411	55	41	1378	35	54
May	14040	719	55				1759	52	07	1279	61	04	1838	55	15
Jun	20374	913	35				2118	72	29	1604	65	50	1682	59	39
Jul	20131	946	00				1897	67	42	2466	90	85	1435	65	02
Aug	20250	930	35				1756	73	53	1606	90	09	1983	61	25
Sep	14756	863	54				1484	52	12	986	63	32	1329	75	26
Oct	3017	444	12				490	21	06	552	39	39	521	26	30
Nov	316	184	19				4	20	20	52	2	10	117	11	45
Dec	557	263	41				365	20	20	182	39	03	0	0	00
	108956	6238	48	74	2	30	11032	438	26	10477	532	54	10501	409	41

1965	DC4 G-APYK pax	hrs	min	DC4 G-ASFY pax	hrs	min	DC4 G-ASOG pax	hrs	min	BRISTOL G-AMLL pax	hrs	min	BRISTOL G-ANVR pax	hrs	min	BRISTOL G-AMLP pax	hrs	min
Jan	0	0	00	139	24	21	422	28	20	3	30	18	1	10	34			
Feb	0	0	00	438	63	09	414	28	40	0	1	55	6	35	07			
Mar	1837	89	37	1	82	48	204	134	33	0	0	00	3	35	48			
Apl	2652	67	33	2443	86	08	2369	48	42				0	0	00	4	9	36
May	3645	167	00	2611	185	15	2901	185	36							7	13	38
Jun	5448	215	05	6116	258	09	3406	242	23									
Jul	5687	226	54	5239	256	36	3407	238	21									
Aug	4823	182	17	4945	255	58	5137	266	53									
Sep	3925	208	25	3724	265	17	3308	199	02									
Oct	1454	129	03	0	133	38	0	94	16									
Nov	0	11	18	9	75	25	134	63	21									
Dec	0	0	00	10	99	57	0	104	21									
	29471	1297	12	25675	1786	41	21702	1634	28	3	32	13	10	81	29	11	23	14

AIR FERRY LTD
PASSENGERS AND FLYING HOURS BY AIRCRAFT BY MONTH FOR 1966

1966	Total pax	hrs	min	VIKING G-AOCH pax	hrs	min	VIKING G-AHOW pax	hrs	min	DC4 G-APYK pax	hrs	min	DC4 G-ASFY pax	hrs	min	DC4 G-ASOG pax	hrs	min
Jan	2	483	10	1	26	30	1	6	10	0	0	55	0	222	05	0	227	30
Feb	0	498	57							0	194	55	0	209	06	0	76	06
Mar	93	206	00							0	60	50	93	130	40	0	0	00
Apl	6018	309	30							712	104	39	2237	82	21	2819	118	10
May	10320	610	46							2653	168	54	1630	141	22	3206	172	20
Jun	29533	1178	38							7292	300	12	7067	309	40	6643	268	06
Jul	39402	1432	13							8898	338	12	9267	338	16	8302	315	35
Aug	37908	1338	23							7893	296	57	9180	334	41	8802	314	35
Sep	28263	1278	41							6490	267	14	6932	288	21	6925	294	40
Oct	2622	561	56							885	167	32	229	25	47	532	158	22
Nov	148	429	27							148	102	22	0	0	00	0	136	50
Dec	0	303	02							0	121	02	0	0	00	0	101	20
	154309	8630	43	1	26	30	1	6	10	34971	2123	44	36635	2082	19	37229	2183	34

1966	DC6 G-APNO pax	hrs	min	DC6 G-APNP pax	hrs	min
Jan	0	0	00	0	0	00
Feb	0	14	00	0	4	50
Mar	0	0	00	0	14	30
Apl	250	4	20	0	0	00
May	2831	128	10	0	0	00
Jun	5467	183	00	3064	117	40
Jul	6203	229	00	6732	211	10
Aug	5892	196	35	6141	195	35
Sep	4583	207	15	3333	221	11
Oct	243	130	15	733	80	00
Nov	0	140	40	0	49	35
Dec	0	80	40	0	0	0
	25469	1313	55	20003	894	31

APPENDICES

AIR FERRY LTD
PASSENGERS AND FLYING HOURS BY AIRCRAFT BY MONTH FOR 1967

1967	Total pax	Total hrs	Total min	DC4 G-APYK pax	DC4 G-APYK hrs	DC4 G-APYK min	DC4 G-ASFY pax	DC4 G-ASFY hrs	DC4 G-ASFY min	DC4 G-ASOG pax	DC4 G-ASOG hrs	DC4 G-ASOG min	DC4 G-ARWI pax	DC4 G-ARWI hrs	DC4 G-ARWI min	DC6 G-APNO pax	DC6 G-APNO hrs	DC6 G-APNO min	DC6 G-APNP pax	DC6 G-APNP hrs	DC6 G-APNP min
Jan	0	291	09	0	0	40	0	0	00	0	53	14				0	132	10	0	33	05
Feb	368	178	23	0	72	38	0	33	15	0	0	0				0	22	40	368	56	50
Mar	564	280	10	356	65	58	0	187	07							2	19	10	206	55	55
Apl	7720	438	50	2495	17	38	2283	68	27							1782	117	47	1160	136	58
May	18897	933	50	4491	115	00	4256	187	25				1867	108	45	4582	216	40	3701	210	00
Jun	34417	1264	53	606	211	35	9400	364	51				7768	314	42	8740	284	20	7903	271	25
Jul	35744	1282	12	0	29	00	10001	403	33				9331	345	55	7827	248	30	8585	284	14
Aug	40365	1343	22		0		11259	415	12				12104	414	00	8553	253	40	8449	260	30
Sep	32468	1238	48				8079	363	30				9489	361	13	7153	241	25	7747	272	40
Oct	5593	457	47				2461	84	40				1737	63	02	732	109	45	663	200	20
Nov	835	249	33				326	38	20				80	23	23	179	119	30	250	68	20
Dec	2815	584	35				0	131	20				0	99	25	204	197	45	2611	156	05
	179786	8543	32	7948	512	29	48065	2277	40	0	53	14	42376	1730	25	39754	1963	22	41643	2006	22

241

AIR FERRY LTD
PASSENGERS AND FLYING HOURS BY AIRCRAFT BY MONTH FOR 1968

1968	Total pax	hrs	min	DC4 G-ASFY pax	hrs	min	DC4 G-ARWI pax	hrs	min	DC6 G-APNO pax	hrs	min	DC6 G-APNP pax	hrs	min	VISCOUNT G-AVNJ pax	hrs	min	VISCOUNT G-AVHE pax	hrs	min
Jan	2618	455	55	0	32	35	2	55	55	234	172	15	2382	190	50	0	3	50	0	0	30
Feb	1264	395	10	0	98	50	252	73	25	1012	124	55	0	89	45	0	8	15	0	0	00
Mar	1523	423	12	500	148	20	0	82	10	0	119	00	108	34	50	251	8	40	664	30	12
Apl	9352	394	02	5055	139	40	1496	81	05	0	1	25	848	99	30	1169	30	43	784	41	39
May	8448	591	43	1309	73	40	2516	119	30	1526	132	55	1111	125	00	842	73	18	1144	67	20
Jun	32919	1227	12	3393	110	45	4509	137	30	7790	284	15	7901	289	45	4671	196	50	4655	208	07
Jul	38383	1345	46	5303	151	30	3654	162	45	8526	279	35	8113	269	00	5810	231	23	6977	251	33
Aug	41655	1350	03	5039	136	35	4860	154	25	9246	283	50	9243	298	50	7131	265	38	6136	210	45
Sep	27517	999	51	2888	77	20	4166	131	55	5366	208	45	6427	213	40	4791	218	18	3879	149	53
Oct	4546	106	40	0	0	00	0	0	00	0	0	00	587	24	10	2756	56	50	1203	25	40
	168225	7289	34	23487	969	15	21455	998	40	33700	1606	55	36720	1635	20	27421	1093	45	25442	985	39

APPENDICES

AIR FERRY LTD
PASSENGERS BY AIRCRAFT BY YEAR

Type	Aircraft	Total	1963	1964	1965	1966	1967	1968
Viking	G-AIVD	27074	12780	14220	74			
	G-AIVF	40137	11910	17195	11032			
	G-AOCH	29474		18996	10477	1		
	G-AHOW	18184		7682	10501	1		
	G-AJBX	7383		7383				
		122252	24690	65476	32084	2		
DC4	G-APYK	122663	21627	28646	29471	34971	7948	
	G-ASFY	190524	24281	32381	25675	36635	48065	23487
	G-ASOG	85448		26517	21702	37229		
	G-ARWI	63831					42376	21455
		462466	45908	87544	76848	108835	98389	44942
Bristol	G-AMLL	40		37	3			
	G-ANVR	10			10			
	G-AMLP	11			11			
		61		37	24			
DC6	G-APNO	98923				25469	39754	33700
	G-APNP	98366				20003	41643	36720
		197289				45472	81397	70420
Viscount	G-AVNJ	27421						27421
	G-AVHE	25442						25442
		52863						52863
Total Passengers		834931	70598	153057	108956	154309	179786	168225

243

AIR FERRY LTD
FLYING HOURS BY AIRCRAFT BY YEAR

Type	Aircraft	Total hours mn	1963 hours mn	1964 hours mn	1965 hours mn	1966 hours mn	1967 hours mn	1968 hours mn
Viking	G-AIVD	1198 09	553 34	642 05	2 30			
	G-AIVF	1637 59	538 42	660 51	438 26			
	G-AOCH	1223 22	2 10	661 48	532 54	26 30		
	G-AHOW	914 31		498 40	409 41	6 10		
	G-AJBX	498 15		498 15				
		5472 16	1094 26	2961 39	1383 31	32 40		
DC4	G-APYK	6001 36	1050 08	1018 03	1297 12	2123 44	512 29	
	G-ASFY	9228 14	950 21	1161 58	1786 41	2082 19	2277 40	969 15
	G-ASOG	4855 32		984 16	1634 28	2183 34	53 14	
	G-ARWI	2729 05					1730 25	998 40
		22814 27	2000 29	3164 17	4718 21	6389 37	4573 48	1967 55
Bristol	G-AMLL	422 46		390 33	32 13			
	G-ANVR	81 29			81 29			
	G-AMLP	23 14			23 14			
		527 29		390 33	136 56			
DC6	G-APNO	4884 12				1313 55	1963 22	1606 55
	G-APNP	4536 13				894 31	2006 22	1635 20
		9420 25				2208 26	3969 44	3242 15
Viscount	G-AVNJ	1093 45						1093 45
	G-AVHE	985 39						985 39
		2079 24						2079 24
Total Flying Hours		40314 01	3094 55	6516 29	6238 48	8630 43	8543 32	7289 34

244

APPENDICES

AIR FERRY LTD
RECORD MONTHS EACH YEAR
PASSENGERS AND FLYING HOURS BY AIRCRAFT

	1963	1964	1965	1966	1967	1968
Record Passengers						
Viking	G-AIVF Aug 3513	G-AOCH Aug 4306	G-AOCH Jul 2466			
DC4	G-APYK Aug 5409	G-ASFY Aug 8240	G-ASFY Jun 6116	G-ASFY Jul 9267	G-ARWI Aug 12104	G-ASFY Jul 5303
Bristol		G-AMLL Oct 11	G-AMLP May 7			
DC6				G-APNP Jul 6732	G-APNO Jun 8740	G-APNO Aug 9246
Viscount						G-AVNJ Aug 7131
Total	Aug 15980	Aug 34638	Jun 20374	Jul 39402	Aug 40365	Aug 41655
Record Hours						
Viking	G-AIVF Jun 107.20	G-AIVD Aug 133.04	G-AOCH Jul 90.85			
DC4	G-APYK Aug 216.12	G-ASFY Aug 215.33	G-ASOG Aug 266.53	G-ASFY Jul 338.16	G-ASFY Aug 415.12	G-ARWI Jul 162.45
Bristol		G-AMLL Sep 75.18	G-ANVR Mar 35.48			
DC6				G-APNO Jul 229.00	G-APNO Jun 284.20	G-APNP Aug 298.50
Viscount						G-AVNJ Aug 265.38
Total	Aug 585.21	Aug 1231.59	Jul 946.00	Jul 1432.13	Aug 1343.22	Aug 1350.03

AIR FERRY LTD
FLYING HOURS BY AIRCRAFT

Type	Aircraft	Before Delivery hours min	Air Ferry hours min	difference hours min	Final Air Ferry hours min	verification
Viking	G-AIVD	18269 05	1198 09	(4 33)	19462 41	Invicta contract
	G-AIVF	16761 00	1637 59	(5 25)	18393 34	Invicta contract
	G-AOCH	8006 45	1223 22	1 28	9231 35	Invicta contract
	G-AHOW	14536 44	914 31	(1 44)	15449 31	Invicta contract
	G-AJBX	not known	498 15			
			5472 16			
DC4	G-APYK	36672 46	6001 36	(11 36)	42662 46	Accident Report
	G-ASFY	44435 34	9228 14		53663 48	
	G-ASOG	30695 25	4855 32	(25 07)	35525 50	Accident Report
	G-ARWI		2729 05			
			22814 27			
Bristol	G-AMLL		422 46			
	G-ANVR		81 29			
	G-AMLP		23 14			
			527 29			
DC6	G-APNO	18938 57	4884 12	10 11	23833 20	Log Book
	G-APNP		4536 13			
			9420 25			
Viscount	G-AVNJ		1093 45			
	G-AVHE		985 39			
			2079 24			
Total Flying Hours			40314 01			

APPENDICES

AIR FERRY LTD
AIRCRAFT OVERHAULS

Year	Aircraft	From	To	Location	Aircraft	From	To	Location
	<u>VIKING</u>				<u>DC4</u>			
1963	G-AIVD	18.2.63	6.4.63	Gatwick	G-APYK	9.1.63	8.3.63	Wymeswold
	G-AIVF	18.2.63	12.4.63	Gatwick	G-ASFY	7.3.63	25.4.63	Wymeswold
	G-AIVF	7.10.63	30.10.63	Manston	G-ASFY	20.10.63	29.11.63	Manston
	G-AOCH	15.10.63	6.3.64	Gatwick	G-APYK	30.12.63	1.3.64	Manston
1964	G-AIVD	1.3.64	25.3.64	Manston	G-ASOG	13.2.64	24.3.64	Wymeswold
	G-AIVF	31.3.64	25.4.64	Manston	G-ASFY	26.2.64	21.3.64	Prestwick
	G-AHOW	17.10.64	5.2.65	Manston	G-ASOG	19.10.64	17.12.64	Prestwick
					G-ASFY	10.11.64	18.12.64	Manston
					G-APYK	31.12.64	5.3.65	Prestwick
1965	G-AIVF	3.1.65	26.2.65	Manston	G-ASFY	16.3.65	6.4.65	Prestwick
	G-AOCH	28.2.65	8.4.65	Manston				
					G-APYK	4.11.65	29.1.66	Manston
	<u>DC6</u>							
1966					G-ASOG	12.2.66	6.4.66	Manston
					G-APYK	16.3.66	12.4.66	Prest/Wymeswold
					G-ASFY	13.4.66	13.5.66	Manston
	G-APNP	14.11.66	17.1.67	Stanstead	G-ASFY	4.10.66	18.2.67	Manston
1967	G-APNO	4.2.67	11.3.67	Southend	G-APYK	21.2.67	23.3.67	Manston
					G-ASFY	24.12.67	25.1.68	Manston
1968	G-APNP	17.2.68	19.3.68	Prestwick				
	G-APNO	19.3.68	1.5.68	Prestwick				

AIR FERRY LTD
FLIGHTS OUTSIDE EUROPE 1963/1964

Aircraft	Date out	Date retn	Route	Time in hours/minutes
G-APYK	24.9.63	25.9.63	M-Manchester-Malta-M	
			1963 total	16 07
G-ASFY	10.1.64	17.1.64	M-Damascus-Baghdad-Damascus-Brindisi-M	29 06
G-ASOG	3.5.64	6.5.64	M-Damascus-Baghdad-M (Baghdad-M 14h 3m)	27 46
G-ASFY	18.12.64	3.1.65	M-Frankfurt-Athens-Heraklion-Istanbul-Beirut-Damascus-Jerusalem-Cairo-Luxor-Cairo-Athens-Frankfurt-M	41 44
			1964 total	98 36

APPENDICES

AIR FERRY LTD
FLIGHTS OUTSIDE EUROPE 1965

Aircraft	Date out	Date retn	Route	Time in hours/minutes
G-ASFY	27.2.65	8.3.65	M-Lyneham-Brindisi-Damascus-Karachi-Calcutta-Changi-Calcutta-Karachi-Damascus-Lyons-M	77 03
G-ASOG	1.3.65	17.3.95	M-Lyneham-Brindisi-Damascus-Bahrein-Karachi-Delhi-Calcutta-Changi-Calcutta-Karachi-Damascus-M	80 29
G-ASFY	2.5.65	7.5.65	M-Lyneham-Brindisi-Damascus-Bahrein-Aden-Cairo-M (Cairo-M 12h 30m)	44 55
G-ASOG	3.5.65	9.5.65	M-Lyneham-Brindisi-Damascus-Bahrein-Aden-Bahrein-Damascus-Brindisi-Lyneham-M	55 24
G-ASOG	30.5.65	4.6.65	M-Lyneham-Brindisi-Damascus-Bahrein-Aden-Rome-M (Aden-Rome 15h 20m)	46 47
G-ASFY	6.6.65	8.6.65	M-Akrotiri-M	21 48
G-ASOG	13.6.65	19.6.65	M-Lyneham-Brindisi-Damascus-Bahrein-Aden-Malta-Tangier-Gibralter-Lyneham-M (Aden-Malta 13h 13m)	53 15
G-ASOG	27.6.65	2.7.65	M-Lyneham-Damascus-Bahrein-Aden-Dubai-Damascus-Damascus-Brindisi-M (Lyneham-Damascus 12h 10	50 57
G-ASOG	4.7.65	8.7.65	M-Lyneham-Akrotiri-Lyneham-Akrotiri-M	45 34
G-ASFY	12.7.65	17.7.65	M-Lyneham-Brindisi-Damascus-Bahrein-Bahrein-Aden-Nicosia-Lyons-M	46 09
G-ASOG	18.7.65	22.7.65	M-Lyneham-Damascus-Bahrein-Aden-Cairo-M	45 20
G-ASFY	27.7.65	30.7.65	M-Lyneham-Akrotiri-M	23 05
G-ASOG	1.8.65	6.8.65	M-Lyneham-Akrotiri-Lyneham-Athens-Akrotiri—M	46 40
G-ASFY	8.8.65	12.8.65	M-Lyneham-Brindisi-Akrotiri-Lyneham-Brindisi-Akrotiri-M	47 06
G-ASOG	22.8.65	24.8.65	M-Lyneham-Brindisi-Akrotiri-M	23 45
G-ASFY	29.8.65	3.9.65	M-Lyneham-Brindisi-Damascus-Bahrein-Aden-Bahrein-Damascus-Brindisi-Lyneham-M	53 21
G-ASOG	26.9.65	7.10.65	M-Lyneham-Damascus-Bahrein-Aden-Cairo-Brindisi(3/10-7/10)-M (Lyneham-Damascus 12h 30m)	44 30
G-ASOG	27.9.65	30.9.65	M-Lyneham-M-Brindisi-Akrotiri-Brindisi-M	28 26
G-ASFY	1.10.65	11.10.65	M-Lyneham-Brindisi(2/10-10/10)-Akrotiri-M	23 50
G-APYK	4.10.65	8.10.65	M-Lyneham-Brindisi-Cairo-Aden-Cairo-M	41 00
G-ASOG	10.10.65	20.10.65	M-Lyneham-Brindisi-Cairo-Aden-Aden-Aden-Aden-Brindisi-M (Aden-Brindisi 12h 45m)	42 35
G-ASFY	15.10.65	20.10.65	M-Lyneham-Brindisi-Cairo-Aden-Cairo-Brindisi-Lyneham-M	42 08
G-ASOG	21.10.65	26.10.65	M-Lyneham-Brindisi-Cairo-Aden-Cairo-Turin-M	40 45
G-ASFY	27.10.65	2.11.65	M-Lyneham-Brindisi-Cairo-Aden-Dubai-Damascus-Brindisi-M	47 18
G-ASOG	15.11.65	22.11.65	M-Brindisi-Damascus-Doha-Dubai-Damascus-Brindisi-M	39 30
G-ASFY	18.11.65	20.11.65	M-Tripoli-Brindisi-M	18 55
G-ASFY	29.11.65	3.12.65	M-Damascus-Bahrein-Damascus-Brindisi-M	33 55
G-ASOG	4.12.65	9.12.65	M-Lyneham-Brindisi-Cairo-Aden-Brindisi-M (Aden-Brindisi 14h 10m)	42 50
G-ASFY	4.12.65	13.12.65	M-Lyneham-Tripoli-Kano-Leopoldville-Livingstone-Entebbe-Jeddah-Benghazi-Milan-M	61 57
G-ASOG	29.12.65	31.12.65	M-Benghazi-Khartoum-Entebbe-Dar es Salaam	26 21
G-ASFY	30.12.65	1.1.66	M-Benghazi-Khartoum-Dar es Salaam	23 37
			1965 total	1319 15

TWILIGHT OF THE PISTONS

AIR FERRY LTD
FLIGHTS OUTSIDE EUROPE 1966

Aircraft	Date out	Date retn	Route	Time in hours/minutes
G-APYK	4.2.66	6.2.66	M-Benghazi-Khartoum-Dar es Salaam	24 10
G-ASOG			Dar es Salaam to Lusaka and Ndola on the oil lift	273 36
G-ASOG	9.2.66	11.2.66	Dar es Salaam-Khartoum-Malta-M	27 15
G-APYK			Dar es Salaam to Lusaka and Ndola on the oil lift	204 25
G-APYK	7.3.66	9.3.66	Dar es Salaam-Khartoum-Malta-M	24 50
G-ASFY			Dar es Salaam to Lusaka and Ndola on the oil lift	505 37
G-ASFY	13.3.66	15.3.66	Dar es Salaam-Khartoum-Malta-M	25 12
G-APYK	17.4.66	21.4.66	M-Lyneham-Rome-Cairo-Aden-Cairo-M	41 32
G-APYK	24.4.66	30.4.66	M-Lyneham-Brindisi-Cairo-Aden-Cairo-Brindisi-M	42 10
G-APYK	9.5.66	12.5.66	M-Lyneham-Rome-Nicosia-M	24 05
G-ASFY	16.5.66	19.5.66	M-Tripoli-Kano-Port Harcourt-Tripoli-Gatwick-M	35 49
G-APNO	12.7.66	14.7.66	M-Lyneham-Brindisi-Cairo-Bahrein-Athens-M	29 50
G-APNP	8.9.66	9.9.66	M-Gibralter-M	9 30
G-APNP	11.9.66	15.9.66	M-Lyneham-Brindisi-Cairo-Aden-Rome-Lyneham-M (Aden-Rome 11h 40m)	34 30
G-APNP	18.9.66	22.9.66	M-Lyneham-Athens-Cairo-Aden-Cairo-M	34 15
G-APNP	26.9.66	30.9.66	M-Lyneham-Brindisi-Cairo-Aden-Brindisi-M	31 50
G-APNO	30.9.66	10.10.66	M-Lyneham-Istanbul-Sharjah-Gan-Cocos-Perth-Adelaide-Perth-Cocos-Gan-Sharjah-Istanbul-Lyneham-M	88 40
G-APYK	10.10.66	14.10.66	M-Lyneham-Brindisi-Cairo-Aden-Aden-Cairo-M	41 02
G-APNO	18.10.66	22.10.66	M-Lyneham-Athens-Cairo-Aden-Cairo-Rome-M	34 10
G-APNP	31.10.66	4.11.66	M-Hurn-Istanbul-Riyadh-Athens-M	27 55
G-APNO	7.11.66	19.11.66	M-Lyneham-Istanbul-Sharjah-Masirhah-Gan-Cocos-Perth-Adelaide-Perth-Cocos-Gan-Sharjah-Istanbul-Lyneham-M	94 00
G-APNO	23.11.66	28.11.66	M-Hurn-Istanbul-Kuwait-Riyadh-Athens-M	28 35
G-APNO	15.12.66	19.12.66	Heathrow-Hurn-Istanbul-Kuwait-Riyadh-Nicosia-M	31 10
			1966 total	1714 08

APPENDICES

AIR FERRY LTD
FLIGHTS OUTSIDE EUROPE 1967

Aircraft	Date out	Date retn	Route	Time in hours/minutes
G-APYK	2.1.67	4.1.67	M-Gatwick-Tripoli-M	15 45
G-APNO	6.1.67	8.1.67	M-Frankfurt-Brindisi-Cairo-M	19 10
G-APNO	19.1.67	29.1.67	M-Lyneham-Istanbul-Masihrah-Gan-Cocos-Perth-Adelaide-Perth-Cocos-Gan-Sharjah-Ankara-Lyneham-M	93 05
G-APNO	26.1.67	30.1.67	M-Hurn-Istanbul-Kuwait-Riyadh-Kuwait-Athens-M	30 45
G-APNP	16.2.67	20.2.67	M-Hurn-Istanbul-Kuwait-Riyadh-Athens-M	32 15
G-ASFY	18.3.67	21.3.67	M-Frankfurt-Brindisi-Cairo-Brindisi-Frankfurt-M	27 45
G-APNO	22.3.67	27.3.67	M-Frankfurt-Milan-Perpignan-Valencia-Malaga-Tenerife-Frankfurt-M	22 45
G-ASFY	24.3.67	26.3.67	M-Benghazi-M	16 25
G-APNO	30.3.67	3.4.67	M-Hurn-Istanbul-Riyadh-Dubai-Istanbul-Frankfurt-M	33 07
G-APNP	8.4.67	12.4.67	M-Lyneham-Rome-Damascus-Aden-Cairo-Lyneham	33 35
G-APNP	13.4.67	16.4.67	Lyneham-Rome-Damascus-Aden-Cairo-M	32 30
G-APNP	20.4.67	21.4.67	M-Lyneham-Malta-M	12 10
G-APNP	27.4.67	29.4.67	M-Lyneham-Akrotiri-M	19 00
G-APNO	1.5.67	4.5.67	M-Hurn-Istanbul-Kuwait-Riyadh-Cairo-M	29 20
G-APNP	8.5.67	12.5.67	M-Hurn-Istanbul-Riyadh-Khamis Mushayt-Jeddah-M	31 30
G-ASFY	23.5.67	24.5.67	M-Tunis-M	10 55
G-APNO	4.10.67	5.10.67	M-Binbrook-Malta-M	12 25
G-APNO	4.10.67	5.10.67	M-Binbrook-Malta-M	12 05
G-APNP	6.10.67	7.10.67	M-Binbrook-Malta-Milan-M	12 20
G-APNP	7.10.67	8.10.67	M-Binbrook-Malta-Milan-M	12 45
G-APNP	10.10.67	12.10.67	M-Waddington-Malta-M	12 40
G-APNP	13.10.67	16.10.67	M-Brize Norton-Akrotiri-Milan-Heathrow-M	20 35
G-APNO			) M-Tangier-M 19 inclusive tour flights	185 05
G-APNP			)	
G-APNO	16.10.67	25.10.67	M-Hurn-Istanbul-Istanbul-Kuwait-Jeddah-Khamis Mushayt-Jeddah-Cairo-M	33 25
G-APNO	18.10.67	21.10.67	M-Tripoli-Kano-Lagos-Malta-M	27 35
G-APNP	21.10.67	24.10.67	M-Stanstead-Nicosia-Dhahran-Nicosia-Stanstead	28 05
G-APNP	24.10.67	28.10.67	Stanstead-Liverpool-Athens-Jeddah-Nairobi-Athens-M	39 40
G-APNP	3.11.67	5.11.67	M-Heathrow-Rome-Beirut-M	18 40
G-APNO	17.11.67	25.11.67	M-Lyneham-Athens-Tehran-Karachi-Columbo-Changi-Karachi-Beirut-M	64 10

c/f 939 32

251

AIR FERRY LTD
FLIGHTS OUTSIDE EUROPE 1967 continued

Aircraft	Date out	Date retn	Route	Time in hours/minutes
			b/f	939 32
G-APNP	20.11.67	24.11.67	M-Hurn-Istanbul-Riyadh-Khamis Mushayt-Jeddah-Cairo-M	32 30
G-APNO	26.11.67	4.12.67	M-Lyneham-Athens-Tehran-Karachi-Colombo-Changi-Karachi-Tehran-M (Tehran-M 12h 20m)	60 40
G-ASFY	4.12.67	8.12.67	M-Brindisi-Beirut-Kuwait-Brindisi-Zurich-M	34 00
G-APNP	9.12.67	16.12.67	M-Gatwick-Frankfurt-Beirut-Kandahar-Kabul-Kabul-Amritsar-Kabul-Kandahar-Tehran-Beirut-Frankfurt-Gatwick	48 40
G-APNO	11.12.67	15.12.67	M-Hurn-Istanbul-Dharan-Khamis Mushayt-Jeddah-Cairo-M	32 05
G-ASFY	14.12.67	18.12.67	M-Lyneham-Benghazi-Bahrein-Brindisi-M	37 40
G-APNO	16.12.67	18.12.67	M-Istanbul-Dhahran-Istanbul-M	27 40
G-APNP	17.12.67	23.12.67	Gatwick-Frankfurt-Beirut-Kabul-Lahore-Amritsar-Kabul-Amritsar-Kandahar-Tehran-Beirut-Munich-Gatwick	46 45
G-APNO	18.12.67	22.12.67	M-Hurn-Istanbul-Dhahran-Riyadh-Ankara-M	30 45
G-ASFY	19.12.67	24.12.67	M-Lyneham-Benghazi-Bahrein-Brindisi-Milan-Heathrow-M	39 45
G-ARWI	21.12.67	24.12.67	Heathrow-Gatwick-Basle-Rotterdam-Las Palmas-M	23 20
G-APNP	23.12.67	1.1.68	Gatwick-Frankfurt-Beirut-Kabul-Lahore-Amritsar-Kabul-Amritsar-Delhi-Amritsar-Kabul-Kandahar-Beirut-Frankfurt-Gatwick	47 25
G-APNO	28.12.67	30.12.67	M-Liverpool-Benghazi-Khartoum-Nairobi-Benghazi-M	36 20
G-APNO	31.12.67	3.1.68	M-Benghazi-Entebbe-Lusaka-Entebbe-Benghazi-M	39 50
			1967 total	1476 57

AIR FERRY LTD
FLIGHTS OUTSIDE EUROPE 1968

Aircraft	Date out	Date retn	Route	Time in hours/minutes
G-APNP	1.1.68	6.1.68	Gatwick-Frankfurt-Beirut-Kandahar-Lahore-Amritsar-Kabul-Delhi-Amritsar-Kabul-Kandahar-Beirut-Frankfurt-Gatwick	50 05
G-APNO	5.1.68	10.1.68	M-Hurn-Istanbul-Dhahran-Khamis Mushayt-Dubai-Istanbul-M	36 40
G-APNP	7.1.68	14.1.68	Gatwick-Frankfurt-Beirut-Kandahar-Lahore-Amritsar-Kabul-Kandahar-Beirut-Munich-Gatwick	42 55
G-APNO	13.1.68	17.1.68	M-Gatwick-Benghazi-Nairobi-Ndola-Nairobi-Entebbe-Benghazi-Gatwick-M	42 20
G-APNP	14.1.68	21.1.68	Gatwick-Frankfurt-Beirut-Kandahar-Lahore-Amritsar-Kabul-Beirut-Frankfurt-Gatwick	44 00
G-APNO	19.1.68	24.1.68	M-Hurn-Brindisi-Istanbul-Dhahran-Khamis Mushayt-Bahrein-Dubai-Nicosia-Brindisi-M	40 45
G-APNP	22.1.68	27.1.68	Gatwick-Beirut-Lahore-Amritsar-Kandahar-Kabul-Amritsar-Kandahar-Beirut-Naples-Frankfurt-Gatwick	48 25
G-ASFY	26.1.68	29.1.68	M-Casablanca-Freetown-Casablanca-M	31 40
G-APNO	28.1.68	3.2.68	Gatwick-Beirut-Kabul-Lahore-Amritsar-Kabul-Amritsar-Kabul-Beirut-Gatwick	43 00
G-ASFY	3.2.68	5.2.68	M-Basle-Cairo-Rome-M	24 55
G-APNO	4.2.68	11.2.68	Gatwick-Frankfurt-Beirut-Kandahar-Lahore-Amritsar-Kabul-Kandahar-Beirut-Frankfurt-Gatwick	46 10
G-APNP	5.2.68	10.2.68	M-Bordeaux-Benghazi-Khartoum-Nairobi-Tamatave-Nairobi-Benghazi-Southend-M	46 50
G-ARWI	10.2.68	14.2.68	M-Casablanca-Robertsfield-Freetown-Casablanca-M	37 05
G-APNP	12.2.68	16.2.68	M-Hurn-Istanbul-Riyadh-Khamis Mushayt-Jeddah-Cairo-M	32 50
G-APNO	19.2.68	23.2.68	M-Brussels-Istanbul-Kuwait-Abu Dhabi-Bahrein-Nicosia-M	30 55
G-APNO	26.2.68	28.2.68	M-Frankfurt-Cairo-Zurich-M	18 20
G-APNO	6.3.68	11.3.68	M-Birmingham-Benghazi-Khartoum-Entebbe-Beira-Durban-Entebbe-Benghazi-M	54 40
G-APNO	12.3.68	17.3.68	M-Birmingham-Benghazi-Khartoum-Entebbe-Blantyre-Durban-Entebbe-Benghazi-M	51 40
G-ARWI	16.3.68	19.3.68	M-Rome-Cairo-Aden-Cairo-M	46 15
G-ASFY	19.3.68	22.3.68	M-Rome-Cairo-Rome-M	23 35
G-APNO	25.3.68	30.3.68	M-Hurn-Istanbul-Dhahran-Khamis Mushayt-Jeddah-Athens-M	33 00
G-APNP	2.4.68	4.4.68	M-Rome-Beirut-M	18 35
G-ARWI	13.4.68	14.4.68	M-Malta-M	12 35
G-APNP	18.4.68	23.4.68	M-Hurn-Istanbul-Kuwait-Riyadh-Khamis Mushayt-Jeddah-Cairo-M	33 05
G-ARWI	23.4.68	26.4.68	M-Casablanca-Freetown-Casablanca-M	31 20
G-APNP	30.4.68	2.5.68	M-Frankfurt-Cairo-Zurich-M	18 35
G-ARWI	2.5.68	5.5.68	M-Athens-Dhahran-M (Dhahran-M direct 17hr 15 m)	34 15
G-APNP	16.5.68	18.5.68	M-Dusseldorf-Dakar-M	22 50
G-APNP	20.5.68	26.5.68	M-Hurn-Istanbul-Kuwait-Riyadh-Khamis Mushayt-Jeddah-Cairo-M	31 55
G-APNO	28.5.68	31.5.68	M-Hurn-Frankfurt-Istanbul-Dhahran-Istanbul-M	29 15
G-APNO	3.6.68	5.6.68	M-Rome-Cairo-Athens-M	18 10
G-ARWI	11.7.68	17.7.68	M-Hurn-Rome-Nicosia-Beirut-Abu Dhabi-Azaiba-Bahrein-Nicosia-Rome-M	43 00
G-APNO			)M-Tangier-M 29 inclusive tour flights, (includes one M-Gibralter-Tangier-M)	283 20
G-APNP			)	

1968 total 1403 00

AIR FERRY LTD

THE NUMBER OF VISITS TO THE TOP TEN AIRPORTS BY YEAR

1963		1964		1965		1966		1967		1968	
Ostend	355	Ostend	1326	Ostend	692	Basle	641	Basle	547	Basle	295
Basle	111	Le Touquet	204	Basle	202	Perpignan	253	Milan	229	Perpignan	280
Dusseldorf	78	Basle	198	Perpignan	188	Dar es Salaam	110	Perpignan	150	Ostend	175
Le Touquet	73	Rotterdam	102	Gatwick	139	Heathrow	91	Manchester	99	Manchester	98
Perpignan	51	Dusseldorf	97	Le Touquet	118	Ostend	79	Ostend	81	Milan	86
Luxembourg	51	Palma	91	Rotterdam	78	Lusaka	61	Frankfurt	62	Gatwick	74
Palma	50	Perpignan	67	Southend	41	Manchester	49	Luxembourg	60	Zurich	46
Dijon	30	Luxembourg	58	Brindisi	33	Ndola	48	Dusseldorf	49	Luxembourg	43
Pisa	23	Lyons	53	Lyneham	32	Dusseldorf	47	Luton	43	Rotterdam	41
Naples	14	Dijon	25	Gutersloh	28	Copenhagen	46	Palma	30	Newcastle	40
										Le Bourget	40
	__836__		__2221__		__1551__		__1425__		__1350__		__1218__

OVERALL

1	Ostend	2708
2	Basle	1994
3	Perpignan	989
4	Le Touquet	400
5	Milan	338
6	Dusseldorf	300
7	Rotterdam	286
8	Gatwick	284
9	Manchester	255
10	Luxembourg	218
		__7772__

APPENDICES

AIR FERRY LTD
NUMBER OF AIRPORT VISITS BY YEAR

	1963	1964	1965	1966	1967	1968	Total
Aden							
Aden			15	7	2	1	25
Afghanistan							
Kabul					8	12	20
Kandahar					4	9	13
Australia							
Adelaide				2	1		3
Perth				4	2		6
Austria							
Linz					1		1
Saltzburg		1	2				3
Vienna		1	1		4	12	18
Bahrein							
Bahrein			13	1	2	3	19
Belgium							
Antwerp		4	7			1	12
Brussels		6	5	5	5	7	28
Charleroi				3			3
Liege		1	1				2
Ostend	355	1326	692	79	81	175	2708
Canary Is.							
Las Palmas					1		1
Tenerife					1		1
Ceylon							
Columbo					2		2
Cocos Is.							
Cocos				4	2		6
Congo							
Leopoldville			1				1
Crete							
Heraklion		1					1
Cyprus							
Akrotiri			11		2		13
Nicosia			1	2	2	4	9
Czechoslovakia							
Brno						1	1
Prague				1	1		2
Denmark							
Aalborg	1						1
Copenhagen	9	14	10	46	7	2	88
Tirstrup			1				1
Egypt							
Cairo		2	12	13	9	10	46
Luxor		1					1
France							
Beauvais	1	7	1	9	9	25	52
Bordeaux		4	4		2	3	13
Calais		6	10	1	4	10	31
Cherbourg	1						1
Clermont Ferrand			6		1		7
c/f	367	1380	787	178	152	275	3139

TWILIGHT OF THE PISTONS

AIR FERRY LTD
NUMBER OF AIRPORT VISITS BY YEAR

		1963	1964	1965	1966	1967	1968	Total
	b/f	367	1380	787	178	152	275	3139
France								
Cognac							1	1
Deauville			4	5				9
Dijon		30	25					55
Dinard		1	1			1	2	5
Le Touquet		73	204	118	1		4	400
Lille		2	2				1	5
Lyons			53	6	4		1	64
Metz					2		1	3
Marseilles			12	5			1	18
Nice			1	2				3
Orleans			1					1
Paris Le Bourget		6	5	14	30	7	40	102
Paris Orly				2	3	4		9
Perpignan		51	67	188	253	150	280	989
Rheims			1	3			1	5
Strasbourg		1				1		2
Tarbes			2	1	2	2	2	9
Toulouse		2	1	5	2	2	1	13
Tours				1				1
St. Nazaire							1	1
Finland								
Helsinki				1		4	5	10
Germany								
Berlin		1	16	1	2	2	6	28
Bremen		1		9		18		28
Cologne			2	6	2		4	14
Dusseldorf		78	97	17	47	49	12	300
Frankfurt		1	10	2	42	62	12	129
Gutersloh				28				28
Hamburg			4	6		3	2	15
Hanover		2	1	15	6	2	2	28
Munich			7	8	4	3	33	55
Nuremburg						1		1
Stuttgart					2		12	14
Wildenwrath				17	1		1	19
Gibralter								
Gibralter				1	1		1	3
Greece								
Athens			1	3	5	7	4	20
Holland								
Amsterdam		2	4	10	7	4	9	36
Maastricht			2	10	2		2	16
Rotterdam		13	102	78	27	25	41	286
Hungary								
Budapest					1	1		2
India								
Amritsar						6	11	17
Calcutta				4				4
Delhi				1		1	1	3
	c/f	631	2005	1354	624	507	769	5890

APPENDICES

AIR FERRY LTD
NUMBER OF AIRPORT VISITS BY YEAR

		1963	1964	1965	1966	1967	1968	Total
	b/f	631	2005	1354	624	507	769	5890
Iran								
Tehran						5		5
Iraq								
Baghdad			2					2
Ireland Rep.								
Dublin			6	8	3	2	4	23
Shannon							2	2
Israel								
Jerusalem			1					1
Italy								
Brindisi			1	33	7	7	2	50
Genoa				3	39		22	64
Milan				8	15	229	86	338
Naples		14	11	6			1	32
Pisa		23	20			1		44
Rimini						1	1	2
Rome				5	5	6	15	31
Turin				1	2	1	1	5
Venice					39	13	13	65
Verona		11	14	6	2			33
Kenya								
Nairobi						2	4	6
Kuwait								
Kuwait					2	6	3	11
Lebanon								
Beirut			1			9	14	24
Liberia								
Robertsfield							1	1
Libya								
Benghazi-Benina				3	1	6	9	19
Tripoli				2	2	2		6
Luxembourg								
Luxembourg		51	58	3	3	60	43	218
Malagasi Rep.								
Tamatave							1	1
Malawi								
Blantyre							1	1
Maldive Is.								
Gan					4	2		6
Malta								
Malta		1		1	3	7	1	13
Morocco								
Casablanca							6	6
Tangier				1		19	29	49
Mozambique								
Beira							1	1
Muscat & Oman								
Azaiba							1	1
Masirah					1	1		2
	c/f	731	2119	1434	752	886	1030	6952

TWILIGHT OF THE PISTONS

AIR FERRY LTD
NUMBER OF AIRPORT VISITS BY YEAR

	b/f	1963 731	1964 2119	1965 1434	1966 752	1967 886	1968 1030	Total 6952
Nigeria								
Kano				1	1	1		3
Lagos						1		1
Port Harcourt					1			1
Norway								
Bergen						27		27
Bodo				2				2
Oslo			1			6	12	19
Pakistan								
Karachi				4		4		8
Lahore						2	6	8
Poland								
Warsaw					2			2
Portugal								
Lisbon					2	3	1	6
Oporto							1	1
Qatar								
Doha				1				1
Rumania								
Bucharest				1				1
Sardinia								
Cagliari						2	1	3
Saudi Arabia								
Dhahran						4	5	9
Jeddah				1		6	4	11
Khamis Mushayt						4	6	10
Riyadh					3	7	3	13
Senegal								
Dakar							1	1
Sierra Leone								
Freetown							3	3
Singapore								
Changi				2		2		4
South Africa								
Durban							2	2
Spain & Balaeric Is.								
Alicante							3	3
Barcelona			2			21	15	7	45
Bilbao				1				1
Gerona							18	18
Ibiza			1					1
Madrid			1		6	1	14	2	24
Mahon							1	1
Malaga				11			1		12
Palma			50	91		2	30	23	196
Valencia					1		1	16	18
Sudan								
Khartoum					2	4	1	3	10
	c/f	785	2223	1455	789	1017	1148	7417

APPENDICES

AIR FERRY LTD
NUMBER OF AIRPORT VISITS BY YEAR

		1963	1964	1965	1966	1967	1968	Total
	b/f	785	2223	1455	789	1017	1148	7417
Sweden								
Goteborg				1	6	1	7	15
Jonkoping			2					2
Malmo					3		1	4
Stockholm					8	1	2	11
Switzerland								
Basle		111	198	202	641	547	295	1994
Geneva		1	10	7	4	1	5	28
Zurich		1	13	7	2	7	46	76
Syria								
Damascus			4	21		2		27
Tanzania								
Dar es Salaam				1	110			111
Trucial States								
Abu Dhabi							2	2
Dubai				3		1	2	6
Sharjah					4	1		5
Tunisia								
Tunis						1		1
Turkey								
Ankara						2		2
Istanbul			1		7	14	10	32
Uganda								
Entebbe				2		1	6	9
U.K. and Channel Is.								
Abingdon				2				2
Binbrook						4	1	5
Birmingham		1	1	2	1		29	34
Brawdy							1	1
Bristol			1			1		2
Brize Norton						1		1
Cambridge			6		4			10
Cardiff						11	8	19
Castle Donington					1		2	3
Coventry				1	2			3
Edinburgh			2		2	2	5	11
Exeter			5	3			4	12
Glasgow								
Abbotsinch					5	6	4	15
Renfrew				2				2
Guernsey				3			1	4
Hatfield							1	1
Hurn			2		3	9	8	22
Jersey		2	8	8	4			22
Lasham			1					1
Leconfield				11	6			17
Leeds							16	16
Liverpool		1	2	5		3	6	17
	c/f	902	2479	1736	1602	1633	1610	9962

AIR FERRY LTD
NUMBER OF AIRPORT VISITS BY YEAR

	1963	1964	1965	1966	1967	1968	Total
b/f	902	2479	1736	1602	1633	1610	9962
U.K. and Channel Is.							
London Gatwick	12	17	139	29	13	74	284
London Heathrow		2	19	91	29	13	154
Luton	2		5	3	43	2	55
Lydd		1	19		1	3	24
Lyneham			32	14	11		57
Manchester	3	1	5	49	99	98	255
Newcastle		1				40	41
Prestwick		4	5	1		3	13
Southampton						6	6
Southend	15	9	41	29	4	7	105
Stanstead	1	3	4	3	4	3	18
Tees-side				2		5	7
Valley			1				1
Waddington					1		1
West Raynham			2				2
Wymeswold	5	2		2			9
U.S.S.R.							
Moscow		1					1
Zambia							
Livingstone			1				1
Lusaka				61		1	62
Ndola				48		1	49
	940	2520	2009	1934	1838	1866	11107

APPENDICES

BIBLIOGRAPHY

Air War over Korea   *Robert Jackson*   Ian Allan 1973
The Big Show   *Pierre Clostermann*   Chatto & Windus 1951
British Independent Airlines since 1946   *Tony Merton Jones*   Merseyside Aviation Group/LAAS International
Civil Aircraft Accident Reports   H.M.S.O. 1968
DC4   *John and Maureen Woods*   Airline Publications 1980
The Douglas DC4   *P. Berry, T Dunstall, M Ford & J A Whittle*   Air Britain 1967
Flight and Flight International magazine   1958 to 1996
Aeroplane magazine
Fly Me I'm Freddie   *Roger Eglin and Berry Ritchie*   Futura 1981
Golden Age   *Charles Woodley*   Airlife 1992
History of the Royal Air Force   *Consultant John D R Rawlings*   Temple Press / Aerospace 1984
The History of RAF Manston   *Rocky Stockman 3rd. edition*   R.A.F. Manston 1986
The Manston Spitfire   *Lewis E Deal*   North Kent Books 1986
Many Reasons Why   *Michael Charlton & Anthony Moncrieff*   Scolar 1978
The Mighty Eighth   *Roger Freeman*   Macdonald 1970
The Narrow Margin   *Derek Wood and Derek Dempster*   Arrow 1979
Nine Lives   *Alan C Deere*   Hodder 1961
The Nuremburg Raid   *Martin Middlebrook*   Penguin 1986
Post-War Britain   *Alan Sked and Chris Cook*   Penguin 1979
RAF Biggin Hill   *Graham Wallace*   Putnam 1957
The Sky Suspended   *Drew Middleton*   Pan 1963
Squadrons of the Royal Air Force   *James J Halley*   Air Britain 1980
The Story of 609 Squadron   *Frank Ziegler*   Macdonald 1971
Strike Force - The U.S.A.F. in Britain since 1948   *Robert Jackson*   Robson 1986
Test Pilots   *Don Middleton*   Collins Willow 1985
V Force   *Andrew Brookes*   Jane's 1982
V Bombers   *Robert Jackson*   Ian Allan 1981
Vickers Viking   *A B Eastwood*   LAAS International 1970
The Year Book,1966 and 1967   The Grollier Society
The Daily Telegraph 1967

Video Tapes:
Lyndon Johnson   Timewatch   BBC
A Year to Remember 1963-68   British Pathe News